The Poet and the Critic

DATE

D.C. Scott

E.K. Brown

The Poet and the Critic

A Literary Correspondence

between

D.C. Scott and E.K. Brown

Edited
with an introduction and notes

by

Robert L. McDougall

Carleton University Press

©Carleton University Press, 1983

ISBN 0-88629-013-9 (casebound)
     0-88629-011-2 (paperback)

Cover/Design: Karen Toner

ACKNOWLEDGEMENTS

Carleton University Press gratefully acknowledges the support extended to its publishing programme by the Canada Council and the Ontario Arts Council.

This book has been published with the help of a grant from the Canadian Federation for the Humanities, using funds provided by the Social Sciences and Humanities Research Council of Canada.

Canadian Cataloguing in Publication Data

Scott, Duncan Campbell, 1862-1947
   The poet and the critic: a literary correspondence
between D.C. Scott and E.K. Brown

Includes index.
ISBN 0-88629-013-9 (bound). - ISBN 0-88629-011-2 (pbk.)

1. Scott, Duncan Campbell, 1862-1947 — Correspondence.
2. Poets, Canadian (English) — 20th century —
Correspondence.   3. Brown, E.K. (Edward Killoran),
1905-1951.   4. Critics — Canada — Correspondence.   I.
Brown, E.K. (Edward Killoran), 1905-1951   II.
McDougall, Robert L., 1918-   III. Title.

PS8537.C58Z542 1983   C811'.4   C83-090138-8
PR9199.3.S36Z482 1983

Distributed by:

Oxford University Press Canada
70 Wynford Drive
DON MILLS, Ontario, Canada, M3C 1J9
(416) 441-2941

Printed and bound in Canada.

for Anne and Christine

Contents

INTRODUCTION

This volume is the record of a remarkable correspondence that took place many years ago between a poet and a critic. The letters began in 1940 and ended in 1947. The critic, quite young, was a professor who held advanced degrees in English and French literature. The poet, quite old, was a retired civil servant who had left school when he was sixteen. Both were Canadians by birth and upbringing, though the critic spent most of his working life in the United States. I shall say something in a moment about how the letters were assembled, but I should like first to introduce the principals in capsule portraits. D.C. Scott and E.K. Brown came to know each other properly for the first time in the summer of 1942. The two Karsh portraits reproduced in this volume were taken in that year. They provide us with likenesses and, being good portraits, probably with a good deal more than that. But who are these men, and what are they really like? I shall introduce them as if they are coming on stage to give a public reading, speaking their pieces in turn, which indeed is what they do in this edition of their letters.

On one side of the stage, then, is the poet and short-story writer, sometime bureaucrat, Duncan Campbell Scott, a name which Scott wryly remarks is long enough to take up most of the space likely to be assigned to him in a biographical dictionary. He is tall, or seems so at five foot ten inches because he holds himself erect despite his eighty years, and as he comes into the light we can see that his sandy hair has thinned to reveal a large and prominent forehead. His eyes, behind rimless glasses, may seem cold, but they can light up quickly with a twinkle that is both impish and warm. He dresses conservatively and wears an English broadcloth shirt with a tab collar.

Scott is an Ottawa man, born in the parsonage at the corner of Metcalfe and Queen, across from the Dominion Methodist Church where his father, the Rev. William Scott, held a charge in the 1860s. Although long since retired, he has been all his life, by an even mixture of necessity and choice, a civil servant. He entered the service in 1879 as a junior clerk in the Department of Indian Affairs and by 1913 had risen to the rank of Deputy Superintendent General, a position which he held until his retirement in 1931. It is indeed less as a poet than as a mandarin of Parliament Hill and a public-spirited citizen prominent in the founding of the Drama League and the Ottawa Little Theatre that his friends have recognized him in his daily progress from 108 Lisgar Street down Elgin and across the Square to the Booth Building where he worked. But his real life is and always has been his writing, and especially his poetry, and the house on Lisgar Street, in which he has lived for just over fifty years, is and always has been the base for this.

The Lisgar Street house is Scott's pride and joy. It is a cluttered, friendly house. It is stacked with books, and there is a good collection of pictures on the walls: a David Milne, a Pegi Nicol, some water-colours by W.J. Phillips, two Emily Carrs, and many fine prints acquired on trips abroad. It is the house to which Scott had brought his first wife, Belle Warner Botsford of Boston, a concert violinist and titian-haired. It is here that he settled again to a new life, more tranquil, after a second marriage, two years after Belle's death in 1929, to young Elise Aylen, a slip of a girl who, as niece to Scott's old friend and neighbour Arthur Bourinot, had grown up, one might say, in his own back yard. But it is to the large music room, one step down at the back of the house, that Scott usually leads his guests. He is a skilled pianist and a musician whose love for music surpasses even his love for poetry. There have been many gatherings, literary as well as musical, in this room. Lubka Kolessa has played here, Murray and Frances Adaskin, on one occasion the Hart House String Quartet. Bliss Carman and Alfred Noyes have been visitors. Lawren Harris and W.J. Phillips have sat here, and here Clarence Gagnon has given the Scotts a private showing of his illustrations for *Maria Chapdelaine*. Newspaper men, amongst them William Arthur Deacon and I. Norman Smith, have come here too; and so also have familiars from the circle of affection: Pelham and Helen Edgar in the early days, in the later days Edward and Peggy Brown, Dorothy McCurry and Madge Macbeth. These names suggest the aura which surrounds this man. He is at all times attentive and hospitable to the arts.

Behind the personal aura is of course the aura of Scott's achievement, unspectacular but solid, in poetry and fiction. Although he is sometimes depressed by the meagre critical attention his books seem to have received over most of his lifetime, he knows his place is secure in the canon of major Canadian writers. He has lived to see 'The Onondaga Madonna,' 'The Forsaken,' 'At the Cedars,' 'The Height of Land' and some of his short stories become part of the education of young Canadians. He is happy enough.

William Arthur Deacon, longtime critic and literary editor for the Toronto *Globe and Mail*, will give us, in an unpublished memoir kept by his family, a glimpse of the later Scott. "For Scott," he writes, "I had the greatest respect; but though I had two hour-long talks with him, I never felt that I knew him. Was he shy? proud? self-satisfied? Or had his life as a civil servant made him wary of newspaper men?" "I visited Scott at his home," Deacon continues, "a few months before his death. He stood straight as ever but was so obviously weak that I begged him not to see me to the door; but he did so out of his unfailing courtesy, though he could scarcely walk. His warm smile in the doorway remains a vivid memory."

This man on stage is teeming with memories: violins and pianos and the sounds of music; Indian place names and the unforgettable expeditions to Moosonee and James Bay in a past as remote as another life; canoe trips, remoter still, with the young Archie Lampman, on the Lièvre and to Lake Achigan; his daughter's improbable death in Paris, an only child, aged twelve; the occasion of the presidential address to the Royal Society in 1922. So much else. The dates are of course not important to him. But he has come a long way. This is D.C. Scott, C.M.G., L.L.D., F.R.S.C., F.R.S.L. And the man opposite him?

Edward Killoran Brown is not unlike Scott in physical appearance, though heavier set. He is about the same height. His hair too has thinned to reveal a strong forehead, and he has bright eyes that can be sharply quizzical. He too dresses conservatively. In his hand is a cigarette, once Scott's indulgence but long since given up. Brown is one man, however, not two or three men as Scott seems to be. He is by profession and vocation, by inclination and will, a scholar-critic. He is at the same time a born teacher and an accomplished linguist who speaks French with the same tailored precision as he speaks English. Asked what his recreations are, he will reply, "Work." Discrimination in ideas and values in literature are his fulfilment and pleasure. He has come on the scene like a meteor, as if he has had foreknowledge of his foreshortened life. From his side of the stage he radiates energy and confidence. He is not yet out of his thirties. He is a Toronto man, though his middle name places him with his mother's people at Seaforth, in the western reaches of Ontario. After his father's death, when he was five, he was brought up by his mother and his maiden aunts; but one has the feeling that, like Melchizedec, he is without parents.

Leon Edel, who was a student with Brown at the Sorbonne in the twenties, gives us an early picture of the man which remains true, I am sure, for the time of Brown's first meeting with Scott. I come back to the present to quote from a recent letter from Edel:

> He was highly articulate and on excellent terms with the Sorbonne professors, who greatly admired him. He was tall and broad-shouldered, clean-shaven, always conventionally dressed. . . . He wore pince-nez at that time, and used to take them off, blink his eyes, and build up mystery when he had a story to tell. "Do you know. . .?" And "What do you think happened?" And so on until he would come out with what he had to tell, which was always some subtlety of observation. And he would chuckle heartily. He watched and observed; he was a close observer of manners and mannerisms. He talked as if he were a much older person, even though he was only in his mid-twenties. . . . He had an impressive stance, erect, smiling, confident, and he was always delightful company.

This is indeed our man in 1942, or so I must believe.

If E.K. Brown ever had a youth, we hear little about it. He has never been an outdoorsman and would scarcely know how to get into a canoe, let alone paddle it. His exercise and his pleasure is walking, and it is a rule which his wife Peggy accepts that where they live must be within good walking distance, not too short and not too long, of his work. If there is a fountain along the way, so much the better, for he likes to stop for a drink of water. He is not at all musical, though he has been known to whistle a tune. He does not dance, and his wife must put up with that. He has never tried seriously to write a poem or a piece of fiction, or paint a picture. The greatest impingement on the spirit of this very self-contained man was probably his marriage in 1935 to a highly talented girl with a will to match his own, Margaret Deaver of Minneapolis, and the birth some years later of two sons whom he adored. Marriage and parenthood are Brown's extra dimensions. For the rest, the line runs straight from his first show of promise at the University of Toronto Schools, through his B.A. at the University of Toronto and his advanced studies in Paris, to a mounting ladder of appointments at University College, Toronto, the University of Manitoba, Cornell and the University of Chicago. The man we see has moved from precocious adolescence to the top of his profession in somewhat less than twenty years. The record of publication along the way, already extensive when he met Scott, is to become prodigious. When it is all over, in 1951, the official obituary notice from the University of Chicago will cite eight books and more than sixty important articles or review essays produced over the relatively short span of his career. Throughout, this man's mark is the sensitivity and crackling intelligence with which his prolific work is informed.

The principals may stand down. They will be back. I want to say something about the provenance of the letters and the circumstances that contributed to the considerable delay in their publication in a complete and authoritative form.

In 1974-75, I was on leave of absence from Carleton University and began a serious study of D.C. Scott as writer, distinguished civil servant and intellectual of the Golden Age of Canadian literature. Since I had in mind a biography, Scott's correspondence would be of the first importance. I turned to two of Arthur S. Bourinot's publications, long out of print. Pursuing his earlier work of restoring the Lampman-Thomson correspondence, Bourinot had brought out in 1959 a little book which he called *Some Letters of Duncan Campbell Scott, Archibald Lampman and Others*, and in 1960 he had followed suit with another slim volume entitled, sensibly, *More Letters of Duncan Campbell Scott*. He had not been able to interest the university or commercial presses in his venture, and both volumes had been privately printed. Bourinot's work showed signs of haste in editing and proofing, and the texts did not inspire confidence; he was in fact not at all well by this time. It was nevertheless work that broke new ground in an important way, making public as it did for the first time a substantial body of Scott's letters addressed to a wide community of literary friends which included Archibald Lampman, E.W. Thomson, Charles G.D. Roberts, Lorne Pierce, Thoreau MacDonald, Madge Macbeth, Bourinot himself, Pelham Edgar and E.K. Brown. If we consider the two little books as one, the principal correspondents by long odds were Pelham Edgar and E.K. Brown. Of Scott's letters to Edgar, Bourinot published seventy-five; of Scott's letters to Brown, thirty. In Bourinot's texts, the letters to Edgar begin in 1899 and end in 1942; the letters to Brown begin in 1942 and end a few months before the poet's death in 1947. Preoccupied with Scott's end of the correspondence, Bourinot published no letters from Edgar, and only two from Brown.

I knew that the originals for Scott's letters to Edgar had ended up in the Edgar Collection at Victoria College, Toronto, where I had examined them some years before. But the Scott-Brown correspondence raised some interesting questions. How selective was Bourinot in this case, and what were his sources? Obviously, there were many more of Brown's letters still to come. The figure of thirty for Scott's letters to Brown, on the other hand, was inconclusive. What part of a putative whole was this? Three-quarters? One-half? One-third? In brief acknowledgements at the beginning of both volumes, Bourinot thanked Mrs. E.A. Scott for permission to use Scott's letters. Did permission necessarily mean possession? Commenting on the texts, Bourinot would sometimes say that a particular letter or set of letters came from "The Scott Papers," but in a parenthetical note buried towards the end of *Some Letters* he went a step further: "These are amongst the Scott papers in the possession of Mrs. E.A. Scott." This was in 1959. Early in 1948, on the advice of E.K. Brown, Elise Aylen Scott had deposited a collection of her late husband's papers with the Library at the University of Toronto. I knew of this collection, as indeed many scholars and students did by 1975. It contained a number of showcase items: letters from John Masefield, Rupert Brooke, Alfred Noyes and the like. But although a few of these had been used by Bourinot in putting together his editions of the Scott correspondence, the collection as a whole gave no evidence of a sustained correspondence between Scott and Brown. This, if any doubts remained, was clearly not what Bourinot meant by "The Scott Papers." Mrs. Scott had left Canada for England in 1948, eventually for India, where she was to find spiritual sanctuary for the next twenty-five years and where she died, at Coonoor, in 1972.

I have probably made the clues sound a bit more puzzling than they were; that is the way it is with stories. They were in fact perfectly adequate clues, and looking back I am surprised that neither I nor anyone else had followed the relatively easy trail to Bourinot's sources in nearly twenty years. The Aylen connection was next. That is not a difficult connection to make in Ottawa, where Aylens abound. As it turned out, at about this time I learned from my colleague Michael Gnarowski that he had in one of his classes a student by the name of John Aylen, who was a grand-nephew of D.C. Scott. That was interesting. But more interesting was the fact that in the parents' home were some boxes of Scott documents and memorabilia. I went to the Aylens' home, was received with great kindness, saw the boxes.

It was obvious, even if I had not already learned from the Aylens that Bourinot had been into the boxes many years before, that two of them contained what Bourinot called "The Scott Papers." They had of course come from Lisgar Street, though their chances of survival in the period immediately following Scott's death had been slim. When Mrs. Scott left Canada, having done the best she could with what she considered the more important of her husband's papers, she had put the Lisgar Street house up for rent. She seems to have left no special instructions about the two boxes of remaining papers. Ten years later, in 1957, she had written from India to authorize the sale of the property. Belongings were scattered: some pictures to the National Gallery, personal effects to relatives and friends, eventually an auction. The two boxes remained on the floor of the music room. Mr. and Mrs. John Aylen, in what must be seen as an inspired moment, scooped them up. Many years later, recognizing the value of the papers, John Aylen Jr. had reorganized and catalogued them. Mr. Aylen Sr., as literary executor to his aunt, in 1972 assumed legal control over what I shall now call the Scott-Aylen Papers. Xerox copies of the complete collection have been deposited with the Public Archives of Canada since the spring of 1978. The originals remain, for the time being, in the hands of the Aylens.

I was by this time fairly hooked, and it was a great excitement to discover in the Scott-Aylen Papers a bulging file of Brown's letters to Scott, and a second file containing carbon copies of most of Scott's letters to Brown. The carbons answered a question which had puzzled me. I knew from an earlier stage of my research that the originals of these letters were in the Public Archives of Canada as part of the E.K. Brown Papers which his widow, Mrs. Margaret Brown, had deposited there several years after her husband's death in 1951. But a comparison of Bourinot's texts of the Scott letters with the originals had shown up some curious inconsistencies. Bourinot had had access to something else, and that something else could only have been carbons. Why had he not used the originals? Since the transfer of Brown's papers to the archives did not in fact take place until 1958-59, it was an easy guess that at the very time Bourinot needed them they were in process of acquisition and not available. The setback was made tolerable by the existence of the carbon copies. Were they not as good as the originals? As it turned out, they were to mislead him sometimes or sell him short (as they did, for example, when Scott had changed the original but not the carbon). As part of a plan to get a sampling of Scott's letters quickly into print, however, they must have looked like God's plenty. Although I would have the originals, the carbons would be useful to me too, in their own way.

The key sources for a complete text of the correspondence were therefore now in place. There would be gaps to fill: a visit to Mrs. Brown in Rochester would turn up thirteen of Scott's letters to Brown which had been inadvertently left out of the archives package; two of Brown's letters to Scott, misfiled in the Scott-Aylen papers, would be retrieved almost by chance at a late date. The rest of the task seemed straightforward: ordering, editing, annotating. The reward would be a complete edition of an important dialogue between a major poet and a major critic that had been tantalizingly incomplete for much longer than it should have been.

The Scott-Brown correspondence reflects a friendship that began with a letter of inquiry by Brown in 1940, when Brown was thirty-five and Scott seventy-eight, and ended only with Scott's death in 1947. Within this period, the two men met scarcely half a dozen times, and even then for the most part briefly. But if this meant a loss of the kind of intimacy that Archibald Lampman and Pelham Edgar had enjoyed in their relations with Scott, it meant also that much was gained for the record. What might have been conversation came to be written. The correspondents were marvellously faithful, answering each other "in chime," as Scott might say, letter to letter, month in and month out, for almost the whole of the seven years. They wrote chiefly about literary matters, and to this extent the dialogue is circumscribed. They wrote about Lampman, of course, whose spirit in a real sense brought and kept them together, but also about books and reading, about work of their own, in progress or contemplated, about the various publishing houses with which they were involved. Scott wrote a good deal about the past. Indirectly, the dialogue reflects the evolving profile of a Canadian literature.

From its inception to the present edition, the correspondence has been as much a product of chance as of design, though Scott's wife, Elise, would have said there is no such thing as chance, and I am inclined to agree. Brown had been introduced to Scott as far back as 1929, in Toronto, where Brown, as a young scholar fresh from post-graduate work at the University of Paris, had just taken up his first academic appointment as lecturer in English at University College. Pelham Edgar, across Queen's Park at Victoria College, an influential figure on the literary scene at this time and Scott's friend for over thirty years, was the connection. But nothing came of this casual meeting, and more than a decade was to pass before Brown, in the fall of 1940 and earning his laurels quickly, wrote Scott requesting a contribution to a Canadian issue of *Poetry* (Chicago) for which he was to act as guest editor. Scott's prompt and even eager response kept this contact open.

Again, however, there might have been no significant sequel had it not been for two crucial meetings which followed. In April 1941, Scott and his wife stopped for a short visit with the Edgars on their way back to Ottawa from wintering on the west coast. An evening was arranged, to which Brown and E.J. Pratt were invited. Scott, though he was tired from the journey east and went to bed early, enjoyed himself immensely. Brown took notes: "DCS told me that Night Burial in the Forest was not intended to suggest Indians but e.g. prospectors." Brown's article on Scott published in that summer's issue of *The Manitoba Arts Review* belongs somewhere with the background of this meeting.

Then, just one year later, in the late spring of 1942, Brown came to Ottawa, and for more than a visit, or at least so it seemed at the time. He had taken temporary leave from Cornell University, where he was chairman of the Department of English, to accept an appointment as "special assistant" to the Prime Minister. It would be his contribution to the war effort. As it turned out, his stay was to be short, and he would be gone again by the end of the summer; but there can be no doubt that it was in July and August of this year that Brown first came to know Scott with some degree of intimacy. There were long talks at 108 Lisgar Street. Important for the future, by the time Brown left he and Scott had explored their common interest in the Lampman manuscripts held by Lampman's daughter, Mrs. T.R. Loftus McInnes of Ottawa. For Scott, the Lampman concern was longstanding; for Brown, it was a new horizon.

I have talked of chance and design. It is an intriguing thought that if Brown had not been called back to Ithaca, and Cornell, or if he had been more enthusiastic than he seems to have been about writing speeches for Mackenzie King, he would in all probability have remained in Ottawa for the duration of the war, and the record of his association with Scott would be meagre or non-existent. The exchanges would still have taken place, no doubt, and at a level of intimacy to which letters can scarcely aspire. On the phone or at 108 Lisgar Street, they would have chatted about successes and frustrations in the publishing of their books: their Lampman volume, *At the Long Sault*; Brown's *On Canadian Poetry*; the first Canadian edition of Scott's *In the Village of Viger*; Brown's translation of *Père Goriot* for the Modern Library; and so on. But the record of the making of these books, and of course much else, would have been written on air.

The wheel turned, however, the counters fell into place and the way opened for the letters. Well stocked with Lampman manuscripts and with notes he had made on the summer's conversations with the poet, Brown went back to Cornell, to his teaching and the groves of academe which he loved. He was to visit Ottawa, and Scott, only twice again, once in the spring of 1943 and once a year later. For the rest, he seemed endlessly busy, moving frequently on short trips from Ithaca (and later from his new base in Chicago) to New York and Toronto; but only twice to Ottawa. Perhaps wartime restraints made travel difficult. Perhaps the wives, very different in temperament and background, did not quite hit it off. Scott, for his part, had pretty well given up travel and would stay close to 108 Lisgar Street. Letters there would be, for sure, and the guarantee for the initial exchange was the Lampman material, which Brown would soon be happily into.

The letters can speak for themselves, and so I shall say little about them beyond what I have already said about their provenance, a subject on which the letters are silent. Having worked with them for a long time, however, I would be mean-spirited if I did not share a few of my thoughts about their import and essential character.

I have spoken of a "young critic" and an "old poet." It would be an over-simplification to say that Scott looked back to an old order passing away and Brown forward to a new order yet to come, but in a sense this is true. Scott was an almost exact contemporary of Lampman, as indeed he was of Charles G.D. Roberts and Bliss Carman, all four of them having been born between 1860 and 1862. He had placed his first short story with *Scribner's Magazine* as early as 1887 and would publish his first volume of poetry, *The Magic House*, in 1893. His last volume of poetry, *The Green Cloister*, had appeared in 1935, and between the first book and the last he had planted, like well-spaced monuments, five additional volumes of poetry (one of them being the collected *Poems* of 1925), a short biography and two volumes of short stories. Fifty years is a large time span for the work of a single author. But whether because of the absence of any dramatic shifts in Scott's development as a writer, or simply (and it may be the same thing) because of a certain quality of timelessness in the work itself, the old poet's considerable achievement at the time Brown crossed his path could be seen as very much one piece of cloth.

What is then to be said is that the taste and sensibilities which had shaped the achievement clearly belonged not to the twentieth century, as the dates of publication for most of the books might suggest, but to the nineteenth. I would myself be very hesitant to say that in 1940 Scott was an anachronism, but I am sure that is what he considered himself to be. Lampman had been dead for forty years, Carman for more than ten; Roberts was to die within the period of Scott's correspondence with Brown. Modernism in poetry and painting and music, about which Scott had had some severe things to say in his presidential address to the Royal Society in 1922, was now old hat and just about ready to be overlaid with new credos bred in the turbulent years of the Great Depression and the Second World War. Scott's friendship with Pelham Edgar remained fast, but time had dimmed its lustre a bit. How strange and exciting Brown's appearance on the scene, fresh and vigorous and confident, must have seemed. Here was a man with a first-rate mind, a critic of wide reading and great authority, who not only took Scott's achievement very seriously, but who also was eager to raise the ghost of Lampman. The dullness of wartime Ottawa (for that is how Scott saw it) was illuminated. It was for a moment like old times and brought back memories of poetry readings at Sir John Bourinot's house on Cooper Street and the literary talk that had for a while fed the Mermaid Inn columns which Scott and Lampman and Wilfred Campbell had written in the nineties for the Toronto *Globe*. The new connection was a great stimulus to Scott, and he rose to it. The letters in this volume make clear, I think, his growing dependence on hearing from his new friend.

Brown's position was of course very different. Although as it turned out the young critic would outlive the old poet by only a few years, that tragic fact seemed inconceivable in 1940. Brown was at the height of his powers and on the threshold of a distinguished career. His degrees from the University of Toronto and the University of Paris had been earned brilliantly. Back in Toronto from Paris, he had joined the staff of the Department of English at University College and had quickly become a favourite son: protegé of W.J. Alexander and friend and confidant of A.S.P. Woodhouse, two formidable figures in English literary studies at the time. As befits a favourite son at the University of Toronto, he had been banished to ''the provinces'' for grooming and quick promotion, the form of banishment being an appointment as chairman of the Department of English at the University of Manitoba. This position he had held from 1935 to 1937. He had then returned to his *alma mater* with the rank of full professor, aged thirty-three. Throughout the decade he had published prolifically: a translation of Cazamian's *Carlyle*; articles on E.M. Forster, Willa Cather, Swinburne, Thornton Wilder; his doctoral studies of Matthew Arnold and Edith Wharton; and what seemed like countless reviews. His was already an important critical voice.

Noteworthy within the larger body of Brown's criticism, moreover, had been his growing commitment to the criticism of Canadian literature. The body of such criticism was not great in those days, but Brown would add to it liberally and with enthusiasm, and he would give it an authority it had not known before. It is in this sense that I think of him as looking forward to a new order. By the time he wrote his first letter to Scott, he had for four years been responsible for the ''Poetry'' section of the *University of Toronto Quarterly*'s Letters in Canada Supplement, a pioneering annual review of poetry, fiction and other forms of writing which he had launched, with strong support from Woodhouse, in 1936. The next phase of his commitment, already seminal in his mind, would be a searching re-evaluation of Canadian poets in which he planned to give particular attention to the work of Lampman, Scott and E.J. Pratt. His classic *On Canadian Poetry* was in sight. The Scott connection was opportune: Brown was as ready for Scott as Scott was for Brown.

Some thoughts, now, of a rather different nature. These letters are good letters because they are written by intelligent and well-informed men who listen to one another and who have matters of some consequence to discuss. Throughout, on the other hand, there are no great issues, and although many questions of judgment are raised there is never any serious disagreement. We may feel deprived in the absence of any abrasiveness in the exchange, but we must put up with this. Brown, relatively young, found himself in a situation where his genuine respect for Scott's achievement merged easily with respect of another kind in the presence of the ''perfect old age'' whose picture he was to catch so movingly in the ''Memoir'' written for the *Selected Poems* of 1951. There was nothing wrong with this situation, and I doubt whether it exacted from Brown any more than the avoidance of a few touchy matters in the field of literary taste (Brown, as his wide-ranging reviews make clear, was much more open than Scott to new trends in contemporary poetry) or, say, the exercise of a certain amount of finesse in probing the delicate area which surrounded Lampman's affair with Katherine Waddell. It was enough to be solicitous and in no mean sense deferential. Scott, for his part, answered in kind. A generous man by nature (except perhaps in his dealings with publishers, when he became easily irascible) it was in the grain of his character to be solicitous about his friend's well-being, his family and his work. Scott's deference had its roots in his immense admiration, doubtless enhanced by the limitations of his own formal education, for Brown's deep learning. There may be moments when we smile a bit, as in the presence of a stately dance of two men who may not get through the door: ''After you, dear Edward''; ''No, No! After *you*, dear Duncan.'' But this will not be often. And why should they not, after all, be gentle with one another? Both were men of reason, and both were disciples of Matthew Arnold to whom notions of sweetness and light and disinterested inquiry came easily. Arnold would have been proud of them.

A much more important consideration is the level of consciousness, if I may use the term, at which the correspondents function. In the absence of diaries, we do not of course know what awarenesses came to the surface in the privacy of their inner lives. We have only the letters. But if we judge by these, what are we to make of the near-invisibility of a world war which spreads its arch of fire over a bed of human suffering throughout practically the whole span of the correspondence? In England at this time, a loaded question put to people who turned on unnecessary lights or wasted food was: "Don't you know there's a war on?" The Scott-Brown correspondence would have had to answer, on balance, "No." There may be a conventional response to a dramatic moment in the war, as there is from Scott, for example, when General Montgomery's Eighth Army turns back Rommel's forces from the borders of Egypt in 1942. There are a number of references to the political arena when the conscription crisis boils up in the Canadian Parliament in 1944. There are glimpses of rationing and billeting. The rest, however, is pretty well silence. The unconditional surrender of Germany on May 7, 1945, goes unnoticed in Brown's letter to Scott of May 8. The dropping of atomic bombs on Hiroshima and Nagasaki on August 6 and 9 goes unnoticed in Scott's letter to Brown of August 11.

I am trying to make an observation rather than a moral judgment, but that may not be possible. The war was not just a series of happenings which, though sufficiently dramatic, to be sure, might or might not be noticed in a letter to a friend. The war meant a profound dislocation and relocation of values. Literary life in London during these years split in a dozen ways over what seemed, to Orwell and Spender and Eliot and many others, grave issues: communism and fascism, the lessons of Spain, the place of the artist in time of war, the plight of the Jews, anarchy and the atomization of the social contract; and to the extent that this life was ever reassembled, the new patterns were almost unrecognizable. We may say that England is not Canada. Yet Canadian poets of the early 1940s, certainly the Montreal group, reflect in their intellectual life and in their poems the turbulence of these years, as does also, to take a particular case, Hugh MacLennan retrospectively in *Two Solitudes* and *The Watch That Ends the Night*. Closer still to home, a young girl named Elizabeth Smart visited her native Ottawa at about the time Scott was preparing a hand-written copy of his poem 'Intermezzo' to send to the Browns at Christmas 1943, and in an agonizing interview with her father recognized the immense gulf that her affair with George Barker, the English poet, and the coming of an illegitimate child, had opened up between her and her family. Elizabeth was one of the first of the new romantics, and there was no part of her own or the world's predicament that was not imprinted on her nerves. She was to write about the pain and the ecstasy of her initiation in a remarkable book, published in 1945, entitled *By Grand Central Station I Sat Down and Wept*. I have particular reason to mention the Smarts because they turn up in the present correspondence. Scott knew them well, Brown slightly. It is as if two spheres of consciousness, one encompassing the two men and the other the young girl, come together but do not touch. The stately procession of the letters moves on its appointed way. The exchanges are frank within the boundaries, reticent beyond. There will be no disturbance of sensibilities beyond a certain level of immediate and practical concerns.

These concerns are proper enough. The shared world of D.C. Scott and E.K. Brown is literature. As poet and as critic, they explore this world eagerly and without artifice. They love to read books, and they love to make books. Best of all, they love to talk to one another about what they are doing. They talk well. We are fortunate to be able to listen.

This edition of the Scott-Brown correspondence is as complete as I can make it. It contains ninety-four letters from Scott to Brown and eighty-seven from Brown to Scott. Two additional letters are from Mrs. Brown to Scott, and I include them because they have to do with Deaver Brown, whose infant presence reigns over an important part of the correspondence. For the same reason, I include a short note from Scott to Mrs. Brown and a short note from Scott to Deaver. The single letter from Elise Aylen Scott to Brown, the last in the volume, is the volume's proper coda. The poem 'Intermezzo' has a letter's place in the collection because it is on one occasion Scott's way, with Elise, of sending Christmas greetings to the Browns. The texts of all the letters are given in full.

Putting the letters in their correct order raised no serious problems. A few of them were undated, others were only partially dated: for example, "Sunday," or "March 16." A few, as it turned out, were incorrectly dated. But because the correspondence is truly a dialogue, the two men answering faithfully to one another in the *poste* and *riposte* of adjacent letters, internal evidence became not only a test for completeness but also, in doubtful cases, an arbiter of sequence. Two very short notes by Scott, both undated, have not been included because of the absence of internal evidence which would enable me to assign them places in the sequence with any confidence. Both say in a few lines, with slight variations, simply that Scott has been indisposed. In three instances, on the other hand, internal evidence suggests that letters may be missing. Appropriate notes signal these apparent gaps in the record.

Editorial procedures have been relatively simple. An unusual characteristic of the material is that by far the greater part of it (148 of 187 letters) exists in author-typescript. The relatively few letters written by hand are identified. But although typescripts offer some obvious advantages over holographs in the preparation of a manuscript, they also create some problems of their own. I pass over the problem of the fading ribbon, which I have come to think of mostly as Brown's problem, or for that matter of the brand new ribbon, Scott's problem on a few occasions, where heavy inking clogs the heads of his *élite* type and smudges on the page. More important is the problem of the typographical error, the "typo," for which there is no real counterpart in script.

It was my early encounters with typos that led me to see a physical difference between Scott's and Brown's letters that seemed worth preserving in the printed version. Brown, no three-finger man (in fact I would guess from the evenness of his page a touch-typist), hardly ever strikes the wrong key. If there is a typo, it is carefully corrected. His spelling, punctuation and paragraphing, moreover, can scarcely be faulted. Such regularity seems consistent with both his calling and his personality. Scott, on the other hand, is irregular. He was, I surmise, a three-finger man. He was also nervous, as he sometimes says to Brown, and he had an arthritic hand. It is therefore not surprising that his letters are strewn with typos. Again in contrast to Brown's practices, Scott's spelling is erratic and his paragraphing virtually non-existent. Punctuation is unorthodox: commas frequent in place of periods or semi-colons. Capitalization is inconsistent and abbreviations are common, or contractions as in "wld" for "would." What help can an editor offer without blurring a very real difference in texture between the two sets of letters? The answer was, of course, for the editor to stay out of the texts as much as possible. Brown's case presented very few problems. What about Scott's?

Scott's unusual practice was to go over his letters, a pen and black ink beside him, after he had taken them from the machine. He might underline a word for emphasis, insert a phrase, provide a marginal comment; and at this stage he corrected many of his typos. But he missed quite a few, and these I have corrected. I have done this in all cases, that is, where I have concluded that a mere typo was involved, as in "tow" for "two." Where there is an obvious misspelling, however, as in "cigarrets," I have let Scott's version stand. Where Scott fluctuates, as he does between "seperate" and "separate," I have taken the spelling as it comes. Misspelled proper names, as in "Rosetti" for Rossetti," are given their correct form in the notes. I have also let stand Scott's punctuation, except in a few cases in which the sense of the sentence seemed in danger of being lost; and I have done nothing with his abbreviations or contractions unless they threatened complete mystification, in which case the form is completed in square brackets or an appropriate note is provided. I have tried to introduce some consistency in capitalization, but I have done nothing about Scott's paragraphing, which seems to me an important signature of this correspondent.

Interpolated material, whether in the case of the filling out of an abbreviation, or in the case of the date of a letter being supplied by me, is placed in the customary square brackets. I have regularized the many different forms in which superscribed dates appear in the originals; thus "2.11.44" becomes "November 2, 1944." I have also regularized Brown's and Scott's practices, both of them erratic, in citing the titles of books, articles, poems and the like: italics for books, double quotation marks for articles and short stories, single quotation marks for poems.

It will be clear from my account of the provenance of these letters that a considerable number of Scott's exist in two versions, possibly three: an original, a carbon copy, and sometimes a printed text in the Bourinot collections. For the most part these sources are identical, but by no means always. This is not, however, a *variorum* edition. The authoritative text, the one used if it is available, is always the letter Scott sent to Brown. On Brown's side, there are of course no alternatives. On Scott's side, if there is no original, which is the case on eight occasions, the carbon copy becomes the authoritative text. Differences

14

between the Scott originals and Bourinot's texts are noted only if Bourinot has omitted material (a marginal jotting, for example, or an insert) because the carbon copy with which he was working was not corrected to conform with the letter Scott mailed, or if he has deleted a passage from his source, as he does, for example, when he encounters unflattering remarks by Scott about Lorne Pierce. On occasion, I have taken notice of the draft of a letter, the draft having been filed by Scott in lieu of a carbon copy. All these procedures are made clear at appropriate points in the text.

I wish to thank Mrs. E.K. Brown of Rochester and Mr. and Mrs. John Aylen of Ottawa for their kind permission to use and publish the letters which make up this edition. Without their encouragement, help and patience, my work would have been very difficult, perhaps impossible. I am grateful also to a handful of relatives of Duncan and Elise who have shared their recollections of the poet with me and let me see letters and documents which they treasure: Mrs. G.M. Graham, the late Dorothea and Lois Aylen, Peter and Muriel Aylen and Mrs. Lewis D. Clement. From the Social Sciences and Humanities Research Council of Canada (it was just plain Canada Council when I began) I received several generous grants in support of the early stages of the project, and this funding enabled me to secure the help of a remarkable group of assistants whose dedication, skill and unfailing cheerfulness I cannot sufficiently praise. My warm thanks therefore go to Claudia Chowaniec, who made a start on the sifting of the Scott-Aylen Papers and the ordering of the Scott-Brown letters; to Judy Pope, who laid the foundations for the notes to the correspondence; to Ofelia Cohn-Sfetcu and Christine Fisher, who for almost a year were at the very heart of the project, and who in that time gave the manuscript much of its first real shape and substance; and finally to Grace Martin, who closed some gaps in the notes which the rest of us had missed along the way. Liana Van der Bellen, Joyce Banks, Robert Taylor, Anne Goddard and others at the Public Archives and the National Library of Canada made the buildings on Wellington Street a pleasant and fruitful place for me to work.

I have talked with many people along the way about the Scott-Brown correspondence. All were helpful. Several took the time and trouble to help me with particular problems: Michael Gnarowski of my department, who put me on the trail of the Scott-Aylen Papers; I. Norman Smith, formerly editor of the Ottawa *Journal*, who had a lot to tell me about Scott and the *literati* of Ottawa in the mid-forties; Bruce Nesbitt of the Department of English, Simon Fraser University, who shared with me on occasion his expertise on Archibald Lampman, as indeed David Staines of the University of Ottawa shared his on E.K. Brown and Sandy Campbell hers on Pelham Edgar; and, in special place, Mrs. Arthur Bourinot, who helped in many ways, but who contributed most by establishing for me a warm and living link with the past. I am grateful to Leon Edel of the University of Hawaii for giving me, in the letter from which I have quoted in this introduction, his impressions of the young E.K. Brown at the time when they were students together at the Sorbonne. I wish to thank Yousuf Karsh for his kind permission to reproduce the portraits of the poet and the critic which appear in this volume. Christine Fisher has been invaluable in the preparation of the index; and I salute Diane Mew, who is without doubt one of the best copy editors in the country.

THE LETTERS

1940

Brown is making a name for himself at the University of Toronto. In October he is invited to serve as guest editor for a "Canadian" issue of Poetry (Chicago). *He writes Scott, asking for a contribution. Scott responds quickly. They make friendly gestures.*

1

6 Glen Edyth Drive
Toronto, Ontario
October 17, 1940

Dear Mr. Scott:

I have been asked by Mr. George Dillon, the editor of *Poetry*,[1] to take charge of an issue of that magazine to be devoted entirely to Canadian Poets and the criticism of Canadian poetry.

It is my hope that you will send me something for the issue: no representation of Canadian poetry could be at all adequate if you were not among those included.

As you probably know *Poetry* pays 25 cents a line, uses no material previously published, and has about 700 lines of verse in an issue. Obviously no poem of very great length could be used; but you perhaps have something not altogether brief that you would care to send to me. I do not like the thought of the best of our poets being represented by one or two short lyrics.

I should add that Mr. Dillon reserves a final editorial judgment; but I am altogether disposed to think that he will take my recommendations without substantial change.

May I take this occasion of saying to you how great my admiration of your work has been?

Sincerely yours,
E.K. Brown

2

108 Lisgar Street
Ottawa
October 25, 1940

Dear Professor Brown,

I would like to be represented in the special No. of *Poetry* as you are editing it and I hope writing any criticism which may appear. I have written so little lately that I have no choice but to send you the enclosed.[1] When we were last in Italy I did several things which have been printed but since then with the exception of the 'Lines for the King's Farewell,' and that as you know was a special sort of thing, I have not written a line.[2] I value your critical faculty very highly and you must exercise it in this connection, and if you do not think that I would be reasonably represented by these lines send them back and I shall be satisfied. I would appreciate a talk with you on the poetry of these times. I have ordered Eliot's new book,[3] the reviews do not give one a favourable impression, and I find it hard to follow his later course. If you are here someday I hope you will "call me up."

Yours ever sincerely,
Duncan C. Scott

3

Baldwin House[1]
University of Toronto
November 12, 1940

Dear Dr. Scott,

Many thanks for your moving and beautifully clear poem which I am delighted to have and shall send to *Poetry* with pride. My expectation is that the material will all go to Chicago in December.

Of late I have been reading with much excitement the collected poems of Kenneth Fearing.[2] I wonder how they would strike you?

If I am ever in Ottawa it would be a great pleasure to have a talk with you. If you are in Toronto and not too busy with your old friends I hope you will let me know.

Sincerely yours,
E.K. Brown

1941

After wintering on the west coast, the Scotts return to Ottawa by way of Toronto, where the poet and the critic spend a lively evening at the home of Pelham Edgar. E.J. Pratt is there. Brown's article on Scott in the spring issue of the Manitoba Arts Review *quickens the flow of letters which follow when Scott is back at Lisgar Street. He is hungry for the kind of sympathetic and authoritative criticism Brown seems able to provide. In between times they discuss Ralph Gustafson's forthcoming* Anthology of Canadian Poetry, *to which Scott is contributing some poems. By September, Brown has moved to Cornell University, Ithaca. It is a promotion, but he will not like Ithaca very much.*

4 [*Holo.*]

108 Lisgar Street[1]
January 19, 1941

Dear Professor Brown,

I should have answered yours of Nov. 12 long ago. I was very pleased that you found the poem acceptable and I shall hope to see the issue. We are leaving home tonight for Victoria B.C. (The Empress Hotel) and will be away until 1 May.[2] I shall try to get Fearing's Poems and will try to tell you how they strike me. I may be in Toronto on my way home in late Apl. as I want to see the Edgars[3] and I'll try to have a word with you. Anthologies are always a nuisance unless the Editor is competent. I had an application the other day from Ralph Gustafson who has been selected by the Penguin people to make an anthology of Canadian Poetry.[4] Instead of getting yourself or Edgar to do this (perhaps you would not accept) they choose R.G. He made a queer selection of 6 of my lyrics[5] but my publishers will have to deal with him. My wife and I got the circular about the "annual survey," but neither of us have books to report. I have only published one poem in '40! the Ballad 'Veronique Fraser' in *Sat. Nt.* Feb. 6.[7] I wonder if you read it. I must close now with regards.

Yours sincerely,
Duncan C. Scott

5

6 Glen Edyth Drive
Toronto
January 30, [1941]

Dear Mr. Scott:

I was deeply touched by your poem, a very delicate and true little thing, and I shall value it very highly indeed.[1] It was most kind of you to send it.

It is very pleasant to look forward to seeing you in April. I hope you can give me a day or two's notice so that I can be free for more than a short time. But come what may I shall make sure of seeing you.

The other day I had a letter from the Editor of *Poetry* in which he tells me his admiration of your poem. He likes the whole issue. It will be the April number of the magazine, so I shall not give him your B.C. address for the present.

Sincerely yours,
E.K. Brown

6 [*Holo.*]

May 10, 1941

My dear E.K.,

This as you will remember is a permitted form of address. I enjoyed that evg greatly and, as I said, I wish such evgs might come frequently.[1] When I came home I found the copies of *Poetry* and have had time to read although, you may remark, no time to write. Being rather critical of verse these times I enjoyed yr prose as I always do, and this sort of criticism is a tonic and I would say a disinfectant of the old style. I think you did a very good piece of work in that and in yr selection. I have my preferences in the verse, certainly; for instance I liked Smith's two last things[2] and E.J.P.'s last,[3] diction I thought particularly fine; but there is no use calling the roll. I hope readers everywhere will find some hope for our future. Dont forget to send me yr *Post mortem*. It is probably that as I am not likely to add much more, and when I get it I will read and write you again. Meanwhile congratulations on yr issue of *Poetry*. I'm sure all contributors myself included are very pleased and satisfied.

Yours sincerely,
Duncan C. Scott

7

July 2, 1941

My dear E.K.,

The Review came to hand and I am much obliged for my copy, and greatly interested in what you have written about my work and the manner in which you have written.[1] You know I admire your prose and your critical power and I am pleased that you have given me the benefit of both. No one has dealt so discerningly with certain aspects of the poems. For example your remarks on page 54, "In his method of thought. . . .etc."[2] This is true but I was not conscious of it. That page deals with the influence of Music and an error has crept in there. You have given me a "Violin" instead of a Piano. The other slip about 'Night Burial' is unimportant.[3] I should be put to it if called upon to take my violin and give you Bach's Air on the G string, although I might make a fist (just now owing to neuritis it would be literally a fist) at one of the preludes from the Forty-eight. I do not like any proficiency I may have in music to be exaggerated. When one of the flatterers wrote of my *profound knowledge* of music he was talking rot in his ignorance. There are few in any time or anywhere to whom those words would apply. I can only claim to be entirely sensitive to Music and to have absorbed a deal of it. When I hear a strain of fine music, I stop thinking. But as for profound knowledge, that is a different matter; that involves more items than in any of the arts. Your reference to this point is just right and the analogies have been so far unnoticed, as you say.

Your remarks about the Indian poems are very good. I had for about twenty years oversight of their development and I was never unsympathetic to aboriginal ideals, but there was the law which I did not originate and which I never tried to amend in the direction of severity. One can hardly be sympathetic with the contemporary Sun-dance or Potlatch when one knows that the original spirit has departed and that they are largely the opportunities for debauchery by low white men.

I like your remarks about my dealings with Nature; quite true, soundly critical, and new in statement. I am very pleased that you have done this article and that you chose to publish it in this connection. Prof. McQueen was a strong man and clearly a lovable character (I never had the privilege of meeting him), and all that is here written about him fills one with regret for his loss. I enjoyed reading the extracts from his correspondence; I realize how you must have valued his letters.[4]

Very many thanks for your appreciation and with renewed regards and best wishes.

Yours sincerely,
Duncan Campbell Scott

[*P.S. holo.*] My typist was very formal. I'll put yr article with Pelham's.[5]

D.C.S.

1942

The highlight is Brown's coming to Ottawa early in the year to pay his dues to the war effort by serving as special assistant to Mackenzie King. The dues are exorbitant, and Brown is back in Ithaca by the end of August. But the nub of the matter is Brown's personal contact with Scott at 108 Lisgar Street during these summer months. They are soon on a first-name basis. The letters fall silent, of course, but the impetus for on-going communication is great. Lampman is the link. Scott introduces Brown to Natalie MacInnes, Lampman's daughter, who has papers and documents inherited from her father. Brown takes a batch of these with him when he returns to Ithaca. Soon he is launched on a project with Scott to bring out a volume of hitherto unpublished poems. This is the genesis of At the Long Sault and Other New Poems. *A lively ping-pong exchange of detail and substance about the proposed volume dominates the rest of the year. In the background, Brown's* On Canadian Poetry *is taking shape. Brown also finds time to write a portrait of Mackenzie King, which* Harper's *will publish in the new year. Scott, more than holding his own in the* At the Long Sault *exchange, writes a short article on Clarence Gagnon for* Maritime Art. *The tempo of the correspondence increases. "You don't know what a nervous and apprehensive friend you have," Scott writes. In passing they share an approval of Earle Birney's* David, *recently published. The quiet note of the year's end is Scott's poem 'Intermezzo,' copied in a fair hand and sent as a Christmas gift to the Browns.*

8 [*Holo.*]

Sylvia Court
Vancouver
January 14, 1942

Dear E.K.,

I must acknowledge yr Christmas card and tell you that I was very pleased that you remembered me. It was long after you had left Toronto that I heard you had gone to Cornell.[1] None of my Toronto friends told me although I know it must have been a serious loss to them. I feel it too, both in the individual and general sense because a good friend of my past work is no longer present and it's a bad loss for Canada. Your critical power was much needed here. However, here's wishing you the greatest success and I hope these Cornell people will understand the worth and distinction of the man they stole from us. As you live in the U.S. we cld not carry out our plan of nominating you for the Royal Soc.[2] We came to B.C. to escape the cold and intended to go to Victoria but we wont get any farther away from home as the Pacific coast is now closer to the war.[3] I shall I think stop at Toronto on the way home to see Pelham as I did last year. I heard from him by letter at Xmas. I have foregathered with Lawren Harris who is living here now.[4] He lent me a small book of poems by Dilys Bennett Laing, a lady he met in New England.[5] I was much taken with some of her things. As you may know his painting has entirely changed direction — no landscapes, no portraits (although he never did many portraits, I think he might have been our greatest portrait painter) just abstract forms beautifully, exquisitely done and full of meaning for him but difficult to *feel* as I like to feel painting. There is no *climate* here — dashes of rain, mist deepening to fog, touches of frost and then some clear days when you get the mountains standing snow-capped around the inlets of the sea and sea distances — and with it all more lovely and strange and shifting atmospheric effects than I have ever seen elsewhere.

With renewed regards and best wishes.

Yours sincerely,
Duncan C. Scott

9 [*Holo.*]

[Ottawa][1]
May 16, 1942

Dear Duncan Campbell Scott:

I learn from A.S. Bourinot[2] that you have returned from the coast. Perhaps you may have heard that I am in Ottawa for a few months.[3] May I come to call some evening?

Sincerely,
E.K. Brown

10 [*Holo.*]

[Ottawa]
May 26, 1942

Dear Duncan Campbell Scott:

Unexpectedly I have to go to Cornell to-morrow and shall be away a week at most. Please don't mention my absence — it's unofficial.

It was good to hear your voice and I look forward to an evening with you when I come back.

Sincerely,
E.K. Brown

11

Cornell,
Ithaca, N.Y.
October 4, [1942]

Dear Duncan:

Will you pardon that informality? After our talks of this summer that is the way I should like to address you despite your eminence and years.[1]

I am sending to you the copies of the poems that seemed to me the best, indeed almost all that I transcribed. If you will add to these the sonnets to his wife-to-be,[2] you will have about fifty pages. I think that fifty pages of text, or a little less, would amply justify a little volume. So much is good, I think.

The tentative arrangement is this: long poems; short lyrics; sonnets. I have not given any thought to arrangement within groups. That should be purely your work, I think. A poet will know. And I don't specially hold to my grouping into three parts. I do think 'Daulac' should come first.

Some poems I have supplied titles for. And again you will do better with these. 'Daulac' might perhaps be called 'At the Long Sault.' There are practically no titles supplied by Lampman himself. I have marked A.L. those few that are his. I have put a few of the *later* love poems in with the lyrics thinking that their import could be concealed. Those that it seemed to me we could not use I have put at the very end. There is one long poem that reveals the object of his love too clearly; fortunately it is not very good, and I have not included it.[3]

We might perhaps include one of the two pieces you published in the *Canadian Magazine*, 'New Year's Eve.'[4] I am enclosing the copies you gave me of the two things you gave to that magazine.

I will send up my rough copies later, so that at a few points you may decide between alternative readings of words and phrases. I have practically always taken the last reading.

You suggested that I do the introduction, and as you will remember I wanted you to have an introduction too. I am wondering how it would be if you wrote a preface, of some substantial length, explaining about the note books and saying why you thought it was worth bringing out some more of the poems, and then if I went on and tried to say what these poems added to our picture of Lampman *the poet* and perhaps attempted a general estimate of him, taking my references as far as possible from our new stuff. That is a suggestion.

In the manuscript book in the Parl. Lib. [Library of Parliament] called "Miscellaneous Poems,"[5] there are two or three things right at [the] beginning that have not I think appeared. Would you have a look at them, and see if you think any of these deserve publication?

I have been dreadfully busy. It is very hard to get junior men with the draft calling so many of them, and although in the end I got enough I was very harassed for a couple of weeks, and I don't know how soon some of those I have may leave us. My own classes are flourishing: 70 for an introduction to the novel, 25 for an advanced course on modern poetry and almost a dozen for my graduate course on the Victorians. I am happier teaching, but I miss a few things about Ottawa, the beauty of the buildings on Parliament Hill and two or three young men I got to know, and most of all my evenings with your wife and yourself. Peggy joins me in my regrets: she fell in love with you both, and indeed with Ottawa.

Sincerely,
E.K.B.

P.S. May I leave the dealings with Musson's[6] to you, or indeed any dealings with publishers other than M. if they are not interested? They will be much more likely to listen to you. [*Holo*] A "Christmas" volume might be worth considering — for Musson's.

12

October 18, 1942

My dear Edward.[1]   The informality was welcome; as I never felt congenial to the initial form of address with any of my friends and as between us I find it flippant I will, unless you have an objection, adopt the above as I think I heard your wife so call you. Neither Elise nor I belong to the sort of people who begin Christian names at the first cocktail party but we reciprocate the feeling you expressed in your last letter. You must indeed have been very busy at the opening of the session and I am surprised that you were able to do so much work on the Poems. You may think me slow in answering yours of the 4th inst, but I have not been idle as you will see from the enclosures. Your suggested arrangement seems right. I found the Greek Sonnets[2] in the first section following on 'The Emperor's Sweetheart'; perhaps I misplaced them, but I take it that you want them to go with the other Sonnets. We should have a note to explain the historical significance of these; will you be able to supply it, or shall I look it up? Your titles were good and will stand; I will try to fill the blanks. 'At the Long Sault' is the proper title for 'Daulac;' I think we should have a few words of prose as a heading to set the stage, as it were. Do you agree, and shall I submit what I think necessary? As for the preliminary matter, my own share might be a *short* preface but I have not yet felt what it should be. Your part will be most important and the outline you give of your introduction is on the right line. This I take it will be a complete study of A.L. You spoke once I think of doing a seperate article for the *Toronto Q*. Perhaps you have given up that idea. I feel more and more strongly, the longer I am in contact with the scheme, that the book ought to justify itself entirely, not alone by the Poems but by the surrounding matter, the editing etc. so that it might be a unique volume. We must work towards that end; I feel a sense of responsibility growing. The punctuation in many of these Poems is nonexistant, I will provide it; A.L. did not favor much scattering about of commas and I think I know what he would do. At present I am in favor of including 'The Settler's Tale' and 'New Year's Eve.'[3]

Now as to a publisher. Loftus reminded me that Musson had sold his rights in all the Poems to the Ryerson Press.[4] Of course I was a party to this change, in fact could do nothing to prevent it; but I didnt like it then and dont like it now, Lorne Pierce not being congenial to me, although we are quite friendly. Maybe he has not done very well with his bargain; his methods are peculiar; he has failed to answer some of Loftus's letters.[5] As I told you I handed over to Loftus all the management of the Poems. I think we shall have to offer the book to the R.P. and I had better deal with the matter when the time comes. What is your opinion? We should have the M.S. complete and perfect before we begin to negociate and that will take some time and we should set a time limit for L.P.'s decision for he is a great dilly-dallyer. If he dont want the book I prefer MacMillan or the Oxford Press. I have seen Loftus once since you left; he came to carry away the M.S.S. That was before I got your letter and I have not told him that I have heard from you but I will when I get your reaction to the Portrait in Six Sonnets; after that I will let him have the Poems and will hope to have their consent without reserve. In corresponding about these Sonnets give me a seperate note. Were you both pleased with Karsh's portrait? We thought it a success but did not approve of the description tacked onto it in *Sat. Nt.*[6] Why will Editors be so foolish? I cut out the Portrait and put it in the front of your *Victorian Poetry.*[7] I made the sugar last as long as I could, felt very pampered and gave thanks every morning. We have been able to give thanks every day for lovely Autumn weather; more than two weeks of golden sunshine; the trees have put up a great show but we have not been into the country to witness it. Now the leaves are falling. "October with the rain of ruined leaves," as our poet has it.[8] Did you see the enclosed PIG correspondence?[9] Gossip asserts that Ilsley was amused but that Our Peerless Leader was furious.[10] Was his letter the sort of thing you were supposed to supply? I hear that Peregrine Acland has joined the staff, he is [the] son of F.A.

Acland once Editor of the *Globe* afterwards King's Printer.[11] Elise joins in
affectionate messages to you both and in the wish that you were here.

Yours ever,
D.C.S.

[P.S.] I send a notice from the *New Statesman* of Spender's new books which I
had kept for you.[12]

13

Cornell
October 28, 1942

Dear Duncan:

Your letter was full of good things. The take-off on W.L.M.K. *et al.* brought
back some memories of servitude. Yes, I used to have almost that kind of thing to
do: I recall a great lot of argument about a note to a woman who was devoting the
rent of her summer cottage to the war-effort. It was one of the man's chief
weaknesses to spend far too much time on detail. All the Canadians I showed the
column to were hugely amused. It is almost in tatters. Thanks too for the Spender
review. I have not yet had time to read the book. What a confused person he is!

And now for Lampmaniana. I like your arrangement of the portrait. Probably
you noticed that in II and III there are references to stoicism which are
superficially at least a little inconsistent. That is my only comment, apart from
delight at seeing so much good verse and congratulation on this method of
enabling us, possibly, to print a good deal about the lady. I refer to the matter in
the enclosure as you ask.

I also like the Ottawa view,[1] in a form which is new to me. 'Despondency'[2]
seems to me a very possible addition; but if you dislike its inclusion I will not
argue for it. I leave the matter wholly to you. The other early pieces seemed to
me weakish or awkward. I am not returning them. If you want them let me know.

'The Usurer' I particularly like: the fantastic image related to the real world
appeals to me. Also I think it would help to show Lampman's variety. The
argument against him that I should like to meet so far as we can is that he shows
so little variety. For the same reason I should like to include 'The Politician.'[3]
But I think I could use here the device you used for the sonnet on Life: quote it in
my article.[4] So though I return it to you it is my view that the best solution is for
me to quote it, and for us to leave it out of the canon.

I enclose a copy of the lines to Natalie.[5] Will you date them if you can?

'The Sunset' is not a good piece on the whole. I agree that it should not appear.
So I don't return it.

I hope you will do the note on 'At the Long Sault.' I shall look up the Greek revolt and send a note. Perhaps you could show the MacI's the material and just mention that such a note was coming. Whatever it is, it wouldn't affect their opinion of our project.

I am so glad that you will look after the punctuation, as you have done with all the other things of L's that have come out since his death. I shrink from doing any of this myself.

I hope your preface will not be over-short. One night you mentioned to us that you did not dislike suggestions of subjects for poetry. Would you do a sonnet on A.L.? That would give a special cachet to our work. It would indeed.

I enclose the chapter on A.L. from my projected book on Canadian Poetry,[6] with the parts that I think should be left out set in square brackets. I think I have written more in the Arnoldian manner than I usually do: but I am always under the influence of Matt. Without being offensively polemical (I hope) I have tried to meet the indictment Collin made.[7] Absorption in A.L. these past months has made me feel that C. was not only ungenerous (I thought that before) but also unjust. You will perhaps be a little disturbed by the number of references to yourself; but I can see no way to avoid them — you have said almost all the important things that have been said on this subject.

Perhaps my article is too long. I can cut it further here and there.

I ought to say that when I wrote the article I had in mind the publication of the book on Canadian Poetry before that of our work. I hope the order will be reversed. If it is, of course I shall wish to leave out from the book on C.P. a good part of what is in square brackets. But until we know what the fate of our work is to be it did not seem worth while changing the article considered as a chapter. I shall wish to have the assurance from the publisher of our work that he won't object to my use of the material in my book on C.P. I will not use it as [a] magazine article.

All the negotiations for publication I am happy to leave to you with the fullest power to act for both of us.

I forgot to say that I think you are right in wishing to omit some of the early love poems. Do what you think best.

Walking through our gorge yesterday I felt that winter was on us: snow on the trees, huge masses of brown water rushing along, and our overcast Ithaca sky. I feel a little lost in the small town. I hope not to end my days here, but Ithaca will do very well for the time.

Our best wishes and kindest memories to you both.

As ever,
E.K.B.

[Enclosure]   Cornell,
                                                   October 28, 1942

Dear DCS:

   Just a line to say that the group of sonnets called "A Portrait in Six Sonnets"
seems an admirable addition to the series. It is one of the best examples I know of
A.L.'s power in dealing with human nature.[8]

                                        As ever,
                                          E.K.B.

14

                                                   October 31, 1942

Dear Edward.

   I have gone carefully through the Poems, have punctuated and in the few
vacancies have suggested titles. I am very keen about 'At the Long Sault.' As I
studied it I felt a certain looseness about it which detracted from its force and
beauty. I have ventured to make a very few changes and a rearrangement of the
lines from "So Daulac turned him anew." I used "town" instead of "burg" in
the 26th line as he uses "town" in the lyric; I dislike "burg." I have done
nothing I would not have suggested to A.L. if we had been together. I think the
Poem is improved in directness and does not lose anything in other ways. Do you
agree? This is a beautiful thing, I am deeply indebted to you for discovering it.
Note the Title as I have it. I think that would be all right. My suggestion of a
prose note at the head of the lines was folly: I think it would spoil the simple
opening of the Poem; if the reader dont know of the incident let him look up
Parkman.[1]
   Please look at the Poem 'Man and Nature.' In the second stanza fourth line
omit "fancy;" fourth verse, second line, "*Save* Nature's only," we get away
from two "Buts" at the beginning of the lines; fifth stanza, third line, "oh"
should be "the;" either the fifth or sixth stanza seems redundant, although the
sixth extends the idea. The repetition of the two last lines in these stanzas seems
weak; would you advise leaving out the sixth, or would you treat the poem as
immature and let it stand as it is? The last stanza, read the two last lines,

   O'er the drowsed head, it hath not soul, but see
   What grace, what strength, what generous dignity!

Would you leave this Poem out? He has often used this theme in a perfect way.
Do you think it would be a good idea to complete the group of Love Sonnets to
his wife by reprinting the three which were in *Among the Millet*, 'Love Doubt,'
'Perfect Love,' and 'Love Wonder,' ending the sequence with 'Love Wonder,'
and including the two, 'Praise and Prayer,' which really belong?[2]

I am sure you are very busy but I shall hear from you before long I hope; how easy it would be for us to decide all questions if we were together. Pelham is in town for the duration, I suppose; he is working with the Censors as a Head Clerk; at present he is living with our friend Col. Osborne.[3] I don't think his wife and Jane are coming just now, I doubt if they could find any place to live. Of course I shall be seeing him often. I hope you and Peggy are well and that her house is settled and that life goes smoothly and excitingly, if you so want it. Here things are smooth and exciting at times. We have been well but we indulged in Colds and could not, in full, enjoy the lovely Autumn weather. I am sending your wife a copy of *Art* with a note on my friend Clarence Gagnon;[4] the National Gallery is having a Memorial Exhibition of his work and this little article is to be used in the Catalogue. I have been reading Sturge Moore in the three vol. edition.[5] I dont get on very well with the long poems but I am finding some lovely lyrics; another poet to whom sufficient attention has not been paid!

Our affectionate greetings to you both and I am as ever,

Yours sincerely,
Duncan

Later. Nov. 1st[6]

Just as I was about to post my letter of the 31st the post brought me yours of the 28th so I opened my envelope in order to add a few words not in complete answer to your good letter. I read your article today and I like it well and I reflected upon it, its place in our scheme, and on the Poems. I wish you would let me know soon what you think of 'The Long Sault,' just a line. For me this poem is lyrical; it does not narrate it describes, and that description is clasped, as it were, between two pure nature lyrics. In fact I would be inclined to leave out the "But," in the line "But far in an open glade," and begin the description with [the] word "Far," i.e. "Far in an open glade." Try reading that aloud. The action described ends with the line, "To gnash their teeth and stare," and then comes the pure lovely lyric of which I think you say the final word of interpretation. The opening and closing lyrics might be printed in italics so detached are they; but I don't advocate that. I am *very* pleased with what you say about this poem and I want to retain it all in your introduction. I will arrange the early Love Sonnets as I think they might be used and send them to you for consideration. I am always pondering on the Canon, and the book takes form in my mind; I mean the whole book, your share, mine and the Poems. I would not care to attempt a Sonnet; I dont object to your setting me a task, but I have never cared to use the form and, as you may have noticed, I have made very few.

DCS

15

Cornell,
November 9, 1942

Dear Duncan:

I had planned to get this letter written over the week-end, but could not. I don't think you will much approve of what I was doing. Before I left Ottawa I made up my mind to attempt a portrait of Mackenzie King; but I felt that I should wait till I was somewhere else where the perspective was surer. I actually drafted the piece in late September; and had it in shape for submission to a publisher by mid-October. I wanted it to appear in the U.S. and in a magazine with a really large circulation; and my inexperience made me hesitate. Finally I decided to send it to *Harper's* first; and to my great surprise on Friday I had an urgent letter asking me to reshape one part and let the editor have the piece back by Monday. So the week-end went to that. He speaks of printing it in January. Please do not speak of it for the moment: after all, it may never appear. I am not uncritical of M.K.: and indeed have some reason to be indignant; but I think what I call the M.K. legend does him an injustice: the truth is not only more complex and intersting, but more attractive. I took the precaution of having the ms. checked by some of my former colleagues who liked it and thought it would do Canada a little good down here.[1]

Peggy left this morning to spend a week or so in Toronto. I should so much like to have gone along; but I am nailed to Ithaca till the Christmas vacation when I hope we can get away to New York, where the Modern Language Association meets.

I like your proposals for 'Man and Nature.' On the whole I think stanza six might go out as you suggest. I like the two small changes: the "neither" followed by three substantives worried me.

In general I follow you in your changes in 'At the Long Sault.'[2] I had better take them up one by one, since this is such an important poem, so important that I would like to suggest that we consider calling the book *At the Long Sault and Other Poems*, by A.L. I am delighted that you think more and more highly of it; so do I. It is one of the great things, I believe.

I would like to retain the "little" in the line where you so wisely replace "burg" by "town." I dislike "burg" and recall Douglas Bush's[3] summing up of Morris's Homer translation in the remark that "he calls Troy the *burg*." Your "away" is better than "back." In the next line I like the introduction of the "of."

I also like the "he" which you bring into the line "tosses them . . . .;" and also the rearrangement of the line just below. I am not quite sure that it is wise to drop the line "And he sinks outworn" though I think I see what you are trying to avoid there.

In the next section comes my only significant dissent. I have become so accustomed to reading it over that I miss the effect produced by all the "ands."

As yet I prefer to keep them, and also not to break the section into two parts as you do just before the line "And then the great night came."

I am disposed to retain the "But" after the opening section of the poem. But I like your idea of perhaps printing the final lyric — what a masterpiece it is, surely one of the best things in this kind — in italics. But this I leave to you.

I haven't yet taken the visit to the history seminar to find out what the Greek sonnets are about;[4] But you shall have the little note before long.

The idea of reprinting the little group of early love sonnets is a good one. I would favor the 'Praise and Prayer' pair remaining separate: they are unlike the others in form.

It is a great relief to me that you like the introductory estimate. It was done with difficulty; but it represents opinions that formed slowly during the months when I was at work on the note-books. For the experience of those I can never thank you enough. They have helped me to develop ideas about many things.

I am sorry that my time in Ottawa did not overlap on Pelham's. He is a grand old fellow. Remember me to him, and all my best wishes are yours and your wife's.

Sincerely,
Edward

16

November 13, 1942

Dear Edward.   Yours of the ninth came this morning. Congratulations on the M.K. article; I shall await it with impatience; MUMS the word. I am writing you this special note re 'At the Long Sault' for that is one of the most important items in our scheme. I return the copy with alterations.[1] I must say I was relieved to know that you had approved so widely of what I wanted to do. As for the Bull Moose section, the phrase "And he sinks outworn" is very weak; you cannot place it anywhere after such a strong line, *"His mighty strength gives way;"* that is the end of the Moose and the wolves get him. "He sinks outworn" is applicable to an old poet attacked by a formidable critic but not to a Bull Moose fighting wolves. In the next section I have put back the "ands," and closed the gap between that and the next section. If you could give up one of the "ands" where I have marked a ? I would prefer the line, "They fell one by one And the world etc." I would excise "from their eyes;" I dont quite like the physical reference there. "Passed like a dream and was naught," seems to my ear beautifully simple. However you may not agree and I never forget that this is *your* poem but I *had* to say what I have said. No italics for the last lyric. Your suggestion for the title of the book is a good one; we will adopt it. There was great joy in the house when the relief supply of SUGAR arrived from Toronto; again Birthday Sugar, for my wife's anniversary is tomorrow.[2] Many thanks to the lady bountiful, must she be rewarded with a poem? I have made a draft of my preface and will send it soon. May I be quite free in making remarks about the Introduction? It is quite perfect as it stands but I want to get a view of it as a prelude to the book. More anon.

[P.S. *holo. marg.*] You will see from this typing how nervous I am this afternoon — but I wanted to write at once — and if possible dont keep me waiting too long for answers — you dont know what a nervous and apprehensive friend you have.[3]

Yours ever,
Duncan

17

November 15, 1942

Dear Edward.   Herewith are the early Love Sonnets. So arranged they show a certain progress and variety and prove that A.L.'s power of expression did not stop short of that feeling. I send copies of two I have left out, you will note my reasons.[1] One other with the Chaucerian rhyme "ylad" I have not bothered to send; the "meads" etc. harked back too far. I dont see any great objection to the inclusion of No. 4; true the rhyme scheme is unusual but I would like to preserve the idea of *service*. I wish you would suggest a title for the series. Could we steal Robt. Bridges' "The Growth of Love"?[2] Why not? The Progress of Love? We would use the dates 1884-1885. I hate the title LOVE SONNETS. I hope the delay in getting the book in order does not prejudice your action in dealing with C.P.'s. I have not been able to work any faster. Did I show you this Sonnet which I call 'The True Life'?[3] I think it good, but you might say it was open to criticism; that a poet advising on the true life would not be so violent and should rather woo the haters than destroy them. And "Damned," is that too forcible? Would you say "Rank" hypocracies? This sonnet gives you another example of force to set beside 'The Pimp' etc. It seems profane to be laying hands on these poems and suggesting changes and the reading and thinking of them has often been painful.

With regards,
Yours ever,
Duncan

18

Cornell
November 17, [1942]

Dear Duncan:

We are so glad that the sugar happened to come at a *special* time: our best wishes to you both accompanied it. Peggy returned last night, after a gay week, in which I should so much like to have shared.

By all means tell me how the introductory essay can be made to serve its end better. It was not written for that end, as you know. It is a chapter in a book.[1] I indicated with square brackets some things I thought should go, and I added a few alternative phrases for the new function. But I did not really reshape the article at all. Part of the function of the chapter might be just as much the function of an introduction: to show that Lampman is a very genuine and very important poet and that he matters to-day as he did fifty years ago. But aside from this there are differences in what a chapter and an introduction might do, and I should be grateful for suggestions.

I accept all the new suggestions about 'At the Long Sault,' except the dropping of the *and*. You will certainly think me mulish! I am so persistent for the *ands*, all of the pesky little things, because it seems to me that the poem with them and the poem without them are different performances. With the *ands* that section keeps something, a good deal of A.L.'s dreaminess, without them it becomes much stronger and a little harsh. I don't think the poem is *better* with the *ands*, but I would plead that we should not alter the general intention, as I think we should be doing if we dropped them. None of the other changes seems to me to affect the general intention: all that the others do is to strengthen something that was left without the last scrutiny of the author. In a word I think A.L. might have done everything else that we are doing, but I am not convinced that he would have dropped the *ands* — though in failing to do so he might have been ill-advised.

I am eagerly awaiting your preface. Let me thank you, for us both, after reading your portrait of Gagnon, which was moving and life-giving. I am sorry that I shall not see the exhibition.

As ever,
Edward

P.S. [*holo.*] The sonnets have just come. Do not feel uneasy about the pace at which we are moving. The *Canadian Poetry* book needs polishing and is not being delayed.

E

19

Cornell
November 24, 1942

Dear Duncan:

I am slower than I wished to be in answering your note about the early sonnets and commenting upon them as now arranged. I have had a specially heavy lot of departmental business, and I have not been able till to-day to be at all confident in my ability to see aesthetic things as they really are!

I never liked the title *Love Sonnets* which I used simply for identification, and then forgot about. I congratulate you on your suggestions. Either *The Growth* or

The Progress is excellent. I approve of all the inclusions, and am quite ready to have the pair of short sonnets broken, one to be included in the other series, and the other suppressed.[1] Perhaps there might be a footnote to the one included saying that A.L. experimented more than once with this peculiar form. Don't take that suggestion too seriously.

I am rather disposed to defend the Keatsian piece that you dislike, "Where many changes fall of gloom and light." It seems to me one of the things that most clearly show what a Keatsian he was much of the time in those early years. It has sincerity, I think, despite the obvious indebtedness. But about this do as you wish. It isn't the sort of poetry on which his fame will come to rest. You might perhaps remember in making your decision that being in the P.L. books[2] it is already available to the public, though, of course, the public doesn't know and won't look.

'The True Life' satisfies me. I had copied it and wrongly thought that you had used it in one of your introductions. I have looked over both, and find that what you used was the one about the crossing-sweeper. The text I found differs a little from yours: it has *basks* for *lolls*; *real* for *true* (in the phrase *true life*) and a comma after *clap-trap*. I like the comma, but in the other matters your text seems better to me. By all means let us use it, and let us keep *damned*.

How changed the face of things has been by the African success.[3] I do begin to think that 1943 will bring great gains, it may be even decisive gains.

As ever,
Edward

20

November 28, 1942

Dear Edward.   I have yours of the 24th. Of course I know how busy you must be and I am not impatient. I must write you a word or two about "The Growth of Love," or "The Progress of Love," or "Love's Progress" — so that we may come to rest on a decision as completely satisfactory as possible. I think these Sonnets have their root in Rosetti; the form of address "My Lady etc." reminiscent of *The House of Life*[1] and sometimes the phrases, but that is a remark by the way. I have changed my mind about these Sonnets as a whole and about their inclusion: I am now prepared to print them all. But I want you to consider several points in this connection. I am ready to include "Where many changes fall of gloom and light" (this seems to me more Rosetti than Keats) and have a good place for it in the sequence. Now for the "ylad" sonnet which I send herewith: I would like to include it, it shows his Lady in a petulant mood and gives a little variety. But that rhyme bothers me and would stump the ordinary reader. There is a sweet, almost childish simplicity in it that I like. What do you think of the line as I have remade it; I dont like to meddle too much, but he could be dolefully "clad" as well as dolefully "carried" or "led"? Or would you advise leaving it out or printing "ylad"? Plwaes[2] decide. I am now inclined to put in the two "Prayer and Praise" Sonnets,[3] if it were not for the beginnings of those two lines in the 1st Sonnet I would be perfectly sure. As they are both short by two lines I would use the title "Prayer and Praise" as a subtitle, as Rosetti did in *The House of Life*. Let me know what you think of this but I shall have to alter those two openings of the 5th and 6th lines I think? *Please return that Sonnet, I have no copy of it, also 'Sweet Trees*, etc.'[4] When you give me your opinion on these points the Sequence will be settled, in fact the contents of the whole book will be, and I can let MacInnes have the M.S. The 'True Life' will go in Damned and all. I will send you my preface and the suggestions I have to offer re your Chapter.

What heartening events, what terror and tragedy, what terrible wickedness and treachery.[5] One [is] breathless these days!

Yours ever,
Duncan

21

Cornell,
November 30, 1942

Dear Duncan:

I have your letter about the sonnets, and am glad that you think of printing rather more than we had decided on. I favor facing the reader with "ylad:" it seems to go well with the "plaining" and the "mead." I also like the music of the phrase "dolefully ylad," which partly vanishes when the "ylad" becomes "clad." I am not quite sure which of the "Prayer and Praise" pair we are debating. So I enclose copies of both. My pencilled mark on the first one in this copy is to indicate that where the book has *soft* the scribbler had *thick*.[1] I like *soft* better: the other seems to me awkwardly sensuous. I know you do not like lines nine and ten in this first sonnet; neither do I. Perhaps you can suggest a change. Lines five and six in the second sonnet are not too good; but the feeling in this sonnet seems to me very fine indeed. I congratulate you on the admirable idea of a subtitle for the "Praise and Prayer" pair to mark it off from the rest.

It is pleasant to think that MacInnes is now to see our work. More and more I grow to think that we are about to do something really worth doing for A.L.'s name.

Have you seen Birney's little volume of verse?[2] Pelham may have a copy. I think the 'David' really fine, and some of the shorter things too. I never took to Birney the person, although I was on amicable terms with him as a colleague during my last four years at Toronto. Always a chip on his shoulder, and always a roughneck. That is a type to which I am usually unjust, I know Birney the poet I take to very well indeed.

In making plans for sending things to me to look at, you may like to know that Peggy and I shall be in New York from December 23rd to December 30th or 31st. I shall later be able to give you a N.Y.C. address, but of course the permanent address is the safer. The snow has come to the Ithaca hills and the view over the lake, which is not frozen, is very lovely. From my study window I look not over the lake but over a valley to the high hills that form a semi-circle to the south of the lake.

As ever,
Edward

[*P.S. holo.*] I am sending the promised "replacement" of the Canadian number of *Poetry* under separate cover. I am reminded that I had a letter from Brockington[3] in which he speaks of a visit he intends to make to Canada and the U.S.

E

22 [*Holo.*]

December 5, 1942

Dear Edward.   I have yrs of 30th inst and will give thought to the Sonnets. I have drafted a short preface and I want to clear a point before I have it typed. *Please answer this by return mail.* I refer to you several times and I want to know, shall I say *Prof.* EKB or *Dr.* EKB? The first mention runs, "In fact if it had not been for *Prof.* or *Dr.* E.K. Brown's admiration for L. etc." Maybe I had better hold everything until you return from N.Y.C. I have suggestions about yr introduction too. I cld probably send this prose by the middle of the month. It is a difficult matter to alter those sonnets. If we are to publish them they *must* be changed. I have seen several things of Birney's that I admire. I'll get his book. The *Poetry* will come to hand, thanks. I thought it was dead but I got a subscription notice the other day. We envy you in N.Y. Will you see Thornton Wilder's new play?[1] I was going to send you and Peggy a new poem for Xmas, but I had better wait until you get the N.Y. air out of yr lungs — but send me a N.Y.C. address.

Yrs ever,
DCS

23

Cornell
December 7, 1942

Dear Duncan:

It is good of you to ask how I like to be styled. I have become used to "Professor" and am reconciled to it, so perhaps you should keep to that although it always reminds me of the first professor I ever heard of, a phrenologist.

We are going to stay at the Biltmore — which offers an amazing reduction to professors. We shall probably be there from Dec. 23 to Dec. 30 or 31. I hope we can have the poem before we go, but in this you must act as you think best. I am sure that ante-N.Y., or post-N.Y., or submerged in the place, we shall respond to it with joy.

All good wishes. I was about to add "of the season," but I shall hope to hear from you again before we leave — it is almost two weeks, no it is more than two, before we go.

This is a miserable note, but I am typing it out at the office before I hurry home, so as to catch the night's mail.

As ever,
Edward

24

December 13, 1942

Dear Edward.   I send "The Growth of Love" Sonnets in the arrangement I propose that we adopt; I hope you will agree. Note the few changes I have made in the "Prayer and Praise" 12-line Sonnets, I take it that you have copies of the first forms and can compare; let me know what you think of these. I also send a copy of 'At the Long Sault' and 'The True Life'; I had all these copies made for you *so do not return them.* With these I hope you have the full text of the book. You do not yet know my suggested titles for some of the poems but you will have these later. Now I hand the M.S. to MacInnes and we shall know the result before long. I have made one change in arrangement. I thought 'Liberty' followed 'The Long Sault' badly, I thought we shd have something rather fanciful there and I have put 'The Frost Elves' second and put 'Liberty' to lead up to the "Greek Sonnets." I think this is better. I have nothing more to say just now. I have your note and Professor it shall be. As for the poem I shall copy it and send it before you go to N.Y.C. We are both well and we are bracing ourselves for a visit from Dona and Jane Edgar[1] who are to spend Xmas with us and Pelham is coming to join them under this roof for those days. We are looking forward to some excitement for we have never had so many visitors together. By the way, I have not said anything to Pelham about our Lampman labours for what I think is a good reason; but he shall know if we are successful and perhaps if we are not.

Yours ever,
Duncan

25

To Peggy & Edward[1]
 Christmas 1942

INTERMEZZO

> Virginal out of the earth
> Rises the Cherry-Tree,
> A slender wand
> With a swerve in the stem;
> Like a Dancer
> Touching earth —, floating on air, —
> With delicate hands forming a wreath
> Over her head.
> This virginal Cherry-Tree-Dancer
> That keeps her poise,
> The turn of her slender stem,
> Her fragile branches hidden,
> Holds her wreath aloft,
> An aureole of blossom
> Woven of rose and snow,
> Around her root the crocuses,
> Firm as if cut from gems,
> Guard an inviolate floor
> For the delicate Cherry-Tree-Dancer.
>
> Silent are these and perfect in repose,
> Yet are they circled and bound
> By memories of lovely sound.

Spring 1941   Duncan Campbell Scott

26 [Holo.]

Cornell
December 30, 1942

Dear Duncan:

We are back from New York only to-day, and I will make this a laconic letter since the typewriter is being repaired and I don't wish to bemuse you with my illegibilities, which must rival your friend Morris's:

Is that Phimister Proctor,
Or something about a Doctor?[1]

I admire your grouping of the love sonnets and raise only one question which has nothing to do with the grouping. In sonnet V, 1. 4, should not the last word be *dight*? I think I must have erred in my first transcribing. *Light* occurs also in 1. 1.

We were charmed by your spring-poem — so delicate and musical and firm at the same time. It stands beside our Schaefer water-color.[2]

We both hope you had a perfect Christmas and that the "company" did not tire either of you unpleasantly.

No more of this scrawl.

Yours ever,
Edward

1943

Much of the year is taken up with continuing work on At the Long Sault. *There are only two problems of any moment: the need for delicacy in the handling of the love sonnets which Lampman addressed, not to his wife, but to another woman, and Lorne Pierce's attempt, from the halls of orthodoxy at the Ryerson Press, to drop some Lampman poems that show the gritty edge of Lampman's social conscience. Brown's* On Canadian Poetry *pulls abreast of the Lampman volume, and the two are published almost simultaneously in the fall of the year. Both the poet and the critic are pleased with* At the Long Sault, *and Scott writes at length of his admiration for* On Canadian Poetry. *The reviews are another matter. "All kind," Brown writes, "but all stupid!" Scott comes out of the winter in not the best of health. He is ordered to his bed in mid-May, and although he is greatly cheered by Brown's visit to Ottawa in the second week of June, he is indisposed again in October. He calls it "nervous indigestion," but it may well be the onset of the angina which is to plague him at the end of his life. Meanwhile, he is becoming increasingly dependent on his friend's letters: "your letters," he writes at the year's end, "keep me alive." It is by the same token clear that Brown's presence plays a much larger part in Scott's life than Scott's plays in Brown's. Brown is unfailingly tactful about this, but he has his teaching, a labour of love which he tackles with tireless zeal, and he has his lectures to give at Yale and Columbia, his scheme to translate* Père Goriot *for the Modern Library, and much else that goes with an active university life. Yet Scott has his ventures too. He contributes to a "Canadian" issue of* Voices, *and his 'Hymn for Those in the Air' is broadcast with music by Healey Willan. He entertains the idea of a first Canadian edition of* In the Village of Viger, *and he begins work on the miscellany which will appear in due time as* The Circle of Affection. *Spurred by Brown, he reads more widely than he has for some time. His heart is warmed by the birth of a boy to the Browns on the 30th of December.*

27

January 8-9, 1943

Dear Edward.　　I have yours of the 30th ult. and I must at least begin an answer this morning although it may not be finished today. You inquire feelingly about our Christmas, hoping that it was perfect, and that our Company did not tire us. I avoided all chance of that by going to bed with a Cold, and remaining there most of the time. I came down for a mid-day dinner on Christmas day, and reappeared and disappeared from time to time, so that Elise had to be host and hostess. It was her thought to bring the family together wh. could not have been so easily accomplished otherwise and she was rewarded for they enjoyed being here and were of the least possible trouble; Jane is a sweet child and behaved beautifully. Pelham went back to Harry's[1] on Monday night and I was left with my affliction wh. I bore with becoming patience. Elise charges me with planning the Stunt with a long view to get rid of all responsibility, but she has forgivingly nursed me back to almost normal. During this interval the weather has made a record both of cold and snow and the city has been almost static so far as public conveyance goes. It is strange that I could read that Sonnet as often as I did and not notice that error; I have corrected it in all the copies I have. I'm glad you think the arrangement good, you say nothing about the few changes I made and I presume they did not offend. I gave the Poems to MacInnes a few days ago with the preface I proposed and also let him have your chapter; I thought you would not object and I thought it well to let them know how highly you valued A.L. Well we shall see what comes of it, approval I hope. I think Earle Birney's 'David' the best thing that has been done in Canadian Poetry for a long time;[2] this is one of the lines along wh. Canadian Poetry shd develop if it is to get anywhere; other things in the book I like and would we could have a chat about them; how oddly reminiscent of 'Grandchester'[3] is 'Eagle Island'; perhaps E.B. wld not care for that association, but all the best pieces in the book are based on tradition. I got an early copy of *Harper's* and enjoyed the article hugely — entirely successful it seems to me, a most difficult thing to do, and is well done. It is finely written, that goes without saying, and cunningly put together, and in many respects revealing. I never got anywhere near the center of the P.M. and your article helps an understanding; unfortunately I always start from a satirical point. Have there been any repercussions (hateful word), will the great man himself pay any direct attention? I send herewith clippings from the *Journal*,[4] no doubt someone has already sent them. I have heard several comments, all favorable. Did you suggest the subject of the vignette at the head of your article?[5] How symbolic. M.K. preserving unity between the two races, figured forth by the river-man with two logs and a pike-pole. Or is he trying to keep them a little apart for political reasons? I hope you dont mind this nonsense. We both admire your article and are proud to know you. But I dont want you to consider becoming M.K.'s biographer.

　　I hope you and Peggy had a good time in the City and have become reconciled to the quiet of Ithaca. It has taken me two sittings to do this poor letter and I am not allowed out today as I hoped because the thermometer is around Zero. Elise joins me in best regards and all good wishes for the New Year.

[*P.S. holo.*] Thanks for yr card & for liking the 'Intermezzo.'

[Duncan][6]

28

January 18, 1943

Dear Edward.   Loftus brought back the poems a few days ago and they had passed the censorship. All my anxieties and heart-searchings on the subject of the "Portrait in Six Sonnets" were needless.[1] When we came to that group in the discussion he said, "Now these poems that were addressed to Miss Waddell, there wld be no objection to publishing them"; so I learned that they knew about the affair (that is too light a word to use)[2] and had given it a place in the life of A.L. Miss Katherine Waddell, born 26th June, '65, was a friend of the family, dead long since. Loftus said there was plenty of evidence that the attachment gave A.L. profound feeling. He said that in this book they did not want us to make too much of it or have anything said that would further stir up conjecture wh. might lead to some journalistic vapourings.[3] He thought my reference in the draft preface was all right, but I dont know whether to let it stand, what do you think? We thought best to go on with The Ryerson Press; Loftus is going to Toronto this month and is to take up with Lorne Pierce the question of cheques for Royalties wh. he has made payable to the Lampman Estate in error; I told him to open the matter with L.P. I send a rough draft of my Preface, I think it might be even shorter and I think I shd leave out any remarks of a critical nature, even the slightest, and leave that to you. Please give me your advice. I send herewith a note on what I think your Intro. shd give us.[4] I have left out 'The Settler's Tale.' I send also a list of Contents. Have you a complete M.S. of the book? I asked a prominent journalist what the reaction to your King article had been and he said it was rather curious for *both* sides were pleased; the Tories thought that you had showed up M.K. in all his weakness, the Liberals thought it was a fine tribute to his strength. So if you have satisfied both their houses you too shd be satisfied. I think very highly of the article as I have already told you. I wonder if I shall hear anything about the N.Y. trip. Yesterday we were enjoying one of the inevitable incidents of such a winter as this is. Masses of snow, roofs shrouded, eaves draped with icicles (Ice "makes daggers at the sharpened eaves";[5] Poor Tennyson as Geo. Moore would say). Well the water invaded our music room at the fire-place end and took the polish off the floor. On Sun. morning I had to find men to come and take all the snow off the roof and open channels for the water. This sort of thing is very annoying just as I had enjoyed a music-experience of the highest. Lubka Kolessa[6] gave a recital wh. stirred me considerably and on Sat.

morning she came here to practise and I cld listen, following the notes, to a real intensive study of Beethoven's Op. 101. While I was in these regions of beauty the water was secretly preparing to come into that very room with reminders of the sordid material. I hope you dont mind this sort of a recording. I refused to review for the *Journal* a book written by Klinck on Wilfred Campbell;[7] I thought there was good stuff in the book but as he did not know C. there was a lack of understanding in it and I cld not review the book without constant reservations. I have undertaken to award prizes for One Act Plays (22) entered in a local Drama League contest;[8] I am surely a fool to undertake this sort of Slavery. We are both pretty well now and I have been out several times. We both send our regards to you and Peggy.

Yours ever,
Duncan

[Enclosure]

Introduction

A few suggestions for E.K.B. to consider with reference to his Introduction. I think the right note was struck in the paragraph in your letter of Oct. 4th. Your article or Chapter is fine and if it is to be improved no one can do it but yourself. But we must not overload these few poems with prose. I think the whole book shd be *new*; therefore I would have you leave out all biographical matter and all quotations from my preface to *Lyrics of Earth*.[9] Omit all references to D.C.S. except that on page 28 perhaps. I dont want to lose any of the critical matter in your Chapter; all you say of 'The Long Sault' pp. 19-21 is excellent, that is the place for the historical note, the closing sentences are just right but I think the last word shd be "resurgence;" you do not need a comparison there with any other poem; quote the closing lyric as you have done. The Introduction is the place for a historical note on the Greek Sonnets. Do not exaggerate L's dislike of urban life, pure horror is too strong. Page 7, a note on a minor matter, L's view of the city towers was almost invariably from the south and east; the heights on the Quebec side were too far away for tramping. He saw mighty few sunrises. A.L.'s frogs were Toads. I have confirmed this fact from a naturalist. He came to know that but found it impossible to be accurate. That long trill we hear in Spring is the Love-call of the male toads. There are several kinds of frogs including bull-frogs and they all have voices but moderate and unromantic and therefore not available for Poetry. It would please me if you left out the words I have bracketed on p. 29.

This is really all I am able to offer, in this connection look up your letter of Nov. 17th, and I dont think I have been of much help. Criticize my draft preface thoroughly.

D.

29

Cornell
January 24, 1943

Dear Duncan:

I am just back from a week in Toronto or I should have written sooner. While I was there I met Ira Dilworth for the first time and liked him at once.[1] We had a common friend in yourself. He was relieved that I could tell him that your illness had not been grave, or at least that you had not admitted that it was. He was distressed that you were, he had been told, unable to take part in the broadcast on the arts in Canada that went on a couple of weeks ago. A very nice fellow.

Not to go to Ottawa was a sad thing for me. I very much wanted a talk with you. But I had not the time, and besides I thought that my turning up so soon after the article might have been misconstrued. I do not need to tell you that the article was not written with any idea of personal advantage, but others might not be generous to me in interpreting my motive.

I like your preface very much. You will note two or three marginal comments, none of them of any moment. Since MacInnes *et al* are willing to have the Waddell sonnets go in, it occurs to me that we might consider one or two lyrics that we did not submit to him. I enclose two. I specially like the one that begins "With those cold eyes my dear."[2]

When I was in Toronto I discussed my book on Canadian Poetry with Lorne Pierce. Since it contains the chapter on Lampman I had to mention the unpublished material. I said as little as I could, and took refuge in the statement that I understood you or MacInnes would take the matter up with him in due time. He was delighted, very much wants to publish the collection, and thinks of a format such as Birney's book has. If MacInnes has not yet gone he might like to know that he will have a good reception.

I have given the week-end to revising my introduction. I agree with you that it was long, even when cut in the ways I had suggested. I have reduced it by a good third. I have also removed the biographical approach, as you suggested, and reduced the amount of quotation (an idea of my own). I have taken out the two references to yourself you specially asked me to delete, and one or two others also. But you can't retire as fully as you wish. Your comments are fundamental so often.

Well, here is everything, preface, introduction, and two new poems for your thought.

Every good wish to you and your wife from us both.

Yours, as ever,
[Edward]

P.S. [*holo.*] I have marked the half-dozen new phrases in the introduction. They are negligible I think: I was cutting out, not expanding.

30

Cornell
January 28, 1943

Dear Duncan:

I have been sitting here thinking a little about our project, and an idea has occurred to me of something I should like you to add to your preface. It is a brief statement of how we dealt with our material. You might say that we followed the same method as you had in the memorial edition,[1] supplying punctuation, and correcting obvious slips, the justification being that we were dealing not with "fair copies" but with relatively rough drafts. I don't think that apart from the sonnets to his wife anything that we are printing comes from the fair copy books in the Parliamentary Library.

The examination you will find enclosed was written by sixty students: I am getting tired of their answers, and it requires unusual brilliance or unusual stupidity to rouse me. I hope to finish them to-morrow.

Sincerely, but in a jaded frame of mind,

Edward

31

January 29, 1943

Dear Edward.   Our letters crossed wh. has happened before. This is merely to tell you that I had a letter from Pierce this morning, cordial, even enthusiastic, wanting to see the copy as soon as possible.[1] MacInnes goes to Toronto tonight and expects to see L.P. tomorrow. I took it upon myself to say to MacInnes that we did not expect any share in the avails and that royalties shd go to the Lampman estate; please tell me that I did right. It is quite probable that we can put in the two lyrics you sent. I would suggest sort of non-commital titles and maybe omit the dates.[2] The terms Preface and Introduction seem rather clumsy but I dont know what to suggest. The Introduction is just what I hoped for and pleased me completely; I need say no more about that. But on page 13 change St. Lawrence to Ottawa; this fight occurred on the Ottawa river, the Indians were coming down the River from their hunting grounds around the Lakes. I have changed that phrase in my preface as you suggest. I'm glad you met Dilworth and liked him. I think I shd be able to send the copy to L.P. next week. I wld have welcomed a visit from you for many reasons but chiefly because we cld have settled so many little points about the book. Best wishes as ever to you both.

Yours,
Duncan

P.S. [holo.] As[3] we intend to print 'The Politician' in the text you'll have to send me a copy at once as I haven't got it.

Would you say Critical Introduction?

D.

Are we to have no note on the Greek sonnets?

32

Cornell
February 5, 1943

Dear Duncan:

Of course I had always assumed that any little sum the volume might make would go to the Lampman estate. That seems wholly right to me. I much appreciate the consent of the MacInnes's to my seeing the note-books, although my chief appreciation goes to you, since I know that it was your vouching for me that opened a door that had long been shut.

It was inadvertently that I included that reference to 'The Politician,' which we had agreed to exclude. If you will strike out the phrase about it and keep that which refers to the 'Epitaph on a Rich Man,' the sentence will do, I think.

At terribly long last I enclose a note on the Greek sonnets. It is not very precise, but it was all I could get from three histories of modern Greece. Perhaps a biography of Venizelos would help, and I shall look for one; it was in this Cretan business that V. got his start.[1]

Your letter to Lorne Pierce was just right.[2] I shall hope that you will be able to assure quick action from him, and I shall take no further step about my mss of the book on Canadian Poetry (which he has) till we hear what he will do about our joint book.

I doubt that I shall order the book on Sir Charles.[3] It sounds like our national criticism at its worst, I think. I have not met the lady. When I was last in Toronto I bought Archer's *Poets of the Younger Generation*, and was interested to note that it was Archer who made that comment on 'The Piper of Arll' on which Masefield made the wise and delightful comment.[4] Our poetry to-day does not interest the English as much as it did when Archer included you and Carman and Roberts in his book.

I have had a good week, lecturing to one class on Browning and to another on Housman and Hardy. I am trying in the course to which the latter two belong to give a brief survey of English literature since 1900, with emphasis on the reflection of life and thought in the literature. In its humble way I think of it as a gesture towards interallied understanding, as they say. Housman always produces a very profound effect, I find, and I think that I do him better than I do Hardy whose poetry always dissatisifed me, or almost always. I break off from poetry to cover the revolt against Victorianism which I shall do via Strachey and Bennett (*Old Wives' Tale*). I find the work wonderfully stimulating to me, and can only hope I convey a half of the pleasure I get.

All good wishes to you both from Peggy (deep in Civilian Defence) and myself.

Yours, as ever,
Edward

33

February 8, 1943

Dear Edward.   I had read my Foreword, as I prefer to call it, several times and with growing dissatisfaction, and when yours of the 28th ult. came to hand making a good suggestion, I made up my mind to revise it. Herewith is a copy; everything is here that was in the old version but in simpler and more direct form which is what I wanted. I hope you will like it better. On page 5 you will find a few sentences which will I hope carry out your idea of what should be said on that subject; if it does not fully carry it out please amend it. The two poems you sent will go in, I send back your copies as I have others. I was a bit doubtful about 'The Secret Heart' on account of the fourth verse.[1] What did our poet mean by that fourth verse? I share your liking for 'Cloud and Sun.' I find I have a copy of 'The Politician,' that was his title I think, but it does not seem adequate. The poem seems to hang in the air without any support. It is a Timon-like arraignment of the whole of mankind, from the Seer to the Pimp: but what is the quality that runs down through all classes?[2] MacInnes had an interview with Dr. Pierce, satisfactory so far as we can expect. He proposes to print *only* 500 copies; that shows what his experience with poetry has been. I told him when I wrote him that we could have the M.S. ready by the end of Feb. Did you speak to him about your copyright in the Introduction? I have nothing to protect in the Foreword. Are you looking up the reference for the Greek Sonnets?

I was much interested in the examination paper and I can well understand the jaded state of your feelings. Was it a pretty stiff paper? It seems so to me who never had any experience with examinations. I have just finished a task for our local Drama league: reading 22 one act plays and awarding prizes. There was nothing brilliant in that competition, I assure you.

As ever yours,
Duncan

Later writing on Tuesday morng February 9, 1943

My letter was ready for the postbox when yours of the 5th came to hand, this has happened before; so the envelope was unsealed and I add a few words. I am glad to be rid of 'The Politician'; I'll alter the sentence. Yes, the advance notice of the Sir Charles book as you say sounds like our national criticism at its worst; L.P. has been one of the chief offenders and I dread to read his contribution to this biography. I told MacInnes to say to him that we would expect to see and approve any advance notices of our book, he did so and L.P. agreed and took it in good part. When I have so little money to spend on books I should like to own, I dont want to part with three and a half for this one. I did not remember that it was Archer that made the remark about 'The Piper'; I have not looked at that book for years. Thanks for the note on the Greek Sonnets. I got a book on Venizelos at the Par. Library this morning. I may write you a special note on this subject but as my mind is not quite clear on what I want to say I dont want to hold this letter until it is. I enjoyed reading your note on your work and to know that you are happy in it. As I write this Elise is resting near me after our expedition to the Library, and sends her greetings with mine. The weather is milder. Icicles grow longer, roofs collapse, we are in expectation of a flood.

Yours ever,

D.

34

Cornell
February 13, 1943

Dear Duncan:

I am most grateful that you and MacInnes are doing all the negotiating with L. Pierce, and all seems to swim along very smoothly. I like the title page. There is something to be said for getting the word or idea of *unpublished* into the title, but it is a long and ugly word. Perhaps you might consider adding the word *new* after *other*. But this is a suggestion and I do not urge it.

The foreword always pleased me, but I like it a little more in this revised form. I think you do me a little too much honor on p. 2 and suggest the omission of a phrase, which may require a little rewriting. Also on p. 1 I think I am given too much credit in one sentence I have marked. Throughout you are exceedingly generous, and I thank you once more.

I hope we can keep the price down to about $1.50. Birney's book was $1.50 or $1.25. It was a sound idea to require that the advertisement etc. be shown us. I have been reading Klinck's *Campbell*. Did you note that they say of Klinck[1] that he held the post of assistant examiner for the Ontario department of education? That honor goes to about 3 or 4 hundred people every year! Reading matric papers for three weeks! Who is fooled by such nonsense? Who does the fooling? Klinck does the best he can by Campbell, but the man emerges as a restless being without the inner solidity that I hoped to find. It seems odd that Klinck was not helped at all by the second daughter (Margery Grey Fleming) whose daughter Jane Grey, with a very notable Pre-Raphaelite appearance, I once taught. I conjecture that you and A.L. had some difficulties with Campbell when you were at the Mermaid![2]

Winter is giving us a holiday here, after a very cold and snowy January. Peggy took some snaps of the trees and bushes that surround us, and give us an air which we shall not have when the snow goes.

Every good wish to you both,

As ever,
Edward

P.S. I hear Grierson[3] is to have scope in the information department generally, perhaps to head it. His shorts are admired down here. No doubt he has "dynamic ideas" about things outside films.

35

February 27, 1943

Dear Edward.   You will see by the enclosed copy of my letter to L.P. of 20th inst. that we are making progress.[1] He acknowledged on the 24th and said he was sending the MS. for a "layout and estimate" and would write me later. You will note that I adopted your suggestion by adding "new" to the sub-title. I made changes in the Foreword to meet your wishes; it was easily done and reads all right. I changed the title of the Greek sonnets to CRETE as that seems to me closer to the subject matter and I have given a short footnote: "These sonnets were inspired by the rebellion of Crete against Turkish rule, which, after years of conflict, ended in the union of Crete with Greece." I dont think I have anything further to report. Yes, Campbell was a source of worry when we were doing "At the Mermaid Inn"; in fact the irritation of some of his stuff on the public and the constant watch that had to be kept upon his opinions went far to stop the Series; but it was pretty well played out, simply because, situated as we were, there was not enough material available to keep the thing fresh. I dont know whether Mrs. Gray is alive. I could tell you much about C. wh. would amuse you. There was much of good in his character and some sweetness perceptible when he allowed it to appear, but the truth is that after a certain date he began to develope into a Snob, and in the end that evil prevailed to a large extent.[2] We have had a warm spell and the snow-piles sank a little; then we had two days of zero weather.

Yours ever,
Duncan

36

Cornell,
March 3, 1943

Dear Duncan:

It is encouraging to hear that L.P. is bending his mind to the problem of getting the book ready. I assume that there is no doubt that he wants it. I could tell from the way he spoke of it when I mentioned it in January that he wanted this for his House. It is a pity that he still thinks (or does he still — you mentioned this in an earlier letter) of just 500 copies. That was too small a number for Birney's book as he soon found.[1] I do hope the price is fair. I am glad you expressed your view of this in writing to him.

Let me say again what a relief it is to me that the negotiations are in your wise and practised hands. I like the note on the Greek poems, and also the change of title. Something of the kind ran through my mind, and I don't know why it didn't stick and lead me to say something. I am glad that you like the addition of "new," which makes the thing more accurate, and of course on the cover L.P. will want only *At the Long Sault*. That would please me, I think.

I have just finished and mailed the survey of Canadian Poetry, 1942.[2] Much of the work for it is dreary, but it is interesting to set one's notes and ideas together. Birney's book seems to me much the best of the year. There were some good things in a little privately printed book of Gustafson's. I am afraid that I was rather harsh to G. in what I said of his anthology.[3] I thought, for instance, that I had to object to his including five of his own pieces in so small a book, which pretends to present the whole range of our poetry. I remember when Pelham at my asking did an article on Literary Criticism in Canada for the *U.T. Quarterly*, I felt, and so did Woodhouse, that his kind remarks about us two editors would simply have to come out.[4] And out they came.

I am putting together a few ideas about my first great teacher,[5] and will perhaps send them to *Saturday Night*. The King piece has made me interested in doing a little lightish biographical stuff.

But what is really in the front of my mind these days is a Browning problem. The value of the ugly, or perhaps of the grotesque. Do you know of any one who has said good things about the U. or the G. in poetry or any of the arts? I have learned a good deal from Ruskin, and of course I know Bagehot's rather unsympathetic study of Browning. But I don't know much else. As I try to define what it is that makes Browning unique I seem to find it in the handling of the U. and the G.

All good wishes to you both, in your even colder climate. We felt warm in spirit, and in body to-day, since we gave a cocktail party for Herbert Davis,[6] once my Toronto colleague, then my predecessor here, now President at Smith. He and his wife were in town for the day, and it was delightful to see them.

As ever,
Edward

37 [*Holo.*]

Cornell
March 8, 1943

Dear Duncan,

This [letter from Lorne Pierce] came to-day.[1] I am replying that I must consult with you. I'll try to reduce my introduction a little further if this seems wise. Your preface *must* stand — it is very short. Royalties are for estate, of course. About format I defer to you.

In haste,
Edward

38

March 15, 1943

Dear Edward.   This morning I want to write you solely about our Book and keep all comments on yours of the 3d for another letter.[1] I am glad you sent me L.P.'s letter which I retain for the present. Loftus came to discuss the correspondence for I had a letter from L.P. dated 5th, in which he said he had written to you.[2] He raises the question as to whether certain of the poems should be included and he makes this list: 'Man and Nature,' 'The Usurer,' 'Epitaph on a Rich Man,' 'Ottawa,' 'Fate,' 'Liberty' and 'Fair Speech.' So we are faced with the suggestions of reducing the Prose and at the same time reducing the Poetry. This seems inconsistent as, if there is to his mind a lack of proportion between the two sections, that is not removed by reducing both. But I suppose there is something he dislikes in these poems. Now let us consider reducing the Prose. He says he would like you to consider how it might be reduced *somewhat* and in his letter to me he uses the word *slightly*. If the sections are to be balanced on a page division there would have to be a reduction of 25% in the prose which is much more than a slight reduction. My Foreword should not escape cutting and there is one Para. which could be omitted. I cannot help linking this suggested reduction in the Prose with the important question as to whether or not he is going to accept your Canadian Poetry. If he is, and if it is, as I hope, to come out soon, you might consider the reduction of the Introduction, and in that event I might have a suggestion to offer.[3] Loftus, whose opinion should be considered, thinks L.P.'s criticism is reasonable from a publishers standpoint. I dont agree if the purpose of the book is kept in view. I would really like to keep L.P. waiting for definite answers to his suggestions until you had heard from him as regards your Book.

As for the Poems, I dont see any good reason for leaving any of them out. 'Man and Nature' is an early effort on what became a favorite theme. The Sestet of 'Fair Speech' has appeared in the Memorial Edition as a six line piece.[4] 'Ottawa' I dont remember and I have no copy of it. He is probably nervous about 'Liberty,' 'The Usurer' and 'The Epitaph'; as for the last mentioned the same subject is worked out in the Sonnet 'The Millionaire.'[5] If we were to consent to any omissions 'Fair Speech,' 'Ottawa,' and 'Man and Nature' might go; but as I have said I would retain all. This question is involved with the irritating plan of L.P. to publish a selected edition of his work limited to about 150 pages.[6] This annoys me, for I had hoped that *Lyrics of Earth* would stand with my Introduction as the final selection. There would have to be severe and unnecessary compression if A.L. were to be cramped into 150 pages. As for the business arrangements I think Loftus and I can look after them and protect your interests.

I hope this rambling letter will not confuse your thought in these matters. Later

I shall write to Pierce and send you a copy. In a day or two I hope to write you again.

Yours as ever,
Duncan

[*P.S. holo.*] Please let me hear from you re the poems, etc.

39

Cornell
March 17, 1943

Dear Duncan:

Many thanks for your letter which came this afternoon. I had supposed there had been a difficulty of some sort. It is odd that L.P. should start writing to us both and in different terms. He made no mention to me of the poems he did not like.

First about my book on Canadian Poetry. I thought it would be well to keep the problem it raises out of the way till our joint venture had been dealt with; and I do not think I have mentioned it to L.P. since my one talk with him about it back in January. But if you think it wise I should be glad to write to him now and ask what he intended to do with it and say that our attitude towards the reduction of the prose in our A.L. book would depend in part upon whether he accepted the Canadian Poetry. I won't write such a letter till I hear from you that you approve of it. And don't hesitate to say you don't approve, if that is your feeling. I assume from your letter that you think I should write to him in such terms, but I am not sure. We must not get our signals mixed!

L.P. did mention to me the idea of a selection from A.L. which would be smaller than yours, when I saw him, but I did not think that this was an immediate interest of his. He spoke of a whole series of such anthologies of Canadian Poetry, and suggested that I do one on Mair and Sangster![1] I wonder I did not tell him what I think of those honorable but unpoetic gentlemen, as they seem to me.

As I said before I should like the business arrangements to go through your skilled hands, not mine.

As ever, but in haste,
Edward

P.S. [*holo.*] I will look over the criticized poems tomorrow and be ready to tell you what I think next week or perhaps this week-end.

E.

40

Cornell
March 18, 1943

Dear Duncan:

I have had a little leisure sooner than I thought I should, and have gone over the poems which L.P. suggests that we omit. Like yourself I hesitate to agree to the omission of anything; *some* of the pieces we are proposing to print are primarily of scholarly interest, showing as they do how A.L. approached his favorite themes at varying times and in varying moods and with varying degrees of power. It seems to me that 'Man and Nature' is a test case. If A.L. is really, as I firmly believe, a poet of great power in his special ways, a poet worth study, then 'Man and Nature' merits publication. It will throw light on other and better work. In itself it is not awfully good, I think. If you judge wise to make some concessions to L.P. I shall readily go along with you, and consent to the sacrifice of 'Man and Nature,' and 'Ottawa' (of which I enclose a copy since you say you are now without one). 'The Usurer' I like very much; I am probably a little silly in my enthusiasm, but I do have faith in that little quatrain. 'Fair Speech' I think we must give since it completes what has already appeared. 'The Epitaph' I also very much want to see included, a fine vigorous thing, and quite as good as the 'Millionaire' sonnet, in my view, and that is very good indeed. 'Liberty' is a very interesting piece and I should like to keep it. 'Fate' I don't feel very strongly about. Well, that covers everything that you mention.

The request to reduce both prose and poetry makes me wonder whether L.P. is not trying to get us into a Procrustean bed: has he fixed the number of pages he wants the book to have and is he going slowly to get us to cut our stuff to meet the arbitrary dimensions he has chosen? I add that nothing I have ever seen of L.P.'s gives me much faith in his critical powers.

Well, be it as you will, and I really mean exactly what I say. After all I have never published any poetry and I don't know how publishers deal with poets' mss. You do know.

Warm and sunny weather and I am feeling joyous. We get too little sun in Ithaca, and one forgets how beautiful this countryside is. Peggy is on a spring trip to N.Y.C. I don't expect to leave town till the middle of April. I have agreed to speak to the Women's Canadian Club of Hamilton on April 19th, and shall try to get to Toronto for a day or so on the trip. You might care to remember that date if it turns out I might be useful in our dealings with L.P.

As ever,
Edward

41

March 20, 1943

Dear Edward.   I reply to yours of the 17th inst. I do not approve of your
writing to L.P. re your Canadian Poetry; I am absolutely opposed to such a
course. The sentence in my last wh. begins, "I cannot help linking etc.," arose
from the closing sentence in Pierce's letter to you of Mar. 5th. I now return this
letter to you, having kept a copy. If he has been able to realize this "hope" you
already have heard from him. When I wrote, "I would really like to keep L.P.
waiting for definite answers to his suggestions until you had heard from him as
regards your book," I was assuming that you would hear from him very soon and
that there would be no delay. Let us forget my foolish idea and go on to a
decision about the contents of "At the Long Sault." I will await your remarks
about the Poems he questions. I dont feel like giving away to him much either in
the Prose or the Poetry. Pierce knows *well* what was our purpose in putting this
book together; I think we are offering him a unique item for his list. We are both
in the unfortunate position of not having before us a copy of the full M.S. and of
being separated in our cogitations, but we will not get our signals crossed. One
word of advice, in your correspondence with L.P. over your Canadian Poetry,
KEEP COPIES OF ALL YOUR LETTERS.

Yours ever,
Duncan

42

Cornell,
March 24, 1943

Dear Duncan:

I think we do a very fine job in not getting our signals crossed. Many thanks
for the line you take about my C.P. This is my line, also.

Enclosed is the letter I sent to L.P. to-day after I heard from you. You will see
that I say nothing except: "Why haven't I heard about my C.P. before now?" I
don't say a word about the reduction in the prose part of the A.L. volume, and of
course nothing about the reduction of the poetry, concerning which he has not
approached me.

Please return the letter when you have perpended it. I hope I shall soon have a
reply from L.P. I forget whether I told you or failed to do so that when I go to
Toronto in mid-April I shall face L.P. with the choice between signing a contract
for the C.P. or giving me back the ms.

Yours as ever,
Edward

43

March 25, 1943

Dear Edward.   I had just returned from posting my last to you when the Postman walked in with the letter from L.P. which I copy here, less the address and signature.

"Just a note to let you know that I have placed the Lampman poems in the hands of Thoreau MacDonald[1] for design and layout. It will be similar to Earle Birney's *David* except that it will be bound in cloth. We plan a very attractive book. We are preparing a contract and forwarding it to Mr. T.R.L. MacInnes." [*Holo.*] Mar. 24th

So we appear to be launched. I had my trouble in typing that letter to him for nothing, although Loftus thinks it was well to have sent it. As to proofs I think I shall ask him to pull duplicate proofs and send one copy to you, one to me, you can send me yours with any corrections and I'll send one copy complete to him. MacInnes is an excellent proof-reader which is all to the good. I wonder what started L.P. from his mood of questioning? Did he think we were sulking in our tents? Have your heard from him about your book?

Yours ever,
Duncan

P.S. I escaped posting this before yours of the 24th was handed in, which was a piece of good luck. I hope indeed that he will take your book and your letter to him was well worded; I return it herewith. I have your April date in mind. I think Elise rather envied Peggy's trip to N.Y. A surfeit of plays would do her good but there is no chance of our moving. Our best to you both. Do you know where this comes from

"The plainsong Cuckoo gray"?

D

44

Cornell,
March 31, 1943

Dear Duncan:

The news you give is a relief. I am delighted to think that all is as good as signed. Your idea about two sets of proofs, and my sending my corrections to you, is excellent. I am glad that the book is to be in cloth, after all.

I have no more news about the Canadian Poetry and shall not move in this till I go to Toronto. Did I tell you that a few weeks ago I answered a months-old letter from A.J.M. Smith, and referred to our book. I had felt that I could not write to him without speaking of it, and yet I did not wish to speak of it so I put off writing. I have not had a reply. But I thought that I ought to tell him. He may perhaps wish to allude to our book in his bibliography, and I think it would be a good thing if he did that, since we have something to gain by all readers of Canadian poetry knowing that this last lot of A.L.'s work is appearing. I assume in this that we will precede Smith in publication.[1]

I have written a sketch of an old teacher of mine [Alexander], and sent it to Sandwell.[2] Perhaps he may print it. It gave me pleasure in writing, at least.

Now I am deep in Carlyle's love-letters, if they may be called so.[3] What a marvellous pair they were, and how born to misunderstand each other!

As ever,
Edward

45

[April 4, 1943][1]

Dear Edward.   I had intended to answer long ago yours of the 3rd ult. which contained observations on subjects other than our usual theme, the Lampman book, but I have been prevented by a combination of indolence and a general feeling of half-indisposition coming from a cold and the general lethargy of shaking off a long winter and being constantly disappointed in the failure of Spring to arrive. I suppose by this time you have solved your Browning problem; I searched my memory for dealings with the Ugly and the Grotesque but without result. It would be hard for me to support your thesis, I seem to feel that wherever R.B. is ugly or grotesque he is least successful. Just how I would apply those words to his work I dont know and I cant say when that quality began to appear, but you would know; it was not in the youthful Browning, was it? What I find unique in him is his strong and unfailing grasp and delineation of character contrasted with his lack of constructive dramatic power. Well, I suppose you will find this stated over and over by other folk and in better form and so I join a procession of the orthodox. In G.H.C.'s[2] notice of Birney's *David* he contrasted it with R.B.'s 'Donald' as to subject, I think, and that led me to read 'Donald' which I hadnt looked at for years. I must confess that I found the poem awkward and the last stanza inadequate; there is a sample of ugliness and it goes along with failure.

I will be interested in what you say in your annual review as to Gustafson and others; I think it was not in the best taste to put in so many of his and particularly to print his portrait; that was gratuitous; why it should have been welcomed with such cries of delight I know not, unless it was for the reason that so much space was taken up by late nonentities. I gave way to him the other day in what I think now was probably a too impulsive fashion. He asked for a piece for a Canadian no. of *Voices* and I sent him something wh. he says is going into the Apl. no.[3] Perhaps you will think I made a mistake as I dont know the standing of this paper, have never seen a copy of it and probably it is taken up with the worship of false gods. I wrote those lines in Oct. last; in Dec. I wrote a sonnet for our friend Brockington[4] and lately some others; so the volcano is not entirely extinct. That Hymn I wrote for the Air Force is to be broadcast with music by Willan[5] on Good Friday at 10.15 p.m. as part of a program. I wonder if you cld hear it. I dont know what Willan has done to it whether he has written a tune or provided a musical background. I hope you will do more of the kind of work you mention and as I take *Sat. Night* I shall watch for it. I hope your correspondence with L.P. is developing satisfactorily, that he is going to take the book on good terms. Dont get tied up with him permanently, there is always a clause in these contracts dealing with future work. MacInnes has got L.P. up to 1000 copies at 1.50 wh. is better, I think they are to meet tomorrow, Mon., and sign a contract, so before long we shall be seeing proofs. In looking over some old letters the other day I came upon a little packet of the only letters A.L. and I interchanged when he had gone off for that rest in the summer of '98.[6] You might like to see them sometime. I have that Apl. 19th date in mind and Elise tells me to say that if you cld come here we would be very glad to have you stay with us.

With affectionate messages to you both,

Yours ever,
[Duncan]

46

Cornell,
April 6, 1943

Dear Duncan:

Just a line in answer not to your good letter but simply to your suggestion, and your wife's, that I come to Ottawa and stay with you sometime in the course of the weekend I shall have in Canada. It is very good of you both, and I should like nothing better, and please give my warm thanks to Elise. But time won't stretch to it. Monday I have to be in Hamilton, and Saturday I have to be in Toronto — there has been a switch — quite unauthorized by us — of the tenants in our house there, and the new people won't pay their rent. It seems such a pity that by train Ottawa is so far from here — 24 hours by any route — and by the now impossible automobile so close.

I am glad to know that the edition is to be 1000. I always disliked the 500. And I do hope the $1.50 price is adhered to. I think the book will make its way. Libraries *must* take it; and people will be at least mildly interested. In Ottawa, perhaps more than mildly.

The other day I wrote to L.P. saying that I should like him to deposit my ms. with a friend of mine in Toronto at the beginning of next week, unless he proposes to contract for it. I will let you know what he says.

We have noted the time of the broadcast. I shall have returned by then, and we shall surely listen. Many thanks for telling us.

I will write again when I have a little leisure.

> With warmest thanks, as ever,
> Edward

47

> Cornell
> May 3, 1943

Dear Duncan:

I am very slow, much slower than I should wish, in writing to tell you how sorry we were that we could not get your poem plus Willan's arrangement on Good Friday at 10.15. Ithaca is a poor radio centre; so much interference. We tried CBL and CBA, but to no avail. I hope the rendition pleased you.

After painful effort I have had a draft contract from L.P., and I now think all will be well. The contract suits me, and I was careful following your advice to strike out the clause about future books. Many thanks. I have asked for a label, as you did for *Green Cloister* since I don't trust Canadian publishers to use good lettering. Even in your handsome *Collected Poems* the gold lettering has faded badly.

May I ask your intercession for the use of passages from your work in the chapter devoted to you? I have been careful throughout the book not to use the full poem, but simply extracts. I indicate on another sheet what I have quoted.[1] Perhaps it would not be necessary to make a request of the publisher? The passages are short.

The Hamilton lecture was a fair success, although I had a very bad day, storm, snow and wind, and rain. I am now trying to polish the address for Columbia which comes next week. It keeps me busy, and I am far from satisfied.

Every good wish to you both from us, who begin to feel stranded here.

> As ever,
> Edward

[*Holo.*] P.S. If I quote anything you would really not like to see singled out do let me know.

48

> Cornell
> [May 10, 1943][1]

Dear Duncan:

A mere postscript to my last. L.P. tells me that he will arrange with McC. and

S.² about the reproduction of passages from your work. I hope that you will not dislike the passages I cited. Of course I will revise if you do.

L.P. also mentions that he has been distressed that the estimate on the Lampman is $1.03, and that he is trying to get it reduced. He is not yet quite sending me the contract for my book but I am so busy at present that I am letting the matter ride, and taking the assurance that he is having final estimate of cost and a layout made. L.P. was disturbed by my roughness to Canadian Puritanism in my introductory chapter; but he seems to be ready to pass it, which shows some courage when one thinks of the non-smoking clerics who might get after him. Did you notice that smoking is not allowed in the building?

Ned Pratt has high blood pressure I learn with immense regret. I hope it will not disable him.

We heard L.W.B. last night and liked the oration. How much we need him at home! For Canada is his home, that is one of the wonderful things about him.

All good wishes on the eve of leaving for N.Y.C. — not just for pleasure (for me, at least) since there is that lecture to give at Columbia.

As ever,
Edward

49 [*Holo.*]

Tuesday [May 18, 1943]

Dear Edward.   I wld have answered your two letters sooner but I haven't been very well and I'm now writing as I lie in bed where the Dr. says I must stay for the rest of the week perhaps and then go slow — a sort of nervous indigestion, that's what I call it.² I was glad to know that you had come to terms with L.P. Of course you may use the quotations and as L.P. is writing to McC & S there is no need of my doing so. I rather dislike the early sonnet on Ottawa but as you no doubt have attached some special meaning to it, probably the first bit of verse I did, certainly the first sonnet — I am quite content. In yr contract with L.P. be sure that a *date for publication* is specified. Now as for the A.L. book I am rather worried — with the cost at $1.03 L.P. couldnt afford to sell at $1.50 wh. his contract with MacI provides for. Now that he has taken yr book I feel considerate for him and wonder if we cld lessen the expense by shortening the prose, but I am not well enough to consider and make any definite suggestions. I'm sure the Columbia lecture was a success and I hope you and Peggy enjoyed N.Y.C. I shall tell L.W.B. what you said about his talk. I think he is leaving for England before long. I shall write you when I am well about the great Scott-Willan Air Hymn.

Regards from us both to you and Peggy.

Yours ever,
Duncan

50

Cornell
May 23, 1943

Dear Duncan,

I was very sorry to hear that you had not been well, and trust you will not let your impatience get the better of your discretion. Ned Pratt, as you have perhaps heard, has been told to slacken his active pace, and coddle himself for a good while. He has high blood pressure; but writes in cheerful mood that he will now have a perfect excuse for saying no to a thousand worthy causes.

It has been a trying spring for every one, and we are still a little doubtful that it is spring, although in the last few days the green has come out on all our trees, and in a walk I took this afternoon I saw some magnificent gardens.

We plan on coming up to Canada next week, and after some time in Toronto will divide, Peggy going to see some friends in Kingston and I moving on to Ottawa. I shall hope for a good talk with you, about many things; and shall see L.P. in Toronto so that I can report how things stand. I have no more news from him.

Our warmest wishes to you both.

As ever,
Edward

[*P.S. holo.*] The line you asked about months ago: "The plainsong cuckoo grey" is from Shakespeare. I don't know from which play.[1]

51 [*Holo.*]

Alexandra Palace
University Avenue,
at Queens Park
Toronto, Canada[1]
June 12, 1943

Dear Duncan:

I enclose proofs of our volume, along with our copy. I have kept the copy of my introduction since I had improved phrasing, here and there, over the text of the A.L. chapter in the book on Canadian Poetry, and I need to have the copy by me when I correct proofs for the C.P. volume.

Most of my marginal marks refer to punctuation; please do just as you think best and regard these marks as mere suggestions. Since you dated the "Portrait in Six Sonnets" it seemed to me right to date the love lyrics.

I will not write at length about anything else, but wait till I can use my typewriter and spare you this scrawl. It was a very great pleasure to be with you

again, and I was specially happy to find you recovering so much vigor before I
left. But don't let the marvellous days we are now having tempt you to too much
exertion.

No need for me to see these proofs again.

Every good wish to you and your wife.

As ever,
Edward

52

June 23, 1943

Dear Edward.   I have not been able to write you before this as I wasnt feeling
any too well. The proofs went back promptly and I asked them to send a revise to
me wh. I have not yet received. There were not many changes; your punctuations
were quite all right. I restored those two lines in 'Liberty' as you miss them. I
think L must have failed to write a line wh. would give a grammatical
construction to the lines; I might have supplied a line but refrained as I would not
wish to add any word. MacI and I have attempted to get over the difficulty by an
exclamation mark; but the opening stanza is not good. I had to leave out 'The
Secret Heart.' 'New Year's Eve' is complete and I could not understand your
note. How useful it would have been had these proofs come to hand when we
were together. I think after the revise is dealt with the book will be letter perfect.
I have not been able to finish the sketch of A.L. I was doing for Quebec but may
resume and finish next week.[1] I hope when you get to your typewriter you will
make a letter for me as I want to hear from you.

Our regards to you both,
Yours ever,
[Duncan]

53

Cornell
June 26, 1943

Dear Duncan:

I was so sorry to hear that you had not been well; but delighted that you were
coming along better. I trust that the proofs will not be a strain in any way. I was
glad that like myself you found them good on the whole. What I meant about
'New Year's Eve' was that I could not find the text of the last two stanzas in the
copy; they were in the proofs, and I suppose I simply did not look hard enough. I
am quite glad to leave the revise wholly to you and MacInnes, though I should
like to see the title page and advertising stuff when it appears. I do not know to

whom they would come first. But I shall have nothing to suggest for the revise, I am sure.

My own book came on well. Being in Toronto and giving L.P. some prods worked miracles. I had the whole of the galleys while I was there, and was able to finish reading them though they did clutter up my last days sadly. L.P. is a little shocked by my rapid treatment of Roberts[1]: he gets about 4 pages. You and Lampman and Pratt have full-length chapters, about 20 pages I suppose. But in the chapter in which I spoke of all the others no one got more than four or five pages. He has asked me to add. I sent him a few sentences on Roberts' role as a sort of official spokesman, but I simply couldn't think of anything else I wanted to say. That is the trouble with Roberts and Carman too[2] — there is so little one wants to say. I do so much hope that you will not find me unperceptive in what I have written about you.

I saw Roberts at a dinner in Toronto. He is in the 7th heaven about Miss P's book.[3] Pratt, by the way, had a letter from the Ryerson Press just like yours, and did not intend to fall for it. Since he raised the subject and mentioned his attitude, I thought I might say, briefly, that you felt as he did, if I had interpreted you aright. I have of course no doubt in my own mind that I did interpret you aright! What shameful advertising.[4]

I am just about to start my summer courses. My only course with civilian students will be a sophomore course on the Great Writers from Chaucer to Burns. I am glad to teach Chaucer again after eight years of absence from him. Spenser I won't be able to do as well. As soon as I get to Swift and Pope (at mid term) I'll be on my own ground once more.

Peggy asks me to say how sorry she was not to see you both. She and I are very fond of Ottawa, and 108 Lisgar St. is one of the prime reasons.

As ever,
Edward

54

July 5, 1943

Dear Edward.   Very many thanks for your last good letter. I send this line not as a full answer but merely to tell you that at once I asked MacInnes to write to L.P. and ask him to send us both a proof of the title page; it should, one would think, have come with the other galley proofs; the revise has not come to hand. MacI had a complete understanding that we should see the advt. stuff but wrote about that again too. I am typing a rough of that article on A.L. for the Quebec paper, so far not very well satisfied with it. Pelham told me that he had been asked to do one on Ned, when that is finished he will have done three. He has gone to Muskoka for a holiday pretty well tired out. I hope Pratt stuck by his resolve not to buy the Roberts book as I have done. Pelham showed me the copy that R. sent him with a most fulsome inscription. P. said, "this is too much"; I said, "*not at all*; you saved his life and he might have said even more."[1] I could say a good deal about what I think was the harm that R. did to Pelham!

I look forward to your book without any personal apprehensions and will of course write about it freely, if you will let me. I hope when we put the A.L. book behind us we will find something else to write about, I would miss your letters.

I have been reading Emmons' book on Walter Sickert.[2] Very lively and amusing; I think you will enjoy this: an honest critic apologized for his opinion; "I had to say what I thought, you know!"; Sickert replied, "It wasnt your saying what you thought that anyone would complain of, but of your thinking what you said." I have written longer than I thought to. Awful weather here, we are so saturated that we'll have to be put through a mangle. Our love to you both.

Duncan

[*P.S. holo.*] Sorry for all these blots. I folded the sheet too soon.[3]

55 [*Holo.*]

July 12, 1943

Dear Edward.   I felt that I *must* send you the enclosed. Comment is needless! P.D.R. sometime ago wrote a general survey of Can. Poetry in wh. he disposed of the poets finally.[1] I have a copy of that, carefully put away, for these pronouncements and decisions must be preserved. The page proofs have gone back and Flemington[2] promises action. *But* I havent had proofs of title page or advt. matter altho' L.P. wrote MacI they were being forwarded. I wrote again on Friday last. Vexatious. We are having [a] heat wave, 90° yesterday.

Yours ever,
DCS

56

Cornell
July 17, 1943

Dear Duncan:

I had a good deal of fun reading P.D.R. on Roberts. It is such an important document, as you say, that I must restore it to you for your archives. I fear that Mr. Ross will not like my book. As I told L.P., our literary history must be rewritten, and some of the landmarks removed. Carman and Roberts will no longer do as landmarks. I think that A.L., and you and Ned Pratt *will* do, and that you three must be the main landmarks. I told L.P. that even if I were wrong about all of you, my book should be useful since it would show that one should and could let one's mind play freely over the subject, and that quite new conclusions could thus be reached.

What worries me is that I don't think the book will get much of a show in the U.S. That is sad because I am always talking and thinking how unfortunate it is that our literature now exists within a national wall; and that it would gain by being discussed more outside the country seems to me certain. The Ryerson Press is represented in this country by a firm I never hear of in any other connection, B. Humphries of Boston. I am trying to interest Pierce in trying to get the agency for my book taken by some larger company.

Sorry to hear you are getting such great heat. Our summer has not been too bad. One desperate week in June; and since then quite moderate. This is a rainy area; and I have never seen such glorious leafage.

I am just finishing my lectures on Chaucer, and about to approach Spenser, whose verse is a never failing delight to me. In my leisure I am reading the *Scenes of Clerical Life*, and playing with the notion of reading G. Eliot through. I have never read *Deronda*, [1] but I know the others pretty well, and would like to see how they would appear taken in sequence, and gone over in a short time.

Your Sickert tale delighted me. I hope you go on with the A.L. piece. It was good news that you have had page proof, and I trust that the title page, advertisement etc. will come through soon. I have not yet had page proof of my book.

As ever,
Edward

P.S. [*holo.*] Of course, I hope that you will write freely about my book. Some of its political implications I fear you will disapprove.

E.

57

July 19, 1943

Dear Edward.   Here is a copy of a letter to F.F. of the Ryerson Press. I hope they have sent you a proof of the title page. There was no proof of the jacket but only a lay-out. Below the sketch of the rapids the words THE LITERARY DISCOVERY OF THE YEAR are to be printed, not too startling but in italics to conform with "and other new poems." I dont quite like this phrase but I cant suggest anything to take its place. On the back of the jacket they will print the explanitory part of my Foreword I.E. the first long para. giving the provenance of the poems. There will be nothing on the inside flaps of the jacket. On the whole I consider this pretty satisfactory, and I think the book will look very well. I explain this Jacket as they may not have sent you the sketch they sent here; it was merely a lay-out in pencil. You will note that I have asked for your O.K. on these points. Nothing more just now; I would like the carbon of my letter as I have kept copies of my correspondence with them.

Yours ever,
Duncan

58

Cornell
July 21, 1943

Dear Duncan:

Your letter has just come. I fully approve of everything that you wrote to L.P. My copy of dust-cover, front cover and title page arrived yesterday, and I at once returned all, saying that I should defer to your judgment in this, but adding that I liked all three. I made one mild suggestion on the advice of a colleague who is much interested in the format of books: that instead of ''FOREWORD,'' we have ''Foreword,'' or the same italicized. The same of course for ''INTRODUC-TION.'' But I said that I did not feel at all strongly.

No copy of the advertising came to me. I think the R.P. is being more sensible and modest than I feared, and I am quite ready to accept ''the literary discovery of the year'' though it is not the sort of phrase that would occur to me. What you will think well of as advertising I know I will like too. You don't like the phrase I quoted, no more do I; but I think we are at one in thinking that it is not objectionable. On the other hand if you should come to *dis*like it, I will of course stand with you.

Unless you raise objections I won't.

Yesterday my secretary dropped in the mail to you my copy of *The Green Cloister*, and I meant to write to you at the time. I suddenly remembered that I had not sent it as I planned to do long ago, so that you might pencil your recollections of dates, as you did in my copy of the *Collected Poems* last year.[1] I shall greatly value your notations. 'The Mad Girl's Song' for instance will always be linked for me with the sleepless night in Montreal to which you refer in a note.[2]

I will stop now since I want to get this to you as soon as I can.

As ever,
Edward

P.S. [*holo.*] I am returning the copy of your letter to Flemington.

59 [*Holo.*]

August 4, 1943

Dear Peggy and Edward,

Your congratulations arrived on the day and gave me the greatest pleasure.[1] I too wish that you had been here and that we four could have had a good visit — let us now begin to hope and plan for next year. We had a quiet & enjoyable day — very hot with the peculiar quality of Ottawa heat.

I have been reading the A.L. page proof this mng. It will be a nice little book. Very soon I'll be sending *The Green Cloister*, with such dates as I know. On the 2nd Aug. I put my name in it wh. will add immensely to its interest and value. My love to you Peggy & our best to you both.

Yrs ever,
Duncan

60 [*Holo.*]

August 12, 1943

Dear Edward.   I am mailing *The Green Cloister* today & have pencilled in dates when I had them. So often lately lyrics were scribbled on bits of paper that were destroyed that I cant date them. You wont find any notes such as I put for the 'Mad Girl's Song.' The poems all have some associations, memories of place and moments but there is no use in making a record of them. "Garland's Hotel,"[1] where I wrote 'The Night Watchman' you may know & you may have stayed there as for years it was the haunt of literary folk. When I arrived Robt Nichols[2] had just left. Rupert Brooke[3] stayed there, and reading M. Sadleir's book on Trollope[4] I find that the great Anthony was there in Nov '82 went out to dinner on the 2nd had a stroke & died on the 6 Decr. A bomb made an end of it & it will never be rebuilt, at least never in the up & down around the corner style wh. made it singular & unique. The page proofs of A.L. came & have been sent back & we shd see the book before long. There was only one thing I did not like — the lyric at the end of 'At the Long S.' was divided & the reader has to turn the page to read the last two verses. I wish the 4 verses cld have been under the eye at once — but there wld have been some difficulty in arranging the type & I let it go without remark. Let us pray, or do whatever is with us equivalent to praying, that it may be a success. I note that you think of rereading G. Eliot. I speculate on the result. Yr resolve led me to look into sections of *Deronda, Middlemarch* & to begin to read *The Mill on the Floss*. I have not gone very far and may stick where I am. You shd have left me with my youthful impressions. Reading Sadleir's book on Trollope led me to look up an essay by G. Saintsbury on Trollope;[5] he places him finally just below the great 4 — Austen, Scott, Thackeray & Dickens. So much for Saintsbury. How is yr book progressing? & have you heard anything of A.J.M.S.'s great anthology? It has taken me days to finish this letter. I was not able to use the typewriter but when I write you next I shall try to type & spare you this ordeal. Our best wishes to you both.

Yrs ever,
Duncan

15.8.43

61

Cornell
August 30, 1943

Dear Duncan:

I am more than usually slow in thanking you for your annotations to *The Green Cloister*, and in replying to your letter. It has not been just negligence. I decided to take a few days out of town; and spent part of last week in New York. When I do that I always have to work harder before and after I go. You will recall the sensation, I am sure. I saw *Angel Street*, a rather cheap thriller with the now customary Victorian background, but the work of a Canadian girl, with the lead, Judith Evelyn,[1] was startlingly good in snatches, and the evening was a good one for me. No chance of getting into the Elizabeth Bergner play,[2] which is not much of a vehicle, anyhow.

When I was down there I brought to a head a project I have been thinking of for a long time: persuading Bennett Cerf, the editor of the Modern Library, to add *Père Goriot* to his library. He agreed to let me do this, coupling another Balzac piece with it, *Eugenie Grandet*. I think Balzac stands as high as any one with me: the life and the construction and the characters are marvels the more I read him. And the style is nothing much, so that one does not feel that a translation ruins him. Perhaps I may translate one of the books as well as editing the whole volume. I shall have to look over the various translations and see what I make of them.

Is Balzac on your list of indispensables?

We shall value the inscription of your name on your birthday more than I can say. And the annotations are precious indeed. Now I should like to hear if you have made any progress with your project of another collection.[3] I hope you will go on with it. It is almost ten years since the last.

I long to see the Lampman book and hold it in my hand, and hear what a few of our friends may say about it. The other day I sent back the page proofs of the C. Poetry book. I think I shall be lucky if it comes out by Christmas. Today I feel a little melancholy. I am about to lose Peggy for several weeks: she is going out to Minneapolis on her annual visit to her father and mother.[4] Somehow I have not made the friends here that I have come on in other places, nor has she, and we both feel unusually lonely when separated. There is something in the atmosphere of this place which won't do for us, and we are tempted to say it is just the small townness: it is our first experience of a small town, and it may be that we oversimplify, and that what is obnoxious is something peculiar to this small town.

Thanks once more for *The Green Cloister*. I have ended my chapter on you with a quotation from *Marius the Epicurean*.[5] I hope that Pater stands higher with you than with most Canadians. Do you know that I was the first to lecture on him at Toronto? As late as 1937? Alexander couldn't stand anything he wrote, and Malcolm Wallace[6] the same. Pelham was more or less indifferent.

Yours, as ever,
Edward

62

September 10-16, 1943

Dear Edward.   Your letter of Aug 30th left you in a melancholy mood. These separations are not good for married lovers, but they have to be endured. Let us hope that these time-divisions discover springs of feeling that might otherwise go undiscovered. As for the local situation, what can be done about it? I have suffered so much from nostalgia that I can sympathize; but perhaps that is not the right word; you have dwelt here and there so you cannot be part of any one place as I have been of this small town. I think you are too close to the academic routine, for one thing, maybe I ought not to offer explanations, your own are sufficient, nothing compensates for the lack of the spirits that are akin, who think like thoughts and have somewhat the same outlook on life. You may become enured to it; you may leave that town for a brighter atmosphere; Turn Fortune, Turn Thy wheel. In all the contents of your letter I was most interested in the project of Balzac for the Modern Library. That was an omission wh. had to be filled; considering his importance it is odd that he had not been present on their list. They could not have placed the work in better hands; I shall watch the progress with interest. Will you write an introduction? A new translation would be welcome. Years ago I wandered through the wilderness of Balzac and have never lost my allegiance to him; it was always in the company of a translator, and I have on my shelves only a few of his books, nearly all in the Wormely translation;[1] two of those books are the ones you mention, *Père Goriot* & *Eugenie Grandet*; I remember being impressed by the subtilty of *The Two Young Brides*; but I cannot judge the worth of her translations. To read him in the original must be exhilerating, but no translation can rob him of the tumultuous life he unfolds or with the vividness of the characters with which he peoples it.

You mention Pater and express the hope that he stand higher with me than he does with most Canadians, he stands very high with me and has kept the sort of shrine I placed him in so many years ago and therefore I am much interested in the close of your article, I must wait a little longer; there are a good many words in Marius and I would not undertake to locate the quotation. I have made some slow progress with that project for a prose and verse Miscellany, the material is so varied that I cannot yet see it as a whole, i.e. as a book developed thro the verse and thro the prose into some harmony. The poems I have got together and they include some early work and I think I can arrange them; but so far I have trouble with the prose. Of course Elise helps me greatly and is urging me on; but the shadow of another unsaleable book darkens my effort. However, it is highly probable that my publishers will not consider it favourably; but it is yet some distance from their clutches.

I had a note from L.P. dated 7th inst in which he said that *At the Long Sault* was still in the work rooms, but Bourinot told me that he had seen both it and your book announced. The purpose of L.P.'s letter was to ask if I would agree to a Canadian Edition of *In the Village of Viger* with illustrations by Thorold MacDonald;[2] I have sent him a favourable answer; they might make a pretty book of it, the sketches are delicate enough and will require tender handling by an illustrator; but as I have always wanted a Canadian Edition this seemed to be an opportunity which came from no pressure of mine. What do you think of this? Smith's Anthology is out for Elise had a cheque from him this morning for her poem[3] and he said he had sent me last week an advance copy of the work but it has not come to hand yet. We shall see. What have I been reading? Turgenev, *Fathers and Sons*,[4] this is a beautiful book; there is a tenderness in Turgenev the other Russians lack; one point of agreement between Geo. Moore and myself is his devotion to Balzac and Turgenev; Renan's *Life of Jesus*; Davis's book *Stella*[5] which I like much, an ex parte statement, is it not? I have an extreme hostile feeling for the personalities of Swift and Pope which does not prevent me from admiring their writings; a book of short essays by Raymond Mortimore, *Channel Packet*,[6] do you know it? there is quite a long piece, Introduction to Balzac, which perhaps you might like. It occurs to me that you would like better a telegraphic form of communication rather than this sort of thing, so unimportant and so rambling. An item of local news, the Bronson-Howards have come to town. In case you do not recognize the exalted name, in its lowest form bed-bugs; an invasion of vermin in that and other forms, a subject of conversation and even appearing in the Press.[7] As yet no arrivals here or amongst friends! I hope you have Peggy at home after a pleasant visit and that she returned to better weather than we have here. Always our best to you both.

Yours ever,
Duncan

63

[Cornell]
September 25, 1943

Dear Duncan:

Here is a copy of the review of Smith's book which I have done for *American Literature*[1] at the editor's request. Perhaps you know that this (published at Duke University) is the journal for scholars in the field of Am. Lit. They don't know anything about our literature; hence I have not gone in for criticism of minor points, but tried, while giving Smith his due, I hope, to warn against some of the distortions he has. I think the section on your namesake FG[2] will serve as an object lesson. Will you look this over and let me have your views, so that I can make changes in proof? I had to send copy today.

I will write of other things later. But I must say how pleased I am that you are getting forward with your own project of a collection, and also mention that I have had a copy of the Ryerson fall catalogue which mentions *At the Long Sault* and my other thing. It is a well presented catalogue, I think.

Peggy is back from the west, I am delighted to be able to say.

Yours as ever — I liked your wife's poem. Although I like 'At the Cedars' very much I don't think it is all that 'Powassan's Drum' is. But the great point is the one that I make in the review that people such as you should have three or four times the space.

Edward

64

September 30, 1943

Dear Edward.   I have read your article on The Anthology several times and with great care and I cannot suggest any modifications or improvements. I am as yet without a copy of the book which Smith said he was sending and I cannot discover any grounds for my expecting such a courtesy, although when it arrives I shall take it for an indication of his real friendliness. The use of the definite article in [the] title is rather questionable; is this the final Scripture to which one must refer in the long future? However I hardly need The Book to appreciate your critique. I think Smith should be pleased: his own position is so firmly taken that he must expect his ideas, I had almost said his vagaries, to be challenged and you do it with such good humour that he must accept it in that spirit. When I get a copy, either this gift, so far merely a shadow-gift, or my own copy bought with my own hard earned cash, I may like to write you again on the subject. I hope Smith's Introduction will serve to clear the air north of the border (I like that sentence on P 4),[1] but I think the general trend of your own writing should be more efficatious. It should become more and more difficult for our chief critics to write as about a Sonnet of Roberts, "with the artistry there is the pulsing of passionate conviction and the ripened fruit of concentrated thought." And note the wording of the Ryerson catalogue re. F.G. Scott's book.[2] I am curious to know what poems of mine Smith has used; is 'At the Cedars' the only one?[3] Elise wants me to say that she was glad you liked her poem; it appeared in the *London Mercury* in '34 when Squire was editor.[4] Did you by any good fortune of the Air hear the Broadcast from Toronto of *Brebeuf*?[5] We listened here until eleven o'clock on Tues. night last. It was admirably presented, Healey Willan's music is very fine and entirely fitting; the narrators made a good job of the words which were well chosen, and the whole was moving; I mean that all went well together and was impressive. I have no personal news but I note that you will write me later and I shall hope for that. I am returning the copy although you did not ask for it but I thought you might need it.

Yours as ever,
Duncan

65

"October with its rain of ruined leaves"[1]

October 7, 1943

Dear Edward.   I hope you are as well satisfied with *At the Long Sault* as I am. The book is attractive in appearance and as I turn the pages the poems look important; I am speaking as if I were a prospective buyer. I am anxious to know how you feel about it. I was rather alarmed at first at the back page of the cover but I think probably it may be a good advt. to give the history of the book.[2] As for our own share of the pages: you remember we thought that maybe the prose would overwhelm the verse, *now* I have not that feeling. I find the right tone in our part, and the verse follows on quite naturally, I think the arrangement of the poems is good. As for your own Introduction — it is admirable; I think I told you when I read it first that it was just what I had hoped for, and now, when I read it in the place for which you intended it, I find it entirely fitting and adequate.

The Shadow has become Substance. The Book was dated in Toronto on the 9th Sept, and the publisher was slow in forwarding it. I have written to Smith acknldg it and said I would write him as soon as I felt able to, which means that as I have not been very well this last week, I must feel just right to compose a difficult letter. I wish I had kept your article, and I must have it in one form or another, so if you have a typed copy to spare send it please. Of course I dont intend to make use of it in writing to A.J.M.S.!

[*P.S. holo.*] MacInnes likes the book. Lovely weather here now & the colour is every day more glorious in the woods. Do you have it in Ithaca? Yesterday we had lunch at the Country Club & sat in the sun for hours. Love to you both.

Duncan

66

Cornell
October 9, 1943

Dear Duncan:

I am delighted to know that you had the same feeling of instant pleasure at seeing the book as I had. I think the Ryerson people did a surprising job, and I like everything about it from the dust-cover to the type. The poems make a good show, and I think our apparatus seems long enough to suggest the importance that we attach to the poems, but not too long for the various functions it serves. Your account manages to say some things about A.L. that you had not said in your many previous comments, and that is a triumph. I am relieved that you have no feeling that my essay is too long. It is of course substantially shorter than when you first saw it, perhaps 25%.

Now I shall be eager to see the reviews. I think the press cannot fail to find some space for it, however much they may wish to comment on the latest piece of economics or fiction. I hope you will let me see what comes to you.

I am sending my review of Smith to you once more, and shall be grateful if you will slip it into one of your letters when it has served your purpose. I also have now a gift copy of the Smith (I assume, though there is no slip to say so), but I shall not acknowledge it by a note, I think, but simply return the compliment by sending him my own book when it comes out later this month (L.P. Volente).

I am leaving later to-day on a trip to Toronto. We are now between terms, and I always like to get away for a few days. I wish it were as easy to get to Ottawa as to Toronto. All I shall have to do is to get on a train well after midnight and get up next morning in Toronto. Yes, our autumn is wonderful to see: there have been killing frosts and yet most days there is a summer warmth. Walks are incredibly fine, these days.

Good to know that MacInnes likes the book. Give him and Bourinot my best wishes. I should like to write a note to Mrs. Jenkins.[1] Would you give me her address? I shall be at the Alexandra Palace in Toronto till the end of next week.

Yours, as ever,
Edward

67 [Holo.]

October 13, 1943

Dear Edward.   Many thanks for yr letter — & enclosure wh. I'll return later. I feel I shd write Smith but I dont want to be critical, at the same time I think I ought to make a few remarks. You will tell me any Toronto news that you think I wld like to hear. Mrs. J's address.

Mrs. F.M.S. Jenkins

80 Driveway
Ottawa.
Yrs ever,
D.

68

November 12, 1943

Dear Edward.   During the last few days I have had your book more often in my hands than any other. I would like to begin to say something about it but not finish today. Many thanks for sending me a copy and inscribing it in that familiar fashion.

This is going to be a famous little book; it is full of ideas and flashes of insight based on a full knowledge of the subject. I want to say a good deal about the first two sections but I write now about the third where my personal interest lies. If I mention first the close of your article on D.C.S. it is because that affected me greatly. (I should say *us* for Elise and I read it together.) It is one of your fine bits of writing and it will keep the picture of the Music Room alive. That room has held many delightful people, has heard much fine music and good talk and for us your visits with your wife are of the best memories; would they could be more frequent and longer. The quotation from Pater pleases me for I am a bit vain in the belief that I have appreciated the Arts and have cultivated my tastes; it flatters that feeling and it makes a moving close to that personal reference. I am in your debt, but have you set me a part that, as an actor, I shall have to play for the rest of my days?

If in the past there has been neglect of my work and a lack of critical insight in discerning any peculiar quality it has been made good by your penetrating study of it, beginning with that first article in the *Manitoba Quarterly* and extended in this book. To have hit upon that phrase, "restraint and intensity," and to have shown its significance in so many examples is the mark of a critic; it was new and illuminating even to myself. I have not been self-conscious in practice; my desire was to make the thing under my hand as perfect as I could make it. I am doubtful whether if you had given me years ago the key to this individuality I could have made constant use of it. I do not find you "unperceptive" (a word you used), but rather discerning and sympathetic and your criticism must take place as the final word.

The MacMechan incident is curious for two reasons.[1] I did not know until I had read your article that such a book was in existence so have never read it; a comment on my general lack of interest in what went on in our literary life. In 1927 I read a notice of the *Collected Poems* in the *Montreal Standard*; very favorable. "A poet of real distinction. . . I was not attracted to Mr. Scott's work; at first I approached it in a very critical mood. Mine is a case of genuine conversion." The notice was in a column contributed weekly and signed "The Dean." I found out that the writer was MacMechan.[2] Now what can one make of that? Spite is too strong a word perhaps. When he wrote in 1924 he was well aware of what I had done; we were members of the Royal Society and friendly enough but I must have done something that annoyed him and he thought he would retaliate. Well, let us forgive him.

A note on 'Spring on Mattagami.' The provanance of this piece was my having taken a copy of the *Oxford Book* with me on that Indian trip; Pelham and I sitting side by side in our thirty-foot canoe had been reading 'Love in a Valley.'[3] I said to myself (or out loud) I will write a love poem in the same form in these surroundings. That great poem was of the English country-side, this will be of the wilderness; I did not think to rival it and I added to the technical problem by using an additional rhyme; and so I did it in three days. I think and hope the passion is sincere but you will have to count the lady as imaginary, the lady of the city and the garden and the Lido; the Venice stanza was written last as I felt some change in colour would be a relief and add to the drama. Does this interest you? There are two places I would like to make changes but I can't do it now. That line about the loon — "Reels remote. . .etc." and the line which ends in "Judgment day."[4] But they will have to go now. By the way as a practical instance of puritanism pages 44 and 45 were torn out of the copy in our City Library.[5]

I have said many times what I think of the Lampman; in this extended form I don't think it could be better. I appreciate to the full your estimate of Pratt; I, too, am an admirer of his and of his special quality which he has brought into our poetry. I think tremendously well of his best lyrics, of their intensity and strangeness. I think he will do even greater things yet; he needs a large canvass and heroic deeds and these time may yet give him — another Dunkirk or a pure invention such as Birney's 'David.' He is only sixty and has twenty years ahead of him.

I hope I have not wearied you. I want to write again about the first two sections of the book.

[Duncan]

69

November 16, 1943

Dear Edward.   I dont know whether you take the *S.N.* so I send this along. A niggardly review, and not a word about the general content of the book.[1] *S.N.* does not make a feature of the book page but this is an instance and a comment on what you say in the first Chapt. of your book. Here is a book by two well known

Canadians presenting new verse of our Chief poet and that is all the space and all the enthusiasm that is accorded it. The attention of the reader is drawn to a few unimportant novels written by foreigners. How strong the emphasis of your first chapter is upon such an incident as this. No satire and no castigation can be effective against such indifference. Well, I suppose we shall have to put up with it. The price of this book should have been 1.50 as specified in the contract with MacI. Without consulting him P. makes the price 2.00; this is an example of how he does business. We had hoped for a price that would make it available for a fairly large distribution.

> Well, dont forget me
> Yrs
> > Duncan

70

> Cornell
> November 17, 1943

Dear Duncan:

I cannot tell you how delighted I was to hear of your pleasure in the article, or rather chapter, on DCS. My only real misgiving as the book was about to appear was what you and Pratt would think of my treatment. Pratt had already told me of his pleasure when your letter came; his brother had come from Nfld, and Pratt's wife had read the chapter aloud in a small quasi-family gathering. Now that I know that you and Elise could read aloud what I wrote of you, I am fully at peace.

The kind of criticism that I try to write calls, at a certain stage, for the most complete objectivity: for instance when I was seeking for that formula of restraint and intensity I was no longer remembering my friend, but looking at the material just as if it had been done a hundred or a thousand years ago. I never know how the result of such cold goings-on will appear to the person most concerned! But I think that the sincerest tribute I can pay to your great art is to deal with it as great art.

You will be pleased to know that Woodhouse considers that the chapter on DCS is to him the most illuminating in the book. My friend Douglas Bush,[1] of Harvard, also singled it out along with one other.

I am trying to catch up with my work here. Last week I was giving a lecture at Yale (on E.M. Forster) and I have to pay now for the grand time I then had. I will write again soon. Now I can only say how happy I am because of your letter, mainly because of what you say of the chapter on yourself, but very much too because of your generous and encouraging praise of the book as a whole.

Clarke should have a copy by now. The Q[ueen's] Q[uarterly] was to get one. I also sent a copy to Brockington, to his Ottawa address, and one to MacInnes, who has sent a very kind letter in return.

Yes, we shall meet and talk. I had hoped to take this term off — November to March — and I now hope it can be the next term — March-June — that I can be free. Whenever I do get more than a few days of freedom you may be sure I'll tap at 108 Lisgar St.

Tell Elise how happy I am she liked the book too. Peggy repudiates her share of the dedication, but I think she liked it. The *Arthur* is Woodhouse.[2]

Do let me know what you think of other parts of the book when you can.

As ever,
Edward.

P.S. [*holo.*] Doubtless you saw *S.N.* on the Lampman. Deacon (*G & M*) was kind but not very interesting.[3] Those are all I've seen.
I value greatly the comments on 'Spring on Mattagami.'

71

[November] 19-23, 1943

Dear Edward.   I dont think you could have stated the matter with more complete understanding or greater sympathy.[1] With the general trend I agree and I am in no way opposed to your "politics" as you thought I might be.[2] Puritanism I dislike as much as you do and I decry the Censor. In Canada we have had our censoring done for us and have merely followed the lead in banning. I hope your remark that puritanism is diminishing is true. Certainly there is naughtiness enough and social conflict and tragedy arising from it in Toronto and Montreal and subjects for drama and fiction are all there. But that literature of perfect freedom I think is a long way off. If it came in my time probably I wouldnt read it; I have never read a book by Hemingway or Dos Passos. If Colonialism is the right word for our deadness, well and good; it requires a definition? Your remark on p. 24 I dont quite agree with.[3] The States had defeated Colonialism and their literature came from a spring of fresh and independent feeling. Our foundations are not built on rebellion and a frontier period of political experiment but on acceptance of tradition and a determination to perpetuate it. Hardship of course and personal independence but no such feeling of Statehood as existed in Mass. or Virginia. Even now, after all these years, we have no positive, actuating feeling in our Provinces, except in Que. or in N.S. perhaps. One element has contributed to foster our Colonialism — the tone of condescencion by notices of our literary efforts both in England and the U.S. That may be changing but running over a long period it has had a discouraging effect. The clinching point of your essay is on pp. 24-25. I have it firmly in mind [that a] literature springs from social pressure and the action, her[oic or] otherwise, that is thrown up by conflict. We agree on this and your sentence "A great literature etc." is a perfect statement.[4] Our future is "incalculable" but I am just now pessimistic because I cannot forsee density of population or intense national impulses in the future. I say "just now" for anyone who is aware of currents in our politics must be disturbed. Your second section is a true development of that subject, moderate in expression, sympathetic to the old and the new. The vigorous young set is given a hard task as set forth by A.J.M.S. on page 74.[5] That and Collin's remarks about Smith seem to me poses, sincere, of course. Measure Collin's words with Smith's accomplishment in *News of the Phoenix*, "His problem is the eternal problem etc."[6] I admire many of the things in this book but I cant feel him at grips with this problem. But I would not alter a word in your development section for I feel you have succeeded in the "objective" ideal you mentioned in your last letter; it is detached and impersonal. You have done a fine thing in this book and as I believe in you and what you will do with your gifts I am proud to have a part in it. I was glad to hear that Woodhouse liked the D.C.S., if he is ever in this town I should like him to call me up. Pelham was here last night, very praiseful of the book and that Section, "a beautiful bit of writing," which it undoubtedly is.

I sent a copy of A.L. to Rowley Frith the florist who has kept flowers on the grave;[7] he was very pleased and said he enjoyed most the Sonnets at the end of the book. I also sent a copy to W.D. Lighthall but he was very ill in hospital and his wife wrote that he could just look at the cover; I have had no further news of him; as you know he was one of A.L.'s first admirers.[8]

G.H. Clarke spent a week end with us, brought his new anthology of War Poetry in wh. Elise and I are both represented. Houghton Mifflin.[9] I would like much a printed copy of your review of Smith's Anthology. Are you going to write to Mrs. Jenkins? I think that would be a good thing to do if you feel like it.

Our love to you and Peggy, I am glad she held you to it.[10]

[Duncan]

72

Cornell
December 2, 1943

Dear Duncan:

I am slow in writing about your comments on the rest of the book. The past week or so I have been caught up in a number of local duties which have robbed me of my time. Also, I ordered and received Froude's four volumes on Carlyle,[1] at which I had merely glanced before, and have found them irresistible. I think that Froude is queerly unfair at times, and too admiring at others; and it is fascinating to watch him veering back and forth.

It was reassuring to know that my approach to the "problem" in the first chapter seemed wise to you. Clearly I must do some re-thinking about colonialism, and I shall.

Collin and Smith will not, I think, like my objectivity, as you kindly call it. They will want a critic to kick the pre-1920 stuff around, I fear. Collin, I hear, is not quite happy about the book; what Smith thinks I haven't heard. It is a pleasure to know that Pelham approves. Lorne Pierce writes of his approval in a letter which came after yours. Sandwell was very kind and comprehending, I thought; but I think too that a book on this subject should have a fuller review in *S.N.* Perhaps the prominent place of the comment will do more for it than a fuller review on the book page, and I feel that it was given as much *editorial* space as it could possibly be thought to deserve.

I was interested to know that you haven't read anything of Hemingway or Dos Passos. It is a chancy business to suggest reading to one who has read so much as you; but I do suggest H's *Farewell to Arms* which you can get in the Modern Library. H. has, I think, a real feeling for words, and for paragraphs, and also a great gift for narrative. I think his account of the Italian retreat, Caporetto etc., is one of the best pieces of narration I ever read. And the sense for language makes his pages live for me. There are other fine things too, although I admit that an element of "smartness" detracts from the total effect.

I am so glad that the pious (in the best Roman sense) florist liked the Lampman book. Perhaps you would be interested in this comment on my account of Lampman from a young communist:

"Lampman's poetry was a reaction of a philosophically mature man, not just to the Canadian countryside, but to Canada as a whole. . . . Conscious of the fundamentally loathesome and inhumane character of society, he became less not more political as he matured. He found a personal solution for the horror he felt about human and social relationships; he found in nature what he missed in society. No other solution was possible in Canada at the end of the 19th century. . . . For a morally perceptive and aesthetically sensitive man like Lampman, delight in nature represented the only possible solution."[3]

High praise, and the higher if one notes the source.

I will not fail to send a copy of the Smith review when it appears. It may be out in January.

> Every good wish,
> as ever,
> Edward

73

[December, 1943][1]

Dear Edward.   Yours of the 2nd came in this morning just as I was sending you a copy of *The Educational Record* with my short A.L. article. My purpose was to arouse some interest in the minds of benighted students and teachers of the Protestant persuasion which might actually lead them to read or even go so far as to buy Lampman. I dont think the idea in the first para. is farfetched;[2] you will note my reference to our book; there is nothing new in this article but I wanted you to see it. Do you get *The Forum*?[3] If so you will have read the article in the Dec. No. on Canadian Poetry. If not I will send you one; let me have your comments sometime. I suppose Northrop Frye is a nom de plume; if so who is he?[4]

I have some idea of how busy you must be so I am not exacting but as your letters keep me alive I like to get them.

As ever yours,
[Duncan]

74 [*Holo.*]

December 16, 1943

Dear Peggy & Edward,

We are sending you a little Phillips color-print with our best wishes for Christmas & the New Year.[1] I wish I cld have had it mounted and framed so that it might look its best when it arrived but I was afraid of the inhumanities of the Customs etc so it goes to you unadorned. I hope it isnt one you have already.

Yours affectionately,
Elise and Duncan

75

Cornell
December 29, 1943

Dear Duncan:

I am just back from a week with Peggy in Toronto. Nothing could have been more charming to find than that exquisite Phillips color print. I admire his delicate work; and we have a water color of his, a gentle green and grey piece. I shall enjoy having this one framed. It came through, untouched, by your skilful planning. Peggy will be equally charmed. Our warm thanks to you and Elise.

By the way my present to Peggy was a Milne,[1] a little later than yours. I learned from Douglas Duncan, an old friend of mine who is now (since 1937) Milne's homme d'affaires, that yours is one of the very earliest Milnes in existence.[2] You might care to know that one something like it, but inferior by far, is priced at $150. Ours is a smaller piece, called "Last Snowdrift," a study in blue, red and black, of his cabin at Six Mile Lake.

MacInnis sent me a copy of the review of *At the Long Sault* in the Civil Service magazine.[3] This is the most intelligent review I've seen, though brief and not too detailed. I dropped into Pierce's office, and read the reviews of this book and *On*

Canadian Poetry. Very discouraging: all the press reviewers want to help the book circulate, but they don't have an inkling of how to review either poetry or literary criticism. It is the same with my book. All kind, but all stupid! Pierce says the A.L. book has sold about 200 and mine about 250, these are mid December figures. He is very pleased with both sales rates.

MacInnis also sent a clipping from the *Citizen* on the evening held in your honor.[4] How sorry I am not to have been there. I do trust that your "indisposition" was slight and trivial. It was nice that Pelham took part.

You will be interested to know that on the strength of two favorable notes in the *Saturday Review of Literature* by W.R. Benet,[5] Knopf has approached Pratt with the idea of a collected American edition.[6] How true it is that only to an American voice do Americans pay heed, but we do not pay heed to a Canadian voice.

Now for a piece of personal news. Peggy expects a baby in January. We both thought it would be better if she were in Toronto, and so did not run the risk of doctor or nurse shortage or inefficiency. Also she has more friends there by far. She has the promise of a good nurse for three months after the baby is born, something we could not hope for here. So she will stay in Toronto till some time in April.

I am delighted to know that she is in the very highest spirits, and now as always in the very best of health.

In the rush of leaving, I may have omitted to thank you for the article on A.L. you did for the Quebec magazine. I was interested in many of the points you raised, of course in the way you worked in the new poems, and just as much in that point about the arrival in Ottawa being a stimulus of the first order to him.

Yours, as ever,
Edward

1944

With At the Long Sault *and* On Canadian Poetry *safely launched, what next? Scott's dependence on his friend's letters makes him fearful the correspondence will die. But the pace of the exchange holds up very well. On the human side of the friendship, a renewal comes from young Deaver; and Scott's concern for this first child of the Browns flows like a warm stream into the new year. It is the gentle side of a man sometimes thought austere, and it is doubtless shadowed with heartache from memories of the loss of his own child, the much beloved Elizabeth, many years ago. It is Brown, however, who takes the helm and steers the ship. In his first letter of the new year, he writes: "You need have no fear that I would forget you. Right now I have a problem for you." He has found a Lampman lecture, hitherto unpublished; and it should "get into print." Later there is the "interesting letter from California," the fascinating "dramatic fragment," and the second-hand copy of the Memorial edition: all Lampmaniana. Brown is never short of "problems." From the storehouse of his active life he draws interesting pieces: the on-going translation of Balzac; his articles on contemporary poetry and E.M. Forster; his broadcast from the Toronto studios of the C.B.C. This is the work of an impresario, though always carried out with great tact and affection. The poet responds wonderfully well. He writes with wit and force, commenting on the present and rummaging about in the past. Meanwhile, Brown has accepted an appointment to the University of Chicago. In April he is in Ottawa briefly to receive a Governor General's award for* On Canadian Poetry. *The old order passes: in May there is a State Memorial Service for Charles G.D. Roberts in Fredericton; in June Brown loses his old mentor, W.J. Alexander, and Scott his close friend Russell Smart. In the Canadian background, the conscription crisis becomes acute. The landing of the Allied Forces on the beaches of Normandy on the 6th of June passes unnoticed.*

76

January 5, 1944

My Dear Edward.   This is great news you have given us and we are immensely interested and we hope you will send us early news of the event. Will you give Elise's love and mine to Peggy; we are delighted to have such good news of her health and her favorable surroundings. You will be lonesome and anxious during this interval and your interest in literary affairs will flag and any thought of Canadian literature will tend to disappear as the first thing to shrink into unimportance, but in the early summer I hope you will begin to remember your old friend in the North and the good days we spent in trying to lighten the darkness of this land.

As you sandwiched your good news between comments on *ordinary* matters I venture to add a few words on like subjects. I am glad you have a Milne, we get great pleasure from ours. MacI wrote the notice you mention. He had a letter from L.P. saying that he was well satisfied by the sale of the Lampman; I must remark he is easily satisfied; that rate of sale for his book and yours does not satisfy me; but comparing it with the sale of my books it is wonderful! I refrain from shocking you by quoting any figures. The reviews so far as I have seen have been contemptible; as I have told you I am pessimistic on the whole matter. I was glad to hear that Knopf is nibbling at an edition of Pratt; I have not got his new book yet but will do so when I am next in Hope's.[1] I did not attend that evg celebration as it would have been impossible to stand it; but every one was very pleased. Brock referred to Elise as "that noble and gifted lady to whom we owe such a debt of gratitude" I told him I felt that was just because I wouldn't be alive now if it had not been for her. I wrote four Sonnets for her on our twelfth anniversary which I may show you some day.[2] The labor of getting my old stuff together goes slowly.

Well, our affection to you both,

Yours ever,
Duncan

77

Cornell
January 8, 1944

Dear Duncan:

Warm thanks for that latest letter. I was much relieved to know that you were absent from the meeting because you thought best, not because you were ill.

I am delighted to be able to tell you that a son has come.[1] Peggy was so well, she could speak to me over the phone the very evening of the birth. All later news is equally good, and when I go up for a week-end on the 15th they will be back from the hospital, and installed with a good practical nurse in an apartment we have taken in Toronto for the winter. It is a very great relief to know that all is over so well.

You need have no fear that I would forget you! Right now I have a problem for you. I have been copying the lecture "Two Canadian Poets" which A.L. gave to the Literary and Scientific Society in February 1891.[2] It seems to me a thing that should get into print, and I think I could get it into the Toronto *Quarterly*. In thanking MacInnes for sending a copy of the review in the Civil Service organ, I raised the question with him. I thought that a short preface, a couple of pages, would be all that is needed to explain the appearance, and if you approve the general idea the notion of what the preface should be like might be held over for later talk or letters. Conner[3] does not list this paper as having appeared anywhere. Did it? And were you there the night it was delivered?

I am interested to know that MacInnes was the author of the review. I had not thought of that, and it is lucky that I praised it in my note to him! I think it is the best we have yet had. Collin is to couple this book with my *OCP* in a review for the Toronto *Quarterly*.[4] God knows what he will say. At least my book is leading a few new readers to A.L., yourself and Pratt. That was always my main wish.

Every good wish to you both,

As ever,
Edward

78 [*Holo.*]

January 11, 1944

My dear Edward,

Our congratulations to you & Peggy on the birth of your son. I hope this note will reach you before you leave for Toronto so that you may give her our love and tell her how pleased we are. It is fine to have such good news of the mother & the boy. I think he is going to be a distinguished member of society and my Shade will salute him from the Beyond. What an interest his development will be to you both. This all reads conventionally, I fear, but there is an underlying feeling that is by no means conventional & we want you both to know it.

Yours as ever,
Duncan

[P.S.] I'll write later about relatively unimportant literary matters.

D

79

January 29, 1944

Dear Edward.   I should like to know very much how you found Peggy and
the boy when you went to Toronto; and in fact the latest news of them. I should
say we because Elise is just as interested. And a matter of importance; have you
chosen a name for him, and what is it? If you would care to give me her address
later on I would write her a note, if you think that would be acceptable.

Now about less important matters. The address "Two Canadian Poets" has
never been published. Is this the source of A.L.'s remark about the effect of
Roberts' early work on him?[1] I [am] sure that I heard him read it, and his paper
on Keats, as I usually went to the meetings. That may have been a day of small
things but they are hardly better now. No more than fifty in the audience in a
room hardly large enough to contain them. MacI wld be favourable to the
publishing and I think I cld offer no reason against it. If you wld care to send me
the M.S. I cld write further about it. Your preface wld we all right, of course. I
am sorry you have used your eyes in copying this; there must have been a fair
copy from wh. he read but MacI says he cld not find one. As I dont know
whether you get the $Q.Q.$[2] I send the notices of the books that were in the last No.
G.H.C. seems blind to the beauties of 'At the L.S.' When he was here we had a
discussion about it and I had to affirm that I was altogether with you in your
admiration, but on the whole I think we might be satisfied. I wonder what you
thought of his review of your book. I was not so well satisfied and I dont know
what he means by "drawing on your imaginative faculty"[3] but if you do by all
means draw on it; but I dont forget for a moment that Clarke admires you and has
tried to show it in this notice. Thanks for sending *The Forum*; I wanted to make
some remarks [on the] reviews[4] but Pelham carried them and the one on Smith's
Anthology [away the] other night and has not returned them yet. I dont care to
hazard any remarks from memory of the contents. What will the clever young
man on the *Dalhousie R.* say;[5] and what will Collin say? I hope the latter wont be
too condescending; I dislike his book,[6] you may think this queer, but I cant help
it; I know you dont mind what these writers say, no more do I; but I wont have
you abused for moving me into the front rank; if they are not cautious I will make
them skip with my old falchion. MacI is in Toronto today and is to see L.P.: if he
reports anything of interest I shall let you know. Brockington went to
Newfoundland to speak at the Burns dinner. He asked Pratt to make a poem for
him to read, as he is of that Island I thought it was a good idea. B. says the poem
is good, fitting and simple. The last quality is sovreign; what idiot said that
simplicity was the varnish of the masters, which showed that he didnt know
much about painting, I think it was that rascal Whitman. The adjective comes
from G.M. Hopkins; Goethe and Burns were also great rascals.[7] This will show
you perhaps that I have been rereading Hopkins's letters. I enjoy them greatly, I
think I have read everything available written by Hopkins and I have an intense
interest in it all. Has anyone of importance tried to interpret the life and the letters

and the poems? Probably. To this ill-furnished critic the *clear* mind [which] shone in the letters and note-books was not carried over into the poems, unfortunately, I think. But why shd I try to express hurriedly what I feel so confidently? Is the Balzac scheme developing? Write me a letter or even a note before long.

Yours ever,
[Duncan]

80

Cornell
January 31, 1944

Dear Duncan:

I have a rather unusually large budget of news and notions for you, and all too short a time in which to set it forth. If the letter shows signs of undue haste, please pardon them, as coming from the sense that I just must get these facts to you.

1. I enclose a copy of a poem of Lampman's on which I came in an odd way. A N.Y. second hand dealer advertised the edition of 1900 at .75, and I bought. The volume interests me in two ways: it is the first copy of the second impression I have ever seen;[1] and it has an inscription from E.W. Thomson to his son B.W.S.D. Thomson, dated Nov. 27, 1904.[2] I wondered, since you knew the Thomsons, if you might recognize the hand; by all means keep the little thing, if it has any interest for you.

2. I read Clarke's review with much interest. I have never been liberal of praise to him, and all in all I think he was kind to me. I don't like the method of comment which suggests error but does not point it out; it is damaging and may be dangerous; and there is a bit of this in the review. I was delighted he liked the chapter on you. His comment on our including too much shows that he did not weigh carefully enough your remark that we were working on the principle of the 1900 collection, not the later one.[3] I was astonished that he did not care for the final lyric in 'At the Long Sault' itself. He is rather too curt towards Smith's own little collection; though I agree with what he says of the anthology. I do not know Clarke, but if you run into him again soon you might mention that I found his review interesting and suggestive, but did not think him right in the main.

3. I am on the trail of the unpublished poetry of Cameron,[4] and have been given new zeal by reading and copying the lecture A.L. gave on Cameron and Roberts. It is now being typed and I will send you a copy. I think of getting Woodhouse to print it if he will. You shall see it of course before negotiations begin.

4. All is well in our midst. Peggy and the boy (we call him *Deaver* — Peggy's maiden name, which I have always liked, partly because it is beautifully

Jamesian) are in the best of every kind of health. And we are about to bid adieu to village life. I have given up my post here to accept a chair at Chicago, which carries the same salary and frees me from administrative drudgery. We are both delighted. The change will come this summer.

5. Last week I was near you by the supposedly straight flight of the crow. (Or does the crow really fly straight? you are the naturalist.) I had to inspect the work for the army at a little college at Potsdam N.Y.;[5] but I found by much study of timetables that I was actually as far from Ottawa in time as if I were here. So I turned back home. It was a lovely mild day even as far north as that.

I hope you are both well and that this extraordinary winter has not brought you any ills. W.J. Alexander who is much your senior writes in very good spirits; his one concern is that it is beginning to be hard for him to read at night. When I think of the dreadful arrangements he calls reading lamps, I wonder that he can read at all at almost 89. I still recall one long evening I spent with him, by the light of one strong bulb completely unprotected. For a man with a strong sensitiveness to beauty, the circumstances in which he lives are unbelievable.

Will Brockington get the CBC after all?[6] I very much hope some really liberal and large way of placing him where he can do his unique work will be found. Give him every good wish when you see him.

As ever,
Edward

81

February 8, 1944

Dear Edward.   Yours of the 31st ult. contained much matter to be commented on; but this morning I am only going to touch on the personal items. We like the boy's name Deaver, it is very unusual, goes well with his surname and will always have those family associations that are so valuable. But you are not to bring him up as a Jamesian character; from such parentage I expect great things of him. Prayers may be out of fashion but I shall put up prayers for him that all good may befall him and that a strong mind and a stout heart may be his to work out his destiny. Is this too solemn? But you must not discount it, and it goes with strong feeling for you both. I am glad that Peggy and Deaver are well; it is too much to hope that I shall see them together one day. As for the other item that you are leaving Cornell I share your evident relief. That situation never seemed to suit you. You are both cosmopolites and the village tone was discordant and the fussing over small details and often I can imagine over vexatious things would be a hinderance to the development of your true interests in life. You might tell me sometime what the nature of the new position is and I'm glad you are not losing any money by it. The copy of the A.L. lecture arrived and a little later on I shall write to you about that and the other points in your last. Do you see the *Dalhousie*? I must send you Martin's notice of your book.[1] Col. Osborne is sending me Collin's article. Brockington and I are attending a meeting this aft. and I will give him your message.

Yours ever,
Duncan

82

February 14, 1944

Dear Edward.   I hope I shall send a proper and decent reply to yours of the 31st ult. as there are several remarks I should like to make in a reasonable and worthy fashion. It was a singular destiny that led that copy of A.L. into your hands. Thomson's son Bernal was Sports Editor of the N.Y. *Times* at the time of his death. He left a son from whom I heard once or twice but I have lost track of him.[1] I seemed to recognize the handwriting of the poem at first but afterwards came to the conclusion that I was mistaken; MacI does not place it and the writer must remain mysterious. I return it herewith. This incident interested me. I hope your search for new poems of Cameron will result in discovering some of his best work. It is not at all improbable that the critical faculty that selected the poems in the Vol. we know[2] was at fault and left out good work. I read the lecture carefully, with surprise and all the pleasure of recollection. Yes, this is the source of the quotation I gave in the Intro. to *Lyrics of Earth*. There is a great cleft between the two divisions of this paper. The Roberts is superior to the Cameron; the writing in the former is vigorous, bold and independent; in the latter it is somehow nerveless and is strongly effected by the quality of the poems he quotes; the examples he gives do not prove his enthusiasm, except in three or four instances. My memory of these far off times is that A.L. was given a copy of Cameron's poems by his (C's) brother and that was his introduction to the author. Note for instance the remark on Page 24 and the stanza that follows.[3] Would A.L. have outgrown this extravagant admiration and come to a cooler view later on? I probably shared his enthusiasm then but now I stand with you in the pages 37 et seq. of your book.[4] I checked up all the poems of Roberts used by A.L. and was interested to find that, with the exception of the two love poems,[5] Roberts [had] retained them all in the collection he made himself in 1936. Did you notice the sonnet quoted from Cameron on p. 21?[6] I am much interested in the rhyme scheme which L. does not pay any attention to. The rhyme scheme consists of two divisions of five lines each, followed by a quatrain. There are two rhymes in each of the five line divisions and two rhymes in the final quatrain. I like this and I dont remember seeing it before, do you? I think I shall try it some day. I am sending the notices in the *Dal. Review*. Maybe you will like to make a comment. I would like to see this Lecture in print and of course I want Cameron to have every chance possible and I trust you may find a treasure. I hope you have good news from the family. I saw Clarke for a while when he was here on a R[oyal] S[ociety] Committee. I was not on the Com. They gave the Lorne Pierce medal to Audrey Brown.[7] I gave him your message and he seemed satisfied. He knew about your going to Chicago. Please write again before very long.

Yours ever,
Duncan

[*P.S. holo.*] I have made some light pencil marks in the margin that can be easily rubbed out. I dont think there is much chance for L.W.B. in the C.B.C. Would to God the govt. had some place worthy of him & would put him in it but "Our Peerless Leader" has something else to think about now.[8]

D

83

Cornell
February 15, 1944

Dear Duncan:

Herewith I return the reviews from the *Queen's*, on which I have already told you my few thoughts.

I wonder if I failed to give you Peggy's Toronto address: 248 Heath St. West. I think of this now because I am sending to her your last letter, with its kind reference to the baby and its name. We won't be too Jamesian, I promise! Peggy was very happy about your other letter concerning the baby.

Well, I have seen Collin's review of the two books, which Colonel Osborne is to bring to you, and no doubt you have seen it too. I don't like it. I don't think it makes sense. I am at once exalted for courage and reproved for timidity (and both qualities seem to be ascribed to me in an eminent degree); and I am praised for being a scientific critic (I don't know what that could mean, unless counting metres and listing subjects etc, and I certainly don't do that) and blamed for having prejudices (for example the "humanist" point of view, which is not defined). I don't see where he comes out, what his over-all view of the book is. One little point that irritated me: I don't think Collin has the right to speak of me as "promising."[1]

He is unfair to the quality of some of the poems we brought out, I think; and he certainly doesn't like having his view of Lampman corrected.[2] Hence the wrath about the praise of the love poems. I stand by what I said about them.

Well, we needn't worry, I am sure. We can rest on what we have done, and what people whose judgment we trust think of what we have done.

I shall answer one or two of Collin's points, but just when and where I don't know.

You ask about the Balzac. I am creeping on, doing a couple of pages of the first draft every night I can find the time. It is agreeable work, and creates interesting and not too perplexing problems. I will let you know when it comes into the more interesting phase, of revising the draft.

I have done a brief review of Ned Pratt's new book and Gustafson's anthology for a *small* New York magazine.[3] I will send you a copy when it appears. The review does not amount to much. This isn't the book of Pratt's I should want to use as a basis for a really careful essay presenting him to American readers. But I never refuse a chance to make our poetry better known here.

Suddenly we are in the midst of winter again. The snow is deep and very white, and there are some fine drifts, but unlike you and A.L. I like looking at snow only through windows.

I go on another inspection of an army program at one of the colleges (this time in Brooklyn) to-morrow night. I will write again when I return. Let me just say that I had a charming note from Pelham, and if you see him tell him, if you will, that I was most appreciative of his congratulations, and will write him too when I get back to town.

As ever,
Edward

P.S. [*holo.*] Many thanks, too, for the *toad* editorials![4]

84

Cornell
February 20, 1944

Dear Duncan:

I was deeply interested in all your comments on the A.L. lecture, as I think I told you in my last hastily written letter.[1] I think I forgot to say that I agreed with you wholly in thinking that there was a great drop in effectiveness when he passed from Roberts to Cameron. The Cameron part does not seem to me to issue out of long thought and love of the poet, but to be rather the expression of a new enthusiasm.

The *Dalhousie Review* makes the charge that I have expected: that I am too much of an enthusiast for the Ontario poets, and too little for the maritimers. The charge is inevitable, and it is put politely, and I have no objection to its being made. But I am impenitent. I weighed things carefully, and came to my conclusions, and I stand on them. I may be a little unjust to Carman,[2] as I know I am not as responsive to Shelley or the Shelleyan kind of poetry as I ought to be. I have tried hard with Carman, as I have tried hard with Shelley. There is nothing more I can do! The *UTQ is* our main critical journal, though I would not go so far as to say it was our best journal of comment on the world in general. The *Dalhousie* and *Queen's* have no one to equal Bruce Clark or E.T. Owen[3] as general critics, and I think that we have others who shine brighter than any of theirs.

The only comment in this review that I resent is the absurd suggestion that your verse is often sentimental. The whole point of my essay is that your restraint is very strong, and that at times it stands in the way of perfect and complete utterance, *but* that this very habit of restraint is *essential* to the perfection you have so many times attained. *No* charge could be more off the mark than that of sentimentality. I just cannot follow the process of mind that would lead any one to say this. Can it be that he thinks you are the Archdeacon?????[4]

I return the review and send an interesting letter from California.[5] Do you know anything about the negotiations mentioned here? I have written saying that you and I (I was sure you would agree) would like to see the articles on A.L. Of course I will send them up if they come.

You might tell MacInnes that Woodhouse at once agreed to publish the lecture in the *UTQ*. He was delighted to have it. You once said that you felt sure there must be a fair copy from which A.L. read it. I wonder. The copy I used, though in pencil, was very neatly written, and could not have been a first draft. Except for a letter here and there it was quite easy to decipher.

All the news from Toronto is good. I hear from less partial sources than Peggy that the baby is becoming very handsome. He has Peggy's darkness, both in eyes and in complexion. A real portrait is promised me for later this week. Next week I get up for three days, between terms here. I wish it were possible for me to go on to Ottawa, but the time is very short. Later in the spring I hope for some weeks of freedom, and I may venture.

As ever,
Edward

P.S. I have had two charming letters about O.C.P., both of which say that the chapter on you seemed the most rewarding. One is from Ira Dilworth, of whom I heard you speak more than once, and whom I met but once, at Pratt's. I took a great fancy to him. The other is from Wilfrid Eggleston,[6] whom I have never met. Dilworth says that the book (and I suppose the A.L. too) had just arrived in Vancouver. How slow and poky the Ryerson people are! I saw a copy of your poems (the collected edition) in N.Y.C. Saturday; but since it had no inscription failed to buy it. It looked very grand on the shelf.

85 [*Holo.*]

284 Heath Street West
Toronto
February 25, 1944

Dear Mr. Scott:

After ploughing through oceans of slush I came home this afternoon to be greeted by a beautiful bouquet of lovely spring flowers and your charming note.

It was awfully kind of you and Mrs. Scott. I showed Deaver the flowers and told him of the good wishes sent by a person whom his father greatly admires. I regret to say Deaver's reaction was to howl for his next meal. All he does is think of his meals. I am sure his dreams consist of wandering through a forest of milk bottles. He's a very healthy cheerful baby. His eyes light up just like his father's when he smiles.

Edward is coming to Toronto at the end of the month. I don't think he can be away from Ithaca long enough to go to Ottawa, but he is looking forward to more chats with you as soon as he *can* arrange it. He was *very* happy that he could work with you on the Lampman, and is always delighted with the letters from you. With my very best wishes to Mrs. Scott and yourself, I am

Sincerely yours,
Peggy

86

February 27, 1944

Dear Edward.   I have two letters of yours wh. I want to answer but I want to write now a Lampman letter and reserve my comments on these reviews until a later time. I enclose something I think will interest you, — a copy of the original circular we issued for the Memorial Edition. It was written mainly by Dr. Dawson.[1] Note the extracts from reviews.[2] I feel strongly like asking you to keep this so do not for the present return it; it shd be pasted in a copy of the book and you might think MacInnes wld be the proper custodian; but when I know that their active interest in these things is so recent I feel that I might give it to you. When I tell you that they had not a copy of the Memorial Edition until I gave them one a month or so ago you will understand.[3] I tell you now that I gave them those two books I had preserved and had specially bound, — the last note-book and the proof sheets of Alcyone, and all the M.S.S. except the two wh A.L. made for me.[4] You will know where these are. Do not think I am nettled about these things, I simply tell them and want them forgotten. I do not know of any correspondence with *Wings* re. a U.S. Edition of A.L. I return his letter. MacInnes and I are proceeding to consider this new edition Pierce wants to bring out.[5] He wld like to limit it to 200 pages. I wld ask you to give thought to these points and let me have your advice.

What poems from *At the Long Sault* wld you reprint; make the list inclusive.

What poems in *Lyrics of Earth* wld you cancel. As you know the first Memoir is to be used and we shall gain space by placing or rather regrouping some of the quatrains and putting them on single pages.

I am very pleased that Woodhouse is going to print the Lecture and so is MacI. I wonder if I might suggest that you think about your short introduction once more; I found it a trifle dry, I mean in treatment; I know you do not want to import any criticism, but wld it be out of place to mention the fact I brought out viz. that all the poems of Roberts were retained by him; and cld you not just trace A.L.'s admiration to the fact of a sudden discovery without in any way criticising his judgment or Cameron's Verse. Then I think you might mention in your footnote the Lit and Scientific Soc. is no longer in existence. Well, perhaps these remarks are uncalled for.

Peggy sent us a snap-shot of Deaver. It is evident that he is a lusty fellow. Elise says he looks like you; I must see him before I decide. I want to write again soon about Collin and the other reviews.

> Yours ever,
> Duncan

[*P.S. holo.*] Did you hear that Hardy[6] has been apptd Librarian of Parliament?

> D.

87

> Cornell
> March 4, 1944

Dear Duncan:

Warm thanks for the circular. I have slipped it into the copy of the memorial edition in which I have entered all the variants I have noted in the mss.[1] It is an admirable circular; I never saw another for such a purpose so well drafted.

Your suggestions concerning my prefatory note are most welcome. I tried to keep it as short as I could; and it was perhaps for this reason that it was dry. I should be glad to note that the Institute no longer exists; but I should like better to be able to give the precise year of its death. Could you, without too much trouble, ascertain that? Also I should be glad to mention, delicately, the point about the recent discovery by A.L. of Cameron through the gift of a copy of the poems. Would you mind being quoted? I thought of some formula such as this: "I owe to Dr. Duncan Campbell Scott the information that Charles J. Cameron, brother of George Frederick, gave Lampman a copy of *Lyrics of Love, Freedom and Death*[2] not long before the present lecture was written." I think that carries the right implications, and does not assail anybody. As for the third point I will think about it. I have already made one change in the ms.: I added a note saying that you had printed in the 1925 edition the paragraph about A.L.'s first reading of Roberts.

I should like time in which to meditate about omissions from the 1925 edition, and inclusions from *At the Long Sault*. A tentative list from the latter would include the title poem, the "Portrait in Six Sonnets," the Crete sonnets, the cold grey eyes poem,[3] and the ivory keys poem.[4] I am writing at the office and with no copy by me.

I spent three days of the week with Peggy and Deaver in Toronto. They are both flourishing, and Peggy was most pleased by your thought and Elise's of sending the flowers. I hope that the boy may have the honor of seeing you; but for the moment he is the mountain and you (as is proper) the prophet.

In Toronto I saw Pierce, but not for long. He wants me to write a few words for the cover of the new volume of D. Livesay he is bringing out.[5] I agreed. This reminds me that I have seen your comment on CGDR for the journal of the Vancouver Poetry Society.[6] It is an admirable pronouncement. I could not imagine a better wording. You must have given sober thought to it.

Thanks for telling me of Hardy's promotion. I am very glad. If you would tell me his initials in your next letter I will write him a note. He was kind to me.

As ever,
Edward

88

March 9, 1944

Dear Edward.   This is just a short note.

F.A. HARDY   LIBRARIAN OF PAR'L

The note re. the Lit. and S. Society might read "Disbanded (or some other better word) circa 1910." I might have found a more appropriate word than "*dry*" by wh. I did not mean uninteresting or boring. I will not now try to say what I meant or I might make the matter worse. I wld not advise saying anything about the Cameron Poems having probably come from his brother; it is merely a vague memory of long ago. Forget my suggestion re. the Roberts Poems. *I* was interested but there wld be no general interest. As for the note about the publishing of that Para. in *Lyrics of Earth*, you may do as you think best, but I had hoped to have this article appear without any reference to me; I am sure people must be getting tired of the association. I am very keen about the printing of this lecture, and I know that your introduction will be all right. You will also do a good thing for the cover of D.L.'s book. I hope I made myself clear on the question of Collin; my feeling is very distinct and very critical.[1]

Delighted you found the family well; I am aware of the pleasure this visit must have been for you both.

Yours ever,
Duncan

[*P.S. holo.*] This is a badly typed letter & my machine seems to have developed a *grease* spot.

D.

89

Cornell
March 13, 1944

Dear Duncan:

I send one of the *Wings* numbers.[1] The other the editor could not locate. I don't much admire the execution; but the will is good, and the passages he picks are often of the best. You will like the slipping in of your beloved quotation, *October with its rain of ruined leaves*. A perfect phrase: *no one* has [done] better than this, no one.

Yes, I did very clearly grasp your view of Collin's article. It was very very reassuring to me that you should have written in those terms. Did I tell you that I had a queer letter from Collin? At the right time and in the right place I shall say something about a few of his points, and I shall give notice of intention in the coming annual review of poetry.[2]

Also, do not think I was troubled by your use of the word "dry" in the comment you made on the prefatory note. I did not take it as meaning uninteresting, but rather as meaning austere. And the note *is* austere, because of its brevity. I may be able to remedy that, and shall try, though now I am hard driven to get the annual review done.

Kirkconnell tells me in confidence that the Gov. Gen. award for "academic non-fiction" will come to me.[3] I am rejoiced at anything that will arouse public interest, and suitably grateful, though I have never had much faith in the worth of things of this sort. As one of my Jewish colleagues here says: there's too much "holly-golly" in them.

Your respect and Pratt's for the interpretations I have offered of your work, and Pelham's for the handling of certain things he has handled so often outweigh everything else.

I shall remember to send you copies when the reviews of Smith and of Pratt *et al* are printed. Another opportunity has come. I sent a copy of the book to William Rose Benet of the *Saturday Review of Literature*. He asks me to do 2000 words for a general poetry number late in April, my theme to be contemporary Canadian poetry.[4] It is a great chance, I think, one of the best journals one could have. I will do my best. I begin a three week vacation towards the end of the month, and hope to do something that will show the Americans what grand things there are north of the line, if they would only look.

Yours as ever,
Edward

90 [*Holo.*]

[March, 1944]

I intend someday to write you again about your book, for I have not yet said enough. I value your letters, and they are of use to me mentally and spiritually, but they must not fatigue you as a task to be undertaken.

[Unsigned note][1]

91 [*Holo.*]

April 16, 1944

Dear Edward,

Just a word to renew my congratulations on the award now that the fact has been published.[1] I am very pleased; as you know my opinion of the book, its worth & its importance, I need not repeat that but I must say that I feel I have not adequately thanked you or given you any proper sense of my appreciation for what you found in my work & the fullness & beauty in the way you set it forth. But I hope you have really understood that from the first; I hope it has not got you into any unpleasant criticism. I think very often of what you may do next. What will be your next book for I think you have much to say worth saying & I dont want to think of you as silent for the larger public. Have you begun to think of that?

I am sending a copy of yr book to Masefield[2] with the right sort of letter I think, & I hope he will say something about it. I hope you approve. Also one to John Purvis.[3] I have sent all the notes &c re Viger[4] to Dr. Pierce & will let you know what comes of it.

Yours ever,
Duncan

92

Cornell
April 20, 1944

Dear Duncan:

Just as I was about to write and tell you a little of the great pleasure I had in seeing you again,[1] your letter comes with its burden of good wishes and congratulations. I much appreciate your steady faith in the book, and in my criticism generally; and I have felt from the first comment you made on my article in the *Manitoba Arts Review* that you were all too generously appreciative of my work even when I have, as at times, failed to seize your full meaning.

I have your gift[2] lying on the desk beside me and the sight of it leads me to say once more that I am sorry if my failure to recur to the subject in the summer of '42 made you suppose I was not eager to have it then. As I recall, what I then felt was that perhaps you had found that no more copies of the brochure remained, and this was why I did not speak of it again.

It is good of you to send copies of OCP to J. Purves and to Masefield.[3] I shall be most interested in the replies. I am sorry that my references to Masefield (they are all in the Pratt chapter, apart from the quotation concerning you) are a little harsh.[4] If I had been making a rounded study of him the note of reservation would not have been so strong; but I was concerned to get rid of the view that Pratt is much like M'd. Clarke[5] holds that, and he did not like my attempt to do this.

You ask, kindly, about the next larger project. Chicago has asked me to replace one of my courses by a set of public lectures: and I have chosen to speak (ten lectures) on the novel in England since 1890. If all goes well I should have a rough draft of a book by a year hence.[6] It is a subject that has long tempted me. I am not now able to do much except fill a few big gaps in my reading, but after July 1, I hope to get seriously to work.

There has been no comment from Benet at the *Saturday Review of Literature* on my ms. of the short article on recent Canadian poetry, due to come out April 29. I have ordered a dozen copies, and will send one to you as soon as they come. I assume the silence means satisfaction. I hope it may lead to a few more American readers for you and Ned. This reminds me that I have had a copy of a very intelligent and long review of *OCP* in *Le Devoir*. It is to be the first of a series of chronicles of recent English Canadian poetry and prose. The author Silvestre,[7] who lives on Wilbrod St., says the next chronicle will deal with *At the Long Sault*. (Perhaps you have seen his new anthology of French Canadian poetry.)[8] I ought to have said that the chronicles will appear irregularly, and it may be that some time will pass before the second one comes out. But to have *Le Devoir* speak well of English Canada is a surprise.

I left Peggy and Deaver in first rate health. They will turn up here next week. It has been a lonely winter, not relieved by much pleasure in friendship, except when I have got out of town. I am free again for three weeks in the latter part of May, and will spend a part of the time in New York, my last visit there before I go west.[9]

I have left to the end the most important point: I trust you are well again, and that you and Elise are finding pleasure in the first really warm days. The hills here are beautiful in the mists.

Yours, as ever,
Edward

93

Dear Edward.   You see I have a fine new ribbon black enough to record my gloomiest thoughts, not that I have any this afternoon, we have a presage of Spring in the first veil of green on the elms but the weather has been anything but Springlike. The poetry no. of the *Sat. Review* was interesting throughout; a genial tone pervaded it and when I read Mr Benet's remark on Masefield, "that great poem of his 'The Passing Strange,' " I felt rather comfortable for much of the verse he printed made me feel the reverse. Your contribution[1] was the most interesting to me and closer to my own life. You there did all you could for E.J.P. and it wont be your fault if his U.S. Edition is not well received. Also you gave me a good hand but nothing is to be expected from the U.S. by me and so there is no chance for a disappointment in my case as there is in Ned's. If the MacMillan's give him as good a page as they did Wilson MacD. for his book[2] it should be acceptable to any N.Y. firm. Benet's review of *Still Life*[3] is very short but then I realize how many American books he had to notice, and it is good so far as it goes. The *Dalhousie Rev.* is just to hand and I notice that B.M.[4] is giving Pratt some advice. He gives *At the Long Sault* a very favourable review. If you dont see this great Quarterly I could send you clippings.

Your book has gone to Masefield but when I tried to find out whether Purves was still at his old address in Edin[burgh] I could not find him; I am sure he was in *Who's Who*. I shall try to get an annual report of the Uni. You understand my wish to send him a copy — he was *really* interested in poetry outside England in the Dominions and I know he would like your book. I am sending a copy to Sir John Squire; he writes a column in *The Illustrated London News* and I hope he might notice the book there or elsewhere, for he must have other connections. He is a friendly acquaintance of mine, I met him in London and we have corresponded; he put several poems of mine and one of Elise's in *The London Mercury*, and put one of mine in *The Mercury Book of Verse*.[5] So you see there is some reason for my sending him a copy. But we must not expect too much from these people, but if I did not hear from them I should be disappointed.

I had a card for the State Memorial Service for Sir Chas. at Fredericton on the 15th inst. but have had to decline.[6] Have you by any chance seen N. Benson's Elegy on Sir Chas. published in *Sat. Nt.* lately;[7] you should know it and I would send it with a comment or two, one line sticks in my memory and it is full of gems of that paste —

"He gave the glacial berg a beating heart,"

But I must remember, "Sweet chucks, beat not the bones of the buried."[8]

Brockington has gone to England for various reasons, one was to hear a Nightingale sing and he promised to send me a note when he did so, he had never heard this famous bird that D.H. Lawrence so abuses. Dilworth was here and before B left we managed to spend an evg here in the Music Room; good talk and you came in for part of it.

When I think of your visit I am disappointed in my share of it; I was not well enough to realize that it was the visit we had both looked forward to and now I think I was not equal to the occasion. As for the books I was to give you, do not think of it again; I had got together copies of most of the old books and if you want them you shall have them sometime.[9]

Lawren Harris was here yesterday, just for a day, came in about half after four, had a cup of tea smoked two cigarrets, cleaned his picture which needed it badly,[10] had an animated talk, went into my bedroom at half after five, slept soundly for three quarters of an hour and then was off to dinner to a meeting and the night train for Toronto. Here is a man I admire hugely.

I have not yet got a copy of *Le Devoir*; I know Sen. Lambert sent you a copy of the Senate debates.[11] I will write a note about the *U. of T. Quart.* when I get a copy.

I hope that Peggy and Deaver are well and that he is laying on his expected ounces. We are both well now but our Spring is slow. My love to you both and to Deaver.

[Duncan]

94

[Cornell]
May 13, 1944

Dear Duncan:

I should have written sooner, but I came down with a heavy cold, and it left me, as those things do, with less energy than usual, and for a few days I did nothing but what local affairs required. Now I feel almost fresh again.

I was glad to have your note about the *SRL* review-article, and look to hear more. Smith and Klein[1] are pleased. I had a pleasant note from Smith the other day. He tells me that from the point of view of the avant garde he and I are sunk in decrepitude, and that we had better get ready for our fate! I said that for my part when the time came I would perhaps do a little fighting. I am not in sympathy with the newest Montreal group,[2] I fear.

Also, how good of you to send the clipping from the *Journal*![3] Senator Lambert (whom I have never met) sent me a copy of the proceedings. I have written to him. I had heard that he liked the article on M. King. This passing mention of me in the place where I used to work, so to speak, reminds me of that remark of N. Robertson's[4] that you passed on to me (and which I have repeated to no one) that he would have found me very useful in his part of the service. I think that I should tell you that when I left the P.M.'s office (where I had an appointment formally in External Affairs) I wrote a note to N.R. in which I said that once I had got some pressing things done down here, I would be available to him, and he replied that he hoped that work could be found. I did not feel that it would be right for me to go farther; but perhaps this comment will interest you as showing that his interest in me was not so very deep! In peace time I prefer my teaching, but in war time I would like to help where I could, and I was a little disappointed.

In some leisure I have had the last few days I have looked through the 1900 Lampman, to see what was left out in the later selection.[5] It seemed to me that almost everything you omitted was best omitted. There are only a very few that I suggest you reconsider, and among these there is none I advocate with great strength. I give the list on the next page.

Meanwhile our devoted love to you, and our warmest wishes that we might see Elise and you soon.

As ever,
Edward

P.S. [*holo.*] I hope you will retain the alphabetical index.[6]

[Page added]

Suggestions from the Memorial Edition.

Winter Hues Recalled. p. 27 Imitative but very interesting to me.
The Dog. p. 121 An unusual mood.
The Land of Pallas. p. 201 The substance is important indeed.
April Night.[7] p. 185

That is all! EKB. [P.S. *holo.*] I am sorry two are such long pieces. Perhaps their length was a main consideration in excluding them twenty years ago.

95 [*Holo.*]

Alexander Palace,
Toronto, May 30, 1944

Dear Duncan,

My typewriter is in Ithaca. Hence this assault upon your eyes.

Sunday night at 9.30 I am broadcasting over CBL on "Our Neglect of Our Literature."[1] It is a practical sort of talk — no real criticism. But there is some mention of Lampman and his 1891 address,[2] and perhaps that may interest you. The talk will be recorded: I shall be back in Ithaca, and may perhaps have courage enough to listen!

I will say just two more things in this scrawl. I have been rereading your stories with great pleasure. Haven't you another you could publish on *Welly*

Legrave?[3] That is a really fascinating figure, and beautifully realized. I don't expect to see Pierce this time — I hope the *Village of Viger* comes as you would like.

As ever,
Edward

96

June 5, 1944

Dear Edward.   We heard you last night with great gratification and we send congratulations; these words needed to be said and they were said with your usual force and I hope they will do some good in lighting up the dark places; there seems to be an interest in trying to develope local centers of Culture, arts and letters, Lawren Harris is the Chairman of some Dominion Comm;[1] but I suppose you heard all about that when you were in Toronto. To give you an instance of the absolute indifference of the local C.B.C.; we tried to get from them definite information as to your B'cast, they knew nothing, did not know that you were the special speaker at *8.45;*[2] if we had not persisted and listened at *that* time we should have missed you; I told Loftus and Pelham, the former phoned that he had heard you and enjoyed the talk but I have not heard whether Pelham was lucky. I hope you heard your own voice, it must have been a curious experience. I would not at first have recognized it, but I soon picked it up and Elise did from the first. What impulse could have led you into such a forgotten book?[3] I am glad it gave you pleasure. I could of course at the time have gone on and invented a series with Welly Legrave as a center; but I would not do it now, not even for you. This story was published in *Scribner's* with illustrations, I think; so was "The Vain Shadow" and "Expiation,"[4] and others in other American Maga's but I never kept a list. As for *The Village of Viger* it is still under consideration by Pierce's "impeccable" artist.[5] I do not expect anything to come of this. I wrote L.P. on Apl. 17, sending him my suggestions; he replied on May first saying he has seen T.M. and would be writing me at length he hoped before *this week* is out; but that week is out and several other weeks and the oracles have not spoken.

Our last letters crossed and there are items in yours of the 13th May that I would like to comment on, and there are some items in mine that might also be referred to but I cannot write any longer this morning. I am probably wearying you with these letters but unless I write them I would not hear from you.

We hope Peggy and Deaver are all right and we send you all our love.

Yours ever,
D.

97

Cornell
June 13, 1944

Dear Duncan:

I was delighted and relieved to know that you and Elise had liked the talk. It was not of course intended for such as you, but for the many who never hear or think about such matters. I don't know whether this sort of thing does the least good, but I am always willing to try. Just the presence of literature in the list of talks is something perhaps.

What a pity about the delay with your book! I saw Pierce after all, but decided not to mention it: it is so hard to communicate with him that I limit myself to one or two topics, and go in for a lot of repetition. I did ask one of the juniors how the book was coming along but he seemed to have no knowledge of it, other than that it was on their list. I am always afraid that Pierce will misunderstand what I say.

What funny folk publishers are. Miss Elliott,[1] who is running the editorial part of Macmillans, could not understand why their book *Who Dare to Live* (by a sailor)[2] did not get the poetry award! It sells, and so it must be good! And yet she thinks she is literary.

I was most interested in the details about some of your short stories. I finished the rereading of them in Toronto, and was very stirred by the representation of lonely Scots in the northland. The mood is very strong, and one does not forget it.

Last week I gave an address here on the future of the liberal arts in university education which caused a good bit of comment because of the suggestions I made.[3] If I publish it I will send you a copy, but for the moment I am satisfied to have made some dint in local complacency. That and the broadcast are all I have been able to do in these past weeks.

The boy flourishes, and is showing himself to be of an inquiring habit of mind. Peggy is in good spirits, and they will have a better summer here than in Chicago heat, to which I go next week. My address will be as you would expect: Department of English, University of Chicago.

Yours, as ever,
Edward

P.S. We were both sorry to hear of Mr. Smart's death.[4] We liked him and admired him.
[*P.P.S. marg. holo.*] I enclose the article — or rather review — on Smith's poems.[5] I am very interested to hear what you think of it. Some of his admirers think the praise faint.

98

June 30-July 5, 1944

Dear Edward.   This is my first letter to Chicago. I hope your lecture-room is large and cool and your quarters very comfortable this hot weather. I imagine it as hot there as it is here; we have had a real Ottawa "spell" of heat and that has really prevented me from writing sooner in reply to yours of the 13th ult. You must prepare for some praise for I have just been reading your article on Forster in the *Yale Review*.[1] I was able to enjoy it to the full for I am familiar with all the books you deal with; I think that is exceptional, for you know I am not a novel-reader; i.e. I dont keep up with the times, and it is unprofitable to read detailed reviews of authors with whose books you are not familiar. I admire the skillful way in which you wind the reader into the main sections of the subject; and the result of the criticism is solvent and most satisfactory. I would like to be a student listening to your lectures. And praise comes to you for the notice of Smith's book. I dont see how any admirer of S. could think the praise faint. You will, I hope remember our talk about his work; I also give it place but I separate it and put it into my own category of what is excellent but I do not expect him to develope; I hope he will surprise me. The avant garde are really fighting a rear-guard action it seems to me and I dont see why you should bother with them. I am returning the notice for it is about the same as that in the *U. of T. Quarterly* which I have. You made crafty use of my remarks about Roberts[2] and it seemed to come naturally enough. I had a copy of the Maga.[3] but have lost it and I do not know what you left out, (if anything), but the quotation and your context makes it plain that we agree, plus of course what you say in the *O.C.P.* I would like a copy of your address "On the future of the Liberal Arts" as I keep everything I can get of yours. We have gone wild on the subject of Culture as I prove by sending you a clipping; this movement was I think originated by Lawren Harris.[4] *Letters* were not represented and I dont know whether Writers can fit into the plan, no prominent writer was at this meeting. I wish they may succeed, but being a sceptic I cannot hope that the Govt will set aside the amount mentioned or even give The Can. Author's Foundation[5] the smaller grant which we ask for the relief of poverty stricken authors.

I was pleased with your remarks about my old stories; there are one or two others I think you might place with them in the batch of prose I was getting together;[6] that project has not been entirely abandoned but has been neglected. Since writing you I have had two letters re. the Viger stories, but cannot report much advance. If this matter fails in the end I would like you to see the correspondence. I feel pity for Pierce in trying to do business with the fearful disability of deafness; and I think it often gives rise to incidents which seem dubious but which are subject to reasonable explanation.

I expected to see A.L.'s lecture in this No. of the *Quarterly*. Can you do anything with his Keats?[7] I am certain Prof. Alexander's death came as a shock to you;[8] it did to me who knew him so slightly. Too many of these veterans are leaving us. I shall miss Smart, he was a member of our little dinner club[9] and the source of much vital talk there for he was, as you know, decidily to the Left; I never knew any one who was so generous to his family, maybe too generous.

On the 26th of June came a letter from Masefield a copy of which I enclose.[10] I am disappointed for I wanted him to say something about the book and perhaps selfishly, something about your remarks on D.C.S. I was not overcome by the association of my name and Carman's with those great ones of the past. As you know, Bliss and I were not ploughing and sowing together. I dont know who is to write this exciting swift poetry or who is to recite it when written. You know he has always been strong on the oral side and I note from the Lit. Sup. of 27th May he addressed the National Book Council to the same effect;[11] the article did not give the idea much support. I know you will understand my feeling about M's letter.

Elise wants me to say that she too enjoyed the Forster and remarks particularly [on] the extract from the letter he wrote you. She sends her love to Peggy and Deaver and so do I. And please give me news of them so that I may not be divided from the divided family.

Yours as ever,
Duncan

99

The University of Chicago
July 14, 1944

Dear Duncan:

Before speaking of any of the things you mention in your letter I want to prepare you for the reading of the enclosure. It will give you pleasure, I am sure, and it may be a novelty. It is a transcript of a poem by A.L. which I found in one of the two notebooks which MacInnes gave to me to read last summer.[1] I think you said that you had not had these by you when you were preparing the collected edition. MacInnes said that he had come on them in the attic. One contained only prose, the Two Canadian Poets lecture and the discourse on Happiness.[2] I sent this notebook back long ago. The other is in bad condition, cover gone, and some pages, very yellow, and is a larger note book than any of those you showed me. From it I have deciphered the poem.

Where A.L. offers alternative readings, I have indicated this in margin; and where I cannot be sure I have deciphered the word, I have set a question mark. It is fascinating to see how he has worked in the love lyrics.[3] I do not think he had great dramatic gifts, but some of the speeches are fine; and of course the fact that in an imaginatively transposed form he was presenting his own grief, and giving it a happy ending adds to the emotional force of the whole.

Should we try to publish this? Did you ever hear A.L. talk of this? I wonder if in the letters to E.W.T. he speaks of this?[4] There is no date, but some of the other pieces in the book are dated, and point, as one would expect, to a relatively late date.

Woodhouse says that the discourse on the two poets is set up, and expected to appear in the July number of the *Quarterly*, which will be late in appearing. I will see that you get some offprints.

I am so glad that you liked the Forster piece. I am much drawn to him, without thinking him a novelist of the first order. The Masefield letter was a disappointment, but I suppose he found himself tired and did not wish to comment on the meaning of the book; I have seen a curious form he has had made for the saving of his time in answering letters. It is a nicely engraved slip saying that he thanks blank for sending him blank, and presents his compliments. Rather ingenious! It would be interesting to know what Sir John Squire might say, and I hope you hear from him.

You must indeed feel the loss of Mr. Smart. Peggy and I used to think that he must have given a lot more than he got from his family. I could not warm to his daughter Jane, the only one I have seen more than once; and Peggy thought she was really rude. But Mr. Smart himself we both liked very much. Yes, the death of Alexander was a great loss to me. I never went to Toronto without going to see him; he was one of my really great teachers, and in these later years he had grown gentler, and I had come to like him very much as a person. He was formidable to the student. There are to be memorial articles in the October *Quarterly* by Wallace and Woodhouse.[5]

I have been busy finding an apartment for the family, and think I have done a good piece of work. I don't know whether you are at home in Chicago; but will mention that the U. is 7 miles south of the centre of the city, near the lake. I have taken an apartment facing east, about a hundred yards from the lake, with a view of the water in the seasons when the foliage doesn't interfere. It is in a park, with such pleasant trees and a nice stretch of grass. Living room and study will look over the lake. The apartment is rather old and very roomy, and we shall not feel too confined, I think.

All the news from Ithaca is good. Peggy has some friends from Toronto with her for most of July. Ithaca is beautiful in summer.

It is such a pity that the Viger book is held up; but perhaps there is nothing more in the matter than the usual dilatoriness of that house which we both experienced last summer. I trust that it will be out well before the Christmas season; for it would, among many other values, make a very attractive gift book. I hope the impeccable artist is correcting his peccata.

Ned's American collected edition is deferred till spring, but the Canadian collected should be out in the early fall, he says. The American collected would seem to be a selection from the Canadian, which will itself be far from complete. I am glad that Knopf will leave out the 'Fable of the Goats' which is weaker, I think, than Ned appreciates, but sorry it will leave out 'The Great Feud'.[6]

You ask about the Keats. I don't know what to do with that. I might do a sort of running commentary, accompanying the most important critical parts. I am going to lecture on Keats in the spring, for the first time since leaving Toronto, and in a vague sort of way I am planning to work on the ms. then and try to place it in Keats criticism. But I may set to work sooner. I have the ms. here.

At present my leisure goes to the writing of the first of my lectures on the modern novel; this is on the early novels of G. Moore,[7] and so far is going along quite smoothly. That is not a difficult topic, and the reading is pleasant, even his failures, like *Spring Days*, are interesting.

Every warmest wish for the happiness of both of you,

Yours, as ever,
Edward

P.S. [*holo.*] If I should not write again in the next few days, let this tell you of my felicitations on your birthday. I wish I might spend it with you.

100

July 27, 1944

Dear Edward.   Yours of the 14th had an interesting enclosure which I intend to make the subject of a special letter later on, for I want to give it more attention than I have been able to up to the present: I was bound to show it to Loftus, and he will write you a letter about it; I dont know whether it will go along with mine but in due course you will hear from us. When I write I will deal with your suggestions for the new Selected Lampman which L.P. does not seem to be in a hurry about.

One chief purpose of this note is to invite you and Peggy to a birthday party Elise is giving on the second instant, to celebrate my 82nd. Just old, tried friends, no representatives of the Diplomatic corps or of The Govt. You would fit into the group and add so much to it that we felt you must be asked although distance makes your presence impossible. Will you tell Peggy, please, and say I am sure she would send me a pound of sugar if she could.[1] Harry and Frances Adaskin[2] are coming to give us some music that afternoon and that will add a good deal to the pleasure of the thing. Many thanks for your memory of the date; I feel better than I did this time last year and will try to last as long as I can. Do keep your friendship warm and that will help me.

The description of your flat sounds as if you had made a good choice; I do not know Chicago at all, have changed trains there and that is all.

The postponement in Ned's book may be to its advantage in the market as I fancy book sales in the States will be affected by the Pres. Election.[3] Our politics are in a dreadful condition and I think our Peerless Leader must have troubled dreams, if he ever dreams. I heard a prophecy the other day that if Godbout was defeated King would pass an O. in C. sending all men to the front; defy Que. and appeal to all good men & true to stand behind the Great Liberal Party![4] But I dont think so.

The Viger book has made some progress; the Impeccable One submitted ten drawings which I have approved, as being fairly suitable; he is now trying for a Jacket Cover;[5] L.P. has been on a holiday; I dont see how they can get this book out for Christmas; they have dawdled over it for nearly a year.

Our Emily Carr's were photographed for a special No. of *The Studio* and one is to be used;[6] these lose much by the absence of color which so well supports the drawing, when that is left naked it seems to me scrappy, but when I got the pictures home and looked at them, I was glad I owned them. I hear great praise of Woodhouse's paper on Milton for the Royal;[7] I hope it will be printed.

I am glad you have constant good news from Ithaca and to learn that it is a good place in Summer; it has been infernally hot here at times.

> Yours ever,
> Duncan

101

> Chicago,[1]
> August 8, 1944

Dear Duncan,

I shall be hoping for a letter describing your 82nd, at which I assisted in the spirit. It was a pleasant rather breezy day here, and I hoped that you would have the same gala weather.

What you say about MacInnes's meaning to write to me about the dramatic poem suggests that he may not welcome publication. He has never referred to the "problem" in dealing with me about A.L., and I have always intended if he did to suggest that it might perhaps be best to bring it out into the open.[2] The history of Arnold suggests to me that when such matters are too carefully concealed for too long a time when the inevitable revelation is made there is a tendency to attach too much weight to it. I need not say that I shall always be guided in anything I write myself by your wishes and his, but this is my own view. But in the long run some one will get on the track. Suppose it were Deacon!![3]

I have asked Woodhouse to send five copies of the address on Roberts and Cameron to you, and five to MacInnes, and I have asked him to send the small cheque ($25) to MacInnes. I don't know if the July number of the magazine has come out yet; mine might go to Ithaca; and of course some time elapses before the reprints go out. Woodhouse will be very pleased by what you report. He was most eager to do well with his R.S.C. paper this year since it followed so closely the announcement that he was to be head of English in University College.

The other day I wrote to H.J. Cody[4] suggesting that the appearance of Pratt's collected would be the right moment to honor him with the Litt. D. He replied saying that while he would favor doing so there was a rule that no professor on the active list should be honored with a degree. He thought that an exception might be made, and he would try to have it done. You are the only person I am telling of this. I know that you will approve the little démarche.

I am deep in the early novels of G. Moore. Some of them are dreadful, e.g. *Mike Fletcher*. I am also reading Huysmans[5] for the first time. No doubt you know him. Very queer but very well done. I am also reading Klein's new poem 'The Hitleriad,'[6] something Byronic and a touch of Pratt I think. I am to do it for *Poetry*.

You will like to know that V. Sackville West gave my book a very warm review in the *Observer*, the first English notice. It is clear that though she lectured in Canada she never troubled to read any Canadian poetry. But she is well disposed, and as is natural in the author of *The Land*, is drawn to Lampman.[7]

Every good wish,

Yours, as ever,
Edward

[*P.S. holo.*] The Ryerson English agent is Hatchard's — I never heard of the house, did you?[8]

102

August 12-15, 1944

My Dear Edward.   I have yours of the eighth. I intend to write just a personal letter, because I have been really suffering from the excessive heat of the last week and I must wait until I can gather what is left of mental energy to deal with the Lampman dramatic fragment about which I shall have something to say. Loftus has written you a letter of wh. I have a copy[1] but I told him to send that on to you and not wait until I cld write. So please understand that it is not from lack of interest that I do not deal with it now.

The celebration of the great National Holiday went off very well; your spirit must have assisted. We had about forty people here, from five to seven. Elise by the cooperation of her friends had assembled enough native champagne for the guests;[2] the Country Club made a Cake; flowers arrived; some generous gifts; the Adaskins made some good music. I am a very fortunate person after all, but you and Peggy shd have been here. Dilworth made a B'cast from Vancouver at 4.30 that day and read some poems, i.e. over the National Network. He read the close of 'The Height of Land,' 'The Fallen,' 'Old Olives,. 'Autumn Evg.' and he spoke very well. I had some letters from people who had lost sons in the war re. 'The Fallen;' wh. I know you like. It was very hot, 93, but day after day the temperature rose until it struck 100 wh. is about the limit for Ottawa. That is all I have to report and I hope you will not consider I have taken up too much time with it.

A few remarks about the contents of your last. I shall expect the offprints. I highly approve of your suggestion as to a Litt. D. for Pratt; one can understand the reason for the general rule but in this case he shd not be thought of as a Prof. but as a creative artist.

When you tell me that you are reading some author for the first time I am always surprised, no matter who the author may be, for I always think of you as having read everything. I have read Huysmans in translations, but not deeply; Geo. Moore as you know I have read most of, but not those dreadful early novels. Elise gave me three books of Turgenev, on the whole my favorite novelist; and I am now reading *Virgin Soil* for the nth time; and I also read *Smoke*. Here is Art if you are looking for it.

How tantalizing to be told of the review of *O.C.P.* without a mention of the date of *The Observer*, wh. I cld easily look up here. Send it please! I have heard nothing from Squire, he is erratic and irregular and may be inebriated. Your note about Masefield's card of acknowledgement let in some light on the text of his letter. I dont suppose I have any idea of the extent he is bothered by poetasters and miscellaneous vagrant authors hoping to get some word of praise wh. they might use. But in our case he might have known that anything he might have said in compliment to a book of that worth wld never have been used. But I am sure that he knew that the book was important, I read between the lines.

The foreign representatives of the Ryerson Press seem to be nonentities, so far as Publishers are concerned. I never heard of Hatchards as Publishers; and a survey of many last nos. of The Lit. Sup. does not reveal any advt except that of the bookshop, wh. is a glorious place to go with fifty Pounds or more in one's pocket;[3] that shop and Bumpus on Oxford[4] were two places I liked to haunt; I know Wilson who is *really* Bumpus, that name having disappeared from the firm.

As ever yours,

Duncan

[*P.S. holo.*] 100 degrees yesterday. I hope Ithaca is never so hot.

103

August 22, 1944

Dear Edward.   I would like to try to reply worthily to your letter of July 14th and to a portion of yours of 8th Aug. referring to the Drama which you succeeded in deciphering from A.L.'s notebook.[1] I say *worthily* because that seems to me the proper word to apply to the "stuff" itself and to the labour you devoted to discovering these lost lines. The poem has merit, very unequal and in some respects questionable, but its interest to me from several points of view outweighs its defects. You express no opinion as to its publication; as you know Loftus is against it and so am I. My opinion is based on its literary demerits alone and not on its treatment of the personal drama.[2] The addition of the fact that it is based on an old story rather increases my interest, because if we consider it as an invention for the purpose of carrying the lyrics it is very weak indeed. I have gone through the MS. carefully and have indicated my preference for the alternative readings. The blank verse is here and there good but is on the whole leaden in tone and movement. The lyrics are inappropriate to the setting. The first (which we have published) and the last are the best; the middle one I do not like, the fourth line seems to me awkward, particularly that in the last verse ("An influence innocently fulfilling");[3] the idea in the middle lyric was well expressed in 'Fate' which we published. The last chorus up to the last verse is good but it was a fatal defect to bring the lovers back again; he should, I think, have closed on the heroic theme of the old king.

Now to answer your questions. A.L. never mentioned this poem to me and he does not refer to it in the Thomson letters.[4] It must be late in production; the blank verse reminds me of 'Vivia Perpetua.'[5] A.L. was subject to the poetic tradition of *subject matter*. He was ever longing for a subject on which to extend his powers; I do not think that arose from a premonition that his life was to be short, but merely from the constant desire to keep on writing; and so he made this little drama out of an old story and put bits of his sad heart into it. If there was any feeling present when he wrote these dramatic lines that his life was nearly over I can imagine him thinking in the opening lines of 'Vivia Perpetua'

I questioned how my soul might best employ
This hand, and this still wakeful flame of mind
In the brief hours yet left me for their use.

He produced an imperfect poem but I do not forget that in the "brief hours" he made some poems that were of his best and in his own manner, some of which we have been instrumental in preserving. The question arises, why did he write the poem? No one can tell. I think it shows that the experience had been put into the past, that he could look at it dispassionately, and that he imagined that he could deal with it in this form and use the lyrics as evidence of a "former state." This is only a surmise, as valid as another.

As for a more open statement of this experience of A.L.'s, I think you could discuss it at any time with Loftus; I dont think he or his wife wish to conceal anything that can be told; there is so little to tell. Miss Waddell and Lampman's wife[6] were close friends up to the time of the latter's death. There was no breach in the friendship owing to this incident; in fact Loftus tells me that they had mutual knowledge of the poems. What I have told you verbally I now put in writing.[7] A.L. never mentioned the affair to me, and there was nothing in his manner or conduct that could have led me to have an inkling of this emotional experience. I was seeing him constantly when he was writing those letters to Thomson, and sometimes in close companionship, for instance on our camping trip to Lake Achigan in 1897.[8] My knowledge came from his office chief, Dr.

W.D. LeSueur,[9] after A.L.'s death, and later from Thomson, long after that event. I think the matter is sufficiently stated for the reading public. There are my references in the Introduction to *Lyrics of Earth*, with the quotations from the letters;[10] there is the more open statement in my Foreword to *At the Long Sault*.[11] I feel like leaving it at that and if anyone wanted to delve into the past let him go to it. I have never been able to relate these circumstances to L's life; they have never seemed very real to me probably because what I remember of his strong emotional experiences in those days are his suffering at the death of his baby, born in 1894,[12] and his joy and pride at the birth of a son in 1898;[13] and his anxieties about his work and his forthcoming book, *Alcyone*.[14] I have never placed very high these late love lyrics; as expressions of passion they will not compare with such poems as 'White Pansies,' or 'The Vain Fight,' or 'To Death,' which all deal with grief.

Now I am sure you are tired of this and I break off but you must understand why I have written at such length. Mainly because I feel grateful for your devotion in deciphering these lines, and in a much less important way because I wanted to get some of the content off my mind. Pierce has not been urging us to get on with the selected poems. I intend to adopt your suggestion re. 'Winter Hues Recalled,' and will write you at the proper time about the other poems you mention.[15]

I am as ever yours,
Duncan

104

[Chicago]
September 2, 1944

Dear Duncan,

I am sorry to be so long in writing. I have been in a scramble for time these past two weeks. Chicago terms are 12 weeks, Cornell sixteen (one doesn't gain by the change, for here one teaches in three a year instead of two at Cornell) and I have been trying to cram my 16 week courses into the smaller mould. You will conceive that the trouble comes most sharply in the last weeks!

My warm thanks for your statement about A.L. I have long wished that you would make such a statement, but I did not like to be pressing, since the judgment I felt should be yours. It is a great relief to have it, and to store it against a day (and I think the day will come, some time) when it may be proper to use it. You are, of course, right in saying that you have written of these matters; but the references you have made, like the brief one I made,[1] have not constituted a communication, for no one has been struck by them so far as I know. Some time some one will be.

I am glad that you think of restoring 'Winter Hues. . .,' a poem I am very fond of.

Your references to the dramatic poem were highly interesting. I too thought the movement of that chorus very queer. "Gilbertian" just hits it.[2] I will speak of these again. MacInnes gave me a most lively account of the material, and I greatly enjoyed his touch. Let us lay the poem aside for a while at least. MacInnes also asked me to let him have my broadcast for his magazine.[3] I had not thought of it as for print; but since he is willing to take it in its oral form I let him have it. If it creates a little interest in the poets among the C.S. that will be to the good.

Pierce and I have come to an agreement about the new material.[4] He was sad that I did not revise any of my judgments, particularly he wanted the Roberts revised, I think. At his urging I added a page on Sherman[5] whom I should perhaps have included before. But the rereading of his work was a disappointment. How odd that he never wrote verse after 1901. Did you know him? and have you any ideas why he fell silent? One would think that his experience of the war would have led him to write. He had some of your interest in the P.R.B.[6] but for me he fails to reach the note which you struck so beautifully in your early dream pieces.

The more I thought of Klein's poem the more sensible I grew that it wasn't very good. I have reviewed it for *Poetry* and will send you a copy when the number comes out.[7] You ask for the date of the *Observer* review: May 21. So far I have seen no other English review. But our English journals are very slow in arriving.

It was pleasant to know that all went so well on your 82nd, and that Dilworth spoke and quoted. I like all those poems. 'The Height of Land' was one of the first of your poems that I read—more than 20 years ago.

Yours, as ever,
Edward

P.S. [*holo.*] I am not printing the address on the humanities in education for the present.[8] I have been asked to speak at a convention of teachers in NYC in November and will use it then, unless, as is all too likely, the convention is cancelled, as it was last year.

E

[*P.P.S. holo.*] I have ordered your works and A.L.'s for the Library here.

105 [*Holo.*]

October 2, 1944

My dear Edward,

I must send you a line to ackl the *U. of T. Quarterly* & the 5 offprints.[1] I am very pleased with A.L. & yr prefatory note is just right. I hope to be able to say more later on. I have had an attack of Flu, have had to stay in bed for 10 days & have my clothes on & am down stairs for the first time today. So you will understand my delay & my brevity.

Hope you & the family are all well. Elise has looked after me as usual perfectly.

Yours ever,
Duncan

106

[Chicago]
October 11, 1944

Dear Duncan,

I was delighted to hear that you were up and about again after flu, but I hope you will take things very lazily for a couple of weeks. Flu leaves one feeling flaccid, I have found the few times I've met the germ.

It was good to know that you liked the A.L. lecture when you saw it in print. MacInnes seemed very happy. By the way have you seen Creighton's *Dominion of the North;* he quotes effectively from the part of the lecture you gave in the *Lyrics of Earth* introduction.[1] I think his is a pretty good book; I learned a good deal from it.

The sheets I enclose are intended for the second edition of *O.C.P.* They are a reply to one of Collin's animadversions.[2] I don't mention C, here or anywhere else that I am replying to him, by name. I hope that you won't dislike my citing you; I was deeply impressed by the phrase you used in telling me of your talk with Clarke, and think it would hold up my hands if I might use it.[3] There is nothing offensive to Clarke, I believe, in the way he is brought in, also unnamed. But if you don't like the way it's done or the idea at all, don't hesitate to tell me, and I'll try to find another line of comment. Would you please send the sheets back as soon as you readily can? Now that L.P. has got moving, I don't want to give him a pretext for delay. Don't hurry unduly, however!

We are enjoying the great city and the comfortable apartment. I am admirably treated, and for the present wholly free from chores. I have more time to read and think than I have ever had. I am going through some of Meredith: *Beauchamp's Career* for the first time, *The Egoist* for the ?th. The baby is in fine spirits.

> Our warmest wishes to you and
> Elise.
> As ever,
> Edward

P.S. If you would like more copies of the offprint do let me know. I have a dozen that I haven't any need to send.

107

October 12, 1944

Dear Edward.   I feel well enough to use the typewriter this morning so I am impelled to write you a line, in reply to your last[1] wh. has never been properly answered. I acknlgd the seperates of the A.L. Lecture, and I intend to drop a line to Professor Woodhouse, particularly as I want to tell him I enjoyed his Milton and the deserved scourging he gave that rascal Graves for his book.[2] Thanks for ordering our stuff for your Library. In that connection I send you a letter I recd sometime ago wh. I have not answered; note the sentence I have marked, do you believe that they have copies of any of my books? It would be quite useless for me to send any of my drafts for I can hardly decipher them myself and Elise would not let the notebooks go. Please return the letter with comments for I must send a polite reply.[3] Pierce was here on the 22nd ult and I had a talk with him; he is aware that he has a strong man in you on the Editorial and Critical side and is anxious to get full advantage of it. He was pleased with the success of *O.C.P.* and was planning for the new edition; he said only a few of the first ed. were left. Needless to say I am delighted and look forward to reading the additions. You ask me about Sherman; I met him only once, he came here and spent an hour or so with me. He was a very likable fellow and we got on well; I could not get him to read or recite any of his verse, and he insisted on my reading 'The Wood by the Sea' and the companion piece wh. he said he liked. Impossible to say why he fell silent; I never got any real pleasure from his work, sorry to say. Pierce was very expansive about his projected series of Selected Poets of wh. the Lampman is to be first. He said he wanted me to decide the format, the binding etc. for the Series. But as you will understand I cannot take on such a task; however I intend that the book will have a decent cover. I think the last ed. of *Lyrics of E.* was abominable but I would like the same page form.[4] I might here and now say something more about the *contents*. Dealing with your selections from the Memorial Vol., I will include 'Winter Hues' and drop 'The Woodcutters Hut' to make room for it. 'The Land of Pallas' is too long, the run-over lines add many stanzas to its length. I dont think I would include 'The Dog'. The Sonnet 'April

Night" is already in *Lyrics of E.* p. 3.[5] Now what would you choose from *The Long Sault,* kindly let me know? Loftus has his ideas about that, and about A.L. generally; for instance he thinks the constant critical reference to Keats' influence overdone; and he thinks A.L. had said all he had to say and that time would not have added anything, with wh. I profoundly disagree. But he has an active mind. I hope you have sent him the Broadcast, this periodical has a circulation of 6000 and I'm sure many will read the article. I did not tell him about your generous offer re. the Lecture[6] so that it might come fresh to him and he did not tell me about sending half of it back to you until it was done, so I am very pleased with the outcome. Do not forget to send me the review of Klein.

[*P.S. holo.*] I know you are very busy just now but write me soon. I sent copy of the Lecture to Mrs. Jenkins.[7]

Yours ever,
Duncan

108

October 15, 1944

Dear Edward.   Since your letter came yesterday morning I have thought much over the additional matter you propose for p. 98. As you know we are at one in our opinion of the poem, and I can join you whole-heartedly. But I want you to consider whether my support comes well just there. I think of this as *your* book, of you as the exponent and critic and I dont think you need support from *anybody.* I like what you have written up to the word "masterpiece," I have gratuitously pencilled the words "despite adverse criticism;" I would suggest a period after "masterpiece."[1] If you want my support, which you do not need, use it *by all means.* But I would like you to leave out the last sentence for it comes too close to our friend. One point I would make, on p. 98 you have already printed my name twice, will your readers dislike seeing it thrice? All this is submitted after due consideration.

I am glad to know that you are all together again and so well satisfied. Our letters crossed again as usual, perhaps you will have something to say to me after my last and this note which I make short so that I may catch the night mail. By the way, Air Mail does not seem to help us much; you posted your last at 10.30 a.m. on the 12th, I got it in the morning mail of the 14th. I am sending this by the usual channel; when does it arrive?[2] More anon, and our love to you all; it is about time for me to have another snapshot of Deaver.

Yours ever,
Duncan

109 [*Holo.*]

[Chicago]
October 22, 1944

Dear Duncan,

I had hoped to write a long letter to you this week-end, but have been asked to give an opinion on a manuscript for the University press and reading it has taken all my time.

But I want to thank you without delay for your judgment on the passage I sent to you. I have revised it in line with what you suggested and am fairly happy with the result.

Also I will say a word about the request from Buffalo. It is best I think to keep the materials for deposit in *one* place. Perhaps exceptions might be made for libraries with which one has a special connection. But this would not be true of Buffalo. I should vote for declining to send anything.[1]

Yours, as ever,
Edward

P.S. I shall write again later in the week.

110

[Chicago]
November 21, 1944

Dear Duncan,

I am slow in writing, but I know you will forgive me for I have been pressed by many things with inexorable datelines. The main worry has been getting into shape three lectures to give on a short trip east that begins later this week. None of them was wholly new but a good bit of tinkering was needed. One of the pleasant sides to the thing is that two of the talks are asked for by former students now teaching, one at Rutgers University (Canadian Poetry to-day) and the other at a convent in Pittsburgh (The approach to fiction). The main job is the one I told you of some time ago, a talk to my brethren teaching English in the eastern colleges.[1]

Then Woodhouse (who much appreciated your letter) asked me to do a review of Ludwig's little book on W.L.M.K.,[2] and this needed rather careful treatment, a poor book or rather booklet, but an occasion for saying something by way of epilogue to my article. I also am to do a review of Ned's collected for the *Quarterly,*[3] but won't finish that till I get home. By the way it's the very ugliest book I can imagine! What Macmillans were up to I don't know, and I am going to speak of the ugliness in the review. What a colour! What blunt lettering! and what coarse fabric!

I was much interested in your remark about Sherman's visit to you. I suppose it was after he stopped writing, or he would not have recoiled from reading some of his things to such an auditor. Smith has sent me an offprint of a curious paper of his to the Canadian Historical people, in which he finds all sorts of interest in those dreary early Scottish Canadian poets.[4] And yet I do not recall that he ever cared for Burns. That's what's so funny! And I think he over-praises Cappon, whose *Carman* seems to me a very weak and sprawling performance, though his *Roberts* has many good things.[5]

I have amused myself in odd hours in the Library assembling a list of the lectures on Poetry that M. Arnold gave in the Oxford chair.[6] One interesting fact is that he lectured on "The Modern Element in Dante," and this has never appeared. I would very much like to know all that M.A. thought about Dante. Perhaps it will appear some day. The post called as you perhaps know for 3 lectures a year; and he had it for ten years. So far I have found in the *Times* the announcements of 16 lectures, and by Christmas I hope to have the list complete. I never tire of M.A.[7]

Peggy has been without a nurse (our one form of help) for the past couple of months, but we expect the nurse back by Christmas and then we shall feel freer. We are all very well, Deaver unfailingly healthful. The last set of snaps were very poor and I am enjoined against sending one: not enough light in the room.

We hope you are both well, and getting what joy there is in these times. I begin to grow doubtful that we shall ever see real peace again, but that is foolish. Still I began to teach in 1929 and from then to now there hasn't been a single year not overclouded in the world by depression, spectres of war or war itself. I envy you who knew the world before 1914. I used to talk in this vein to Hermannsson[8] the grand old professor of Old Norse at Cornell.

Yours, as ever,
Edward

111 [*Holo.*]

Friday
November 24, 1944

Dear Edward,

I was glad to hear from you. This is not an attempt to reply to yours but to ask you, as soon as you get home from your trip, to answer the query I made in mine of 12 Oct. "What wld you choose from *The Long Sault* for the new Selected Ed?" The ans. is important because L.P. is now urging me to send the copy. So please reply & you may be inclusive but arrange the titles in order of preference & I shall hope that we may concur on the main items.

Yours ever,
Duncan

112 [*Holo.*]

[Chicago]
November 29, 1944

Dear Duncan,

Just a dashed-off note immediately on returning, in answer to your question. A few weeks ago I made a selection and fully intended to send the list. Here it is:

1. 'At the Long Sault'
2. The two poems preceding 'Fate' and the two following[1]
3. 'Crete'

Perhaps the best of the second sonnet sequence should also be given.[2]

I had a good trip. The Rutgers University audience was *keenly* interested in Canadian poetry, to my surprise and great pleasure.

Yours, as ever,
Edward

113

December 24, 1944

My dear Edward.   I am sending you in a *"roll"* a copy of Vertue's Copper-plate of Pope[1]— I was going to say of your favourite Poet but I refrain. Its condition bespeaks its age, and I think it must be a fairly early print of the plate and gives one a feeling that the little Great Man looked something like that. I hope you will care to have it and pin it up in your Studio at the University for I dont think Peggy would welcome it. I will mail it as soon as I can get to the P.O. to have it weighed;* as it was printed in 1741 there should be no duty on it. Just pull out the green tissue and the print will come along.

Our best wishes for the New Year. I will be writing you on more general subjects soon. [*Holo.*] & thanks for yr card.

Yours sincerely,
Duncan

*[*Holo.*] that may be several days as it is cold here now, but this is just a warning ltr.

D.

114 [*Holo.*]

[Chicago]
December 30, 1944

Dear Duncan,

It seems a good long while since I last heard from you — aside from the card from Elise and you, for which our thanks. I trust you have not been ill. I had a heavy cold the first half of the month, but am now in perfect form. Today is Deaver's birthday, and we are happy to think he has come through the most dangerous year so well.

Our nurse is back after an absence of three months. The return is well-timed, for Winter is my season of relief from teaching; and Peggy will now be able to join me in a short trip to Toronto next month. I fear our time will not stretch to a longer trip. I am very happy that Peggy can get away for even a short time.

I have now finished the first draft of the *Goriot,* and am taking the keenest pleasure in revising it so that it may read more like idiomatic English.[1] It is a pleasant task for these holiday weeks, and one that enables me to be at home.

I have also been reading, for review, Matthiessen's new book on H. James,[2] of which Pelham has no doubt talked to you. Much interesting new material — another interesting fact is that it comprises the Alexander lectures at Toronto last fall.

I see W.L.M.K. has beaten out the storm once more.[3] But I think he'll lose the general election, at least will lose a clear majority.

Every good wish to you both for the New Year, in which Deaver would join if he knew what these artifices of time are.

Yours, as ever,
Edward

1945

Now the pace begins to slow, although in the fewer letters there is no diminishment in warmth and interest on either side. Lampman's presence is assured early by the unexpected appearance of a collection of manuscript poems which Lampman seems to have prepared as a gift for the "other woman" in his life. It is offered for sale to the University of Toronto. The occasion prompts Scott to clear up some of the details of the Waddell affair. Other matters move slowly. Scott's elaborate scheme to present bound holograph copies of two poems by Lampman to Trinity College, Toronto, drags on until October. It is meant as a surprise for Brown, but surprise is lost and Scott is grumpy. Meanwhile, his edition of selected Lampman poems, a project never much to his heart, creeps at a snail's pace through the Ryerson Press. But the Canadian edition of Scott's Viger is out in May, handsome in its brown cover, and gives much pleasure. A short story, "The Circle of Affection," written the previous year, goes to Queen's Quarterly in July. The house on Lisgar Street is growing very old, like the poet himself, and Scott is appalled at the cost of repairs. Brown's preoccupations, as usual, are many, and he is dutiful in giving Scott some account of them. The appearance of the American edition of Pratt's collected poems sets the critic off on a campaign against the neglect, public and academic, of Canadian literature on both sides of the border. In August he is in Banff, where the group of Alberta writers there assembled so depress him that he takes no pleasure in the beauty of the setting. In November he is "buried in the proofs of Goriot." But he has his teaching, and that is going well. He is, moreover, re-engaged with Matthew Arnold, of whom he never tires. Scott will prick up his ears. It is also a new track for Brown which will lead to an important book. Scott is eighty-three on the 2nd of August. There is a party at the Country Club, and Dilworth gives a broadcast reading of Scott's poems from Vancouver.

115 [*Holo.*]

[Chicago]
January 3, 1945

Dear Duncan,

How good of you to send the admirable ''Pope.'' It is the most ''poetic'' Pope I know: the eyes, the prophetic (tho' not Hebraic!) nose, and the more than sensitive fingers. My 18th century colleagues, to whom I showed it, were full of envy. It will be on my walls, probably of my study at home, when craftsmen can be found! My study is very small but it begins to look well — a Turner water-colour of the Arch of Trojan, framed ms. poems of A.L., yourself,[1] and Ned, four small water-colours by (of all men!) J.A. Froude,[2] and a water-colour reproduction of Bellini's head of Christ which I picked up in Paris ten years ago.

I perhaps told you that the January *Quarterly* will have a review of Pratt's collected edition by your friend.[3] I decided to abuse my seniors the elderly professors in Canada for not having done more to make Pratt recognized at home and abroad years ago. I have taken his, clearly, as a type-case. Pelham should not feel hurt for I have published my praise of the help he gave Pratt. I am thinking of men like Broadus and Sedgewick and Malcolm Wallace and Cy (the *Hon.* Cy) MacMillan.[4] Well, it was fun to write and made me feel very virtuous. I referred to your work in the first couple of sentences.

With my warmest thanks, in which Peggy joins,

as ever,
Edward

116

January 30, [1945][1]

Dear Edward.   I have been weeks carrying out my promise to write soon which I made in the note sending you the print. It is not too late to wish Deaver Many Happy Returns. I did not know the exact date of his advent so I could not send you a message in time; if I knew and forgot I would have felt as if I had failed. However you and Peggy know that he has my love and best wishes; it is fine to have you write that he has come through his first year so well; I hope he will live as long as I have and feel as well as I do now and be living in a better world.

I was glad to know that the print got to you safely and that you liked it; no doubt, in its long journey from the impression, it has had many owners but not one, I think, who has understood the Poet as well as you do. I am all impatience to read the *Goriot;* for me it is one of the great novels and I know it only in English; now you are giving it to me again and I must say I anticipate even greater satisfaction.

I would like to have news of the Toronto visit. Did you see Pierce, and have they made any advance with the new edition of *O.C.P.*? I am sending a copy to South Africa to a poet there who has sent me several copies of his book of so called poems which is said to have gone through many editions; his name is A. Vine Hall.[2] I have passed the gallies of the Viger book and expect page proofs before long; they are trying to make a nice book and I hope you will like it. It is to be bound in BROWN cloth and that should bring it luck; but I do not expect that it will be a "best seller," horrid term; you know how this edition came to be published.[3] I have read all Chas. Lamb's letters lately and in one I find a sentence that is applicable to my case; to this effect, Nothing with my name will sell, *"there is a blast upon it."* Well, as he said in another letter, "Damn the age; I will write for Antiquity."[4] I will send you one of the first copies I get which wont be until Spring comes. We have had a cold winter, and I have not been able to go out very often. I have been reading quite a lot of different things. One book that interested me was the *Letters of Pissarro to His Son Lucien,* they are far superior to the letters of Cézanne[5] wh. I also read. P. gives you a feeling of intimate life and the struggle of an artist who knew that he was right; there is nothing of the rottenness of Bohemianism; there is nothing of that either in Cézanne, his friendship with Zola is interesting, and the closing pages when he is dealing with the problems of his art. Now I am deep in J.B. Yeats letters[6] wh. I find well worth while; and Sir Donald Tovey's book on Beethoven;[7] you observe my reading is varied. I suppose no man had a deeper knowledge of the structure of music than Tovey, so that he is often too deep for me, but I am nearly always on dry land. Sometime ago a friend gave a Dr. Thompson who was in the Air Force a letter to me and I saw something of him. He is a friend of Spender, who he admires greatly and a closer personal friend of Auden. When he went to the States on his way to England he sent me a copy of Auden's last book wh. A. had put my name in.[8] I wish we were together so that we might discuss this book. Did it get good, understanding reviews, have you read it? I am sending you a half-tone of a portrait of Spender wh. was in an Ex. of British pictures. It was a good picture and loses much from the absence of colour. I hope to hear from you soon. Elise joins in love to Deaver and to you all.

Yours, as ever,
Duncan

117

February 10, 1945

Dear Edward. 	I have been reading your review of Ned's book and am very pleased with it; I wish it had been longer and more detailed but the content of appreciation is there, and you dwell on his strong points and, after all, that is most important. Your remarks about the arrangement are no doubt just but I have not followed them out to come to any conclusion; if you had been with him when he was laying out the book you might have advised him.[1] Will the U.S. Edition follow the same line? I hope your reliance on the American critics is well founded,[2] but I have no faith in them or the British critics to do justice to a Canadian work. I liked your personal references on p. 213 and you have in *O.C.P.* dealt with that quality in his character. You have left the Academic critics at sea and I can think of them all from Vancouver to Halifax scratching their heads to find out whom they should praise now to redeem themselves. I am at a loss too but then I have no responsibility and can only wait to be told; still I can guess. When Edgar comes here next I am going to ask him whom he should praise; it may be hazardous, for Pelham and I do not indulge in literary conversation. And thank you for bringing in my name just in the way you did; always thoughtful and considerate for my credit.[3] But I wonder what you will say if I attempt to print the poems I have by me; for none, I fear, are in the style you like. In this connection I will tell you that Dilworth was here the other day and brought a message from the Oxford Press that they were ready to publish this book of Miscellanies whenever I have it ready.[4] Dilworth had brought a copy in advance of his Anthology of Twentieth Century Poetry, Canadians are represented;[5] it is published by Oxford and *just between ourselves* the book is dedicated to ME. I hope that wont stop the sale of it. I got yesterday the page proofs of Viger and I think it is going to look like a nice book. I must say that Pierce has been interested to make it so. Some time ago Child wrote me about MSS of A.L. for Trinity.[6] Loftus and his wife will consider it; but it may be some time for she has gone to Cal[ifornia] for four months and all their papers are packed up before moving into a new flat. I have a little scheme of my own to give Trinity something but I shall tell you about it if I find I can do what I want, as I wish the MS to be *properly bound.* Child told me, much to my delight, that the Plaque of A.L. was safe in the temporary Chapel and that when the new Chapel was built it would be placed in position.[7] Our politics have reached the lowest level I can remember. I think the episode of King, Ralston and MacNaughton is a shameful one. The election in Grey North gave King something to think about and if he were to appeal to the country now he would get a set-back.[8] There is nothing he wont resort to in order to retain power; I even expect him to extend the life of Parliament if he thinks he can get a majority of the Houses.

I find J.B. Yeats' Letters full of interesting remarks. I give you one on Balzac from a ltr to W.B.Y. ''I am still reading Balzac. I have only four or five of the forty vols left to read. How he hates a vague man — there is a certain poet in one of his books, Canalis by name, who is Russell, without Russell's honest heart.''[9]

Well I have indulged my bad habit of writing you long letters and so I conclude with love to Peggy and Deaver in wh. Elise joins.

Yours ever,
Duncan

118

Dear Duncan,

If this letter suggests a battered mind, I will tell you that within the past seven days I have read through *Ulysses*.[1] I had not read it through, though I often dip into it, in ten years. I must be a better reader than I used to be for I followed the sense without stumbling, though here and there I miss a phrase or sentence. I think it is a powerful work, but not one that people are likely to read a hundred years on.

I appreciate your wish directed at Deaver. We would settle for less. If he could achieve one half your eminence and two thirds of your age, his would be a fortunate life. The rest, as Dr. Cody likes to say to show what knowledge he has picked up in the market place, would be velvet.

I am glad you approve so many things in the critique on Pratt. You may be right that I am too hopeful of the Americans, but I think that they are very likely to take to Pratt's work. No, the American edition will not be the same: much will be omitted.[2] Knopf does not want too large a book. In general, so far as I know them, I approve of the omissions for the purpose. I hope you are right, and that the senior academics will scratch their head: they ought to. I shall be amused to hear whom Pelham will praise if he will say! But though the paper is more violent than I usually am, I fear I did not dot the i's: and many professors will think they are not aimed at.

It is very good to know that *Viger* progresses. Pierce was pleased with the project when we spoke briefly of things in train: but I fear he will not easily get what you want for binding. The Canadian publishers are in a bad way; ceilings prevent their importing what they want from the U.S. and Canadian stock is unlovely. At least I heard this from the U.T. Press.

By now I trust you will have a copy of my 2nd edition. Pierce says he has sent it. There is but [one] slight change in the section on you; but here and there throughout the book I have made additions, and I hope that I have improved the work.

I shall be looking for Dilworth's anthology. Give him my warm wishes if you see him or write. I like him. I shall keep your secret. I also much hope that the *Miscellanies* will come out, Oxford would be a good publisher I think. Clarke is active.[3] Too Oxfd. group[4] and imperialist for me, but he cares for books, a rare thing in publishers.

I had some talk with Coats,[5] who has become a close friend of my good friend Harold Innis.[6] Amazing breadth of reading Coats has, and the R.S.C. address he gave last year almost staggers under the burden, I thought.[7]

Our best wishes to you both. You will like the change of season which cannot be more than a month off even in Ottawa, after so early and so hard a winter.

Yours, as ever,
Edward

P.S. [*holo.*] I shall be eager to hear what you think of my additions which are chiefly in the latter part of Ch. 2 and in the essay on A.L. I am glad to hear of the plaque. I did not get over to Trinity on this last brief visit.

119

March 5-6, 1945

My Dear Edward.   Many thanks for my copy of the second edition of *O.C.P.* I have put the inscription where it belongs on the front page, and I treasure both my special copies.[1] I have gone through the book carefully and have noted all the changes I hope. Of course I looked at my own section first. I was glad to see the change from definite to the indefinite on p. 138, in the sentences at the top of the page;[2] and it warmed up my old heart to read the section again. I could not trace any changes in E.J.P. I think you enriched the A.L. by the reference to the lecture;[3] and I think the wording of the para. on 'At the Long Sault' is an immense improvement from the para. you sent me. I like the expression of delight you have in this poem, which, as you know, I share. In the first divisions of the book I note your remarks about Sherman, and I think you have done him justice as you wished to do. A.J.M.S. should be pleased with the space you have given him and the generous praise and appreciation. As for your book as a whole now that I review it in its second edition, I have nothing but admiration; it will be an everfixed mark for many years.

I was going to begin this letter by an explanation for my delay in ackldge the book; I gave Loftus a message to you wh. I cannot be sure he delivered, as he was in doubt whether he cld stop in C. I was not able for some days to use the typewriter as I had not been just up to it, but I am feeling better now. He spent a half-hour with me on the Selected A.L. I shall write again to you later about this. Did you hear of the death of Emily Carr? I liked to think of this brave spirit still with us working, planning and ever believing in the message of her art. Dilworth was of great help to her and I am sure he felt her loss. His Anthology is on the market now, but I have not seen a copy yet; when I write him I will give him your message. The only remark I care to make about Coats' address is that it showed the vice of the parenthesis unrestrained; it is a way of writing that I detest; I dont think there is a single parenthesis in *O.C.P.* It pained me to hear that Clarke of the Oxford Press was an *Oxford-group* adherent, but as he loves books we will overlook his fault. I dont pity your battered state of mind after reading *Ulysses;* I cld never get on with that; I smuggled one of the first copies into Canada from France when it was thought daring to even mention the work, and it is around here somewhere in seclusion if not in hiding, but I will not meddle with it.[4] You will have one of the first copies of *Viger*. They have bothered me a good deal about it and sent me a proof of the titlepage for my approval; and I had to tell Flemington that I thought it was poor; but they shd not bother me about these details when they have so much impeccable taste scattered around the office.

Try to write me again before long and we send you, Peggy and Deaver our love.

As ever,
Duncan

120

Chicago
March 24, 1945

Dear Duncan,

I have wanted to write to you for several days, but wished to get permission to mention to you a matter that seems to me exceedingly interesting, and the permission came only to-day. I will touch on this first.

Miss Marjorie White of your city has offered to the U. of T. Library a book bound in green calf and cloth, and containing 92 poems in manuscript; the book was presented by A.L. to Miss White's aunt, whom she styles the "Lady of the Six Sonnets." She asks $100.[1]

The price is certainly not high, and it is not about that that I specially wish to consult you. What I am wondering is if the U. of T. Library is the best depository for the treasure. I have no convictions, but you may have. Stewart Wallace[2] and Woodhouse would be the real custodians (Woodhouse because he is now head of English) and I think we can depend on their good judgment. But you might have other views. I should be glad to buy the book myself, but Miss White says that she is offering the book to the U. of T. because if a private person came to possess it there would be no assurance against its leaving Canada where she wishes it to remain.

Also I wonder if you know anything about this particular book of ms.

I have asked Wallace to ask Miss White for the titles, and, where there are no titles, for the first lines. So there will be plenty of time for me to hear from you, before Wallace writes again to pass on the list.

You might be interested to know that Miss White is selling the book because she needs the money, and that the price was fixed after consultation with Mr. Fee[3] of the Archives.

Now I think you know everything that I do!

I was elated by your praise of the 2nd edition. I am so pleased that you like the changes you have noted. The only one you have missed is the next to last paragraph of the Pratt, where I speak of Collin (unnamed) and of the qualities in 'Dunkirk.'[4] I was glad to add a word of praise for that poem, though I know that

Pratt is happy at my choice of 'Brébeuf' and 'The Cachalot' as his ranking works.

It is also very good to know that the materials for the new Lampman volume are with Pierce. Loftus MacInnes telephoned me and we had a good talk; his train had been delayed, and he had not the time for a meeting; he also seemed pleased with the additions to the Lampman essay in *OCP,* which, no doubt, were drawn to his notice by you. I am sorry he is feeling seedy, and hope that when he comes back via Chicago I shall see him and find him better.

A little later I shall write you about some other things that are in my mind; but I am just beginning a busy week-end, busy not with revelry, but with last minute preparations for classes — my quarter off is ending, and I go back to teaching on Monday. A fine program: a course on Wordsworth and Keats, another on Browning (repeated from last summer) and the public course on the modern novel.

We are all in fine spirits, Deaver indeed looks healthier every day. We hope you will find warm days for pleasant walks, and that for you and Elise this will be a beautiful spring. Here it is already very warm, and the buds are coming in the park beneath my windows.

Yours, as ever,
Edward

121

March 26, 1945

Dear Edward.   Your letter of the 26th inst.[1] came this morning and I reply at once for there are, to my mind, no complexities in the problem that require long consideration.

Now as to facts: I did not know of the existence of this M.S. Book. Miss White's mother was a sister of Miss Katherine T. Waddell; her father was James White[2] a useful Civil Servant in his time. Her mother died not long ago and I suppose Miss White finds herself in straitened circumstances.

Now as to my reactions; you ask my opinion on only one point and I give it. The Library of Toronto University is, under the circumstances the *best depository* for the book. The only rival *might be* Trinity College. I use the phrase "under the circumstances" because the M.S. has been offered to the U. of T. and the proposal is a clear one and Trinity should not be brought into the discussion. I give my advice although you did not ask for it. Let Toronto buy the book and pay her reasonable price and not haggle about it. I see that you do not consider the price high and it is not high. I dont suppose there would be any attempt to offer a less sum but I mention the price because I have had an illustration of what our accursed parsimony has accomplished in the management of the National Gallery and I am indignant; they tried to beat Mrs. Gagnon in her price for the *Maria Chapdelaine* pictures and they have lost them.[3] My indignation is not extended to Wallace and Woodhouse or yourself for an intention that is not in prospect but my mind is suddenly heated by late occurrences, and that affects even my typing.[4] You will recognize the unique character of this book but I bring it up here for herein the special value lies. It is the selection of Poems by A.L. for the girl he loved by which he wanted her to know his worth and the depth of his feeling for Nature and the truth of his feeling for her.[5] The number of the poems seems extraordinary, 92! They must include much of his best work. Let the University buy the book instanter.

I hope you will write me soon again. You need not boast about weather; we took the Brockingtons to the Country Club yesterday and had tea on the lawn.

Dear Deaver; he will develope quickly now and soon he will carress you with his eyes, and you and Peggy will see that look in a child's eyes that cannot be otherwise expressed but which cannot be at all expressed.

> Our love to you three and Elise joins,
> Duncan

P.S. In writing you about the Waddell episode I mentioned LeSueur, I want to make it clear that he only knew of the affair by happenings in the office. E.W. Thomson was A.L.'s only confidant.

[*Holo. below postscript*] I did not mention the Library of Par. because that is not to be thought of. Imagine the delays, the quibbling, the sniffing of our Peerless Leader if it ever got so far.

[*Holo., top of first sheet*] Much of this ltr is for yourself alone but my opinion & advice are given without reserve.[6]

122

> March 27, 1945

Dear Edward.   This is a P.S. to mine of yesterday to mention a point I thought of after I had posted it. Loftus never mentioned this book to me; he and his wife knew that Mrs White had copies of the special poems and he said they were rather proud of the association. Miss White must be about Natalie's age,[1] and they may be friendly. It seems to me strange that when the MacInnes's are both away she should try to sell the book;[2] but there may be nothing in that idea. If they were here you would undoubtedly take the matter up with them, as you and I have always been careful to meet their wishes. There is no legal difficulty for I think the lady has a perfect right to sell the book; that does not involve the copyright question. Loftus said he would send me his Cal[ifornia] address and if I get it you might write him, if you thought it advisable. So please give this point consideration.

Dilworth spent an hour with me when he was rushing here on C.B.C. business. He was glad to get your message and told me that he had asked Clarke to send you a copy of his anthology.

> Yours ever,
> Duncan

123 [*Holo.*]

April 2, 1945

Dear Edward,

I had a brief Card from Loftus today. His address is

4121 First Ave.
San Diego, Cal.

He said he hoped to see you on his way back. I think he had two months leave.

Yours as ever,
D.

P.S. I dont intend to write Loftus during this short absence.

D.

124

[Chicago]
April 3, 1945

Dear Duncan,

Thanks for both letters. I am glad that you are pleased by the suggested disposition of a volume which must seem to you a part of your custodial trust, even if you had not previously known of its existence. I wrote to Wallace before your second letter came, urging in the strongest terms that the book be bought, and that the price was low, and I said you associated yourself with me in both points.

As for the question of the interests of the MacI., which you mention in the second letter, I think we have nothing to regret. Miss White (who by the way began to correspond with Wallace early in February, *ie* before MacI left Ottawa) declared that she would not sell to any private person since she thought the piece too valuable a piece of Canadiana to leave the country. Accordingly, our one concern was with the question whether the U. of T. was an ideal, or at least a highly suitable depository. We both thought it was, as compared with any other public depository. In expressing that opinion we could not be thinking of the U. of T. versus the MacI's, for the MacI's were ruled out of consideration just as you and I were. I wish you would take the matter up with MacI. if I do not see him en route back. If I do, I'll explain it to him, and drop you a line at once. I think it would be useful to impress on him that Wallace and Woodhouse are both very conservative gentlemen and can be trusted to act sagely. Woodhouse I know will always wish to consult me since he knows little of Canadian literature and has come to rely on my judgment in all that touches it.[1] I may get to Toronto in

September, the next break in my teaching. If I do, I'll spend a good deal of time with the book — always providing that negotiations go well, as I trust they will.

Did I tell you that I am to go to Banff for a week in August to conduct some conferences (as they call them) with the Alberta Writers (God save the mark!).[2] The expenses of the meeting are paid by the Rockefeller F'D'N, which loves regionalism. I shall value the chance to see the Rockies for the first time.

Later I will write more at leisure, and shall try to have copied the list of the contents of Miss White's book. There are 93 poems, but the love poems do not seem to be there.

We all flourish, and were glad to know that Ottawa was warmed to the degree that you were sitting on the lawn at the club. Recall me to Brockington's memory. All good wishes from us both to you and Elise.

As ever,
Edward

125

[Chicago]
May 8, 1945

Dear Duncan,

I use this paper out of vanity.[1] I never heard of the association till I got a packet of this paper, and saw what they had done to me. But I like the paper.

I am much in arrears in writing to you, but the writing of these lectures on the modern novel has kept me on the run. Novels do take me such an endless time to read, if I am to talk critically about them.

MacInnes called me by phone on his way through. I was sorry we could not meet: there were only three hours between the time of his call, and the time he would be leaving; and I had my weekly lecture on the novel that evening. I told him about the ms. book, and he was very pleased. I believe he said he would talk to Miss White. I stressed that she wanted to commit the charge to an institution, since she intended that the book should stay forever in Canada. He also spoke of some interesting letters he had picked up, and which he would show to you.[2] In good time I shall hope to hear more, the reference to personal relations was interesting as MacInnes reported it.

Ned Pratt got a good review in the *S.R.L.* from Robert Hillyer (who has just been forced out of his Harvard chair because of drink, I hear).[3] That is the only review I've seen.

We are all well. We think Deaver is handsomer all the time, and he is certainly supremely well. As to brightness, we don't know, and so far we don't care! I'll be here through the summer, and unless the heat becomes dreadful I shall keep my family with me, the park in front of us and the lake a few yards away are strong points, and travel is the devil. Peggy has no wish to try it with a baby.

I did not see our peerless leader on his day here.[4] My political career is over, and I have no wish to keep fences in order. I did have a pleasant hour with G. Dexter,[5] who always seems to me a thoroughly fine fellow.

> Our best love to you both,
> Yours as ever,
> Edward

126

May 28, 1945

Dear Edward.   I have two letters of yours which I have neither acklgd nor answered which is unusual. Loftus has just phoned me that the purchase of the Book went through; he and his wife saw Miss White. Natalie had seen the Book but L had never seen it, and as it had gone to Toronto did not have a look at it. I shall be interested to know what you think of it, as no doubt you will be in Toronto before long. I am glad it has found a secure and wholly friendly resting place. Now, if something could be done for Trinity; the MacI's saw the plaque in place in the temporary Chapel and said it looked very well.

In yours of Apl 3rd you told me you were going to Banff in Aug. In your last you said you were to be in Chicago for the summer. Has the Banff trip been given up? I hope not, for I liked to think of you having a first look at the Rockies. While you might not be impressed by the writers I am sure you would meet with some friendly people. I am glad Ned Pratt got a good review in the *S.R.L.;* of course I see no U.S. reviews; but I trust the book will go well. How utterly stupid of Hillyer to lose his place for such a reason.[1] I do not know anything of his work, either prose or verse. I was much impressed by your new letter head and the list of names; you surpass them, and I'm sure they knew they were getting strength by calling you in. Yes, I know Odell Shepard's book; that seems a long time ago. Loftus spoke about the letters from A.L. and he will let me see them as soon as they get unpacked. I sent you a copy of *In the V of V* the other day; the first copy off the press. I hope you did not object to L.P. using a quotation from *O.C.P.*[2] I did not know that he was going to do this and as it refers to verse it does not seem very appropriate. But I suppose he wanted to get strong support for an unsaleable book; but he is responsible for it.

I am sure that Deaver grows in beauty and strength—how I should love to see him.

> Yours ever, and with all our best to you both;
> Duncan

127

Chicago
May 29, 1945

Dear Duncan,

We both send thanks and congratulations on *Viger* in its new dress. When I took off the dust-cover and pointed to the color of the binding, its texture, and the lettering, Peggy gave what I think is the sincerest compliment that any one can pay to a Canadian-made book: she said it looked as if it had been designed and manufactured in this country or in England. On this occasion I think you really have circumvented all the evil ways of the Canadian publisher. The match of the dust-cover and the true cover is admirable, and one feels that this is a binding that will really last. The impeccable one could not quite rid himself of the sense that all this was somewhere north of Chicoutimi;[1] but some of his effects are pleasing: for instance the head-pieces for "The Little Milliner" and "Sedan." It was very pleasant to renew acquaintance with the tales and sketches in the new garb. I read two each evening till I ended, all too soon. I enjoy all, of course; if I have a favorite it is "The Bobolink," a very charming and moving sketch indeed. But all are fine, all.

One query. I note that you call the girl in that sketch "Blanche" which is also the name of the river.[2] Am I reading too much into the piece when I find meaning in this? I noticed one typographical error: the first two words on p. 26 are run together.

We are proud indeed of the inscription. The book lies on our living room table, and is much picked up by those who come.

I hope that something like the due attention is paid to it in the press.

Deaver becomes more of a person, and seems to become cheerier all the time. I am sorry that Chicago is so far from Ottawa.

Yours, as ever,
Edward

[*P.S. holo.*] Elise will be sharing your happiness that after so much effort and in the face of so many difficulties the book has such excellence in appearance to express the excellence within. I am proud that some words of mine appear on it.

128 [*Holo.*]

Chicago
June 2, 1945

Dear Duncan,

This is no reply to your letter, but just a note to cover the enclosure. I should like to have your suggestions for this draft of a note to introduce the selections from A.L.'s essay on Keats.[1] I judge from Connor's comment that although it was planned as a lecture it was never delivered.[2] Is that so? Perhaps you may have a comment on A.L.'s motives in writing it. Later I may have a clear text of the extracts to send to you. I am now checking the quotations.

As ever,
Edward

129

June 14, 1945

Dear Edward.   Many thanks for your generous praise of the little book and for letting me know that you and Peggy enjoyed it; I shall write about that subject later, perhaps in reply to the letter you seem to promise; I shall wait for it because I dont want our letters to "cross" again.

I write now about the Keats Essay. I wish I could discuss it with you for I am very keen about having it published, and it is so long since I read it that my comments may be of no earthly use to you. Your Introduction is, as usual, very interesting, but I thought you would submit to a few observations which cant be called criticism. This production of L's was not written as a lecture and was never so delivered. I feel certain in saying that he prepared it for publication and hoped that one of the U.S. Magas would print it; but I dont remember that he ever offered it anywhere.[1] I have placed faint pencil figures before the sentences on which I want to comment.[2]

No. 1. Were the letters to Fanny Brawne available to L? They were not published in any but a private edition until 1895.[3] I have before me two rough notebooks in which L wrote this essay and the last book contains several drafts of poems he was working at — 'Vivia Perpetua,' etc. — and the latest dated poem is Mar. '95. In the early parts of this draft L does not deal sympathetically with F.B. He gives the then current opinion of her character.[4]

No. 2. Would you consider reprinting in full the quotation I gave on pp. 31-32 of *Lyrics of Earth?*[5] You have not quoted it in *O.C.P.* and I feel that it would amplify your statement, be appropriate to the tone of your Introduction and would make it available for a reader who would never probably look at *Lyrics of E.* You might think this over.

No. 3. I have paid a great deal of attention to this section and I thought I would try to give you my opinion for what it is worth. I do not believe that L's affinity for Keats' work was influenced by any seeming similarity in their circumstances; if one leans on that L's critical position is weakened. But I notice you say for the *man* Keats so I am no doubt reading too much into the sentence. A word in comparison to their circumstances or a reference to L's: he was poor but he never had serious money difficulties, he was never in debt; until L overstrained his heart by useless physical exercises his health was fairly good; his heart was weakened by his early attack of rhumatic fever, but if he had been reasonable about this fetish of exercise he would have lived for many years. True he felt the lack of success *for he had literary ambitions,* but he never had to stand the outrageous attacks that Keats suffered, I dont think he ever had an entirely unfavorable review. This is really all I have to say about the Introduction which will no doubt be a fine prelude for what is to follow.

I have several matters to write you about but must do that later because this letter has been too long delayed.

Yours ever,
Duncan

130

Chicago
June 20, 1945

Dear Duncan,

Your comments are exceedingly helpful. I have adopted every suggestion save one. The quotation on pp 31-32 of your memoir goes very well, and I have taken it in. Your comment that it was not by reason of likeness in circumstance that A.L. was drawn to Keats the poet has led me to change several sentences, and to make it clear that I am speculating only on his attitude to Keats the man. This is, as you recognized, a point of importance, and I am glad to get it right. About the Fanny Brawne letters I think you are mistaken; I am not going to the University this week (my week off, between terms) but in my Rossetti: *Life of Keats,* 1887, the bibliography distinguishes between a privately printed and a public edition of the letters in 1878. As you say, A.L. did not think at all well of F.B.: no doubt some thoughts of his own life were in his mind as he wrote, but on these I don't plan to say anything. I have noted, with thanks, your indication of the way in which MacI. likes his name written: that sort of thing is important to get right. I am very proud of your approval of the two sentences in which I spoke out as a critic.

You may have wondered why there is so little criticism or evaluation in the prefatory note, or perhaps I told you the reason.

When I first mentioned my project of doing something with the essay to Woodhouse, what I had in mind was a critical paper of my own, in which I would quote rather substantial extracts from the essay. Woodhouse urged me to print as much of the essay as seemed wise, and to leave my comments for another occasion. I welcomed the chance to get some more of A.L.'s criticism into print; and acceded at once to his suggestion.

I have been enjoying my week of repose. The weather is so uncertain, or rather so sadly certain to bring rain at least once a day that I have stayed close to home. I have been reading Stendhal's *Red and Black*[1] for the first time, with some amusement, but without feeling that this was much that I had missed. I still don't understand the cult. Are you a worshipper? Also Douglas Bush's new book *Paradise Lost in our Time,* (Cornell Press). You should get Hardy[2] to get this. It has some fine stuff, though he is more of a lover of the Miltonic substance, and harder on those who care chiefly for the form, than I could be. Pelham will be interested: D.B. was his brightest student. You would be stimulated by this little book, I think.

I sent my lecture on James and Conrad to the *Yale Review,* and they have agreed to publish it.[3] I was pleased not only by this, but by their suggestion that I develop the pages on Conrad a little farther. My view, without being hostile to James, is that not enough has been made of the other master, whom in my heart I admire more. I have also sent the closing lecture in the series, "Recent Tendencies," to *Harper's,* but I doubt that it will suit them.[4]

Mention of *Harper's* reminds me of the inglorious fate of the P.M. To be the only member unseated by the soldier vote is rather hard.[5] There will be joy among the heathen!

We are all happily well and looking forward to sunnier days. Where on this continent are there long successions of sunny days in which the temperature does not climb above 82 or so?

Our best wishes to you both,
As ever,
Edward

P.S. I will send the text of the Keats, plus my preface, when it has been retyped. Yes, I do go to Banff, anyhow, taking a week off from my teaching here — I am sorry to be rushed in the trip, I should like to have stopped at some points I won't see for a long time, if ever.

131

July 6, 1945[1]

Dear Edward.   You were generous in your praise of *Viger* and I am very glad that you and Peggy liked it so well. It was a bit of a struggle to get the book produced in its present form; there is one error in "make up" which I could not get them to correct, although I marked it on the page proofs and wrote a special letter about it; the lines "Whoever has from toil and stress," should face the Table of Contents and there shd be a *blank page* before the first story; just think of the preliminary pages in this order and you agree; this is as it was in the old edition; but there is no use bothering about it. As yet The Impeccable One has not said a word. I am sure you will understand that I did not approve of the stuff on the inner flap of the cover; I never saw it; the word "gloat" is very objectionable, but thoroughly Pierceistic, to coin a word.[2] Some attention is being paid to the book by the Press and I have had a few interesting letters; later on when you are less busy I may make up a sheaf of them and send it for your perusal, if you wld care to see them. Last winter I wrote a short story wh. I call "The Circle of Affection,"[3] it amused me to do it and Elise to read it, and Clarke is printing it in his Summer No.[4] I will send you a copy. Pierce and W.J. Phillips have got me to consent to do an article for one of the Canadian Art Series, on P's work of course I mean. You may see him at Banff, when he was here I told him how much you and Peggy liked the color-print of the Indian Village under snow,[5] he said there were only two left of the edition, there may be an opportunity for you to get one of these. It seems a real task to write this article, or "brochure" L.P. calls it, but as I like both the man and his work so much I did not seem able to refuse. I am glad you are going to Banff and are having a look at the Rockies, I wish I were going too but I dont expect to see the West again. Some comments on yours of the 20th June; I am not a worshipper of Stendhal; very lately I read *Red and Black* and then failed to get into *Chartreuse de Parme*[6] and gave it up; it seemed to me artificial so I let it go; neither of us seems very friendly to him. I get the *Yale Review* from the Lib. of Parl. and I shall watch for your contribution. There are certain things of Conrad that I prize and can read and reread; but James and Meredith, both of whom I once read completely, have lost their hold on me. I hope you will send me the text of Keats with your Foreword, I want to see it very much. The new edition of Lampman hangs fire; everything is ready here but until L.P. says "I am ready now to go on" I wont send him the M.S. I want you to approve the short Foreword and shall send it someday soon.

King has weathered the storm as I said he wld; it was amusing to see Quebec "come under the barn with the rest of the boys."[7] He is going to make a speech in Gaelic in Glengarry. I dont want to say what I think about his conduct, political, during these last months but Canadians do not seem perturbed; we forget easily because we have no public opinion. Elise has charged me to say that what we chiefly need is a good snapshot of Peggy and Deaver. We are pretty well and, now, we are having *perfect June* weather and that is one of the best months for Ottawa. When King referred to himself and Smuts[8] as "we two rebels," he said the ultimate absurdity; dear old Smuts was never a rebel and as for the other artful dodger he would never get into a firing line. Our best to you both and I am as ever yours.

Duncan

132 [*Holo.*]

Chicago
July 9, 1945

Dear Duncan,

Here, at last, is A.L.'s paper on Keats. I have revised the introduction, recalling your remarks. I should be glad of your comments on any point, but specially ask you to consider the last page. Do you think the passage in square brackets should be cut?

I enclose a letter from Sandwell. Taking the very short notice of *Viger* as my text[1] I wrote a criticism of the books page and suggested that *as a first step* he might have a substantial review to head the page in each issue. I am not convinced by his reply. Please return the letter.

Yours, as ever,
Edward

133

July 18, 1945

Dear Edward.   Have I seemed dilatory in dealing with the Keats? We have had such sudden changes in weather lately that it has affected me. A plunge almost to freezing point is not very pleasant, is it? Then I wanted Loftus to read it; but as he only kept it for a day I cant blame delay on him. I send it now with expressions of the delight it has given me to read the Essay and yr Note and I am glad that it is being published. I need not comment on the Essay but I wld say that his pithy description of the purpose of the story in 'Endymion,' p 10, is better in its finality than Bridges' long analysis.[1] As you say he spends much space on the early poems and the Essay is hurried to a conclusion. That is our loss I think. The quotations from 'Endymion' are good but some lover of Keats shd make an anthology of that poem and the extracts wld not seem as if divorced from a context; each extract would be a poem in itself. I would advise leaving out the para. you have marked on the last page. It spoils the close and as a tribute from his friends it is quite inadequate. On p. 1 you will find an 's' left out of "realists." On p. 9 Loftus marked the word *port,* thinking it might be *part,* but I dont think so: I left it for you to erase.

As I said before I shd have liked to find more of E.K.B. in [the] Prefatory note but I understand the reasons and if your comments are left for "another occasion," well and good. I should like very much if you wld modify or altogether leave out the words "beset by money difficulties etc." wh. give an undue emphasis to these circumstances; I tried to give you my own opinion based on what I think are facts; please look that over; but you must do as you think best.

Dealing further with A.L. I enclose the Foreword I propose to put in the Selected poems.[2] And I want your approval or criticisms for improvements.

You will observe what I am including from *At the Long Sault;* Loftus tells me his wife wants the Series "The Growth of Love" to be included; and they both want the "Portrait in Six Sonnets" left out. I am placing 'At the Long Sault' in the place of honour in the third section and following it by 'Between the Rapids.' 'Winter hues recalled' goes with the Nature poems in the first part.

You were very right on general grounds to attack B.K.S. on his literary reviews and I think that even after he gets rid of the "very elderly gentleman" there will be not much improvement. I suppose this anonymous individual is about 60 years of age! He certainly cut his remarks re. *Viger* to the bone. I was not surprised for I think the very elderly person is Middleton, the Poet Laureate of *Sat Nt.*[3] *Viger* was a new book with its illustrations and shd have been given a little more space; even as a bit of book-making it was worthy of praise. I am afraid L.P. will be disappointed with sales but I warned him. Sandwell is a good friend of mine and I hold nothing against him, but his letter is queer; what does he mean by "retiring from active service"? Is he going to the C.B.C. as Governor?[4] I return the letr herewith. It was good of you to draw Sandwell's attention to the review.

Yours, as ever,
Duncan

134

[Chicago]
July 29, 1945

Dear Duncan,

My thanks first for the careful eye with which you read over the *Keats*. I am pleased that my doubts about the adequacy of the passage on the last page concerning his repute among his friends are confirmed by you. I have struck out the reference to A.L.'s being distressed for money, and substituted an anodyne general phrase. You were right that "port" was not a misprint; it is oddly used, but I am sure that it was what A.L. wrote and I think he intended it. We are, as you say, the poorer for the hurried fashion in which A.L. dealt with the later poems. How I wish there had been ten pages on the odes! The paper has gone to Woodhouse, and I trust that he will like it.

I am sorry that you were not so spry some parts of the last month, and trust that the indisposition was fleeting. It has been a queer summer everywhere. We have not come anywhere near the freezing point; but there have been cool windy days that are very unlike Chicago in July.

The main reason for this letter is to carry our wishes for a fine and happy anniversary. I hope you will have as happy a time as you wrote of a year ago, and that due homage will be appropriately rendered you over the air and in the press. Peggy and I are sorry that we cannot be where we were in 1942, on this occasion. Why, I would even put up with the P.M.'s office for the month if it gave me a chance to drop in at 108 Lisgar St.

There is much else in your penultimate letter that I should like to write of; but I want to make sure that this reaches you by the great day. I will merely add that I shall be eager to see "The Circle of Affection," and that I see nothing to change in the foreword to the new volume of A.L. I do not agree (nor I think do you) with the desire of the family that the sequence of sonnets to Mrs. L. should be set forward as part of A.L.'s best work; but their pleasure in it (and their reluctance to include the other sequence) does them credit in a way, and if I were in your place I think I should yield as you have done. It is a great pleasure to me to have my name appear in the fashion it does.[1]

Our kindest wishes to you and Elise,
As ever,
Edward

135

August 11, 1945

My dear Edward.   Yours of the 29th ult. came just in time and I was able to enjoy Peggy's and your congratulations as the chief pleasure of many messages I had that day. The Press played up my age and past endeavours to good advantage. I was interviewed by a *Journal* Reporter, a very attractive girl,[1] who as she talked had her eyes wide open. We did not know what to expect from the child but I am sending a copy herewith. Elise thinks you shd see it and feel partly responsible for she was a pupil of yours at Toronto, and understood what an advantage that was; she had with her a copy of *O.C.P.* and went away quite happy with a copy of *The Green Cloister;* I told her that was the only way I had of disposing of my books. Dilworth B'cast from Vancouver; read "The Bobolink" and 'Old Olives'; he also read one of the Sonnets I wrote for Elise on our Twelfth Anniversary, that did not come over so well, and cannot be read out of the sequence;[2] of course he made some very warmhearted remarks. Altogether I was too well treated. We had a dinner of 20 at the Country C. Just tried and sifted friends. Would you and Peggy had been there!

I am glad you pointed out my slip in the Foreword to A.L. I can easily make that right and will send you a copy of the amended words. Later I shall send you some clippings re *Viger,* if you care to peruse them. As you never mentioned a date for the Banff trip I cant tell whether you are gone, however when you come home write me. I am sending a copy of "The Circle of Affection" in a separate Envelope, if it doesn't reach you with a one cent stamp let me know and I shall ensure its delivery. With affectionate messages to you and Peggy and Deaver in which Elise joins—

Yours ever,
Duncan

136 [*Holo. postcard*]

Banff
August 24, 1945

A pleasure to talk with your friend W.J.P. and see the region. Otherwise a disappointment. Am glad I don't normally teach writers. The C. of A. arrived just before I set out.

Yours, as ever,
E.K.B.

P.S. We came by *Gull Lake* at night.[1]

137

Chicago
September 8, 1945

Dear Duncan,

I returned from Banff the middle of last week, and have not got back into the swing of my work here. It was an agreeable interlude, though the "writers of Alberta" seem to me a rather sad lot. The best of them, and she is very promising, is Gwen Pharis, whose plays you may perhaps know.[1] She has real ideas, and great integrity. I thought it rather pathetic when she said in conference with me, that it was not unnatural that most western writers did slick mechanical things, and no more — with the absence of an intelligent audience, the absence of the best books, or any knowledge what they were, it was safer to do the formulable trick thing. But I have hopes of her. I also enjoyed the elderly Georges Bugnet, whose novels you have doubtless read.[2] I mean to read them. He gave me his fine prose poem, 'Le Pin du Maskeg.'[3] It has noble rhythms, and is not without significant resemblances to some of your own work in the evocation of the primitive in man and nature. If you have not read it, I recommend that you risk it.

For an encyclopedia here I have done an article on Canadian literature, French and English, in 800 words. The dimensions are dreadful, but I was consoled when I was informed that 800 words was the allotment for French literature. I had the pleasure of mentioning you and A.L. I also did the articles on M. Arnold, Meredith and the Brontës.[4]

Woodhouse tells me that the *Quarterly* will print the Lampman article on Keats in January. I will drop MacInnes a line about this later, but if you see him, you might tell him. I am very happy to think of its coming out.

Peggy is particularly joyful to-night because our nurse has returned after three and a half months of absence. Deaver is not a hard child to look after, and the park that faces our door, and leads to the lake shore, is a very pleasant place to loiter. But it will be fine for her to get back her freedom for a while. He still does not talk, but he seems to grasp most of the main things we say to him, and we think he is intelligent as well as handsome. There have been no snaps for a long time, but when Peggy takes some you may be sure I will send one to you and Elise.

And now I want to tell you of my great pleasure in "The Circle of Affection." It has great charm, in the fusion of realities with a note of the fairy-like which comes partly from the great purity of the style and tone, and partly from a certain approach to character. Old Ottawa has a special appeal for me, little as I know of it, and I liked the very slight localization.

I am revising my paper on James and Conrad for the *Yale Review*. That is all I am doing apart from classes. But I have borne a rather heavy summer with no depression of spirits such as would overtake me at Cornell.

Yours, as ever,
Edward

[*Holo.*] P.S. At Banff I met A.Y. Jackson.[5] We enjoyed talking of you. L. Harris had just left Lake O'Hara.[6] I wish I could have seen him. A.Y.J. spoke of you and of L. Harris with great affection.

138

September 25, 1945

Dear Edward.   Your P.C. from Banff and yours of the 8th inst were most welcome. I think your visit to Banff was spoiled by Writers for I dont note any trace of love for the Rockies but no doubt you had time to see the region to advantage; but did you have any physical advantage from the change? I prefer the Selkirks to the Rockies because there is greater variety in atmospheric effects; but there is no place I cld visit now in the Selkirks; I was very fond of Glacier wh. is now wiped out by improvements. I will try to find Mr. Bugnet's poem and I am in ignorance of Miss Pharis's plays. I am scanning yr last ltr as I write. Thanks for giving me a word or two in the article for the Ency. My name is too long for any condensed notice; when *it* was written all your space was occupied. Let me know when the article appears in the *Yale Review,* I can get it from Hardy. I have told MacInnes re the A.L. Keats and he was properly pleased. I am glad that Peggy has the nurse again; Deaver is no doubt a good boy but it is a strain to have the constant care of a child; as for his seeming slowness in speaking there is nothing in that, the male child is always backward in using his tongue. Peter Aylen's boy did not attempt to talk until he was nearly three and he says enough now to make up for any previous silence.[1] We expect the first good snapshot of Deaver. Only a slight change was needed in the Foreword to the new A.L. to set it right and I have made it; but I have not sent the MSS to Pierce; I would rather wait till he asks for it because that would be an evidence that he was ready to go on with the book and I dont want to think of the MSS lying around in his office. He wrote me the other day that the *Viger* sales were good, and the reviews splendid; would that the terms were reversed for the sake of the publisher. I am sending you some of the reviews herewith. Dont you think that Clarke might have been a trifle more friendly in the *Queen's Quarterly!*[2] I presume that B.M.[3] means that there is a broad streak of sentimentality in the stories; but he did better this time. You will be interested in the extract from the letter, being an expert in Balzac; I suppose Mr. Beston has a right to his opinion and I hope you wont be too hard on him. Do you think as a reward I shd send him a copy of "The Circle"?[4] I cant tell you how pleased we were that you liked that story wh. was an amalgam of a few incidents and characters. You said just the things I hoped you wld say about it and so I am very satisfied;[5] I shd do more work of that kind, it amused me to do it; I have heard some appreciative comments, even the Principal of Queen's liked it;[6] the Canadian Balzac shd work harder. Your ltr to Sandwell has produced results and he wrote an agreeable para. wh. I send along in case you have not seen it. I wrote him, for B.K. is a real friend of mine and has said many kind things about me.[7] Pelham's work with the Censors is over and he is at loose ends;[8] I am sympathetic with his present position, between ourselves, as he has a very small flat here and cannot get into his house in Toronto; as it is impossible for him to work in the flat I got my friend Lanctot[9] to give him a room at the Archives where he can be quiet; he plans to write a book for Lorne Pierce and this is what is *between ourselves* as I dont know whether he wants it talked about.[10] My love to Peggy and Deaver, Elise joins, and I am ever yours.

Duncan

139

Chicago
October 15, 1945

Dear Duncan,

It was most interesting to me to look at the reviews you sent, and which I now return. I liked being associated with you once more in Ford's column.[1] He gave me a very pleasant review a couple of years ago. I do think the quarterlies might have been a bit more generous with space, and something else, let us say discrimination. By the way I have been going through some of the magazines of the '90s tracking down Pater items, and it was agreeable to come on so many of the Viger pieces in what was, I suppose, their original dress.[2]

MacInnes will perhaps have told you that I profited by a short visit to Toronto to mail him the Keats ms. book.[3] I had to go up on business: I inherited from my father some time past a poor business property in a decayed area. No one ever wanted to buy it till the past couple of years. There had been offers, and at last a man began to telephone me again and again; and I thought I had better go up, get some valuations and see whether I should get quit of the matter. I sold. For more money than I had hoped to get; but you will see I am no war profiteer by my telling you that I was given one thousand more than my father paid about 1910! But it is a great relief.

I had very little time to myself, but I did spend a few hours at the University Library, inspecting the Ms. book from Miss Waddell.[4] As I told MacInnes in my letter, it bears no mark of her possession, or of its having been addressed to her. There are none of the "love poems." I am disposed to question that it was a selection made for her. I think he made it for himself, and then it was given to her. It covers 1889-1892, but there are some revisions dated as late as 1895. I have still a good deal to do. So far I had not found any poem that is not in the 1900 volume. The book is of rough surface, black, thicker and broader than the scribblers, with a tan leather spine.[5] Perhaps you have seen it.

A fellow citizen of yours Guy Sylvestre, who edits a review with the rather absurd title *Gants du Ciel,*[6] has asked me to contribute to a special English Canadian poetry number. I told him I would write on the elder poets, which in this case will be a selective group, A.L., you, and a briefer passage on Carman. I have nothing new to say, but since the articles will be translated, and will perhaps reach a new public, I thought I might consent. Pelham is writing on Pratt, and Pratt on D. Livesay, Smith on Klein, and Collin on Smith.[7] So the editor tells me. The deadline is December 1, and I have nearly completed my article.

I did not see Pierce. I am sorry that the new A.L. drags, but then everything drags in that house, and so far as I know, in every Canadian publishing house. My American years are making me more of a bustler, I trust it will not grow offensive!

Pratt was somewhat discouraged by some of the American reviews. The review in *Poetry* said that he was roughly 1850 vintage![8] and at that more modern than Carman! I told him that time was not such a criterion as certain people thought, and I think Pratt himself does not take it as a criterion, but he naturally resents a bit (or rather is a bit upset) when some one turns him into his own grandfather. He does not think well of his latest poem.[9] I did not read it as yet. It has come out as a brochure.

I also found time one evening to take part in a short wave panel to England. I was glad I did, for one of the associates was Arthur Irwin, the new editor of *Maclean's.*[10] I had that same sense of being immediately attracted when I met him, as I had had a couple of years ago with Dilworth. If he is let do what he wants, I think *Maclean's* will improve a lot. As Dr. Johnson would say: there is great need for it.

I am reading Proust seriously for the first time. I have just finished the first section, and am about to start the second. There is a wonderful picture of jealousy, one of the most moving and real things I ever read.

I like all my courses this quarter: the two I gave last fall: Introduction to the Novel, and Matthew Arnold, plus one I gave last summer in cooperation with colleagues in other departments, a discussion course on great novels.

Peggy is getting ready to take Deaver and the nurse (whom we shall have till Christmas for sure) to Minneapolis to spend a week with her family. He is a remarkably happy child.

Our best wishes to you both,
as ever,
Edward

[*P.S. holo.*] In the article I am quoting that wonderful stanza which ends with the line I have heard you quote: "October with the rain of ruined leaves,"[11] also the beautiful close of 'The Onondaga Madonna' and the first stanza of 'Grand Pré'.

140

October 30, 1945

My Dear Edward.   I wrote you last on 25th Sept. I hoped my next letter would have an item of special interest to brighten the usual dull context. But I learn that Loftus forestalled my plan, quite innocently of course, and no harm has been done except to my sense of something achieved in which he had no part.[1] You remember I had three of A.L.'s Ms which he gave me and of wh. I gave you one.[2] I thought to have the others bound and given to Trinity; I was aided by Major Lanctot the Archivist who allowed his binder to work out the scheme (by the way he does *not want his name mentioned*).[3] Well he made a fine job of it; we got near to the College colours; I wrote a note of presentation, of wh. I send you a copy;[4] as the paper of the poems was frail the binder had backed it all with Japanese silk. I sent the book on the 24th, just a week ago, and yesterday I had a letter from the Provost thanking me for the "magnificent gift," "bound up so elegantly with a message from yourself." Why am I making such a fuss about this now? Because I had intended this as a sort of surprise for you, who are interested in all that pertains to him.

I would make a few comments on yours of the 15th inst. I hope Peggy is back from her visit; it must have been a great pleasure to her. I am glad you sold the property, real estate is always a nuisance; as you know I own this house, having built it in *1887*, and since the war it has been difficult to keep it in proper repair, I have just spent over a hundred dollars in having new eavetroughs and cld with advantage spend five hundred in other ways. I cannot remember seeing the A.L. book; and have no explanation to offer; does it show any signs of being prepared for submission to a publisher? Sylvestre asked me to contribute "souvenirs" of what he called the "Golden Age of Canadian Poetry," memories of Roberts, Carman, L and my self; but I declined very politely and subscribed to his paper with the silly title. He asked me for a poem to be translated, of not more than sixty lines. I sent him 'Old Olives,'[5] wh. wld puzzle him to translate. Pelham thought I was severe in refusing and he showed me his piece on Pratt; you were very good to him (Sylvestre) but then I was always hard to get along with. Smith was here the other day and came in to see me with Pelham; I thought I might do something for him and his wife whom he expected to come from Montreal, but their child fell ill and he went to M— and that was the last of it. I am sorry Pratt was somewhat discouraged by some American reviews. The periodical *Poetry* is negligible so far as I am concerned; its influence if it has any must all be evil so far as the interests of poetry are concerned, this is a very badly written sentence, but I tried to say something caustic. I have never got on with Proust but Elise is devoted to him, but she has not been able to get the two last vols of translation;[6] the Customs Authorities will not admit them to this pure land. I have just read the second of Santayana's autobiography,[7] and am reading page by page Doughty's *Arabia Deserta*[8] for the third time. Do you realise that it is three years since we began this correspondence? I have not yet begun my sketch of Phillips for Pierce's Art Series. I intended to say above that the Quebec Govt has given Sylvestre 160 subscriptions to his *Gants*.

> Our best wishes always to you three,
> Yours ever,
> Duncan

141

> [Chicago]
> November 29, 1945

Dear Duncan,

I am slow in writing: this past month I have been buried in the proofs of the *Goriot*. I never care for proofs, and when the work to be checked is a translation, I find the need for a double check. Fortunately the publishers have not been goading me. I think another week will see the end. I shall be eager to know how you think the book reads.

Your presentation to Trinity was a perfect idea, beautifully carried out. I shall certainly call and ask to see the volume when I get to Toronto again. Child wrote to tell me his pleasure in the outcome of his desire to honor A.L., and to link him more closely with the College. Child is a fine person.

You ask whether the notebook now in the U. of T. library has any sign of being prepared for submission to a publisher. There is no obvious sign, unless you would think a table of contents was such. One thing that would tell against the idea that it was so designed is that on the *back* of some pages there are new versions of lines and stanzas, bearing dates later than the original.

Yesterday I saw some copies of Smith's *News of the Phoenix*[1] on a remainder counter. I was surprised for Pierce told me that he kept in Canada most of the first and only edition, and it ran only to 1000 copies or less. Smith is not a poet to be understood or liked by many people.

After your animadversions on *Poetry* do I dare to tell you that they have asked me to review Walter de la Mare's new volume?[2] I have never been down to their office, which is about ten miles from us. I would like to honor de la Mare, by a sympathetic review, and agreed. It is a very interesting volume. I think you would like some of his handlings of retrospect. He is a poet I have not read as much as I should, or should like.

I was shocked to hear that the last volume of Proust is still withheld from the Canadian public. Don't you think you and Elise, living where you do and knowing the people you do, might have a try at getting the ban relaxed? I suppose the ban on *Ulysses* still holds.[3]

This is my last quarter of teaching before my annual vacation, and research period. I shall not be sorry to regain some leisure; but I wish I were clear in my mind which of two projects to pursue. I want to revise and complete my lectures of last spring on the novel, and move towards a book. I also want to bring out a critical edition of M. Arnold's first series of *Essays in Criticism.*[4] There are many interesting variants as between the four editions published in his lifetime, and also there is much to say about queer little errors of fact, and, what interests me most, no one has yet said what I think should be said about the art Arnold shows there. I hope I won't be like Buridan's ass.[5]

You applaud my idea of selling the property. That is good news. The thing is sold. All the property I now have is my mother's house in Toronto, which she left to me, and in which a respectable and undemanding tenant lives a blameless life. If I had any notion what to put my money in, I might take it out of the house; but I am quite at a loss. In this country money is losing its value fast — price control was never half as effective as in Canada, further it was attempted late, and has already gone in part — and yet the rates on investment are very low.

Let me dispel these somewhat gloomy thoughts by telling you that Deaver is on the verge of speech, and is interesting us more all the time. Peggy was somewhat astonished to find that our invaluable nurse has scraped an acquaintance with the nurse to a great granddaughter of old John D. Rockefeller, and that Deaver had lunch today in the Rockefeller nursery. The child's mother is here to study at the University. We trust that Deaver will not try to leave his class!

> Our warmest good wishes to you both,
> as ever,
> Edward

P.S. I have sent my article to Sylvestre. It will not be liked by some of the other contributors, but I think Pratt and Pelham will like it. It has nothing in it that I have not said before, except that I say I have not been generous enough to B. Carman.

142 [*Holo.*]

December 18, 1945

Dear Edward,

   Here is just a conventional card to give you & Peggy greetings.[1] This note is to warn you that Elise & I have sent a little gift for Deaver by Book Post & you may not get it in time for Christmas but surely in time for his birthday: it is a combination present. We thought the bright pictures wld attract his attention. We have been delayed with our holiday plans for we have both been rather ill with colds & that prevented all activities. My first ltr of the New Year shall be to you. I hope you wont be bothered by The Authorities & have to pay any duty on the book.

Yours ever,
Duncan

1946

The letters are quite frequent at the beginning and at the end of the year, but in the spring and summer the exchange falls off a bit. Scott remains the supplicant, protesting at the same time that Brown must write only when he has time to do so. Brown does not have much freedom of this kind. Compulsive in the area of scholarly communication, he publishes three articles and four reviews in the course of the year. He is well into the manuscript of the book on Arnold by the end of January, but the complex argument of this "study in conflict" will make claims on his time and energy for many months to come. From the beginning of July until the middle of August he teaches the summer session at Columbia University. By the end of the summer he has, in one of his articles, paid homage to Willa Cather, whose work he has come to admire; and a biography of Cather is in sight. He does not forget Scott, nor is his attention ever perfunctory, except perhaps when he suggests that Scott initiate plans for a commemorative stamp in honour of Lampman, a suggestion to which Scott does not respond. Scott is busy enough himself in the practice of his own craft. He writes the "brochure" on W.J. Phillips, labours over the design and composition of what will become The Circle of Affection *and puts the finishing touches on the selected Lampman. All three are in press by the end of the year. His "lines for Deaver," sent to the Browns in June, is a fine product of his mature art. The death of Deaver's grandfather in a car accident in September, to which Scott responds with deep concern, somehow tightens the cords of friendship between the poet and the critic. From October on, the correspondence is on track again. Perhaps Brown's greatest gift to Scott towards the year's end is John Watkins, the brilliant and charming career diplomat he introduces to the Scott household. Watkins' visits will be a boon to Scott in the closing months of his life.*

143

January 10, 1946

Dear Edward.   I would like to run through yours of Novr. 29th and make a few comments. I will watch for the issue of *Goriot,* in wh. I am doubly interested; it is one of my favorite Balzac's and this will be your version made for an ignorant chap who cannot read it in the original. We get here the Modern Library quite promptly. The gift to Trinity College culminated in an issue of the *Review* in wh. they printed the whole matter and gave a good reproduction of verses of 'April.'[1] They sent me only two copies and I felt I had to give one to Loftus, I hope Child sent you one; if he didn't I will get one for you. I cannot think that Pierce printed 1000 copies of Smith's book. You dignify my ill considered fling at *Poetry* as an "animadversion," I was influenced by their stupidity in choosing a reviewer of Pratt's book; they have restored the balance by asking you to do the de la Mare, wh. you will do excellently well; I shall try to see it. *Poetry* has its place, I dont forget their Canadian No. But I can find no consolation in much of Contemporary Art, either poetry, painting or music; occasionally I find a man who knows where he is going and how to get there; extremes of Painting and Music seem to be hopeless; Poetry seems to have the advantage. I enclose a copy of an extract I made from one of Mozart's letters in which that greatest of all musicians sums the matter up conclusively for me.[2] I note the two projects for your relief from teaching; both attract me and I would not attempt to influence you in either direction; but we must have the Arnold sooner or later. What may come of Deaver's contact with the Financial Magnate's Family, God alone knows. I hope he got his birthday book without causing you any trouble; if it did let me know and I wont do it again. Elise wants you to know that she has recd the two last vols of Proust from England and is now deep in them.

There is only one item of interest in my active literary life. You will recall the idea for a Vol. of prose and verse. I finally made up the copy and sent it to McC[lelland] and S[tewart] without any hope that they would be favorable to it; but much to my surprise I got a *very cordial* acceptance; the copy was not out of my hands for ten days. I feel that you were not very much taken with this idea, and you must be prepared for a disappointment as it is a mixed lot; but for better or worse and sooner or later you will have to pass upon it; there is only one thing that will give you comfort — you will not have to review it. I am gradually writing that booklet for Pierce on W.J. Phillips; Pierce shows a great indifference to it; weeks ago he said I am sending you a Contract but it has not yet come to hand; this firm has a desultory way of doing business.[3] I hope you will continue to write me during '46; I would miss your letters but I must not be a burden.[4] Elise joins in best wishes to you all for this year.

As ever yours sincerely,
Duncan

144

Chicago
January 15, 1946

Dear Duncan,

Not having any lectures to give has made me a worse instead of a better correspondent. I think this is just because I needed some time to get into a new routine. We want to thank you and Elise most warmly for the beautiful book. For the time being we keep it, and two other books that came at Christmas, out of Deaver's hands, for books at this time appear to be things to tear, rather than to look at. But a little later we shall give it to him. The favored toys are a small toy-car which he can carry even when he goes out for a walk, and a dilapidated and incredibly unsightly doll. You might be interested in one tale about the doll. It became so unsightly that Peggy tried to remedy the face by a couple of strokes of red and black at appropriate places. I have never seen Deaver so disturbed; and though he did not cry he was utterly unhappy till the strokes were removed. I took the occasion to point out to Peggy that Man's devotion to Woman is not quite so surface a thing as Woman often supposes. I think she is half convinced!

Child sent me a copy of the Trinity magazine. I think the thing was nicely done. I am specially glad they reproduced A.L.'s admirable script.

I am glad that McC and S dealt so quickly with you. You have perhaps taken my comments on your project more seriously than they were intended. I am glad of it: I simply thought that two volumes, one of verse and one of prose, would be even better. But the better is the enemy of the good; and I am delighted that we are to have more of your work in the convenience of book-form. I suppose that spring will be the time of publication.

You will probably be out before the Goriot. At least I have no more news of that book. There is nothing left for me to do to speed its appearance.

I have finished the draft of the de la Mare article — a short one — and shall lay it aside for a couple of days before a final revision. I had never read the *Memoirs of a Midget*.[1] I did so, and thought it a most real as well as most charming work. I had not known that he could handle a *long* thing as masterly as this is done. And the style is d.l. M. at his very best, I thought. It has less of the sinister undertone than most of his things, though this is not absent.

Before I turned to the d.l. M. I had written about 10,000 words on Arnold, and think I have at least as many left in me. I shall go back to it at once. I am having the happy experience, one of the happiest a critic can have, of finding that my central idea is throwing light on things I did not have in mind when I formed it. This gives one a reassuring sense that one is not having a pipe dream, but is instead really seeing into the author's consciousness. I am hoping that I won't run dry at 20,000, but may get a short book. It is still too soon to tell. Meanwhile all ideas about the novel are laid aside.

I hear that one of my prettiest ex-students has married the son of poor Henry,[2] W.L.M.K.'s secretary. I hope that the son is not such a beaten being as his father. I seldom felt sorrier for any one. Do you know him?

A.L.'s Keats was to be in the *UTQ* for January; but I judge there has been a change of plan, for I have not had proof. I am sorry, and the sorrier because it cannot be in April, where I must be represented by the survey of the year's poetry.[3]

We must not let our correspondence languish in the new year. It has opened very well for me, with mild days and many thoughts. What a blessing that I don't have the worries or the sense of hemming in that I suffered from at Cornell. I hope that you threw off the cold that you had before Christmas. Have you access to the kind of injection against some kinds of flu which the Americans developed in the war? Many of our friends have taken it, and it is said to offer complete immunity to about 75 per cent of the "injectees." We have not taken it. I find that so long as I don't have wet socks I seldom get any kind of respiratory trouble. And I am a real old woman about wet socks.

Our love to you both, and our thanks on behalf of the illiterate member of the family.

As ever,
Edward

P.S. [*holo.*] Has Pelham gone to the coast? Do give my best wishes to him; and to Brockington if you still have him in Ottawa.

145

February 23, 1946

My Dear Edward.   It is more than a month since I recd your last letter and that looks like neglect; as one of my chief pleasures is to hear from you I must do my part in such fashion as I can. Will you allow a few remarks on items in your last? Does Deaver's affection for the original face of his doll foreshadow that he will always be constant to his first loves? We were amused at your account of his dislike. As for my projected book I have heard nothing since I last wrote; this is not quite correct for I had a ltr from John McC's[1] secretary warning me not to expect anything "too immediately;" dont you like that phrase? I have learned that the difficulty all the Toronto publishers are facing is Binding; in fact my firm has had to go to Vancouver to get some of their binding done. As for the Staff of Our Peerless Leader, I heard sometime ago that shortly after Turnbull[2] left there was a mild strike and he slackened somewhat in his exactions. I hope the A.L. Keats will come before long; I consider the April No. with its review important so that I can agree with the postponement. Did you note that the tenth of this month was the 46th anniversary of L's death; the general aspect of *this* tenth was almost a copy of that and the succeeding days, brilliant sunshine and intense cold. I have not tried any innoculations for Colds and dont intend to; I propose to enjoy them as they come along, but we have both been fairly well. A domestic crisis has arisen for our maid the faithful Ann[3] is marrying a returned soldier and we have to find a substitute wh. may be difficult; this piece of information is more for Peggy than for you. As for Pelham — he has not gone to the Coast and there seems to be no immediate possibility of his change. I feel sympathetic for him for many reasons wh. I cant elaborate here; he was in Toronto the other day and saw Ned and some of his old pals, but in this Can. Authors Foundation he has raised up a sort of Problem wh. is vexing; to think that the Govt is going to give us a grant is visionary, and if they dont, we shall have to depend on private subs. I gave him and Brock. your messages. The latter has been away so much lately that I have not seen much of him; how he stands the travel with all his disabilities[4] and keeps up his constant cheerfulness seems to me heroic.

You will know from this writing that I am not in custody as a Spy; our papers are full of it;[5] and it wld be quite a waste of time to give you any of the rumors, or my own reactions to it all. The only name I have heard mentioned is Poland[6] who was in the Ex[ternal] Affairs. Did you know him? I am making progress with my MAGNUM OPUS: I sent the biographical part to Phillips who was very pleased with it and I have completed the part dealing with his Water-Colours, now follow his Wood engravings and his Colour-wood-cuts. I have not heard from L.P. since he told me on Nov. 16th that he was forwarding a contract; I intend to write him soon and find out whether another author is writing the booklet; but I must not be hard on him or his firm; he is a charatable soul, without him Pelham and his schemes wld be lost in Toronto. Has Dilworth sent you a copy of his Anthology? If you have it not I will send you a copy.

I do my usual haphazard reading. Now I am going through the two vols of Thackery's letters wh. have been issued of the four projected.[7] They were sent to me by Norman Smith Jr.[8] of the *Journal*. The most interesting of those I pick out are those to his mother and to Fitz. These letters deal with the tragic loss of his wife; and the hand of Fate is visible when you know of T's daughter Harriet as the wife of Leslie Stephen and the mother of Virginia Woolf. All these early letters show Thackery's big heart and his consideration for all his connections. It is amusing to find him bargaining with his publishers and asking his friends for good notices of his books. The Lit Sup lately had a long article on J.W. Mackail and that led me to get his life of W. Morris.[9] I was as much interested in him and his friends as I ever was and that as you know is a great deal. What a noble fine fellow Morris was. His verse and designs may have gone out of fashion; but not for me. I found a quotation from him in Mackail, where he describes the monks working on the West Front of Peterborough Cathedral, wh. I intend to drag into my travel note on seeing the monks working on Buckfast Abbey when we were going to Dean Prior.[10] But I shall give Morris credit for it. I notice a tendency in our contemporaries to use quotations from well known passages in other writers without even quotation marks. There are several instances in this book of Mackail's. One I remember from M. Arnold, the well known words about

Oxford;[11] but the most flagrant is the closing para. where he quotes those beautiful words from the margin of 'The Ancient Mariner' about the stars entering their appointed rest — as lords, etc.[12] It makes a very lovely close to the book but Coleridge gets no credit for it; the ignorant might think it was written by Mackail. I am glad you are making progress with the Arnold. Write me again before long and do not lay it up against me that I have been so lazy in answering your last; and I send our love to you three, with the largest share to Deaver.

As ever yours,
Duncan

146

[Chicago]
March 27, 1946

Dear Duncan,

I am back to teaching this week, after my months of trying to blacken paper as fast as possible, and eager to answer your long and most interesting letter. We had a very fine week in northern Kentucky (minus Deaver), our first sight of the southern states. The spring was so far on there that we felt as if it were Toronto in May. The magnolias and many of the fruit trees were in full splendor. We made the acquaintance of smoked ham, kept two years before serving, and took to it. The beauty of the Greek-colonnades was a thing of wonder. We have seen nothing else in the U.S. so interesting. Yet Kentucky was just a pioneer settlement, and we now want to see something of the Carolinas and Virginia.

We were both relieved to note the absence of your name from the list of soviet lovers and hope that you have preserved no record of your long distance communications with Moscow. I am sorry to see so many foreign born people involved, or children of the foreign born; this may lead to a kind of super-nationalism, especially if your friends, the followers of John A., come in again. I do not see why there was such reluctance to deal with the matter. According to Percy Philip in the *Times* it was very hard for the cipher clerk to get a hearing, from any Canadian official, and finally he had to go to the city police.

Despite the warning not to expect anything "too immediately" I hope that you will by now have heard something from McC and S. I am eager to see the book. I have had an odd experience about publishing which might amuse you. In 1936 Macmillan's in Toronto brought out an anthology I had prepared from Arnold's prose. This last fall because of the paper shortage they refused to run a new edition; and I brought one out with the Manitoba press. I wanted to take out the copyright in my own name; and learned that despite the statement that the first edition was copyrighted (which appears in the usual place) it never was. This is a thought to strike a sort of terror into one. It had never occurred to me that a publisher could slip on a thing like that.[1]

I have completed the survey of poetry for the year. I thought Frank Scott's volume the most interesting of the year.[2] But there were other very good things, Charles Bruce,[3] very attractive indeed, and some of Anne Marriott's[4] good, but I don't think she is growing as I had once hoped. I believe she is in Ottawa now. I never met her. I noticed Dilworth's book so far as it concerned Canada. It should do great good. The Canadian poets needed an anthology in which they might stand side by side with the Americans and the English. I also liked his notes. Perhaps the introduction is a trifle "vague." In general I liked his selections from the Canadian poets, though I cannot easily spare, among your shorter pieces, 'The Onondaga Madonna'. I was delighted to see 'The Forsaken' and the Air Force Hymn. The A.L. selections differed from those I would have made, but I liked them. I think he might have spared another page for A.L.

Did you ever think of issuing a selection from your work, I mean a volume of about the size of Arnold's selection from his poetry.[5] Say 100 or 125 good sized pages? I think there might be an advantage in this. Undoubtedly it did Arnold a great deal of good.

What you said about the Thackeray volumes was most interesting. I feel really guilty that I have not yet read the letters; I shall get to them some time this spring. I have been reading a Meredith novel with much pleasure, *Harry Richmond.*[6] It seems much more straightforward and more vigorous than any I can now call to mind. I have also been reading Harrold's new book on Newman,[7] but do not find it does much more than recapitulate what was already said, and said in more satisfying prose by others.

I have been asked to review Hilton Brown's book on Kipling,[8] for the *Yale,* and have agreed, perhaps incautiously, for I have never been a Kipling reader, and shall have to turn to.

This quarter my courses are on Browning, and on the structure of fiction, both favorites of mine, and the classes look alert and pleasant. It is good to see the pre-war ratio of men back; my groups are half and half, which is the way I like them.

Deaver was photographed the other day, and when the results come Peggy says I may have one for you. He is a winning child, and we have been lucky in having for so much of the time a nurse of the best sort. We were very sorry to hear you were about to lose your admirable maid, whom we remember. Poor Woodhouse has not been able to get any help except a cleaning woman, and his mother is of your age, and suffers from pains in the legs. It almost seems as if the age of any sort of domestic help was over. Do you recall Ruskin's remark in *Unto this Last* that money is of no use unless it assures you some power over the time of some one else? Otherwise the man with possessions is worse off than the man without them, for possessions take time and energy to maintain.

I was delighted to know you were so well on with the work on WJP. If you write him, will you tell him of my kindly and grateful memories of him and his family last summer?

> With our love to you both,
> Yours, as ever,
> Edward

P.S. [*holo.*] Your remark on the P.M.'s staff was illuminating. I don't care for Pickersgill[9] as a person but am sorry for him because I can't see where he can land after WLMK departs. He has made many enemies in External Affairs, where his job theoretically is. Have you seen the severe remarks on the Royal Society in Brebner's little book *Scholarship for Canada?*[10]

147 [*Holo.*]

> April 14, 1946

Dear Peggy,[1]

You have an adorable boy and we fell in love with him at the first glance. We think he has his mother's enchanting smile and his father's serious brow. He will have something to give the world from that noble strong head.

I have not followed the Truman family exploits. We have enough commonness here. But our new Gov. General's wife is already reported to be well dressed.[2] No Governor General's wife will ever equal Lady Bessborough[3] in charm or in "clothes." Mackenzie King continues to be the best dressed man in Canada, "our Peerless Leader," and he has lately proved himself capable of rising to unexpected heights of passion and indignation. Our spys seem to be all in duress and are being sentenced one by one. We hope to see you all in Ottawa before dear Deaver grows up. Elise joins me in many thanks for the Photo and in best wishes to you all.

> Yours very sincerely,
> Duncan C. Scott

148

> May 1, 1946

Dear Edward.   I begin this month with the good intention of writing you a long and very interesting letter and I hope that not many days of the month will lapse before I send it to you. When we got Deaver's photo I wrote at once to Peggy to tell you how much we admired him and how loveable he was; he must be a great joy to you. Not long ago I got from Hardy the *Yale R.* for winter and we have both enjoyed your article on James and Conrad. I am on the Conrad side and I think Elise is too; she had been dipping into James lately without much pleasure and my days for reading him are past but I offer no criticism, you have done for him pretty finally; and there are certain things of Conrad that are firmly established in my liking. I note you were reading *Harry Richmond;* I wonder if it held its interest to the last. Looking back over my Meredith period that was my favorite novel; but I dont think I could tackle it now, simple as it is comparatively; my jaded old head asks something rather short, uncomplicated and masterly if I am to read fiction at all; and for this combination I have to go back to the past; I wish you would write me a novel on this specification. I notice your remark about your review of the year's poetry; Anne Marriott is here in the film board and I heard that she was working hard there; we have not seen her because we dont float about in her pool; she is I know delicate and I have not expected any great development although I would wish for it.[1] Birney has gone to the English Dept of B.C. University, whether as head of the Dept or not I dont know,[2] Edgar has written him and will probably have news. As for my own small events, I chronicle that the W.J.P. book is finished much to his satisfaction and mine as to getting it off my hands. As the Ryerson Press has allocated all its paper for '46 the booklet wont be out this year. Apropos of the R.P. I enclose a clipping re Hatchards. You will be interested to know that I have a poem in Noyes' *Anthology of Catholic Poetry;* he wanted some poems by those he called non-catholics and asked for 'Compline,'[3] I did not know that it had been included until I got a royalty from McC & S the other day; Noyes said he would send me a copy of the book but it has not arrived; after all that is a good deal to expect and I never thought of it. I have been reading with much pleasure Bush's book in *The Oxford History of English Literature.*[4] The sections wh. gave me most pleasure were Jonson, Donne etc., and Milton. In the section I mention I was pleased with his references to Vaughan as if I had met an old friend; I cannot tell why this poet has so appealed to me from my earliest reading, and I am not called upon to do so.[5] Herrick I liked, and Donne. He might have dated the beginning of Donne's influence before 20-25, on p. 135, because I remember well Rupert Brooke in 1913 telling me what an influence he was and how he had influenced his own work.[6] Perhaps that influence (too many "influences" here) would be hard to trace now, in the work of the Georgians. I got Brebner's pamphlet and read what he had to say about the R.S. but he expects too much from such a body and does not do justice to what the Soc'y is doing. I wonder what your friend Woodhouse thought of it; he is one of the worth while members of my Section. Looking over the membership and counting the names in Sec II I find that 58 are professors at Canadian universities and 20 non-academics; in the other Sections (except the French Sec) the proportion is still greater.[7] This is I suppose to be expected but one would think that there were more than 20 persons who would qualify on the score of authorship alone. If I read Brebner carefully I would probably agree with much that he says about the subject. And this Conference on Taxes they are holding now fills one with foreboding;[8] this Govt has got us into a financial impasse and I dont see how we can meet our obligations, however all that I can do is to pay with the rest of the victims. I send you a clipping from last night's

Journal.[9] There will not be many in the number of the quality of you and Bush but we have lost you alas!

As for this proposed new book of mine, it is still quietly reposing in the publisher's hands. I got the MS back to make some changes and inquired what progress had been made, as to format etc. The lady who coined the phrase "too immediately" replied that the MS had been in the printer's hands and wrote "I shall be very happy to keep you informed about any progress which takes place, directly it becomes apparent. We will hope for the best." I think this lady should be in Mac. King's private office. I have thought sometimes of making a selection of my poems but will never do it; and I dont think that anyone else will; there is so much that I should like to drop; but I dont think you would like some of my inclusions; your choice wld be of immense help; but I cant think of it now. We both like your James and Conrad and your task in the Kipling will be accomplished; I shall be on the lookout for it.

Our domestic problems seem to have been solved by Divine Intervention, our new maid is named Celestine, and I hope she wont vanish to her natural home in the Sky "too immediately." I find it somewhat difficult to accomodate my memory to the new name and have called her Celophane and Clytemnestra (why the latter comes into my mind I cant explain), but so far so good: she moves with angelic swiftness and silence. We hope she'll remain on our spot of earth for sometime. An item of first rate musical importance [was] the Opera B'cast of the new work, words by Coulter, music by Willan;[10] it is truly very fine and I so praised it to Frigon that he sent me the Gramophone Album with Willan's Piano Concerto which they have issued for their International Service.[11] I think I have bothered you long enough so I say I am ever yours, [*holo.*] and with love from us both to Deaver, Peggy & you.

Duncan

149

June 10, 1946

Dear Edward.   I am glad you sent me the review of *The Burning Glass,*[1] otherwise I might not have seen another of your good things; there is always something distinctive in your criticism that is new and invigorating. I like particularly the close of this article. You had the whole of his work in mind, I cannot claim that knowledge. You are rather discouraging to one who approaches his 84th, but I do not anticipate the end of all things and have never felt it approaching; I think my trust in Music has much to do with my outlook but that would be hard to explain to you and I wont attempt it. I was absorbed with the poem 'The Vision' on p. 90;[2] it seems to me a summing up of his inner feeling and is for me important. Then I have always got more out of the mystical side of de la Mare, e.g. in such things as 'Said Flores';[3] 'The Blind Boy'[4] has exquisite sensation and the closing verse tells much of what I might try to say about sound in Music. The book as you say is full of beauties. What a different task you have in the review of Kipling; I have read Hilton Brown's book and will watch the *Yale R*. wh. I get from Hardy.

As you have no doubt read the enclosed lines before you have read my letter you may be seeking for some special explanation not for writing the lines for Deaver but for sending them just now. I would like to include in the Miscellany some verses I had written for children and Deaver must be there.[5] Unless you and Peggy have any objection I would print them in the book on which progress is not yet apparent. I send a copy of the Table of Contents so that you may see the arrangement. 'Deepwood' is the name of Arthur Bourinot's summer place at Kingsmere;[6] the Bach piece is addressed to Ethel Bartlet and Ray Robertson,[7] who first played this for me in London when it had just been arranged for two pianos for them. Of course this list of contents will not mean much to you, but it will expose the extent of the proposed book and will not be likely to restore your confidence.

Walter Phillips has been here for a few days and I was able to give them your message; they said they were delighted with your visit and sorry that there seemed no time to see more of you.

We send our love to you three and as ever

I am yours sincerely,
Duncan

[*P.S. holo.*] Of course in copying the poem I had to make an error in copying Deaver's name merely thro' nervousness.

D.

150

Chicago
June 11, 1946

Dear Duncan,

Peggy and I are deeply touched by your beautiful poem for Deaver. I read it to her over the telephone from my office as soon as I received it, and she was so delighted she asked me to read it again so that the great beauty of detail could begin to come through. This is one piece by which I cannot do my duty as the detached and impartial critic, but I am sure that if I could I would place it among the purest triumphs in your work. It will always be a unique treasure for us, and, we trust, for Deaver as he comes to know it. I read it to him in the evening; he stood absolutely still and listened very intently; and he seemed to appreciate that it was in some special sense related to him. The poor boy was miserable all last week with laryngitis; but he is now well again, although still unnaturally pale from being indoors so many days.

On the wall of my study, just over the section of a book case devoted to Wordsworth and Keats, hangs the poem 'These are in the beginning' which you addressed to me on 18.1.41. I am wondering if you would write out the poem to Deaver, and we would then have it in its most personal form to hang in his room.

The table of contents of your forthcoming book — I hope that forthcoming is not too optimistic — is very attractive. I very much like the idea of including a few of the really early pieces, so that they can stand beside the recent ones. Several of the poems, two of the stories, and the RSC address[1] are old friends of mine, and I shall be very happy when they come out in new attire, and together. Canadian publishers appear to become slower and slower. I heard of a book yet to appear at the U. of T. press, on which the author was reading proof almost two years ago!

I am delighted to think that you found something in the article on de la Mare. I made that point about his most recent things being not quite so good as some of the earlier ones because I wanted to make higher claims for him than this last volume taken by itself would support. Many of the readers of *Poetry* are young, and I was afraid that if they were to judge him solely by *The Burning Glass* he would not matter to them as much as I think he should. He has less thought than most poets I care for, and I think that an older poet who is not strong in thought is likely to be disappointing. I have said before now that I think this is one reason why the later poems of Roberts do not satisfy as much as some of the earlier ones.

The Kipling review is very brief; I was held down to rather narrow limits. It should appear one of these days. I have sent another of last year's lectures on the novel to a magazine, *College English,* and it is due to appear in the fall.[2] I believe that I shall have reprints this time. One will surely go to you. It is entitled: "Two Formulas for Fiction: Henry James and H.G. Wells."

I have been adding to the ms. on Matthew Arnold, and think I can now see my way to the end of the book although I shall not have it in shape for a publisher before Christmas. But it is very reassuring to know for certain at last what the end will be. Parts of the book sound severe; but I think the total effect will be to make Arnold seem a more interesting person, to whom one feels closer, and for whom one has sympathy. I am deriving much pleasure from this work.

Your remark about the place that music plays in your thought is tantalizing. But perhaps you do well not to explain it to me, for in music I am scarcely even a novice. Of all the arts I am most lost when it comes to music. I was fearful in writing even what little I did about it when I did the chapter on you; but I felt that it would be impossible to omit all reference to music. I envy you your intimacy and knowledge.

We are coming to Toronto towards the end of the month. How we wish you were there! It will be the first time Deaver has travelled since he was a small infant. I shall be there only three or four days and must then go to New York to begin my teaching at Columbia. Peggy will stay a while longer. My address all summer (till Aug. 20) will be Department of English, Columbia University, New York, 27. I am greatly looking forward to being in New York for so long: I have never had more than a few days at a time in earlier visits.

Our love to you both, and our thanks for your devotion to Deaver. If we are not mistaken, he is an unusually gentle and good child (though with an iron will beneath this) and we could not hope for anything finer for him than that he should justify your love.

Yours, as ever,
Edward

P.S. [*holo.*] I was delighted to hear of your fine progress with the W.J. Phillips book — and also interested you saw them again. I liked them very much and they were very warm and kind to me.

151

June 18, 1946

Dear Edward.   I had very keen pleasure in reading your last in which you and Peggy accepted my lines to Deaver, what I would have felt or done if you had rejected them I cannot say. As you wanted me to write out a copy for him I thought I shd do it at once and send it before you left for your journeys and here it is. I took great care with it for the poet of The Golden Age has to form each letter with his pen; the lines I sent *you* were I'm afraid very badly written for I did not think of you preserving them. The lines to Deaver came very naturally and without any fussy reconsideration. I was interested in your description of his attitude in hearing them, and cld make a picture of the group. Poor Deaver, I know laryngitis is very weakening but I hope the change of air will put him strong again, and that T. will be kind to Peggy too. You are having a very interesting life and I wld like to be in N.Y. for awhile or go to T. to have a look at you; but all these places are equally inaccessible to me now. You will note that the "Gloves" have arrived,[1] and I thank you for the reference, I cld understand it pretty well but Elise who reads French translated it for me. But nothing wld induce her to translate the long portions dealing with the real Poets. We attended the Massey wedding[2] and at the Chateau reception I was hailed by the redoubtable J.F. Pouliot in a loud tone of voice, "Here is my favourite Canadian Poet;" he assembled a group and repeated the announcement; I felt as if I had been crowned by the French Academy.[3]

I note the N.Y. address, drop me a line if you feel like it and I will write if I have anything important to say wh. wld be unusual. We will both be interested in the Arnold, but do not be severe on him; keep your severity for the writers, or some of them, of contemporary verse; but I add that there were a few things in *Poetry* that I liked. We had Anne Marriott here last week, a pleasant girl, but without enough mental energy to put her forward; I am ever surprised how little these poets know of English poetry and the literature appertaining to it; she had never read Hopkins' letters, and expressed some curiosity about them; I told her I thought them amongst the best letters written by an English Poet and told her I wld ask Hardy to let her have them. Noyes' Anthology is in the house but it seems a mis-title; it is a collection of Poems *written* by Catholics and an addition of non-catholics; there is some very fine verse in the book including my 'Compline,' wh. stands up well with selections from Shakespeare, Tennyson and others but then they also belong to The Golden Age. I wish sometime Peggy wld write me whether this nonsense annoys you and I wld refrain, as I shd from writing such long letters. My love to you both and to Dear Deaver and I wish you a successful trip and due power in your lectures.

Yours ever,
Duncan

152 [*Holo.*]

Toronto[1]
July 1, 1946

Dear Duncan,

A word of greeting and thanks. Your autograph copy of the poem to Deaver came to us before we left Chicago and was securely lodged in a file to await our return. In your bold calligraphy it is very handsome and will look fine on our walls.

Ned Pratt came for lunch today and was modestly happy in his *CMG,* an order and a rank in which — if my memory serves — he joins you.[2] We spoke of you affectionately and admiringly, as always.

Please give my felicitations to Brockington when you see him. I leave tomorrow for New York and will write a proper letter when I overtake my typewriter there.

Peggy joins me — and Deaver would — in all kind wishes to you both.

Yours, as ever,
Edward

153 [*Holo.*]

[Toronto]
July 6, 1946

Dear Mr. Scott —

I am enclosing a souvenir from the Ryerson Press dinner.[1] We sat at the head table, and in 99 degree heat I was wedged between Lorne Pierce and a doctor who'd lost his hearing in the ear adjoining me! To complete the gala occasion the firm's president, one Mr. Dickinson (?)[2] introduced those present and refused (at whose request?) to make a speech, as he spent 15 minutes advising the authors to "Keep it clean, boys!"

I think Edward has told you how delighted I was at the nicest thing that has ever happened to Deaver — your poem. We were both deeply honoured that you would write it and of course most charmed with its beauty and the image you used.

I am afraid Deaver wasn't greatly impressed. He prefers Little Jack Horner, *especially* the last line which he thinks is written *about* him. No modesty at two. Edward writes that he has very nice quarters at Columbia. I hope they will be cool. With my kindest regards to Mrs. Scott and yourself.

Most sincerely yours,
Peggy

154 [*Holo.*]

Butler Hall
88 Morningside Drive
New York 27
July 31, 1946

Dear Duncan,

My warmest greetings on your birthday. I remember how happily you said everything went off last year and hope this year will be as pleasant. I wish we could be with you in Ottawa as in 1942.

I sent a copy of the article on de la Mare to the subject and have had a most kind and "happy" letter in reply. He said he would like to read other "literary studies" of mine so I sent a copy of *On Canadian Poetry* and specially directed his attention to the chapter on you, with the remark that I believed your poems would have a special attraction for him.

I read proof on A.L.'s "Keats" two weeks ago and believe it will appear in the (delayed) July number of the *Quarterly*. I asked that two offprints be sent directly to you — apart from some to go to T.R.L.M.

I am having a good though extremely busy time and am glad that I came. But the purpose of this note is not to describe my doings, but just to wish you everything good on your birthday.

Yours, as ever,
Edward

155

August 8, 1946

My Dear Edward.   Many, many thanks for your good wishes; they arrived in the afternoon mail on the second, and joined some others but none more thought of than yours. I am sure you were joined by Peggy and Deaver. I had a delightful note from her in early July sending me the menu of the C.A.A. dinner.[1] We enjoyed that day and in the evg had some few friends, fewer than last year, for dinner at the C.C.[2] Really it was very nice and I wish you two cld have been with us. I had rather expected a typed letter from you following a remark in your last wh. you have properly forgotten, for you must not be burdened by this correspondence when you are so importantly busy, so dont think of writing me until you are quite at leisure. I was anxious to write you for I felt that I was too casual in my reference to your article in *G du C*. I did completely appreciate your reference to me as you must have known. I thought the issue was so remarkable that I was moved to send a note to Sylvestre, a copy of wh. I send you. He sent me a very cordial note in reply. I am glad to hear of your letters to and from de la Mare; I hope he knows the importance of *O.C.P.* and it was entirely like you to direct his attention to *my* Section. I was incited by your review to look up his collected poems and have had rare pleasure in many of the things there, but I cannot load this letter with titles. It comes in naturally here to mention one of my birthday congratulations, and I send you a copy of the letter I had from Masefield.[3] I did not copy the heading giving the Vice-Presidents but they are so many of the men I admire, including de la Mare, that I mention a few: Augustus John, Vaughan Williams, G.M. Trevelyan; Geoffrey Faber is the Chairman,[4] I met him when he was here. Masefield in writing gave me a Knighthood, dubbing me Sir Duncan, but I had to disown that honour. But dont you think the letter is very flatteringly worded? I shall send them a copy of Karsh's photo of this battered countenance, it will surprise Masefield I think who has probably never seen my visage.[5]

I got a copy of the *U. of T. Quarterly* with the Keats and shall be glad to have offprints; I sent this copy to Loftus to read. You certainly did a good deed in having this published; what good prose Lampman wrote; the whole thing, including your admirable introducing note, is fine; it seems to give A.L. a solid background; there was *mind* there and a great endowment of imagination; if he had lived to gather experience he wld have gone far; but I have said all this before.

Pratt sent me a warm note in response to mine sending him our congratulations on his C.M.G. and I gave Brockington your message wh. pleased him much. And in Ned's letter he mentioned his liking for the lines to Deaver wh. I was glad to read. My publisher has gone into the ranks of the Seven Sleepers, and I have heard nothing from them. Nor from the Great Pierce about the Phillips book; in fact that firm seems in a muddle; but I suppose they will pull through. Pelham is in P.E.I. with his family and I had a letter from him on the Second wh. read as if it had been written from Paradise; such a combination of golf, bathing, bridge, can never occur again; he sent me a description of a sunset wh. he said was worthy of Turner. I am glad they are enjoying it so much for Pelham has worked very hard and needed a rest; I think he will spend another winter here but he has said nothing definite about that. The Govt has given the Writers' Foundation a grant of $2500.00.

Have I tired you? Do not think of writing me at length until you are free of all these extra duties.[6]

Yours ever,
Duncan

156 [Holo.]

August 9

Dear Edward.   I was just on the point of supplementing mine of yesterday when I was delightfully interrupted by a Birthday Card from Deaver: now this was most thoughtful of him! I enjoyed it & I had affectionate thoughts of Peggy & of him — will you say so when you write. An omission in my ltr was no mention of "Goriot" & whether we cld expect it soon. I send a clipping from today's Montreal *Gazette*.[1]

Yours ever,
Duncan

[P.S.] You need not return that note I sent Sylvestre.

157

Butler Hall
88 Morningside Drive
New York 27
August 21, 1946

Dear Duncan,

I was delighted to hear how pleasantly your anniversary had gone. What a fine thing it is to have been born in mid-summer, not in November or February.

It was good to know that as you read the "Keats," in print, the idea of its publication still appealed to you as a sound one. I do not know how much good such steps may do now, but in the end people will be grateful that these essays of A.L. are available. It is rather saddening that so little interest is taken at the time.

Mention of A.L. reminds me of an idea which came to me a couple of weeks ago when I happened in the Sunday *N.Y. Times* to look at the "stamp" page, where there was a display of the new series of Canadian stamps. Would it not be a very nice thing if in 1949 a stamp were issued to honor A.L.? His long years in the Post Office make the idea specially appropriate. Now if you agree, I think that you would be more likely to succeed than any one else in approaching authority. Mulock[1] is an illiterate, but he might be interested. Perhaps Brockington would care to speak to him. I would be glad to write to Turnbull[2] if you thought it wise.

My own offprints have not come yet. I trust that they and yours and MacInnes's will come in due time. Mine may be in Chicago, of course.

I was touched by your generous praise of me in your letter to Sylvestre. It was like you.

My main undertaking this summer has been to do an article on Willa Cather (who will be 70 this December) for the *Yale Review*. It is six years since she published a book, and she is so much out of the public eye that I thought an article of homage would be appropriate.[3] I have always liked her fiction, and I found that it stood rereading very well indeed.

To be in New York for several weeks has been a pleasant experience. That was why I came — not for the teaching, which is conducted in classes so large that one does not feel that much is accomplished. Perhaps things are better in the regular sessions — I hope so. The weather has been extraordinarily moderate; and since my tasks were not too onerous, I do not feel tired at all. Chicago seems like an aggregation of small towns after New York; but I miss our green in this city of pavement. Chicago has not been so avaricious of space, and almost everywhere there are at least small lawns, and there are also boulevards, and the green rests the spirit.

To-morrow I am going to New Haven to spend a few days looking at the Yale collection of Arnold manuscripts, much the best in the world, and something I have long wanted to see. I will then come back here for a few days, and may go home via Toronto, I am not sure.

My congratulations on the honor which came via Masefield, and which you will, I think, enjoy.

> All best wishes to you both,
> As ever,
> Edward

P.S. [*holo.*] The *Goriot* is now expected to appear in September, but I shall not believe in its appearance till I see a copy. I hope Pierce has awakened from his midsummer sleep & McClelland also. I am very eager to see those books.

158

August 24, 1946

Dear Edward.   Your letter arrived yesterday aft. just as we were starting to see C. and Cleopatra[1] with the Brockingtons. When I read your possibility of going home via T. I thought at once that you shd come here on your way; and Elise tells me to issue a very cordial invitation for you to stay with us. Cant you manage to do that? It wld give us so much pleasure.

You will be surprised to know that Pierce came to life, and I have just sent back the gallies of the little book; I hope you may like it. I will not write any more now but I shall be hopeful of seeing you.

Yours ever,
Duncan

159

Butler Hall,
88 Morningside Drive
New York 27
August 27, 1946

Dear Duncan,

When I returned from New Haven last evening I found your kind note, and it made me very sorry that I had not told you earlier of my plan to return via Toronto.

I have already made plans for the 29th, the day I am to arrive there, which cannot be postponed, since some of the people I have to see will be leaving for the long Labour Day week-end, and not returning till I myself expect to leave for Chicago. It would give me great pleasure indeed, to have a couple of days with you, and it is very kind of you and Elise to ask me, but this time I cannot make it.

It was good to hear that Pierce has come to life, and I shall be looking for the book on W.J.P. I wish there were equally good news from McClelland. I am sure the W.J.P. will be out before the Goriot.

Arnold's notebooks were of the greatest interest, especially one long piece in which he reflects, communes with himself, about some of the ideas which he later put into the preface of 1853.[1] I think the communings are even more interesting than the great preface. I tried to persuade my friend at Yale, Chauncey Tinker,[2] to edit the notebook containing this passage, and I think I succeeded. It would interest you a great deal, I know.

In the next week or so I am to be something of a dental cripple, but I shall feel happier when the dreadful work is done. So you won't miss much in not seeing me just now.

I send a snap of Deaver, not because it is a good one, but because it shows him entering the "little boy" phase, and gave me quite a start.

Yours, as ever,
Edward

160

[September 9], 1946[1]

Dear Edward.   It was a disappointment but we had to bear it, and we hope
that someday you will come. This is just a note and I will not touch on some
matters that need comment. We were delighted to get the Snap of Deaver wh.
gives an idea of his ''growing up,'' I want to keep track of him from year to year
and I have put this with the first, no it was the second, and shall keep them (3)
together. I got my two ''off-prints'' and they look very well in their covers; I
gave one to Brockington; if he makes any remarks on reading it I shall report.
How he stands this life of his I cannot fathom; constant travel, ever dealing with
rough problems, and determined labor people. I do hope the dental operations go
on without much trouble. After a while I'll write you another letter. Pelham
returned from The Island enchanted; he ought to make a study now of Hunter
Duvar.[2]

Our best to you both,
Yours ever,
Duncan

161

Chicago
September 26, 1946

Dear Duncan,

I am glad I did not plan on a visit in Ottawa, for the very morning of my arrival
in Toronto I had the sad news of the death in Minneapolis of Peggy's father, and
of serious injuries to her mother in the same motor accident. I left at once, and
was with Peggy in Minneapolis for a week or so during which her mother made
very excellent improvement. I then came back here, and after another week
Peggy returned also. We are very hopeful about her mother, but shall not be
without anxiety so long as she is in the hospital.

Deaver will not remember his grandfather at all, I believe. My father died
when I was three years and nine months old; and the earliest memory I have is of
nine months before his death; a memory I can date because it involves a
row-boat, and a pier, as well as my father. Deaver last saw his grandfather last
February when he was just over two.

Peggy takes comfort in the fact that her father (who was 77) would have been
helpless to occupy himself if he were not able to be at his business and that before
long he would have been obliged to give up being active in it. He was a very
remarkable man — much more of the type that flourished in the northwest in the
generation before his own than of any type I have known. He had absolutely no
civic sense: all taxation was robbery etc., and the J.S. Mill idea that to do best for

oneself was ultimately to do the best for others. I do not think he had more than two or three friends in his whole life; and they were rather business associates than friends. You can imagine that his old age would not be a happy one.

Peggy has borne up very well indeed. I hope that after a while when her mother is out of the hospital I can persuade Peggy to take a trip for a change of scene; but that cannot be before Christmas, I think.

This is not a proper letter; but I have had so many to write in connection with Mr. Deaver's death that I must wait a while before I can really gather my thoughts together.

I was delighted to see your W.J.P. book listed in the fall Ryerson list, and that its excellence has led to a replanning of the series. I am betting that it will be out before the Goriot. Perhaps you would be interested in the article I did on Willa Cather which is in the autumn *Yale Review*. I think it is perhaps more personal, partly because it has less intellectual complexity to treat, than most of my fiction articles. What time I have had this past month I have given to writing the conclusion to the Arnold book, but it is not yet done.

Our love to you and Elise. Deaver is now finding a lot of pleasure in the book you sent him at Christmas.

As ever,
Edward

P.S. An old friend and classmate of mine, John Watkins, is now for a couple of months in Ottawa, being broken in by External Affairs, before he is sent to Scandinavia. He is prodigiously well read in late 19th c. literature, and a very likeable person. I did not suggest to him that he call on you, but if you happen to feel like seeing him I am sure he would be very pleased.[1]

162

September 29, 1946

My Dear Edward,

Yours of the 26th came by the last post yesterday and I write you at once; your news made us very sorrowful and we send our sympathy to Peggy for her loss and anxiety; this sympathy is sent in no conventional terms but truly comes from the heart; these losses strike at the very basis of life and are not to be compared with any others. I hope the anxiety for her mother's safety grows less every day and that as I write she is quite out of danger. You shared this time of trial with her and it is indeed fortunate that you were not so far off as Ottawa when you got the message. Our loving sympathy to Peggy and you and if you can drop me a line to tell me how Mrs. Deaver progresses I shall be obliged. These motor accidents are too frequent and too devastating and you did right by not dwelling on the circumstances. Peggy should certainly have a change of scene and I hope she will be able to accomplish it. Perhaps dear Deaver will remember his grandfather. It has been impossible for me to remember mine for both were born in the eighteenth century; my father was born in 1812[1] and if his father was twenty at that time his birthdate would have been 1792, but I know he was born earlier than that; I remember my maternal Grandmother, being held up to see her on her death-bed; then I was about five, and I can see an old face and a head with a lace nightcap; she had The Gaelic, as they say, and I've been told that her pet name for me was Gagey.[2] I thought this note might interest you and even amuse Peggy.

My use of this machine is worse than usual this morng for I am even more nervous than usual.[3] I'll send you the first copy I get of W.J.P. and I shall also say a few words about Pierce. I shall look up the *Yale Review* and later I will send you another sort of letter. There is "apparent movement" about the other book and The Impeccable One has sent me a design for the Jacket.

> Again our sympathy and our love to you all,
> Yours faithfully,
> Duncan

163

October 17, 1946

Dear Edward,

I have not heard from you since the 28th ult.[1] and we have been anxious to know how Peggy's mother is recovering, speedily we hope and in all ways satisfactorily. I write "we" advisedly for Elise is as interested as I am. You will let us know when you next write me.

I may have one or two items of interest. Pelham was very praiseful of the A.L. Keats; I never heard from Brockington wh. is understandable; he is difficult to catch these days; he flew to Eng. and is expected back by air this Sat. I hope to God he arrives safe and sound for there have been so many accidents lately. He gave us seats for two special showings of Henry V. The second show was a very special affair and the *Journal* made an Editorial on the occasion a copy of wh. I send for your amusement, wh. you must return as it is the only one I have.[2] I go very seldom to the Movies but this one is so good that we are tempted to go a third time, so you may care to see it.

I hope de la Mare replied to your letter as he shd do but these people are I think rather remiss. There was an entirely inadequate review of Ned's *Collected Poems* in the Lit. Sup. of Sept 14th;[3] I cld send it but I know that Weekly must be available for you. I dont like it at all; to head the review "Stories in Verse" shows a lack of comprehension and from my point of view a sort of unfriendliness.

I got a copy of the *Yale Review* and found your article on Willa Cather done in your very best style; Elise wants you to know that she joins in this praise.

Fortunately I know her two books *Shadow on the Rock* and *How Death Came to the Archbishop;* I think I read *My Antonia;*[4] you know how little fiction I read but I had not missed those books and I agree with your opinion as to their chance of permanence. I am sure she must have been pleased with your Homage and was conscious that here she had a critic who was worthy of her.

I have not mentioned that in July I had a letter from Arthur Stringer[5] saying that he had been assigned the task of writing a Biography of Rupert Brooke by the father of the late Richard Haliburton who had collected a great mass of material and had planned to do the book.[6] A.S. asked me to give him any memories of R.B.'s visit to Ottawa. Well you know that after 33 years one's memories of such a visit are dim and I told Stringer that anything I said wld be factual, I meant that I wld not contribute anything imaginary. I sent him a few facts and a copy of a few of Brooke' letters.[7] But I ask you confidentially, was the choice of A.S. for this work not extraordinary, for there seems to be no sympathy between the work of the two men, placing them side by side; and can you tell this ignorant person who the late Richard Haliburton was?

The Ryerson Press sent me a pasted-up dummy of the W.J.P. booklet with the illustrations in place and I think it will look well. I had a note from Thoreau MacD. He said that the other book wld come to 415 pages wh. rather alarmed me;[8] but this is McC & S's risk and if they have developed signs of madness those who are nearer to them than I am shd have noticed it and taken action in time.

The other clipping I send because you are always interested in this family;[9] it will not be advisable, certainly not necessary for you to take any notice of this. Please return.

We both join in affection to you three; and hope that Deaver still enjoys his tricycle.

Yours ever,
Duncan

164

Chicago
October 27, 1946

Dear Duncan,

I was as always much interested in everything in your letter, as in the enclosures. It is pleasant to think that one newspaper in Canada has a scale of values in which Governor General and Prime Minister are set well down. I was reminded of the Washington stories concerning how there are many Presidents whom the society of the capital has not accepted. And very right too, when one thinks of who some of the men have been for whom the presidency has been possible. But I wonder if any American president was more of a mediocrity, or worse, than one Canadian P.M. you served under, Sir Mackenzie Bowell?[1] Or do I do him an injustice?

Peggy's mother continues to improve. Peggy was with her for most of the week not long ago. She has made out slowly that her husband is dead; and will thus be spared the shock of a sudden disclosure, of which we have been afraid. Until her leg is removed from its cast we shall not know whether she will regain its use. (I should have said "until the cast is removed from the leg.") But all goes at least as well as we have had any ground to expect. Peggy much appreciates the interest Elise and you have shown.

I was delighted to hear that the book on W.J.P. is so far advanced. I trust it will appear before Christmas. It will make a fine Christmas book. The sales manager of the Ryerson Press (a sensible woman, named Elsinore Haultain[2]) was here last week, and told me confidentially that the Press was making another connection in the U.S. I have urged from 1943 on that B. Humphries was almost useless; and Pierce has at last come around to seeing that this is so. When I ordered a copy of *At the Long Sault* for the Cornell Library, Humphries replied (two weeks after publication!) that the work was out of print. Mrs. Haultain did not tell me who the new agent was to be. I am sorry the Lampman book is to be delayed. I had a pleasant letter from MacInnes, in which he speaks of this.

What is more important than even the WJP, I was so pleased to hear that the McC. and S. people have made some progress with your collection of prose and verse. I am delighted that it is to be a book of liberal size, much larger than *The Witching of Elspie*.[3] I suppose it is too much to hope that it will appear in 1946; but 1947 should see it, at the worst. It will indeed be an event; but I wish we had literary editors in Canada who knew an event when they saw it, and would make of it what is deserves.

B.K. Sandwell and his wife spent an evening with us early this month. He was very cheery, and it seems that he will not be withdrawing from *Saturday Night* for at least two years. Plumptre, who is to succeed him, will take over gradually. Perhaps you know him; he has been a good deal in Ottawa during the war years, although I think that he spent even more time at Washington. He is a Toronto graduate in political science; I doubt that he has anything like B.K.S.'s interest or competence in matters of literature or any of the arts. But he has some general culture, was brought up in a cultivated family (his father was rector of St. James's Cathedral in Toronto, and his mother was interested in almost everything — I put them in the past, for his mother has been an invalid for years and his father has receded from the scene); and has had literary friends.[4] I suggested to B.K.S. that he take over the book section when he no longer cared to carry the full editorial load.

MacInnes mentions that he and you made a search for the essay A.L. did on the Pre-Raphaelites, but without success. As you may recall, Connor refers to this essay.[5] I thought it would be well to publish it or a part of it, and then I could feel that all of A.L.'s prose of a critical kind would be available in print. Probably it will turn up somewhere sooner or later.

I have been more than usually busy with my university work. We have a very large number of students, like every other university, and the autumn brings in more new faces than any other season. My two colleagues in American literature are rarely out of residence at the same time; but they are now both in California; and it has fallen to me to deal with their students and intending students, not in class but in conferences. So I have had much to do; and have been reading, out of necessity, some novels of Upton Sinclair and Howells, which I would rather have left on the shelf. More attractive reading has been Kinglake's *Eothen*,[6] which I had somehow missed. There are very fine passages, both passionate and comic in tone. But no doubt you know the book. I have also read Balzac's *The Old Maid*, which was full of suggestion, although I seldom care for his provincial books as much as for the Parisian ones.

Your remarks about the paper on Willa Cather were very cheering. I sent a copy to her rather late, just a couple of weeks ago, and I am hopeful that I may hear from her. No, I have had no reply from de la Mare. But book-post is slow, and he doubtless has much to do. Speaking of poetry, I thought the first of Frost's poems in the *Yale Review* number which had my paper was very fine indeed.[7]

The *Chambers' Encyclopaedia* editor has acknowledged my article on Canadian literature and pronounced it excellent for their purposes.[8] I hate having to do a subject such as that in so small a space. I was allowed 3000 words, out of which I had to take what I needed for biographical sketches and bibliographical references. I spent 1100 words on biographies of Haliburton, A.L., D.C.S., Carman, Roberts, Pratt, Leacock; and in the 1900 remaining had a very hard time touching on the essentials. At the last moment I decided to slip in a sentence on your fellow-Presbyterian Andrew MacPhail, and another on Hugh MacLennan,[9] and had to pare away some other things I valued.

Yes, it is indeed odd that the Rupert Brooke should be committed to A. Stringer. The only R. Halliburton I know of is a travel writer; but I have been able to live without reading any of his things. A full life of R. Brooke would be very valuable, and even fascinating.

I was pleased that Pelham liked the A.L. Keats. Give him my best wishes when you see him. I am glad he has not yet gone to B.C. Perhaps he will relinquish the idea.

Our best wishes to you and Elise, in which Deaver would join if he understood such courtesies. He is very merry these days, and acquiring an interest in flowers.

Yours, as ever,
Edward

165

November 24, 1946

Dear Edward,

You are very indulgent in giving so much of your time to writing me when you have so many urgent things pressing on you but as I cant get along without your letters I try to be indifferent as to the trouble it gives you. As you know I have seen your friend Watkins who lodges just a few doors east on this street; his landlady is a real lady and an old friend of ours and his first visit was with her by his own intention. I had neglected looking him up for my dear old sister[1] fell and broke her hip on Octr 6th and has been in hospital ever since and is likely to be there for some time yet; and this put us to anxiety; I call her *old* for she has two years advantage of me; I do not want to dwell on this. We both like Watkins and hope to see him often, he is a man to whom I can speak of books and writing and they are rare. He brought us a copy of *Goriot,* so I have had a glance at it;[2] I did not keep it to read for I expect Hope's to have some copies before long and I shall postpone any remarks until the book is really with me; I will say however that your Foreword is most excellent. I was glad to learn from W. that Mrs. Deaver was better, and I hope to have more definite news from you when you next write. As for my own Literary Activities, the Phillips book is advertised in all the R.P. notices but I have not seen a copy yet; the first one I get goes to you. The galleys of "The Circle" have gone to the printer, but no page proofs yet; still progress has been made; I had a note from Thoreau MacDonald sending me proofs of some vignettes they intend to use on the pages separating the sections of the book, and I approved them; he had chosen a green cloth for the cover; if they get the book out for the Spring market (how I hate that word) they will do well; I hope you will not be too surprised by the contents and will feel kindly towards it. Much to my astonishment I recd from the R.P. the *whole* of the galleys of the Collected Lampman. Pierce has fixed on the general title for this series, The R.P. Library of Collected Canadian Poets; as he has control of only four or five Poets the word *Library* is hardly well chosen. As you know I am hostile to having Lampman published in a Series and have a contempt for all boxed up Poets; in derision I call the Series Pierce's Plucked Poets. Pelham is labouring over the book of reminiscences he is doing for Pierce, he complained to me that Pierce was urging him constantly about this book and I told him he could put a stop to that by asking P. for an advance of 500 dollars[3] on royalties. Pelham did not think well of that suggestion. There is no likelihood of his going to B.C. and he is going to spend the winter here, in fact Ottawa seems attractive to him, even as a place of residence. How did the idea ever get into your wise head that I was a Presbyterian? I was born into the Methodist Connection when the adherents were called Wesleyan Methodists and were close to the revered founder of the sect; they seem to have forgotten him in their Union[4] and I have forgotten them all having wandered far away and am lost in a wilderness, but I have a strong Faith of my own, you see I spell Faith with a capital. I am interested in Deaver's notice of flowers, that will be a foundation for his love of beauty in this drab world. I like to think of your working at the Arnold and your remark about the notebooks; I was always intensely interested in the extracts from his diary wh. I have had by me for years;[5] Arnold was certainly a great influence with me in the 80's, and yet is for that matter.

It is snowing here this morning but we have had beautiful weather in Octr. and Novr. and that seems to shorten the Winter but Winter for me is still Winter and I cant hope to get around and about.

> Our love to Peggy and you and Deaver.
> Yours ever,
> Duncan

166

> Chicago
> November 27, 1946

Dear Duncan,

We were very sorry, and are full of sympathy, to learn of the accident to your sister. I know how long the recovery is from such mishaps when one is no longer young. Peggy joins me in the hope that you are by now reassured, and that your sister will make a good recovery. Mrs. Deaver's progress continues to be very slow; but at the end of November she is certainly much stronger than she was at the end of October. I think Peggy is much more optimistic and we are both more tranquil.

I am very glad that you and Elise have seen J. Watkins. He is one of my oldest friends; even to one of your years, a friendship of 24 years without the slightest ruffle will seem a thing of tested worth. It has been a great pleasure to me that Peggy is as fond of him as I am. He is indeed a "friend of the household."

In order to save you any bother with customs, I asked Britnell's Bookstore in Toronto[1] to send you a copy of the Balzac. B. replied that it would be two or three weeks before he had stock but he would then send it. If you do not hear from him by mid-December I hope you will remind me. JW tells me he left a copy for you to look at.

I do not get much writing done these days. I am reading instead. I have decided to offer a course on Carlyle next quarter, and need to read and reread much. It is more than a decade since I read the *French Revolution;* and I am glad that it seems even better now than it did then. I am also trying to get back my German, and am spending half an hour each evening on simple prose. It is scandalous the way I have let German lapse; and I now must have it.

I had a very fine letter from Willa Cather, who appears to have taken great delight in the article. She shares my view that *Death Comes for the Abp* is her best book. I also had a most friendly letter from W. de la Mare; but unfortunately he makes no direct reference to Canadian poetry. He refers to the difficulties I have outlined as having impressed him deeply; and speaks of his shame at knowing so little that has been written in Canada; but there are no references to individual poets or poems.

This is not a true letter; but an expression of our sympathy and hope that your sister may make a good and quick recovery.

Deaver flourishes.

Yours, as ever,
Edward

P.S. [*holo.*] We showed your poem to Deaver to Chauncey Tinker from Yale who was here for dinner and he was much moved by it. He is a grand scholar and critic, the best perhaps in English Studies of his generation (*aetat.* 70).

167

December 14, 1946

Dear Edward,

This is just a note enclosing our Christmas Card[1] with our love to you and Peggy and Deaver. Under separate cover we are addressing you a book for Deaver's Birthday and for Christmas. I hope he may like it now or later. I marked it Christmas Gift and I hope your Customs will let it go and that you will have no bother with it. We have a touch of real winter this morng with a swirling storm of snow and wind. We are both well and intend to have a quiet holiday season.

With affection for you all,
Yours sincerely,
Duncan

1947

Scott is feeling his age, and the drag of winter which has always wearied him taxes him severely now. The only two letters he attempts in late winter and early spring are both broken off and resumed much later. He is in bed a good deal of the time. By May, The Circle of Affection is still not out, and in early June his older sister dies in an Ottawa nursing home. But then there is a turn for the better, and the guttering candle flares brilliantly before its light fades. Scott's last letters are among his best. Brown has a copy of The Circle by the end of June, and his delighted response to the book is Scott's tonic. Watkins, now a favoured friend, is a frequent visitor at 108 Lisgar Street. He and others gather in the music room on an evening in July to savour the superb playing of Géza and Norah DeKresz. Scott's eighty-fifth birthday passes happily, and a highpoint of it is a card from Deaver, signed in a child's hand, ''like a tracing by Matisse.'' The last long letter to Brown is an outpouring of recollection and comment sparked by Brown's detailed response to The Circle. Scott is alert and in good spirits. Perhaps encouraged by this renewed vitality in the poet, Brown comes up with another ''problem.'' He has been able to identify the date of composition for a great many of Lampman's poems. Will Scott help with those he cannot date? He sends a list. Scott is more than willing but puts off the task. Loftus MacInnes is very ill. The next letter from Lisgar Street, written six weeks later in the spidery scrawl of a stricken man, is a few lines of warm congratulations to the Browns on the birth of a brother to Deaver. That is the end of the correspondence.

168

Chicago
January 19, 1947

Dear Duncan,

I am slow in writing, and the more of a procrastinator that I have wanted to thank you and Elise for the charming book you sent to Deaver. He has marched about with it, and asked for readings, and has shown that he thinks of it as something special. I wish he could see you; but those of your age, and those of his are not travellers.

We had a splendid day at Christmas, the first Christmas that meant anything to Deaver. It meant a great deal. He was delighted with everything, particularly with the lights we had for the tree, some of which had a faculty quite new to my experience, the liquid within them streaming and bubbling. We had in a family we see much of, a Jewish colleague with his wife, and two teen age sons. The boys feel the lack of Christmas, and it was a pleasant evening.

Somehow I have needed longer than usual to make a good start in organizing my two new classes — one of the nuisances of our short twelve week terms is that no sooner do you get an understanding of a group than it has gone, and another takes its place. But I have now got things moving, and can relax. The first weeks of a term are always bad ones for my letter-writing.

I am giving my advanced course on the novel, and have begun with *The Old Wives' Tale,* in which I see more every time I read it. The *Times* said when A[rnold] B[ennett] died that to write this book he grew wings. It is unaccountable to me that he could then go on writing such miserable tenth rate stuff in other novels. I am going on to Forster's *Passage to India,* another old favorite.

The other course is on Carlyle. I have never taught his *French Revolution* and indeed only gave it a quick reading years ago. Its power has been a surprise, and I am glad I undertook to do it. C. is not high on my lists of favorites, but I like to get into him now and then. And some chapters are wonderfully beautiful in a strange way.

Poetry asked me for a review of four recent Canadian books: Birney, Coulter, Dudek, and Souster.[1] I have done it, but could wish the fare had been better. I gave most of the space, about 1000 words, to Birney. The new editor of *Maclean's*[2] has asked me to do a piece on Ontario. That is an attractive subject, but I don't know whether I could express myself within the terms of a *Maclean's* audience. I am tempted to try. The magazine will have a series, one on each Canadian region. All the other writers are journalists. I am afraid that for good and bad my piece, if I wrote it, would stand apart. The fee is colossal: $300. That would be more than I got for the King piece.

Watkins writes with pleasure of seeing you from time to time. He appears to accept his unexpectedly long stay in Ottawa with equanimity, although his only reason for entering External Affairs was to live for a while in Scandinavia. He ran into Pearson on a journey and found that Pearson had not forgotten the relation with Scandinavia, but that was about all Watkins could say.[3] Watkins is wonderfully well-read and has liberal enthusiasms for many kinds of letters. I know that you will enjoy him, as he enjoys you. You can conceive what a pleasure it was for us both to have him in the aridity of Ithaca.

We are changing the departmental chairman. Here there is a triennial review of the chairmanship; and it is possible to change without a fight. I think the new man will be a better focus for us than the outgoing chairman, but am chiefly happy that I am to be allowed to go on in my own way doing the things I care to do, and not returned to the cares of administration.

I expect my Arnold ms. back from the second Arnoldian scholar to read it sometime this week. I shall then give it a final polish before trying to publish.

Our kindest wishes to you and Elise, in which Deaver joins. May I hear from you soon.

Yours, as ever,
Edward

P.S. [*holo.*] Macmillan sent me Grove's new book *In Search of Myself.*[4] I think he is trying very hard to tell us he is illegitimate but can't quite decide to say so!

169

February 19, 1947

Dear Edward,

This day is just a month since the date of your last letter and I must at least begin a reply this morning although I know I wont finish it for perhaps a few days. There are certain points in your last letters on wh. I would like to comment. It was good to have heard from Miss Cather and de la Mare; as for the latter I remark that you never get anything from English authors by way of literary criticism, at least that has been my experience. Even in their publications they deal but scantly and in some cases misunderstandingly, about American and COLONIAL books. As a case in point you no doubt saw the Lit. Sup. notice of Pratt's *Collected Poems;* it was headed "Stories in Verse;" my own modest *Viger* was listed under the head of "Country Life."[1] Well, we must bear up, and carry on our own show. I was very pleased that Prof. Tinker liked Deaver's lines; Watkins did too and I am glad for all sorts of reasons that I made them. The book drags annoyingly, and I am waiting for the final page proofs. I submitted the Foreword to Watkins who suggested two changes wh. I adopted; a period instead of a colon, "and" instead of "which." I was anxious to know how the Foreword impressed him; was it too fanciful or sentimental, but he passed it as neither. As you know Thoreau MacDonald has made drawings in his well known manner to seperate the sections, I noticed that he had one for the first blank of the book where he used a rainbow in the design, I want to think that he had read Deaver's verse.[2] There is something queer about the Phillips book; there was a review of it in the *Globe & Mail* of Feb 10th or 11th ? of wh. I send you a copy;[3] it was accompanied by a rough print of one of the pictures.

These words were written on Feb 19th, and now it is the Ninth of March; the interval has been spent in company with a sort of mild 'flu and a general feeling of inability to do anything so you must forgive the laches. The typewriter bothers me and this letter may be more telegraphic than usual, disjointed too. The Ontario book wld give you a lot of trouble but you wld do it so well and I wld commit (like the French Lady) a mortal sin for 300 Dollars. I want the latest news of your Arnold book in wh. I am deeply interested. There is no copy of *Goriot* either from Britnell or Hope. You tempted me to read *The Old Wives Tale,* and I was repaid; of course Bennet wrote a lot of pot-boilers but there are certain of his books, mighty few, that I cld reread; but not now for I am reading translations of Euripides. What an Impressionist Carlyle is, in the Painters sense I mean; but I wont follow you in reading the *FR* just now. I am enclosing two extracts. Can you imagine the state of mind that wld lead parents to call their child Ben Hur?[4] And where does the Lampman come from? As the other note refers to A.P.S.W.[5] I thought I wld send it along; no doubt he has seen it. The paper by Foot is good I think. I send you under seperate cover one of the publications of my new affiliation,[6] I thought the note on translation might interest you; do not return it. If you get a copy of the R.P. Spring List you will see that the Viger book goes into the class of *Anne of Green Gables;*[7] one cannot object if one's book is a failure; I dislike the price of $1.69; it seems like the price of a sale of men's underware; but I do object that the only reference is a note of *A.J.M. Smith's* and I think it is scurvy treatment of Thoreau MacDonald and of the general makeup of the little book wh. we all thought was a good piece of bookmaking.[8] I was amused by two letters I had from Flemington[9] re. the change in price. The first told me that my royalty wld of course be on the new list price, *18 days* after he writes me that "of course" the royalty shd have been on the NET price. So all is well. My opinion of Pierce has not been altered by this incident, it was low enough before.[10]

Watkins is now a familiar of the house and he sat with me an hour when I was in bed, when I was merely tired out, no danger of 'flu. He had dinner with us not long ago, the fourth at the table was a lady who has a lot of bright talk, we thought it might leven the dull lump of *my* conversation. They seem to be willing to keep him here but I think he wld like to get away, but I shall miss him when he goes.

> Our affection to Peggy, Deaver and yourself,
> Yours ever,
> Duncan

[*P.S. holo.*] Please write soon.

170

[Chicago]
March 19, 1947

Dear Duncan,

I delayed answering your fine full letter until the book on WJP had arrived. I found it this morning, and read the first half of it while my students were writing their examination on the novel, the second half more appropriately at home to-night. It is an admirable work. You make the technical processes both clear and significant; and you diffuse a feeling of what is essential in WJP's work and in his personality. I took particular pleasure of course (liking WJP and being interested in his work, but caring a great deal more about DCS) in the few personal passages.

I thought your kinship in being sons of the Methodist parsonage was beautifully handled, and your little tribute to the way you were aided as a child was very pleasant to me.[1] This about cheese is also good,[2] though Peggy is not with me on that. Plain Cheddar etc. I like but I loathe the rest; and in Paris used to say that those who wanted the special cheeses should be made to eat in special rooms. Their odor spoiled many a pleasant moment in a Paris café. Your way of taking WJP's remark on a picture-hung wall was also admirable.[3] It evoked your house for us very vividly.

You have never written prose I have liked so well. You have added to the fine qualities you have always had something of suggestion, of softness, that is *very* rare indeed.

WJP will be delighted. I trust the book will get half the circulation it deserves. More than that no Canadian publisher will give it! I was sorry to hear about the reduction in price of *Viger*. But you must not tell Pelham; for his *H[enry] J[ames]* was on sale for 35 cents for quite some time at Eaton's, and $1.69 will seem like crowing.

We are very happy to hear that you and Elise have come through your sicknesses. This is the truly bad time of the year, and I hope you will take specially good care of yourself till April comes. A year ago now it was warm here, and very sunny, and cheering; but we are still in winter, though the snow lingers only in sheltered places.

I am at work on the Canadian bards, and expect to end my sessions with their year's work next week, if I do not flinch.[4] There are a few good things in Page: *As Ten as Twenty;* Robert Finch has some very delicate and suggestive things in his *Poems* that you would I think enjoy; and I have come on a couple of poems by Sister Maura[5] that are better than anything she had done before. All in all, not a bright year.

Watkins speaks with much pleasure of his times at 108 Lisgar. He is an admirable friend in every way. Has he told you of his sad problem with his sister? One sister died of tuberculosis about fifteen or twenty years ago; the other, having had it, developed mental trouble. At Woodstock,[6] I think, at present. His father died when the family was young; his mother kept the farm going; and died at a ripe age a few years ago. She was a very fine, determined, and also cultivated woman. Watkins has had a hard life. He failed in a doctor's oral at Columbia about 1932 or 3; and was deeply discouraged for years by this. I worked on him to come up to Cornell and try again; and I think his immediate success (with a fine thesis, which I read) gave him new confidence. I thought you might now like to know these things about your new friend.

I am glad that you liked the *Old Wives' Tale*. It has no real fellow.

It is good of you to ask again about the Arnold. It is now with our University Press, but they will not have their readers' reports for some time. I am chairman of the academic committee on the Press and felt I had to give the mss. to them as a mark of confidence and loyalty; but I secured the promise that, should the reports be at all lukewarm, I should be free to withdraw the mss., for I would not trade on my position. I am also insisting no one should tell me who the readers are.

I wish to get this in the mail at once, to tell you of our pleasure in the book.

Deaver will be invited to look at the pictures tomorrow. He is very charming just now, and we find him more of a delight all the time. Your poem hangs in his room, between his window, and his dresser. He knows it is about him.

> With our love to you and Elise,
> Edward

171

March 29, 1947

Dear Edward,

Goriot arrived from Britnell on Thursday and this is merely to ack'l it and to say that it was received with joy. The inscription has been fixed in place and adds much to the value of this personal copy. I shall write again about it but I am a slow reader and cant devour a book so I wanted to let you know that I have it.

My other book approaches completion. I must say that McC & S have taken some pains to make a good-looking book of it and I hope you will be pleased with it.

In my last letter I indulged in some sharp remarks about The Ryerson Press and Dr. Pierce.[1] You will have begun to understand me and know that I sometimes yield to irritation; but you know I have no such strong feeling against Pierce as my remark would imply; so forget my censures. Did he send you a catalogue of the Queen's Univ. treasure?[2] What a collection of Carmaniana; Bliss was the sort of personality that leads to these accumulations; the people who met him liked to have something of him and treasured it whatever it might be; but I must say that he was generous to other Canadian writers when he was in a position to be generous. We are in the midst of a snowstorm and it seems as if winter wld never cease.

My love to you all,
Yours ever,
Duncan

[*P.S. holo.*] I have no decent envelopes so forgive the Commercial form.

D

172

April 23, 1947

Dear Edward.   It is more than a month since I read your last and would have answered before this had it been possible; but I wasnt very well and spent some part of every day in bed and when I was up and about I couldnt face the typewriter. So here is my explanation, I give it because there are certain things in your last that required comment; there is nothing seriously wrong with me but the winter had tired me. I told you I had got *Goriot* and since then I have read it and thought a good deal about it. Your introduction is admirable, you say all that needs to be said and you say it with the clearness wh. I so much admire in your writing. If Balzac gets his sentences mixed up your translation reads as clear as your own prose and like the original. I can give it no higher praise. As for Balzac how powerful and supreme he is when he comes to deal with a crisis; I dont propose to entertain you by any amature criticism of this genius, but I was overpowered to come in contact with him again. I will treasure this copy of *Goriot;* I have phoned to Watkins about *Grandet,* I have not seen him for some time as he has been very busy, are *They* really plotting to keep him here? He would not like that. Your praise of *W.J.P.* pleased me; you recognize what I tried to do for him, and he and his wife are very grateful and the whole family are touched by the way in wh. I referred to the son who was killed in the war. He and his wife had tea with us on Monday, he is on a picture selling trip and showed a lot of his water-colours. We spoke of you being at Banff and he said how glad he was to see you, he is building a house there and intends to live at the foot of the mountains.

To continue a few remarks re the little Phillips booklet. He could not find any copies for sale in the Montreal bookshops, and I dont think there are any copies here. When Flemington advised me about the reduction of price he said my royalty wld be 10% of the new list price (ltr dated Jany 22); a month later he said that he stated this royalty "inadvertently." "This [is], of course, 10% of the net price." So I asked him what the *net* price was; he replied "1.69 less one third, or 1.13." So you will understand that I get eleven cents on all copies sold; so you will know the reason why I cant visit Chicago this year. Another instance of the stupidity of this firm: they advertised the price of *W.J.P.* bound as 1.25; when I

ordered some extra copies they charged them at 1.50, with the information that
they had been compelled to raise the price due to additional manufacturing costs
in connection with the coloured plates; one wld have thought that they cld have
found that out before they advertised the booklet. I hope this may amuse you; if
not, see all the time I have wasted.

                                                      [May] 7, 1947[1]

Dear Edward,   I have not been able to do any work since I finished the
portion of the *good* letter I had planned; but there was no help for it. Adverting to
your last, Watkins had never told me about his sister's condition but had casually
mentioned that he had a sister who was in hospital; indeed I am sorry for him;
such a responsibility is an awful drag upon him in every way. The matter came
up when I mentioned my own sister's case. I have not said anything to you about
it lately as I dont want to bother you with my anxieties, she shows no great
improvement, she lies in bed, quite well looked after, but at times her memory
fails, then again she will be quite as lively as ever; as she is just near us on Cartier
St. we can see her often and I am glad to be able to look after her. I have not
asked after Peggy's mother lately from no lack of interest but to avoid for you the
necessity of writing; perhaps you will let me know how she fares toward perfect
recovery.

   I hope that your next will give me some good news about the "Arnold" as I
am anxious to read that book. As for *The Circle* they seem to be having trouble
about the Jacket cover; the last ltr on that subject was dated April 8th, a month
ago, but I dont intend to write them about it. I understood from one of their letters
that the book was already printed, cloth for the cover chosen, and only the Jacket
to be decided. Well, you will have had more than enough of the trials of an
unsuccessful author. I think there is a character in one of Saroyan's plays, "The
world's greatest unknown Poet."[2]

   I wish I had a more cheerful ltr to send; the weather has been very hard on us;
last night freezing and we are promised snow for today!

                                    With our love to you three
                                    Yours ever,
                                              Duncan

173

                                                      [Chicago]
                                                      May 29, 1947

Dear Duncan,

   It was as always a great pleasure to have your letter. I am sorry that you have
been a bit "seedy;" but this delayed season has not given any of us much of a

spur. Think of it, even in this more southerly spot, we are to have frost to-night.

Your news about the carryings on at the Ryerson Press does not surprise. They do not seem to have any consistency. Here is a little item from my history. I was eager that *OCP* should not sell for more than $2. This sum was fixed in the contract. The book was published at $2.25; and has always sold at that; but my royalty is on $2. Of course I have never expected to make much by the book; so I have not protested. But what a way of doing business!

I am sorry that your miscellany is delayed. I am most eager to see that book. My Arnold has at last been formally accepted for publication by our Press. I am now reading it over and making the alterations of phrase which a year's delay since most of it was composed makes easy to desire. We have not yet worked out even a provisional date of publication. I still hope it may have a 1947 date.

Much to my surprise *Maclean's* took the article on Ontario almost as it came to them. They cut out a couple of passages, they say, as going a little beyond the range of their readers. In every way I have found their new editor, W.A. Irwin, a good man to deal with. The cheque, incidentally, came before publication! I hope it may entertain you. I have asked for some copies, and will send you one, when they arrive. I have mentioned you and Ned Pratt in one sentence as the leading poets of the time, a reference perhaps a bit "drug in"; but there is a paragraph on Ontario as the centre of Canadian intellectual and artistic life.

This article is a trifle, and I would not wish you to give it thought.[1]

Poor Watkins. I fear he will see another year pass before he gets to his heart's desire. A member of the External Affairs department who was recently here said that he thought W's chance of getting abroad was not bright. He claimed that wild promises were easily made in that department, in which he has served a long time. But Watkins is very adaptable; and he does not seem to repine.

I am sorry that your sister's recovery is not more definite. We have been very happy this past month or so about Mrs. Deaver's progress. After so long an anxious time, she began suddenly to improve very much; and is now sitting up, and will take to a wheel chair some time this summer. To us this seems almost incredible. When I leave for New York about the middle of June, Peggy will go to Minneapolis and will stay there at least a month.

Fortunately there is no lack of money in the Deaver family and the huge costs of Mrs. Deaver's illness will be borne by the estate without any stringency. Mr. Deaver (a very strange man, whom I never could understand in the least) lived a very quiet life and amassed an amount of money which is a surprise to every one.

I had a note from Pelham enclosing his review of Wells's book on Pratt.[2] It (the book) seems a crazy performance; and Wells, a nice fellow, is somewhat crackbrained. Pelham calls him professor of Comp. Lit. at Columbia; the truth is that he is an "associate," a peculiar rank, which implies that not much work is expected of a man, and his role and salary remain small. I do not know of any equivalent arrangement anywhere else. But the conferring of this rank is always an adverse judgment on a man. I liked Pelham's review. I wish he had done the book.

This quarter my great pleasure has been a seminar class on Pater: four good students. We have informed one another on many things, and have all become more enthusiastic about Pater than when we began. I am still turning over the idea of a book on him. How strangely little we know of his life! You probably know the "oral legend" at Oxford that he was homosexual. I sometimes wonder if there is some scandal which accounts for the withholding of such knowledge as we have of almost all the other Victorian lives.

If you do not happen to write until late in June, I may now give you my N.Y. address, the same as last year, Butler Hall (not a part of Columbia despite the name and location), 88 Morningside Drive, New York, 27. I am due there on the 23rd.

Peggy is out at present, but when she comes home, I am going to ask her for a snapshot of Deaver taken a couple of weeks ago. He continues to give us much pleasure from day to day; and more to himself. At present the recent gift of some goldfish, by his grandmother, is his chief joy.

Our love to Elise and yourself, and when you see LWB tell him I do not forget him.

As ever,
Edward

174

Sunday, June 8, 1947

My Dear Edward,　　　Your last with such good news of Peggy's mother was very welcome. I have not such good news; my sister died on Sunday last; I would have written you before but there has been so much to attend to and so many notes to write. Her accident and its consequences have been an *immense strain* on us both and we are still feeling it but we must get back to our usual routine again. My sister had every possible care and attention, she was just near us in the Nursing Home on Cartier St. and we could see her after a walk of five minutes. Elise has been a wonderful comfort to me and to her during this time. I will answer your letter soon I hope. We were delighted to have the latest photo of Deaver on his Charger, he looks quite at home on a saddle, I was, and still am, terrified of horses. God bless him and give him control of all animals.

I am sending you by this mail your copy of *The Circle*. I dont think I have any luck in this because you will be so occupied in N.Y. that you wont be able to look at it. But I send it all the same. I hope you and Peggy will like the look of Deaver's 'Lines'; it is extraordinary how much readers like them and seem to transfer that liking to him, wh. pleases me.

With love from us both to you all,
Yours faithfully,
Duncan

175

Butler Hall
88 Morningside Dr.
New York
June 30, [1947]

Dear Duncan,

You will have set me down for a most ungrateful and unfeeling friend.

Your magnificent book, with the beautifully inclusive "dedication" to the three of us[1] came the day I left Chicago, and of course I have it with me. But your letter with its sad news came later, and caught up with me only a day or so ago.

I need not tell you of my sympathy with you in your loss. But it is a great deal both for you and your sister to have lived so near to each other, and for you and Elise to have been close by, and able to see her, in the final illness. No comfort seems very substantial, of course, so soon after the event; but in retrospect the closeness and the accessibility will seem a real consolation. My mother died after an illness of ten days, almost seven years ago; and I am eternally grateful that I was able to be with her for the last week.

If I may turn now to the book, I would say that Dryden's remark on Chaucer is the best initial comment; here is God's plenty! How varied the treasures are, and yet how they are all parts of one treasure, directed by a true principle of organization. You know how I admire the title piece. The early stories, unknown to me, are almost as fine: I have taken great delight in "The Return,"[2] managed with such beautiful restraint, so sound, so sad, and yet so fine. The paper on "The Last of the Treaties" is an admirable thing, so deft and so rich in suggestion. But I must not begin to particularize, I would go on forever. The poems I will speak of in another letter.

I showed Deaver the page which celebrates your love for him. He was much excited, and clung to it. The McC. & S. people kindly sent me another copy, and this I gave into his charge, to his joy and pride. He is a very understanding child. A week before I left I suggested to the nurse and Peggy that I tell him when he wanted me at night not to cry but to call "Daddy." They were very dubious, but I tried it, and it worked with him at once.

But this letter is to concern you and no one else.

With sympathy and admiration,
Yours, as ever,
Edward

176

July 4, 1947

My Dear Edward,

This is just a note to thank you for your understanding sympathy which I am grateful for. I hope you will make the promised observations on the verse in *The Circle* and I will then reply and write you a letter about the book and several other things I want to say to you. I hope N.Y. is giving you good weather, we almost had a fire in the grate last night.

Yours ever,
Duncan

177

July 24, 1947

My Dear Edward,

I am afraid you will exclaim "Another letter from this troublesome old fellow," but something constrains me to write and I do so. Maybe it was because our mutual friend John was with us last evg and we were of course speaking of you. We enjoy having him "drop in" like that informally; but last week we gave him a real party. Gésa De Kresz, who you will remember as leader of the Hart House Quartet when it was at its best, and his wife Nora Drewett the pianist, having got themselves out of Hungary are here in Canada and hoping to stay here if there seems to be an opening for them.[1] So we had a choice few of their friends and some other musical people to welcome them and they played for us for an hour and a half, and John was of that choice group.

My last short note seems now to me unappreciative of your glorious welcome of *The Circle;* it reads to me now as "Oliver asking for more." But you probably, who are so understanding, will have read it aright. You were yourself to blame by writing that you would in another letter refer to the poems; and I hope that you will although it may be a difficult task. Nothing could have been more congenial to a neglected writer than the words you wrote. John too picked on "The Return" but he also fastened on another story, the one that was (allegedly, as the newspapers say) pronounced by one of our foremost short story writers, as the best short story written in Canada.[2] It has already been suggested as the basis of a Movie but I dont intend to venture into that field. "The Return" was written at the time of the Viger group, and I cannot remember why it was not included. I made a one-act play out of it with the help of Lampman's old friend J.A. Ritchie,[3] and it is published in that first and only Vol. of the Plays given at Hart House Theatre;[4] why his name was not finally associated with the play is too long a story to tell but it was purely his own fault. If you find it possible to say anything further about the book I shall be pleased. I am sending a review by Norman Smith Jr. wh. appeared in the *Journal;*[5] I have not heard that the *Citizen* has made any comment. There was a short patronizing notice in the *Gazette,* and a very friendly col. in *The London Free Press.*[6] But that is all I have seen so far, when the book gets into the hands of the younger writers I may expect a scoring. Later on I shall perhaps ask Miss Hutchinson of McC & S to let me have all the notices, good, bad and indifferent. I think my name has been a great handicap — no one with a pen-name like that shd go before the public. Now if I had a name like Bliss Carman, what a success I would have had.

As for the other things I wanted to say to you, here are some of them. My delight in knowing that the Arnold book had been accepted and that we should have it before long. I obtained on my own initiative a copy of your Ontario article[7] and found it very entertaining; it was remarkable how you accomodated your style to readers of that Sheet without sacrificing any of your own personality. Thanks for hauling in my three-barreled name and thanks too for telling the Ontario folk to read Emerson on Self Reliance; how much that essay meant to me forty years ago[8] and I reread it with some profit at this date for when one gets to my age he needs something even more than Self Reliance. I intend when I can spare time from reading *The Belton Estate* to read *Dr. Thorne*[9] in one hand and *Vilette*[10] in the other. The Dr. is not a favorite of mine and I have not read *Vilette,* that confession will come as a shock to you! How foolish of Sadleir to make such absolute claims;[11] he has a good enough case, why spoil it by these sweeping assertions. My present absorption in *The Belton Estate* comes from the discovery that my friend and neighbor Mrs. Russell Blackburn[12] is a devoted Trollopian and has all his books and when she offered to lend me two I had not read, *Miss MacKenzie* and *The B.E.,* how could I refuse? So at present I am varying that reading with S. Sitwell's new book *The Hunters and the Hunted,* wh. I dont like much not nearly so well as Sir Osbert's last books.[13] I lay it down with relief and take up *The Belton Estate.*

I enclose a late article by P.D. Ross on the latest Selected Lampman;[14] by the way I suppose Pierce has sent you a copy, if so tell me how it impresses you; if not I shall see that you get a copy. As a bit of bookmaking it wont compare with the Musson *Lyrics of Earth.*[15] Ross poses as a discoverer of L. but I never knew him as a *friend* of his in the way we count friendship. When Ross ventures on criticism he is ''somewhat overparted'' but I have no objection; he has only *very lately* mentioned me as a poet, he hardly likes to admit me and his review gives no idea of what the book is; he shd have quoted from my Foreword. But Ross is now a most generous man; he has considerable wealth and he tries to use it well and supports strongly Pelham's Writers' Foundation. He may have an opportunity soon of showing how deeply he is concerned in the L. tradition for I have the sad news that Loftus is most seriously ill, in the Hospital, and the outcome of his somewhat obscure condition is as yet doubtful. A stomach ulcer burst and he had an immediate heart attack Natalie is very brave and hopes for the best, she says, and so do I; and I do not want to think of her future without him and wont do it; but you will see why I drag Ross into this connection. Maybe I shd not have mentioned this to you but I know you like Loftus.[16]

Elise invites Peggy and Deaver and you to a party on the 2nd Aug. at five of the afternoon to drink some Canadian champaigne to my health, John will be there and some 40 or 50 other friends and it wld be a joy to have you. I shd like to see you; "The stars are setting, and the Caravan starts for the Dawn of Nothing, oh make haste."[17] Well whether you are here in person or not I shall think of you Three as here and will drink a full glass to you.

Did Gustafson send you a copy of an article he wrote on Lampman and did he ask you to comment on it?[18] Will you write me sometime at your convenience and believe me ever yours affectionately,

Duncan

[*P.S. holo.*] I shd have mentioned that all *T. Sat. N.* did for *The Circle* was to print an enlarged copy of Karsh's photo with a short description of the book below it! One might have expected B.K. to deal with it but at least I escaped one of their hacks.[19]

D.

178

[New York]
July 26, 1947

Dear Duncan,

I am slow in writing to you.[1] And I must now first convey the very warmest good wishes on your approaching birthday. I trust that once again you will have a party at the Club, and that you will be able to see in many eyes the pleasure that thousands of people will feel in the fact that you reach your eighty-fifth anniversary so hale, and so cheerful, as well as so wise. I wish I could be there.

Every one of the poems in your miscellany appealed to me and gave me pleasure with the single exception of the 'Farewell to Their Majesties.'[2] Not even you could win me to the mood there. I am too strong a republican to be capable of response. I don't like "majesties," and if I am to endure them at all they must be simple folk like the late King of Denmark or brilliant folk like Frederick the Great.

I was specially delighted with 'Old Olives at Bordighera,' which I knew before. I think this is one of your happiest poems, with the idea moving in and out of the symbol. It is a great favorite of mine. The last lines are peculiarly fine. 'Amanda,' which I do not remember reading before, is very moving. I happen to like the name as much as you, and so got off to a running start in my pleasure. 'To go with March amarching' haunts one with the overtones you manage so well in so many of your works. It is in one of your veins that I have always admired.

'At Derwentwater' is moving, too, but I am not yet quite clear how to read the final line, and that is very important in that poem.[3]

For one who does not often use the sonnet (as you once pointed out to me) the sequence on your anniversary is all the more remarkable. You have gone very far there in your insight and your wisdom.

I enjoyed the early poems also. 'Early Summer Song' is a beautiful piece, and in one of your most masterly manners. A poem of youth, and beautifully so. 'At Murray Bay' was no less a delight. The suggestions of landscape, and of feeling, are exquisite.[4]

You know my pleasure in the beautiful lines to Deaver, and of them I shall say no more now.

This has been a fine summer for me, and I am delighted that I came. I have been prowling around the city — it is not too hot for that — and finding nooks and restaurants that I did not know of.

My class is responsive, and though having so many hours of teaching cuts into my writing — even into the writing of letters — I think the experiment has been a grand success.

Peggy has returned home from a month with her mother. Deaver spoke to me over the 'phone last week, and seems more cheerful than ever. I wish he could see you. But this summer Peggy plans to stay not far from Minneapolis.

With warmest good wishes to you and Elise, and felicitations far from conventional on the anniversary.

Yours, as ever,
Edward

179 [*Holo.*]

August 5, 1947

Dear Peggy,

It was good of you to remind dear Deaver that he had a duty to perform. I am sending him a printed reply to his card. I like to follow his development from little hints that Edward puts into his letters. You will be together again soon. I have had two generous letters in praise of *The Circle* & I hope you found something in it to approve of. If you & Edward *and* Deaver cld have been at our party on the 2nd it wld have been perfect. We had John with us & I have ordered him to report to Edward about our "goings on." We like him well.

We do hope you have no cause for anxiety over your mother's condition and that she continues to gain in all ways.

Yours sincerely,
Duncan

180 [*Holo. print*]

DEAR DEAVER.

THANK YOU FOR THE LOVELY BIRTHDAY CARD WITH YOUR NAME SO WELL PRINTED. I THINK WE ARE IMPROVING IN OUR PRINTING.

I LIKE TO HAVE THE GOOD NEWS OF YOU WHICH YOUR DADDY SENDS AND I HAVE THAT SNAPSHOT WITH YOU ON YOUR HORSE WHICH I LIKE. AT YOUR AGE I NEVER DARED TO MOUNT A HORSE.

LOVE ALWAYS
DUNCAN

181

Chicago
August 31, 1947

Dear Duncan,

It was a very keen pleasure to have news of you and Elise, and especially of your *fête,* from JW. It was almost as if I had been there, as I wish I could have been, instead of finishing my labors at New York University. I was also delighted that JW should report you as feeling so well, and doing so much without fatigue.

Perhaps I should first say a word about the enclosure. A. Creighton,[1] the editor of the *Canadian Forum,* is unknown to me. He asked me to do a brief notice of your selection from A.L. I explained that it was somewhat difficult for me to do so, as he would see from your preface. But he insisted; and the book has had so much less attention than it should that I decided that I should do as he asked, while, of course, indicating clearly that I was not really qualified to be judicial. I hope you will not dislike the result. It is meager; but C. limited me to 200 words and I have gone over 250. I did not dare go higher. [*Holo. insert*] My warm thanks for your "inscribed copy" — it will be treasured on the Lampman-DCS shelf.

It is good of you to bear with my lack of enthusiasm for Trollope. I am reading *The Small House at Allington,* with enjoyment. I hope if you do *Villette* you won't be disappointed. JW is a lover of the Brontës. I have also read, for the first time, *The Mystery of Edwin Drood.* It did not seem to me of the best Dickens, but I enjoyed parts of it. I have also reread an old favorite of mine, *Silas Marner.* What a magical power she has at her best, humor, and feeling, and fact all fused as so few can do! I am writing a paper for the English Institute[2] which meets every September, the subject being "The Interpretation of Victorian Fiction." It is just about done; and I think I have made a couple of points. I shall hope for your reading of it, when I return from delivering it, and get it re-typed.

I was very much interested to learn that like me you had found "Self-Reliance" a great thing. I used to enjoy my classes on Emerson when I taught at Toronto, and must some time return to teaching him. Carlyle wears much less well, I find, though he is the greater literary artist, I believe.

When I was in Toronto I bought a set of Borrow, and your pages on him were the main reason.[3] I must read him through: I have known him so little. The six volumes sit opposite me now; but I cannot touch them till my paper is done.

Deaver has grown a great deal this summer, and is better company than ever. We had a longish walk together this afternoon. He is becoming very sensitive to the beauty of flowers, and this is a grand summer for them.

We have had oppressive heat; and I have not been downtown since my return. I stay at home, and read and lounge. But September will bring back my energy.I find that I mind the cold less and the heat more than I used to do.

> With our love to you both,
> Yours, as ever,
> Edward

P.S. [*holo.*] When you write please tell me how Loftus progresses. And please give Mrs. MacI my sincere sympathy. I always liked Loftus and we seemed to get on from the beginning. No: Gustafson has not sent me the article. At the *Toronto Quarterly* we once rejected an article of his on A.L.

182

September 2-8, 1947

My Dear Edward,[1]

Now that you are home again I can write with a clearer conscience, I think my letters must have been a nuisance when you were so busy in N.Y. Yours of 26th July about the verse in *The Circle* gave me infinite satisfaction, for I did not expect you to like it all so much. I may be forgiven my burst of loyalty, wh. was sincere;[2] there are reasons wh. I need not try to set forth. What pleased me best of all was your remarks about the four sonnets, "Twelfth Anniversary;" I expected you, of all my friends, wld understand those sonnets; there is a portrait, and there are reflections and a declaration of devotion, but as good as I cld make them they are not worthy of Elise. As you have been interested in my method of doing verse I will tell you that I wrote the first three and the beginning of the fourth on one evening, 12 Mar '43.[3] E. was not well and I was down stairs alone and the idea suddenly hit me to do something to show her on the 27th March, two hours of intense feeling and a sense of freedom in expression led to the result; there was ever so little tinkering and I was able to make a fair copy for her. I felt that you wld understand but I wanted to be sure. May I make some remarks about the others you mention. 'Amanda' was printed in *Voices* in a Canadian No.[4] It was first called 'A Dream,' but we must give Pelham the credit of suggesting the present title. The actual dream I had the night you & Peggy were here (so long ago!) but I did not think I wld try to do anything with it, until months afterwards, Oct '42, the idea struck me to work on it, I must say I like it and I am glad you do.[5] The early poems were done so long ago that I have no dates but of course after *The Magic House*,[6] but I did not think it worth while to print them in any of the other books and they wld not have appeared here if it had not been for Elise who decided the matter; she was particularly taken with 'Early Summer Song' wh. I dug up and wh. I had really forgotten about, I think it was printed in some obscure paper but I have no printed copy of it.[7] Now for the last line of 'Derwentwater,' of course you know well that I have no knowledge of prosody. I suppose the difficulty comes from my dropping one accent from the last line and thus, in a sense, disturbing the uniformity of the stanzas. Well, I have done it before, to my ear the line is a perfect conclusion to the lyric and to have lengthened it wld have been a mistake; it shd be read with the preceding line without pause; in the two lines there are five accents. But perhaps you mean that I have not expressed an important idea clearly, please let me know. If you want other examples of my confirmed irregularities, compare the third and fourth stanzas of 'Veronique Fraser,'[8] or the 18th and 19th (p. 58), I read the last two lines of 19[9]

She had forgotten her lovers
    And their quest.[10]

Please give this matter your attention. As for 'The March amarching' lyric: it was written to order from no less a person than Wm. Arthur Deacon years ago for some special number, was it of *Sat. Night*?[11] Forgotten, but Elise insisted it shd go in. Why dont you order a Poem on some special subject, say the marriage of Princess Elizabeth, i.e. if the CBC wld pay me for it![12] I would try to be worthy of any commission from you, a difficult matter. I wld like to remark on the 'Slumber Song,'[13] I printed it as her parents wanted it; this baby only lived a little over a year, and died after a two hours illness in July of '46; so I was doubtful whether they wld care to see it in print, but they were keen about it; I thought I shd tell you about this. L.W.B. often asks after you and sends his regards. Deaver's poem still delights me, how easy it was for me to write it. Your latest news about him is interesting; it must have been exhilarating to hear his voice over the phone. Now I thank you for yours of the 31st ult. I hope the *Forum* prints the notice without cutting it, as ever you were praiseful of my care of L's work and you have done your part lately too and fully. Loftus is out of hospital but is in very bad shape, his wife is very courageous, we were able to get a part-time nurse for her. I hope you will be patient with Borrow, he is often most tedious but at his best there is no one quite like him. There is no use my lecturing about Trollope, he also is tiresome, but in his own range inimitable, I dont think

The Small House is one of my favorites. Yes, *Silas Marner* is a work of genius. In a book of Gorki's I read "That dull novel *Middlemarch;*" and so opinions differ. We had a delightful evg with JW on Friday and had the latest news about you; he is a great addition to our inner circle. This is one of my usual long screeds; the garrulous outpourings of an Ancient; I have made a vow that in future I shall vie with you in conciseness.

Just a last word about your birthday greetings; I had a card from Deaver with a signature that looked like a tracing by Matisse, there was a sense of *design* in it; I replied by printing a reply and sending it to Peggy with a short note; I wld like to know that it arrived, no good wishes were so welcome as yours. I also dislike HEAT,[14] we were prostrated by the intense heat in Aug. I had felt nothing to compare with it in all my Ottawa days; and the sudden changes in temperature have been very trying. One can fight COLD but Heat when it is mixed with HUMIDITY is intolerable, one just expires. I had a note from Masefield about *The Circle*[15] wh. I thought you might like to see, so I send a copy; make some remarks if you feel like it. When can we expect the Arnold?

> Our love to you all.
> Yours ever,
> Duncan

183

September 6, 1947

Dear Duncan,

A small thing that can be done for A.L. has occurred to me: the listing of as many of his poems as possible according to date of composition. Such a listing will be of great help to the study of the development of his art and thought.

I find that from my notes on reading the mss. and your additions I can date no fewer than 157 poems within a month; and about 25 more within a year.[1]

The list I enclose is of the poems I cannot date, though in some cases I might guess.[2] The two entries in ink are from our Long Sault volume. The final entry in pencil is a notation of yours. I do not find a poem so entitled (perhaps just the looking for it has blinded me).[3] All the other poems you noted on the same sheet were easily found.

If you find any material that is relevant in the little book you have[4] would you note it for me. And also any general ideas or memories?

When I get things into shape, I shall of course send you the rough draft of the list for comment.

I am just finishing a revision of my paper on Victorian Fiction for delivery next week.

> In some haste,
> Yours, as ever,
> Edward

184

[September 16] '47[1]

Dear Edward.   I had just posted my last to you when yours of the 6th came to hand. Of course I will be ready and glad to help with your scheme wh. I think an excellent one. You must not expect any results "too immediately," to quote that classic phrase. I will go over your list carefully and give whatever dates or information I have; that will not take long. But our *delay* will be with Loftus; I gave Natalie the little book you mention, the bound copies of *Alcyone* with the corrected proofs, and *all* the MSS that were in my hands, there were only a few.[2] I thought she had better have them as I had no ownership in them. I think we exhausted the little book for dates when you saw it, or afterwards I did. But there are the Scribblers. These shd be gone through again. Now the point is that Loftus is a *very sick man,* he is improving but he is in bad shape, as we say, and struggling back into life; I have phoned to Natalie once or twice but she does not want to be disturbed much, he cant see any one. Under these circumstances you will agree that I cant bother her about the notebooks etc, *at present* and I dont know when I shall be able to. I would hope that Loftus might improve so greatly that it would be an occupation for him to go through them and get all the dates, but we can only wait a bit. I think it remarkable that you have found 157 dates. I had a chap here yesterday looking after my machine; he put on a new ribbon and left some oil of wh. I give you a sample; but I could not recopy, I knew you wld excuse the blemish. Do not forget to send me a copy of "Victorian Fiction."

Yours ever,
Duncan[3]

185

[Chicago]
September 28, 1947

Dear Duncan,

Your two letters gave me a great pleasure. All that you say of the poems in *The Circle* was of the deepest interest. I think on farther analysis, that what slightly disturbed me in that last line was a sense that the attention caught for it by the metrical irregularity was not quite justified by the expansion of the thought, I mean that a thought of that depth cannot perfectly be captured in those words. I like your irregularities in general, as those of other poets.

The Masefield letter was friendly and has his pleasant touch; but I wish he had been somewhat fuller, just as I wished that de la Mare had been fuller in his to me. The English are not much given to the real and direct approach to an intellectual or aesthetic matter — a lacuna in their culture.

I am relieved to hear that Loftus is out of hospital but sorry to gather from your letter that he must face a long recovery. I shall write to him one of these days. There is no reason to speed the inquiry into the A.L. dates. It is a slight matter; and can wait indefinitely. You are ingenious and also wise in suggesting that this might be a pleasure to Loftus during the long weeks ahead.

I shall see that a copy of the lecture on Victorian fiction goes to you, when printed. But when that will be I don't know. I think that the lectures given at that Institute are bound in a volume about a year later. I have been revising since I returned.

Pierce has agreed to take 250 copies of the Matthew Arnold,[1] which he says he likes better than anything of mine he has seen. He is in my good graces just now! I believe he has taken all he should, for a book of this kind on this subject cannot be expected to sell very widely in Canada.

I am reading *Dombey and Son* for the first time. Critics had rather discouraged me from trying it; but I find it full of interest. The treatment of the "rejected" child Florence Dombey is very powerful. This interests me particularly because my "trade" reason for reading the book was that it immediately preceded *Copperfield* on which I have an essay in the rough that I want to complete.[2] He was very much preoccupied with the orphan or quasi-orphan child at that time.

Tell JW I shall write to him very soon. It was a great pleasure to see him even if so briefly.

Classes begin to-morrow. This quarter I am to repeat Browning, give a general course on methods of literary study which is also a repeat, and try a George Eliot for the first time here. It is a pleasant prospect.

Our love to you both. Deaver liked your birthday greeting, or rather response to such a greeting, and so did we all.

Yours, as ever,

Edward

P.S. [*holo.*] I am glad you approved the notice for the *Forum*. I don't know when it will appear.

186 [*Holo.*]

November 30, 1947

Dear Peggy & Edward,

We send you congratulations with love & all good wishes and to dear Deaver too, it will be fine for him to have a brother! Let us know in a letter of yr very own what his name will be.[1] I have been fixed here in bed for 5 weeks exactly today! With our love.

Elise & Duncan

187 [Holo]

November 30, 1947

Dear Mr. Brown,

I am putting a note in with Duncan's letter, for I think I should tell you that he is much more seriously ill than he realizes. He was having bad heart attacks all last week — angina — and although he is much better these last three days he is naturally much weakened. It was a pretty bad experience for both of us.

We are not telling any one what it is, apart from the family and one or two old friends — people are apt to be so tactless in their inquiries — and I'd be glad if you would not mention it. He does not know himself, and we are so anxious that he should not be alarmed about his condition.

Our love to you and Peggy,

Yours sincerely,
Elise A.S.

(Duncan Campbell Scott died December 19, 1947)

NOTES

The following abbreviations are used in these notes.

> PAC   *Public Archives of Canada*
> SAP   *Scott-Aylen Papers*
> PEP   *Pelham Edgar Papers*

LETTER 1

1. *Poetry: a magazine of verse* had been launched in 1912 under the editorship of Harriet Munroe and had soon become a flagship of the modern poetry movement in the United States. Among the new poets introduced in its monthly issues were Vachel Lindsay, Carl Sandburg, Amy Lowell, Ezra Pound, T.S. Eliot and Hart Crane. Pound was for a time foreign correspondent for the magazine. The "Canadian" issue cited was published in April 1941 (vol. LVIII, no. 1). Brown's contribution was an article entitled "The Development of Poetry in Canada, 1880-1940."

LETTER 2

1. The poem was entitled 'Power.' It was to be published later in Scott's *The Circle of Affection* (Toronto: McClelland & Stewart, 1947).
2. The Scotts had been "last in Italy" in the winter of 1937-38 (December to February). In a letter of May 5, 1939, Gladstone Murray, chairman of the Canadian Broadcasting Corporation, had written to ask Scott to compose a "special poem" to be broadcast on June 15 at the time of the departure of the King and Queen from Canada through Halifax (SAP). The title of the poem, as it appears in *The Circle of Affection,* is 'A Farewell to Their Majesties.'
3. Several Eliot titles were issued in 1939 and 1940. In a letter written a few days later to Pelham Edgar, Scott identifies the book he has ordered as *East Coker* (PEP). It was published by Faber & Faber in the spring of 1940.

LETTER 3

1. Brown is using office stationery of the *University of Toronto Quarterly*. This was to be his last year as editor.
2. Kenneth Flexner Fearing (1902-61), an American poet noted for his proletarian sympathies and for the three volumes of satirical poems which he had published between 1929 and 1938. His *Collected Poems* was brought out by Random House in 1940.

LETTER 4

1. After the first few letters of this correspondence, Scott's address is seldom on the letterhead, only the date, and sometimes not even that. Throughout, he was at 108 Lisgar Street, Ottawa, in the house in which he had lived for more than fifty years. I see no point hereafter in repeating the address. The one exception (Letter 8) is noted.

2. Escape from the rigours of the Ottawa winter was a routine well established. Italy, which the Scotts loved, was now ruled out by the war. In 1940, they had wintered in Phoenix, Arizona. The present winter was to be spent in Victoria, B.C. In 1942, they would have one more visit to the west coast, staying this time in Vancouver, where Mrs. Scott's mother and three sisters had settled.

3. Scott's friendship with Pelham Edgar dated back to the turn of the century. They had been closely associated first as joint editors of the Makers of Canada series, later as co-workers in establishing the Canadian Writers' Foundation. The son of Sir James Edgar, for many years Speaker of the House of Commons, Pelham was born in 1871 and educated at Upper Canada College, the University of Toronto and Johns Hopkins University. He was a student, as the young E.K. Brown was to be many years later, of modern languages and literature. In 1902, Edgar became head of the Department of English at Victoria College (Toronto) and he continued in that post until his retirement in 1938. He was a bringer-on of talent: E.J. Pratt, Marjorie Pickthall, Northrop Frye and even Scott himself were in some sense his protegés; and as teacher and critic he was highly regarded by his peers. He published *Henry James, Man and Author* (1927) and *The Art of the Novel from 1700 to the Present Time* (1933). For Scott he provided an entry into the world of the academic which the poet so greatly admired. Edgar died in 1948.

4. Ralph Barker Gustafson (1909-), poet, teacher, anthologist, was educated at Bishop's University and Oxford. At this time he was living in New York. Now retired after many years as professor of English at Bishop's University, he has published more than a dozen books of poetry, five anthologies and numerous short stories. The assignment Scott refers to produced *Anthology of Canadian Poetry* (Penguin Books, 1942).

5. In the end, five poems were published, not six: 'After Battle'; 'At Delos'; 'Watkwenies'; 'The Half-Breed Girl'; and 'The Sailor's Sweetheart.'

6. Probably the Letters in Canada Supplement to the *University of Toronto Quarterly*. Brown had been joint editor of the *Quarterly*, with A.S.P. Woodhouse, since 1932.

7. Later published in *The Circle of Affection*.

LETTER 5

1. In addition to the poem for *Poetry*, Scott had sent another to Brown personally. The occasion is recalled by Brown in Letter 150, where he gives the date as January 18, 1941. If there was a covering note, it has not been preserved. 'These are in the beginning' was subsequently published in *The Circle of Affection*. It appeared also in *Queen's Quarterly*, vol. 50, no. 1 (Spring 1943), p. 63.

LETTER 6

1. The Scotts, as planned, had stopped in Toronto for a visit with the Edgars on their way back from Victoria. From a letter Scott wrote to Pelham Edgar on May 5, 1941, we learn that E. J. Pratt had joined the group at the Edgars' home. Scott was delighted: "I enjoyed my evg with you, Ned and E.K. and wish I cld have prolonged it but I was tired after a long trip — 10:30 is not my limit usually" (PEP).

2. A.J.M. Smith (1902-80), poet, critic, anthologist. Professor of English at Michigan State University since 1936, Smith had maintained close connections with Canada, where he had been born and educated, and had by this time already done much to set the pace for the coming of modernism to Canadian poetry. His first volume of verse, *News of the Phoenix*, was to win the Governor General's Award for 1943, and in the same year he would publish his critical and historical anthology, *The Book of Canadian Poetry*. See Letter 44, note 1, Letter 60 *et seq*. The poems which Scott refers to are 'The Mermaid' and 'The Cry.' These are the "two last" of the three poems which Smith contributed.

3. E.J. Pratt (1882-1964), poet, teacher, raconteur. Pelham Edgar was the link between Pratt and Scott. As early as 1918, at Edgar's urging, Pratt had written to Scott expressing his great appreciation of the work of the older poet (SAP). In the years which followed there were many occasions for contact — through the Royal Society, the editing of the *Canadian Poetry Magazine,* the work of the Canadian Writers' Foundation and the like. Pratt was to publish four volumes of verse within the period of the present correspondence: *Dunkirk* (1941); *Still Life* (1943); *They Are Returning* (1945); and *Behind the Log* (1947). It was not his best period, and both Scott and Brown seem to sense this. Pratt contributed two poems to *Poetry.* The first is 'The Invaded Field.' The second (''E.J.P.'s last'') is 'Come Away Death.'

LETTER 7

1. "Duncan Campbell Scott, An Individual Poet," by E.K. Brown. *Manitoba Arts Review,* II (Spring 1941), pp. 51-54.
2. "In his method of thought there is a trait, clearly related to his musical approach, but so far unnoticed, although it is perhaps the most individuating of all the qualities in his verse. In his last collection, *The Green Cloister,* again and again he proceeds by setting forth two clearly separated and contrasted positions, sometimes brought into an ultimate reconciliation" (p. 54).
3. Writing of 'Night Burial in the Forest,' Brown says that the three principals of the story ''are all, doubtless, Indians, but the nexus is a universal one'' (p. 53). Among some papers passed on to me by Mrs. E.K. Brown in 1975 were a few notes Brown made at the time of, or soon after, his first meeting with Scott at the Edgars'. The date given is April 28, 1941, and one of the notes reads: "DCS told me the 'Night Burial in the Forest' was not intended to suggest Indians but e.g. prospectors.''
4. Robert McQueen had been killed in a plane crash while travelling from Ottawa to Winnipeg on February 6, 1941. He was forty-five years old. At the time of his death he was serving as a director of the Bank of Canada and held the position of professor of Economics and head of the Department of Political Economy and Political Science at the University of Manitoba. The issue of the *Manitoba Arts Review* in question was a memorial number dedicated to Robert McQueen.
5. The typist had put, for Scott's signature, "Duncan Campbell Scott." I think this is the only one of Scott's letters in the present sequence which he had typed for him. The article by Pelham Edgar is "The Poetry of Duncan Campbell Scott," *Dalhousie Review,* VII (1927-28), pp. 38-46.

LETTER 8

1. In 1941 Brown had accepted an appointment to Cornell University as professor of English and chairman of the Department. He was to remain in Ithaca until his move to the University of Chicago in 1944.
2. Scott had been elected a fellow of the Royal Society in 1899. He was honorary secretary from 1911 to 1920 and served in the same capacity again in 1925-26. He was president in 1921-22.
3. The Japanese had attacked Pearl Harbor on December 7, 1941, and the United States was now at war with Japan. There were rumours of Japanese submarines operating off the west coast of Vancouver Island.
4. Lawren Stewart Harris (1885-1970) was born in Brantford, Ontario. He studied art in Berlin and in other European centres in the first decade of the century, returning to Canada in 1909. He was an original member of the Group of Seven, of the Ontario Society of Artists and, from 1933, of the Canadian Group of Painters. By 1942, he was settled in Vancouver.

5. Dilys Bennett Laing, wife of the American poet and novelist Alexander Kinnan Laing, had published a volume of poems entitled *Another England* in 1941 (New York: Duell, Sloan & Pearce).

LETTER 9

1. The original of this and the following letter is on notepaper bearing the seal of the Office of the Prime Minister of Canada. On the back of the page Scott has scribbled a number and the words ''EKB's phone.''

2. Arthur S. Bourinot has an important place in the Scott story. His father, Sir John Bourinot, had been Clerk of the House of Commons from 1880 until his death in 1902. The Bourinot home on Cooper Street, which lay almost back-to-back with Scott's home on Lisgar, had been a rallying place for intellectuals and writers of the day: Archibald Lampman, the young D.C. Scott, W.D. LeSueur, Wilfred Campbell, Gilbert Parker and others. Arthur Bourinot was of course much younger than Scott, but the ties had been close from the beginning and became even closer when, in 1931, Scott married Elise Aylen, who was Bourinot's niece. Bourinot himself had a solid reputation as a poet, and it was natural that Brown should turn to him for information about the Scotts.

3. In the spring of 1942, Brown accepted an appointment as ''special assistant'' to Mackenzie King. Exact duties were unclear, though speech-writing was probably meant to be a part of them. But from the beginning Brown seems to have felt great frustration, and by the fall he was back in Ithaca. The important outcome, however, was the contact with Scott — and through Scott with T.R. Loftus MacInnes and his wife Natalie, who was Lampman's daughter.

LETTER 11

1. The talks of that summer had been highly productive. The written record falters and falls silent, of course, as Brown and Scott put their heads together at Lisgar Street, but a later letter from Scott to Lorne Pierce, dated January 26, 1943, gives us some idea of what has happened. Since the letter helps to fill a gap in the correspondence, I give the text in full in Appendix A (p. 280). It is clear that Lampman has figured largely in the conversations between the two men, and Scott has told Brown about manuscripts still in the hands of Lampman's daughter, Natalie MacInnes. Natalie has been cooperative. Now, back in Ithaca, Brown has beside him Lampman's scribblers and notebooks and is beginning to put together a manuscript of hitherto unpublished poems. This is the genesis of *At the Long Sault*, which was to be published by the Ryerson Press in 1943.

2. At the time Lampman wrote these sonnets, he was engaged to Miss Maud E. Playter, second daughter of Dr. Edward Playter of Ottawa. The group of poems referred to was to be called ''The Growth of Love.''

3. The ''later love poems'' were to appear in *At the Long Sault* as a sequence called ''Portrait in Six Sonnets,'' and the import to be concealed was that they were clearly not addressed to Maud Playter, now Mrs. Lampman. This is the first reference we have to Lampman's love affair (if that is what it can be called) with his co-worker in the Post Office Department, Miss Katherine Waddell. It was a sensitive matter for Loftus and Natalie MacInnes and, to a degree, for Scott. From his conversations with Scott, Brown knew of Lampman's extra-marital attachment but did not know the identity of the lady (E.K. Brown Papers, PAC). For a full though not entirely reliable account of the Waddell affair, see Dr. Margaret Whitridge's *Lampman's Kate* (Ottawa: Borealis Press, 1975), pp. 11-23.

4. 'New Year's Eve' had been published in the January 1914 issue of *Canadian Magazine*. The other poem referred to is 'The Settler's Tale,' published in the December 1913 issue of the same magazine.

5. This manuscript book is one of four deposited with the Library of Parliament after Lampman's death in 1899. They are all "fair copy" books and therefore represent a final, or nearly final, stage in Lampman's composition.

6. The Musson Book Company had published the 1925 edition of Lampman's poems.

LETTER 12

1. This letter exists in three distinct forms and may be taken as a good illustration of the problem of textual variants on the Scott side of the correspondence. The text printed is the one Brown received. In the SAP I found Scott's draft of the same letter. There is no carbon copy. Scott made very few such drafts, or at any rate very few have survived. I see them as signals of his special concern, made when he wanted to be sure he got things right. The third version, differing in some particulars from the other two, is the text derived from Scott's draft and published by Bourinot in *Some Letters of Duncan Campbell Scott, Archibald Lampman and Others* (Ottawa, 1959), pp. 17-18. Variations between the three texts show clearly: (a) Scott feeling his way through some uncertainties; (b) the difficulties which confronted Bourinot when he faced the draft rather than the carbon copy of a Scott letter; and (c) one of the main principles of Bourinot's editing, which was to delete passages he thought might give offence to persons still living.

2. The Greek sonnets, three in number, were published in *At the Long Sault* under the heading CRETE.

3. cf. the text of the draft version referred to in note 1: "I am in great doubt about 'The Settler's Tale,' but I shall write again about that. The other piece might go in." In the end, 'The Settler's Tale' was not included.

4. The Musson Book Co. Ltd. had acquired from Morang & Co. the rights to Lampman's poems for the publication, in 1925, of *Lyrics of Earth: Sonnets and Ballads,* a selected edition, drawn from the "Memorial" volume of 1900, with an introduction by D.C. Scott. The beginnings of the Ryerson Press lie deep in the nineteenth century and come forward through a succession of Book Stewards of the Methodist Book and Publishing House under whose imprints the house presented its lists. Perhaps the best-known of these imprints is that of William Briggs, who was Steward between 1879 and 1919. In 1920, Lorne Pierce was appointed editor of the Ryerson Press, and the Ryerson imprint soon became familiar as a hallmark of Canadian publishing.

5. Bourinot omits, without any indication he is doing so, the entire reference to Lorne Pierce, as also the later one to "L.P." as "a great dilly-dallyer." Lorne Pierce was editor of Ryerson Press until shortly before his death in 1961. Author of *An Outline of Canadian Literature* (1928), *A Canadian People* (1945), etc., he was a tireless promoter of Canadian writing. T.R. Loftus MacInnes was born in Victoria, B.C., in 1901, the son of Tom MacInnes, poet. He entered the federal civil service, in the Department of Indian Affairs, in 1914. In October 1915, he married Natalie Charlotte, only daughter of Archibald Lampman. At this time he was still with Indian Affairs and had acquired an excellent reputation as editor, since 1928, of the *Civil Service Review*. He died in 1952.

6. Yousuf Karsh, distinguished photographer. The work which brought Karsh international recognition is represented in *Faces of Destiny* (1947) and *Portraits of Greatness* (1959). He became friendly with Scott soon after coming to Ottawa in 1932, and in the years that followed he did several portraits of the poet. He was amongst the select group who attended Scott's funeral at Lisgar Street on December 22, 1947. The portrait referred to here is of course of E.K. Brown. It had appeared in a recent issue of *Saturday Night* (October 3, 1942). The caption to which Scott takes

exception begins: "This quizzical-looking gentleman is Professor E.K. Brown, one of Canada's most eminent academic authorities on English literature, photographed by Karsh after six months service in Ottawa in a position somewhat similar to that held by Leonard Brockington."

7. *Victorian Poetry,* edited with an introduction and notes by E.K. Brown (New York: Nelson, 1942).

8. This is the last line of Lampman's 'September.'

9. I have not had much success with the "PIG correspondence." I am not even sure that I am reading "PIG" correctly, the typescript being blurred. In the October issue of *Saturday Night* there had been several letters from farmers angry about new controls on pork and beef imposed by Finance Minister James Ilsley and James Gardiner, Minister of Agriculture. But the "take-off on W.L.M.K." identified by Brown in the next letter, together with what was apparently a rejoinder by King, are not there. The references remain obscure.

10. James Lorimer Ilsley had been named Finance Minister in 1940 and was to hold that post until the end of the war. He was inevitably the author of many unpopular measures: high taxes, rationing and a variety of restrictions and controls. In the later years of his life he was to become Chief Justice of the Nova Scotia Supreme Court. "Our Peerless Leader" is the mocking term Scott used (doubtless very much in private) for Prime Minister Mackenzie King.

11. Peregrine Acland (1892-1963) had had a distinguished career as a soldier in the First World War. In 1929 he had published *All Else Is Folly: A Tale of War and Passion* (Toronto: McClelland & Stewart). The preface was by Ford Madox Ford. In the National Library there is an autographed presentation copy of the novel which has the following inscription: "To the Right Hon. W.L. Mackenzie King in appreciation of the friendship he has always shown Peregrine Acland."

12. Spender's *Ruins and Visions* and *Life and the Poet* were reviewed by G.W. Stonier in the *New Statesman and Nation,* (August 1, 1942), p. 79.

LETTER 13

1. See the poem 'Ottawa,' *At the Long Sault,* p. 20.

2. There is no such title in *At the Long Sault.* Since most of the titles were supplied, however, and doubtless many of them second-guessed, the poem in question may be 'Loneliness' (p. 26): "So it is with us all; we have our friends, etc."

3. No poem called 'The Politician' appears in *At the Long Sault,* nor does Brown refer to or quote from a poem with this title in his introduction. Scott is to comment later (Letter 33) on the inadequacy of the title: "It is a Timon-like arraignment of the whole of mankind, from the Seer to the Pimp: but what is the quality that runs down through all classes?" Is this then the same poem Scott calls 'The Pimp' in Letter 17, suggesting it to Brown as another example, together with 'The True Life,' of Lampman's "force"?

4. Brown was referring, not to "the sonnet on Life," but to the so-called "crossing-sweeper" sonnet, quoted by Scott, under the title 'Reality,' in his introduction to the 1925 collection of Lampman's "sonnets and ballads" (p. 30 of that edition). Brown corrects his mistake in Letter 19.

5. It is difficult to identify "the lines to Natalie"; perhaps the lines were not included.

6. *On Canadian Poetry* (Toronto: Ryerson Press, 1943). *At the Long Sault* was published first, as Brown hoped. It is interesting to compare the two texts, in particular the introduction to *At the Long Sault,* pp. xi-xxix, and Chapter Three of *On Canadian Poetry,* pp. 80-108.

7. The reference is to W.E. Collin's treatment of Lampman in the first chapter of *The White Savannahs* (Toronto: Macmillan, 1936) pp. 3-40. The essence of Collin's argument is that Lampman, in a misguided response to Arnold's call for men of good will to "Hellenize," had turned his back on humanity and taken to the hills and streams.

8. The "enclosure" is the only part of this letter printed by Bourinot. See *Some Letters,* p. 18.

LETTER 14

1. Francis Parkman (1823-93), American historian, chronicler in several volumes of the story of England and France in the New World. Parkman tells the story of Daulac (or Dollard des Ormeaux) in Part Fourth of the series, *The Old Régime in Canada.* In the 1899 edition (London), see pp. 124-39.

2. *Among the Millet* (Ottawa: Durie, 1888) was Lampman's first volume of poems. The three sonnets mentioned appear there in the order given. When they took their place in the *At the Long Sault* sequence, the ordering, always a fine point with Scott, was changed and the sonnets separated: 'Love-Doubt' (I), 'Love-Wonder' (X), and 'Perfect Love' (XI). See *Among the Millet,* pp. 123-25; and *At the Long Sault,* p. 37 and p. 42.

3. Colonel Henry Campbell Osborne (1874-1949) had had a distinguished career in the First World War. For many years Secretary-General of the Canadian agency of the Imperial War Graves Commission, he played a prominent part in the construction of the Canadian Memorial at Vimy Ridge. At the time of the present correspondence his immediate connection with Scott was their shared interest in the development of the Dominion Drama Festival. His wife Marian, who died in 1931, had some reputation as a poet and a dramatist.

4. See D.C. Scott, "Clarence A. Gagnon, recollection and record," *Maritime Art,* 3 (October-November 1942), pp. 5-9. The article was republished in *The Circle of Affection,* pp. 148-56. Gagnon, etcher and painter, was born in Montreal in 1881, studied first under William Brymner in Montreal and later at the Julian Academy in Paris. He became a master of the art of etching but is perhaps best known for the 54 paintings he produced for Mornay's 1933 edition of *Maria Chapdelaine.* The Gagnons and the Scotts were long-time friends, and after the artist's sudden death in January 1942, it was to Scott that Madame Gagnon had turned for help in the disposition of her husband's paintings, etchings and papers. There is a substantial Gagnon File in the SAP.

5. Thomas Sturge Moore (1870-1944): English poet, man of letters and wood engraver. Moore, whose first volume of poetry appeared in 1899, was to become prominent amongst the Georgians celebrated by Edward Marsh in successive editions of *Georgian Poetry* between 1912 and 1922. His work reflects the Georgians' delight in quiet and disciplined perfection in art.

6. There is a draft of this addition to Letter 14 in the SAP. Bourinot did not print it, presumably because its many cancellings, inserts and scrawled phrases made it difficult for him to guess Scott's final intentions in the absence of a carbon copy of the letter sent to Brown. But the very existence of the draft is itself an indication that Scott is writing under some emotional stress, and the many changes between the draft and the original confirm an agitation which we may guess was induced by his hearing again the voice of his old friend Lampman in this fine poem passed over and so long silent in the notebooks. The letter seems incomplete without the draft and I have therefore placed a copy of the latter in Appendix B (p. 281).

LETTER 15

1. The article was published, as promised, in January. See E.K. Brown, "Mackenzie King of Canada," *Harper's Magazine*, 186 (January 1943), pp. 192-200, (reprinted in David Staines, ed., *E.K. Brown: Responses and Evaluations*, New Canadian Library No. 137 [Toronto: McClelland & Stewart, 1977]). J.W. Pickersgill, in *The Mackenzie King Record*, gives an interesting account of King's reactions:

> On January 4 he "was very much hurt" on reading an article in *Harper's Magazine* by Professor E.K. Brown who had spent six months on his secretarial staff earlier in the war. What Brown had sought to do was to give an objective portrait of Mackenzie King. But the Prime Minister felt it was unfair and held him up to ridicule. Brown, he wrote, "was trying to show that the public had one point of view whereas, in reality, if they knew me, they would find I was quite different. In seeking to make his contrast, he fell into the error of painting one side solely as it is represented by Tory propaganda. He even went the length of speaking of my being disliked in all the English provinces." Mackenzie King never ceased to resent this article of Brown's. On January 7 he noted: "I have been thinking a good deal in the last forty-eight hours about the future. In part perhaps as a result of the effect of Brown's article and the sort of talk to which it will give rise" (Vol. I, p. 475).

2. Included in the residue of Brown's papers to which Mrs. Brown gave me access in 1975 is a typescript of the 'Daulac' poem which I believe has the same basic text as the copy Brown now has before him. It shows a few changes ("burg" to "town," for example) and some added punctuation, but by no means all the points Brown talks about in this letter are noted. One may postulate a more advanced copy, probably the one Scott sends with his next letter (Letter 16). The typescript that has survived is at any rate interesting in that it lets us see plainly the differences, now emerging, between Brown's transcript of the Lampman poem and the version which is to be published as the title poem of *At the Long Sault*. See Letter 16, note 1.

3. Douglas Bush was born in Morrisburg, Ontario, in 1896. He earned his B.A. at the University of Toronto in 1920 and his M.A. in 1921. By the time Brown came to University College, Bush was off to Harvard, where he earned his Ph.D. in 1923 and where he was to spend most of the remainder of a very distinguished career. But the University College network was close, and the two men were to meet and become friends in the thirties. Bush, by 1942, had already published three important books: *Mythology and the Renaissance Tradition in English Poetry* (1932); *Mythology and the Romantic Tradition in English Poetry* (1937); and *The Renaissance and English Humanism* (1939). See also Letter 70, note 2.

4. See the reference to Venizelos and "this Cretan business" in Letter 32.

LETTER 16

1. For the reader who wishes to follow more closely Scott's suggestions for the improvement of later sections of the poem, I have included relevant lines from the 'Daulac' transcript in Appendix C (p. 283). This part of the poem gave Scott more trouble than any other, and he was to make many changes (cf. the final version in *At the Long Sault,* p. 3).

2. Elise Aylen was born on November 14, 1904. Daughter of a prominent Ottawa family and niece to Arthur Bourinot, she had married Scott in 1931.

3. Bourinot prints this letter in *Some Letters* (p. 20) but does not include the marginal note. Here, as elsewhere, is evidence that he was working from a carbon copy rather than from the original, which alone had the holograph postcript. Scott's nervousness is

indeed plain to see. He has had to correct, with a spluttery pen, eighteen minor mistakes or omissions in the original.

LETTER 17

1. The selecting and ordering of the "early Love Sonnets" which begins here is continued in Letters 19, 20 and 21. In the absence of the enclosures which Scott has sent to Brown (the layout itself and the note giving "reasons") it is difficult sometimes to be sure what is being proposed and why. The important point to recognize is that in the end *all* the sonnets mentioned or discussed were to be included in *At the Long Sault.* Of the completed sequence, the poems with which Scott and Brown are chiefly concerned here are sonnets IV and V, and the two parts ("Praise and Prayer") of sonnet VI (*At the Long Sault,* pp. 38-40).

2. Robert Bridges, *The Growth of Love: A Poem in Twenty-four Sonnets* (London: E. Bumpus, 1876).

3. See *At the Long Sault,* p. 35.

LETTER 18

1. See Letter 13, note 6.

LETTER 19

1. The "short sonnets" have twelve lines each. The rhyme schemes are highly irregular. Together they make up the two parts of the "Praise and Prayer" sequence, as published in *At the Long Sault* (VI). What is not clear is which "sonnet" is being dropped at this stage, and indeed Brown himself is to be confused on this point later. Perhaps some of the difficulty lies in the ordering of the components in the sequence. The two poems have discrete subjects: i.e., "prayer" and "praise"; and Brown seems to accept the pair as being arranged in that order. But Scott may have already moved to reverse that order since the superscription which appears in *At the Long Sault* reads "Praise and Prayer." I do not know what Brown means by the "other series" to which one of the poems is to be assigned.

2. Lampman's "fair copy" books in the Parliamentary Library.

3. Allied forces had landed in Morocco and Algeria during the second week of November, and the success of that operation now seemed assured with their rapid advance into Tunisia. General Montgomery's Eighth Army was meanwhile continuing its pressure on the German forces from the east.

LETTER 20

1. Dante Gabriel Rossetti's *Ballads and Sonnets,* published in 1881, contained a sonnet sequence which he called "The House of Life."

2. Clearly typed in the original. Although Scott usually corrects his "typos" by pen, he lets this word stand. I assume it is a phonetic device used for emphasis. Scott sometimes indulged in this kind of verbal playfulness in his early letters to Pelham Edgar.

3. There is a marginal note at this point, indicated by an arrow. It is in Scott's hand, and it reads: "You made a pencil note on the copy wh I could not make out. D." Brown is careful to give a typed version of his next pencilled note.

4. This is the "ylad" sonnet: " 'Sweet trees,' I cried, in plaining dreams astray,/Through mead and woodland dolefully ylad, etc.'' It was to be placed fourth in the published sequence.

5. Late 1942 was a turning point in the war. In October, General Montgomery's Eighth Army had turned back Rommel's forces at Alamein. There were Russian victories in

the Caucasus, and the Americans had opened a new offensive in the Pacific theatre. In France, the Vichy government of Marshal Pétain and Pierre Laval was engaged in various acts of collaboration with the Germans.

LETTER 21

1. By "book" Brown probably means one of Lampman's fair-copy books. Brown had seen these books in Ottawa and had taken notes. His main sources in Ithaca, however, were "notebooks" and "scribblers," both representing early stages in Lampman's composition. See Letter 30, where Brown justifies editorial tinkering on the grounds that he and Scott are dealing "not with 'fair copies' but with relatively rough drafts."

2. Earle Birney, *David and Other Poems* (Toronto: Ryerson, 1942). This was Birney's first collection of verse, and it was to win the Governor General's Award for Poetry in 1942. At this time, Birney was serving as a personnel officer with the Canadian Army Overseas. His university career had begun with an appointment as lecturer in English at the University of Toronto in 1936. He was later to settle in Vancouver, where he taught Creative Writing at the University of British Columbia.

3. Leonard W. Brockington, broadcaster, administrator and writer. A graduate of the University of Wales, he came to Canada in 1912. He studied law in Calgary and was called to the bar in 1919. From 1936 to 1939 he was chairman of the newly established CBC. After a brief period of service as special assistant to Prime Minister Mackenzie King in the early years of the war, Brockington had become a kind of roving ambassador of good will for Canada abroad, and in general a booster of wartime morale wherever he went. His rich voice and lofty style were in tune with the temper of the times and soon won him wide popularity as a war correspondent and radio commentator. At this time he was in England, where he had recently been appointed to the British Ministry of Information as special adviser on Commonwealth Affairs.

LETTER 22

1. *The Skin of Our Teeth.*

LETTER 24

1. Jane was Pelham Edgar's daughter by a second marriage, in 1935, to Dona Waller.

LETTER 25

1. Scott and Lampman had been in the habit of sending to a circle of friends Christmas greetings in the form of original poems privately printed as Christmas cards. Scott continued the practice, though I think not with complete regularity, after Lampman's death in 1899. Professor S.L. Dragland gives a partial list of these occasional poems in the bibliography to his *Duncan Campbell Scott: A Book of Criticism* (Ottawa: Tecumseh Press, 1974), p. 194. I found the present poem amongst the residue of Brown's papers passed on to me by Mrs. Brown in 1975. It seems an integral part of the correspondence, Scott's way of greeting the Browns at Christmas, and I therefore include it. The words "To Peggy & Edward, etc." are in Scott's hand, as is also the entry, "Spring 1941," presumably the date of composition. 'Intermezzo' was to be published in *The Circle of Affection*.

LETTER 26

1. Edmund Morris, the painter, had joined Scott's second Indian Treaty expedition into James Bay in 1906. They had become good friends. The passage Brown quotes is from Scott's 'Lines in Memory of Edmund Morris,' a poem which he wrote soon after receiving the news of Morris's death, by drowning, in an accident off Ile d'Orléans. That was in 1913, and the poem was published in *Lundy's Lane and Other Poems* (1916). The lines occur at the beginning of the poem, and their context is the struggle

of the poet to read the all but indecipherable handwriting of a letter from his friend which he had put aside to answer later and now can never answer. In the SAP there is only one letter from Morris to Scott filed. It does not seem likely, from internal evidence, that this is the letter Scott had beside him when he began the "Lines"; but it was probably written about the same time, perhaps a month or two before the final letter, and it may show us how the name "Phimister Proctor" got into Scott's head. The letter is on Canadian Art Club stationery, no date, and the handwriting is indeed very bad. It is an invitation to the Scotts to attend a "viewing" in Toronto, and it reads in part: "The private view is on the 9th of May. The Proctors and Ernest Lawson come from New York, the other Lawsons from London." Phimister Proctor, Canadian-born, did most of his work in the United States, where he was well known as "the sculptor of the pioneer West." The "other" Lawson is probably the Scottish-born portrait painter, J. Kerr-Lawson, who, although he had come to Canada at the age of three and was to become decorator of the Senate Chambers in Ottawa, was by this time well established in London, England. William Colgate in *Canadian Art* (1943) cites both men as members of the Canadian Art Club in its early years.

2. In mid-career, Carl Schaefer had come to be recognized as one of Canada's leading exponents of water-colour painting. He had recently been appointed war artist, attached to the RCAF.

LETTER 27

1. Colonel Henry Osborne. The use of the name "Harry" suggests Harry Orr McCurry, civil servant and longtime friend of the Scotts. McCurry had joined the staff of the National Gallery in 1919 and had become its director in 1939. In 1925 he had married Dorothy Jenkins, daughter of Mrs. F.M.S. Jenkins, Archibald Lampman's younger sister. But the reference in Letter 14 to Pelham "living with our friend Col. Osborne" settles the matter.

2. Some years later, Scott was to be in touch with Birney, when the latter was editor of *Canadian Poetry Magazine*. He expressed his admiration for 'David' at that time (January 17, 1947, SAP). Birney replied (January 31, 1947, SAP): "I prize indeed any praise from you since your own work in both prose and poetry has always given me great pleasure and I have come to think of you as our prime artist-in-words in this country."

3. Rupert Brooke, 'The Old Vicarage, Grantchester' (Café des Westens, Berlin, May 1912). Scott's interest in Brooke had its roots in the latter's visit to 108 Lisgar Street in the summer of 1913. See "Notes by Duncan Campbell Scott re Rupert Brooke's visit to Ottawa," in A.S. Bourinot, *Some Letters*, pp. 58-60, reprinted here in Appendix I (p. 292). These notes were written in the summer of 1946, in response to an inquiry from Arthur Stringer, who was preparing a biography of Brooke.

4. The Ottawa *Journal* was very much Scott's newspaper. The political colouring was right (Conservative) and there were journalists on staff whom he had come to admire: I. Norman Smith, for example, and Norman Smith Sr. and Martin Burrell from earlier days.

5. The "vignette" is from a small engraving, scarcely an inch square. Scott catches the essentials in his next sentence: the figure of a river-man balanced on a log and reaching towards another log with his pike-pole.

6. There is no original in the E.K. Brown papers for the second page of this letter, i.e., the portion which begins "I got an early copy of *Harper's*. . . ." and runs through to the end. Fortunately there was a carbon copy of the complete letter in the SAP. The carbon is of course not signed.

LETTER 28

1. This may be a good place to say a bit more about the appearance in the present correspondence of the wraith-like figure of the "other woman" in Lampman's life. It is easy to see why Scott should have experienced "anxieties and heart-searchings" at this particular point. In the conversations of the previous summer, though he had not given the girl's name, which he said he could not remember, he had nevertheless passed on to Brown a good deal of information about Lampman's affair and how he came to know about it. In a memorandum written for his own benefit soon after one of these conversations (E.K. Brown Papers, PAC) Brown makes it clear that Scott's sources were Lampman's working papers, which had come into his hands soon after the poet's death, and W.D. LeSueur, colleague in the Post Office Department where Miss Waddell and Lampman worked, who had discussed the matter with him. Scott seems to have got it into his head that Natalie and Loftus MacInnes, representing the next generation of the Lampman family, did not share his knowledge of the affair. Scott's relations with the Lampman children, Natalie in particular, had from time to time been strained. Now he must approach Natalie on delicate ground and in such a way as would make it seem that he had spoken out of turn to Brown about a matter of private concern to the Lampman family. Hence his great relief at finding that the MacInneses not only knew of the affair but "had given it a place in the life of A.L."

2. The clause in parentheses is omitted by Bourinot in his version of this letter; see *Some Letters,* p. 22. It is evidence that Bourinot has contributed a good deal on his own initiative to the blurring of the image of the Waddell affair in the record which has come down to us; cf. Margaret Whitridge's introduction to *Lampman's Kate* (pp. 16-18), where she makes Scott the instigator of a number of ploys designed to suppress important information about his friend and Miss Waddell.

3. The entire sentence is omitted by Bourinot. Margaret Whitridge, quoting this passage from the original letter in the E.K. Brown Papers, makes her own omission — with perhaps some eye to the main chance, the clause "wh. might lead to some journalistic vapourings."

4. The "note" (as Bourinot judged, printing it, *Some Letters,* p. 24) is important and is reproduced here as a continuation of the letter.

5. Tennyson, *In Memoriam,* cvii, 1. 8.

6. Lubka Kolessa-Philipps came to Ottawa in 1940 with an international reputation as a concert pianist. Born in Austria of Ukrainian parents, she received her early training in Vienna. In Ottawa she gave concerts in the ballroom of the Chateau Laurier and in the Art Gallery, now the Museum of Man, at the head of Metcalfe Street. She became professor of the Faculty of Music at the University of Toronto in 1942 and remained there until her appointment to the Conservatoire de musique et de l'art dramatique de la province de Québec in 1952. She was a frequent visitor at 108 Lisgar Street in the early years.

7. Carl F. Klinck, *Wilfred Campbell: A Study in Late Provincial Victorianism* (Toronto: Ryerson, 1942). Campbell, born in 1861, came from the Bruce Peninsula on Georgian Bay. For many years a Church of England priest, in 1891 he withdrew from the ministry and moved to Ottawa, where he became a civil servant and a member of the group of intellectuals that included Scott and Lampman. A voluminous writer of both poetry and prose, he collaborated with Scott and Lampman to produce the "At the Mermaid Inn" column for the Toronto *Globe* between February of 1892 and July of 1893. A good selection of his poetry has been brought together recently by Carl Klinck in *Wilfred Campbell: Selected Poems* (Ottawa: Tecumseh Press, 1976).

8. The Ottawa Branch of the Drama League of America was founded May 9, 1913. Scott became an influential member and served as president from 1922 to 1935. The Drama

League changed its name to the Ottawa Little Theatre in 1952. See "Drama for the Love of It: Ottawa Little Theatre Marking Anniversary," by Jean Southworth, Ottawa *Journal,* April 6, 1963.

9. Scott's selection of Lampman's poems, published in 1925 with the sub-title "Sonnets and Ballads," not to be confused with the volume Lampman published under the same title in 1895.

LETTER 29

1. Ira Dilworth was at this time regional representative for the Canadian Broadcasting Corporation and manager of Station CBR in Vancouver, an appointment which he had held since 1938. Before that, he had been professor of English at the University of British Columbia; before that again, teacher of literature and principal at a Victoria high school. He was a man of fine sensibilities and sophisticated tastes. Critic and anthologist of poetry, an accomplished musician and connoisseur of art, he had much in common with Scott. They had not known each other long, but Dilworth had long been an admirer of Scott's poetry, and by the early forties he was a visitor to be counted on at 108 Lisgar whenever business brought him to Ottawa. It was he who was largely responsible for putting Scott in touch with Emily Carr. "Ira nearly always mentions you when I see him," Emily Carr writes to Scott in the fall of 1944. "He is very fond of you and proud that Canada has you. . . . If Ira comes back from the East without having seen you there is always a ring of disappointment in his voice" (SAP). Dilworth's *Twentieth Century Verse,* which broke new ground in 1945 by placing Canadian poets without much fanfare in the company of contemporary British and American poets, was dedicated to Scott and included a selection of his poems. In 1947 Dilworth was appointed supervisor of the CBC's International Service, Montreal, and in 1950 he moved to Toronto as National Director, Programme Planning. He died in 1962.

2. Presumably Brown drew these lyrics from one of Lampman's scribblers. More than a year later (July, 1944) he is to come upon them in a different context when he turns his attention to an unpublished "dramatic fragment" on the subject of King Seleucus which he finds in a "notebook" passed on to him by MacInnes the summer before (see Letter 99). MacInnes is at this point asked to comment, and it is from this later intervention that we are able to identify the "two lyrics" Brown is presently sending to Scott. See MacInnes's letter to Brown of August 8, 1944, Appendix F (p. 287).

LETTER 30

1. The edition of Lampman's poems which was published by George N. Morang in 1900. Brown is referring specifically to the "Memoir" which Scott wrote for this edition.

LETTER 31

1. This letter, and others relating to the Ryerson Press publication of *At the Long Sault,* can be found in the SAP.

2. 'With those cold eyes, my dear' was published in *At the Long Sault* as 'Cloud and Sun' (p. 25). Despite Scott's suggestion that the date should not be given, it was: October 18, 1895. 'You cannot answer to my love' was not published in *At the Long Sault.* Margaret Whitridge, however, includes it in *Lampman's Kate* (p. 36), supplying a title, 'The Virgin Spirit,' and dating it October 15, 1895.

3. In the original, Scott writes "If," then scores the word out in favour of "As."

LETTER 32

1. The "Greek sonnets" appear in *At the Long Sault* under the heading "Crete." Eleuthérios Venizélos was just beginning his political career at the time the sonnets were written in the fall of 1896. He led an unsuccessful insurrection against Turkish

rule in 1897, and played an important part in the troubled evolution of Crete in the first decades of this century.

2. There is no mention of the letter to Lorne Pierce in Scott's previous letter. It may have been sent separately, with a covering note, perhaps coupled with an advance notice of the Charles G.D. Roberts biography, referred to by Brown in his next paragraph.

3. Elsie Pomeroy, *Sir Charles G.D. Roberts: A Biography* (Toronto: Ryerson, 1943).

4. William Archer, *Poets of the Younger Generation* (London and New York: J. Lane, 1902). In his wide-ranging survey, Archer included short chapters (they were in fact critical comments stitched together with liberal quotations) on Bliss Carman, Roberts, D.C. Scott and Richard Hovey. He calls 'The Piper of Arll' ''a singularly beautiful fantasy, full of jewel-like colour and tenuous, unearthly melody.'' ''I scarcely know,'' he adds, ''where to look for a more brilliant flash of romantic imagination'' (pp. 392-93). Masefield's ''wise and delightful comment'' may have its roots in a letter he wrote to Scott in 1905. In it, he described Scott's poem as ''the most beautiful sea-poem of modern times'' and asked permission to include it in a collection of ''poems of the sea.'' But a more likely source is the foreword Masefield had written for the English edition of *The Poems of Duncan Campbell Scott,* published in 1927, where he says: ''But of all the poems in the book my favourite is still the romantic fantasy 'The Piper of Arll,' which I read for the first time, with intense delight, in my boyhood. It was the first poem of romantic fantasy ever read by me, and I love it still as I did then.'' He was to give the background for the experience in his autobiography, *In the Mill* (1941). See Letter 91, note 2. The original of the Masefield letter of 1905 is in the D.C. Scott collection at the University of Toronto Library (The Thomas Fisher Rare Books and Special Collections Department).

LETTER 33

1. It seems reasonable to identify 'The Secret Heart' with 'You cannot answer to my love,' the companion-piece to the lyric 'With those cold eyes, my dear.' Scott could, however, be referring to a poem which Whitridge prints in *Lampman's Kate* under the title 'Would You Care?' It begins, ''Couldst thou but know my secret heart.'' Both this poem and 'You cannot answer to my love' (which in *Lampman's Kate* appears on the opposite page) have four stanzas, and in each case there is some fuzziness in the final stanza. But on balance I conclude that the source of Scott's puzzlement is the fourth stanza of 'You cannot answer to my love.'

2. 'The Politician,' not published in *At the Long Sault,* comes partly into focus here with Scott's description of it. See Letter 13, note 3, where I suggest the possible identification of 'The Politician' with the poem Scott calls 'The Pimp' in Letter 17.

LETTER 34

1. Dr. Carl Frederick Klinck was to have a distinguished career as teacher, scholar and editor in the field of Canadian literature: co-author, with Henry W. Wells, of a book on E.J. Pratt (1947); from 1948-55 head of the English Department at the University of Western Ontario; co-editor, with R.E. Watters, of *Canadian Anthology* (1955); general editor of the *Literary History of Canada* when work began on this important project in 1968.

2. Between February 6, 1892, and July 5, 1893, Campbell, Scott and Lampman wrote a literary column weekly for the Toronto *Globe* under the title ''At the Mermaid Inn.'' Bourinot published a selection of these short essays in 1958. A complete text is now available in *At the Mermaid Inn,* edited by Barry Davies (Toronto: University of Toronto Press, 1979).

3. John Grierson, pioneer Scottish film-maker, had worked with Robert Flaherty on the development of the documentary during the twenties. He came to Canada in 1937 at the invitation of the Canadian government, his assignment being to write a plan for government film production. His work led to the establishment in 1939 of the National Film Board, of which he was first commissioner. At this time he was awaiting formal appointment as general manager of the Wartime Information Board.

LETTER 35

1. For Scott's letter to Lorne Pierce of February 20, 1943, and the latter's reply of February 24, see Appendix D (p. 284) and E (p. 285).
2. The final clause (''but the truth is, etc.'') is deleted by Bourinot in the text printed in *Some Letters* (p. 25).

LETTER 36

1. The first printing of *David and Other Poems* in October 1942 was only 500 copies, and Ryerson were obliged to do a second printing within six weeks.
2. Brown had launched a ''Letters in Canada'' supplement to the *University of Toronto Quarterly* in 1936. Its purpose was to provide an annual review of publications in the humanities and social sciences. The section on poetry had been Brown's responsibility from the beginning.
3. Ralph Gustafson, *Lyrics Unromantic* (New York, 1942). The anthology is the Penguin *Anthology of Canadian Poetry* to which Scott had been asked to contribute.
4. Pelham Edgar, ''Literary Criticism in Canada,'' *University of Toronto Quarterly*, VIII (July 1939), pp. 420-30. A.S.P. Woodhouse had been a member of the Department of English at University College, Toronto, since 1929. He was to become head of the Department in 1945 and would continue in that post almost until his death in 1964. Brown had known him as mentor, then as colleague and close friend. Together they shared responsibilities, throughout most of the thirties, for the *University of Toronto Quarterly*, and although Woodhouse would probably at this time have bartered the whole of Canadian literature for a piece of Spenser or Milton, it is nevertheless to him as much as Brown that credit must go for making the ''Letters in Canada'' supplement a regular feature of the journal. His main interests, which were in the field of history of ideas, are admirably illustrated in his edition of *Puritanism and Liberty* (1938). A major work on Milton, unfinished at his death, was edited by Hugh MacCallum and published by the University of Toronto Press in 1972 as *The Heavenly Muse*.
5. The reference is to William John Alexander, born in 1855, educated at Toronto, the University of London, Johns Hopkins and the University of Berlin, patriarch of the Department of English, University College, Toronto, during his long period of service there between 1889 and 1926. Brown had graduated from the University of Toronto in the same year Alexander retired. Much later, Brown was to contribute his ''Rhythm in the Novel'' to the distinguished Alexander Lecture series begun in Alexander's honour in 1929-30. Alexander's death in 1944 is noticed in Letter 99. The sketch proposed in the present letter was written and sent as planned to *Saturday Night* (see Letter 44).
6. Herbert John Davis (1893-1967) was a professor of English, born and educated in England, and perhaps best known as an authority on Jonathan Swift. He had held a temporary appointment at University College, Toronto, in 1922 and had joined the staff again for the two years, 1935-37, during which Brown served as chairman of the Department of English at the University of Manitoba. But Davis was a frequent visitor at other times to University College, where he had many friends. He went to Cornell University in 1937 (Brown having returned from Manitoba) and became chairman of the Department of English there in 1938. Brown, as noted, was Davis's successor at Cornell.

LETTER 37

1. Pierce's main suggestion was that the introductory material, being long in relation to the poetry, "might be reduced somewhat." The letter is dated March 5, 1943.

LETTER 38

1. There is a draft of this letter in Scott's files, and its many barred words and revisions suggest Scott's agitation at the proposed reductions to the "Long Sault" volume.
2. Pierce's letter to Scott is dated March 10 and not March 5, as stated here.
3. Brown's introduction to *At the Long Sault,* it will be remembered, was to be lifted from the "Canadian Poetry" manuscript. In the meantime, the problem of reducing the introduction might be eased if a fuller version were to appear in print ahead of the shorter one.
4. Published as 'Good Speech' in the Memorial Edition, p. 226.
5. Published in the Memorial Edition, p. 276.
6. An early glimpse of Ryerson's "Canadian Poets" series, to which Scott would in due time contribute *Selected Poems of Archibald Lampman* (1947).

LETTER 39

1. Charles Mair (1838-1927), poet and adventurer, author of *Dreamland and Other Poems* (1868) and *Tecumseh: A Drama* (1886). Charles Sangster (1822-93), pre-Confederation poet, author of *The St. Lawrence and the Saguenay and Other Poems* (1856) and *Hesperus and Other Poems and Lyrics* (1860).

LETTER 43

1. Thoreau MacDonald was born in 1901, near Toronto, the only son of J.E.H. MacDonald, founding member of the Group of Seven. He became art editor and illustrator for the *Canadian Forum* in 1923, and his linoleum cuts, mostly nature scenes of great simplicity and strength, are a mark of the magazine throughout the twenties and on into the thirties. He had been involved in the design of the 1925 edition of Lampman's *Lyrics of Earth*. Later, he would design and illustrate both the first Canadian edition of Scott's *In the Village of Viger* (1945) and *The Circle of Affection.*

LETTER 44

1. Smith's *The Book of Canadian Poetry* was in preparation at this time. As it turned out, the Lampman book was not to precede Smith's, though they were to run neck-and-neck. The University of Chicago Press released the anthology on September 9 (see Letter 65). Ryerson Press brought out *At the Long Sault* on September 25.
2. B.K. Sandwell (1876-1954) was editor of *Saturday Night* from 1932 to 1951 and an influential critic and journalist of his time. He had been a newspaperman in Toronto and Montreal, a teacher of economics at McGill and of literature at Queen's. He was elected to the Royal Society of Canada in 1925.
3. Alexander Carlyle, ed., *The Love-Letters of Thomas Carlyle and Jane Welsh.* 2 vols. London & New York: J. Lane, 1909.

LETTER 45

1. I have no original for this letter; it exists only as a carbon copy in the SAP. Internal evidence places it in the present sequence. Written across the top, I think in Bourinot's hand, is "Undated (March 1943)." Bourinot, at any rate, gives this month and year when he prints the letter in *Some Letters* (p. 28). The letter must have been written after March 25, which is the date of Scott's previous letter to Brown. It had not, on the other hand, reached Brown by March 31 since Brown's letter to Scott of that date makes no mention of it. By April 6 it has been received and acknowledged. The letter

222

was written on a Sunday: "tomorrow" (the day of MacInnes's appointment with Lorne Pierce) is a Monday. According to the calendar for 1943, the first Sunday after March 25 fell on March 28. Given the speed of the mails in those days, however, a letter mailed in Ottawa on March 28 would almost certainly have reached Ithaca by March 31. Brown does not have Scott's letter by March 31. Hence the date supplied, which is the Sunday next, April 4.

2. George Herbert Clarke (1873-1953), poet, critic and teacher. Clarke had been professor of English and chairman of the Department at Queen's University since 1925. Now on the point of retirement, he was still active as chairman of the editorial board of *Queen's Quarterly* and in the process of putting together *The New Treasury of War Poetry: Poems of the Second World War*. See Letter 71.

3. *Voices* described itself as "a quarterly of poetry." It was edited by Harold Vinal and published in Vermont. Ralph Gustafson was guest editor for the special "Canadian Issue" which appeared in the spring of 1943 (No. 113). Scott contributed 'A Dream' (pp. 6-8). This was the poem later called 'Amanda' and published in *The Circle of Affection* (pp. 61-63). For more about 'Amanda,' see Letter 182.

4. Published in *The Circle of Affection*, p. 73: 'To My Friend—Leonard Brockington.'

5. Published in *The Circle of Affection* as 'Hymn for Those in the Air' (p. 51). Healey Willan, born in England in 1880, had come to Canada in 1913 to take up an appointment with the Toronto Conservatory of Music. His connection with the University of Toronto remained close throughout his life. Organist and prolific composer, he was to write incidental music for a broadcast of Pratt's *Brébeuf* in September 1943, and the score for John Coulter's opera *Deirdre of the Sorrows*, produced by the CBC in 1946.

6. Bourinot included three of these in *Some Letters*, pp. 2-6. The originals are in the Thomas Fisher Rare Book Library, University of Toronto.

LETTER 47

1. The list is preserved in the SAP. Scott has pencilled in the number of lines involved in each case. There is no check-mark opposite the quotation from 'The Closed Door,' but the lines were evidently agreed to since Brown uses them in *On Canadian Poetry*. There is likewise no check-mark opposite the lines from the sonnet 'Ottawa,' a poem which, as we learn from Letter 49, Scott was not fond of but which he allowed Brown to use.

LETTER 48

1. This letter is undated, an unusual omission for Brown. I have arrived at the date given by establishing that Brockington's "oration," delivered "last night," was broadcast on Sunday, May 9, 1943. Brockington had just returned from visits to Australia, New Zealand and the Pacific theatres of war.

2. McClelland & Stewart had published all of Scott's poetry from *Lundy's Lane* in 1916 to *The Green Cloister* in 1935. Publication of the collected volume of 1926 had given them copyright extending back to Scott's first volume, *The Magic House*, of 1893.

LETTER 49

1. This is an undated holograph letter, headed only "Tuesday." Internal evidence places it securely between Letter 48 and Letter 50 in the present sequence, and the precise date is supplied indirectly by Scott himself, who has written in the margin of Brown's last letter, "18 May '43" — his way, frequently, of recording the date of his answer to a particular letter.

2. In the SAP there is a pencilled draft of the main body of this letter in Mrs. Scott's handwriting. It begins with the next sentence and stops four sentences from the end of the letter as we now have it.

LETTER 50

1. It is in fact from *A Midsummer Night's Dream* (III, i, 134).

LETTER 51

1. The address is letterhead, hotel stationery.

LETTER 52

1. Scott had been asked to write an article on Lampman for *The Educational Record,* a publication which described itself as "a quarterly journal in the interest of the Protestant Schools of the Province of Quebec." The editor was W.P. Percival, an ardent supporter of Canadian literature, and his plan was to run a series of short biographies of Canadian poets which would by this means be made available to teachers. Pelham Edgar had already contributed one piece on Bliss Carman (May 1941) and another on D.C. Scott (Jan.-Mar. 1942). In 1948 the series was published in book form by the Ryerson Press, under the title *Leading Canadian Poets.*

LETTER 53

1. Of the poets of the Confederation, it was Roberts who had received the lion's share of attention and critical acclaim prior to the publication of Brown's *On Canadian Poetry* in 1943. After more than twenty years abroad, Roberts had returned to Canada in 1925 and had quickly assumed the role of *doyen* in the ranks of Canadian writers. He had been knighted in 1935.

2. In the older pecking order, Carman had vied with Roberts in popularity. The Canadian Authors' Association had seen to his elevation to near sainthood in the six or seven years prior to his death in 1929.

3. His biography by Elsie Pomeroy.

4. The "letter from the Ryerson Press" seems to have involved the promotion, perhaps in the form of an endorsement solicited from Pratt and Scott, of the Pomeroy biography. But Scott does not mention such a letter in the preceding sequence. It is possible that a note written to accompany an enclosure is missing.

LETTER 54

1. When Roberts was in financial difficulties in 1931-32, the Canadian Authors' Foundation made a payment to him of $2500. Pelham Edgar was chiefly responsible for this intervention.

2. Robert Emmons, *The Life and Opinions of Walter Richard Sickert* (London: Faber & Faber, 1941).

3. Scott has had his pen out, as was his custom after he drew the sheet from his typewriter, correcting mistakes, putting in punctuation marks, etc.

LETTER 55

1. Philip Dansken Ross, eighty-five years old at the time of this correspondence, was still active as editor and publisher of the Ottawa *Journal.* In a Saturday column ("A Booklover's Corner") published July 10, 1943, he had reviewed E.M. Pomeroy's *Sir Charles G.D. Roberts.* Roberts, the subject of this "fine biography," was unquestionably "the chief figure in Canadian literature." The "survey of Canadian Poetry" to which Scott refers is probably *Canadian Poets and the Short Word* (Ottawa: the author, 1938).

2. Frank Flemington was at this time assistant editor at the Ryerson Press.

LETTER 56

1. George Eliot's *Scenes from Clerical Life* was published in 1857, very early in her career. *Daniel Deronda* was Eliot's last novel, 1874-76.

LETTER 58

1. The copies of *The Green Cloister* and the *Collected Poems* to which Brown refers remain in the possession of Mrs. E.K. Brown of Rochester, N.Y. They were of such obvious importance to scholars interested in Scott and the chronology of his poems that I put together the information they contained in an article subsequently published in *Canadian Poetry* under the title "D.C. Scott: The Dating of the Poems" (No. 2, Spring/Summer, 1978, pp. 13-27).

2. In Brown's copy of the *Collected Poems* (p. 226), the poem is dated 27 May, 1924, and carries the notation, "A sleepless night in the Mt. Royal Hotel!"

LETTER 59

1. Scott had turned eighty-one on August 2.

LETTER 60

1. Garland's Hotel, London, stood at the head of Suffolk Street, near Pall Mall East. It was destroyed in the air raids of 1940. The date which Scott attaches to 'The Nightwatchman' in Brown's copy of *The Green Cloister* is December 1934.

2. Robert M.B. Nichols, born in 1893, was a minor English poet and dramatist.

3. Rupert Brooke was born in Rugby, England, in 1887. Author of *Poems of 1911* and the posthumous *1914 and Other Poems,* he counted himself one of the Georgians, a group of poets with whom Scott had many affinities. In May 1913, Brooke set out for a year of travel which took him first to New York and Boston, then in early July to Ottawa, where he visited D.C. Scott with the prompting of an introduction from John Masefield. After further travels, which included stops in Victoria and San Francisco, he returned to England in 1914. Here he enlisted. He served in Belgium and then was posted to the Dardanelles. He died in the spring of 1915 and was buried on Skyros.

4. Michael Sadleir, *Trollope: A Commentary* (London: Constable, 1928).

5. "Trollope Revisited," in *The Collected Essays and Papers of George Saintsbury, 1875-1920* (London: J.M. Dent, 1923) II, ix, pp. 312-43.

LETTER 61

1. Judith Evelyn (Allen) was born in South Dakota in 1913. She was a graduate of the University of Manitoba and took her M.A. there in 1933. She made her radio debut in Toronto in 1935 and the following year received the Lady Tweedsmuir Award at the Dominion Drama Festival in Ottawa for her performance in Patrick Hamilton's *Angel Street*. Her later work was to be mainly in the American theatre and films, but she was to return several times to Canada for special appearances.

2. Probably *The Two Mrs. Carrolls* by Martin Vale. It was described by Lewis Nichols of the *New York Times* as a "who-done-it" which was "saved by the Bergner performance."

3. This is the first suggestion we have in the present correspondence of the collection to be published in 1947 under the title, *The Circle of Affection*.

4. Mr. and Mrs. Charles S. Deaver.

5. Walter Pater's *Marius the Epicurean* was published in 1885. At the end of the section on Scott (*On Canadian Poetry,* p. 132) Brown recreates the impression he had of the poet in 1942, the year in which he was most often in the poet's company. The date was close to Scott's eightieth birthday.

Here, I thought, as Pater presents Marius thinking of Fronto, was "the one instance" I had seen "of a perfectly beautiful old age — an old age in which there seemed . . . nothing to be regretted, nothing really lost in what the years had taken away. The wise old man . . . would seem to have replaced carefully and consciously each natural trait of youth, as it departed from him, by an equivalent grace of culture."

6. Malcolm Wallace succeeded W.J. Alexander as head of the Department of English at University College, Toronto, in 1926. He served as principal of the college from 1928 and retired in 1944. He died in 1960.

LETTER 62

1. Katherine Prescott Wormely (1830-1908) translated the works of Balzac for the Centenary Edition (Boston: Roberts Brothers, 1885-1897), 42 vols.

2. The first edition of *In the Village of Viger* had been published in Boston, in 1896, by Copeland Day. I have let Scott's misspelling of "Thoreau" stand.

3. Elise Aylen's poem was entitled 'Ode.' It had appeared originally in the *London Mercury* under the title 'Dusk of the Gods: a poem' (*London Mercury,* 30 [July 1934], pp. 199-200).

4. Later (Letter 102) Scott is to call Turgenev "on the whole my favorite novelist." *Fathers and Sons* was published in 1862.

5. Herbert Davis, *Stella, A Gentlewoman of the Eighteenth Century* (New York: Macmillan, 1942).

6. Raymond Mortimer, *Channel Packet* (London: Hogarth Press, 1942). The book is a selection of papers and reviews reprinted from periodicals.

7. A two-column spread in the Ottawa *Journal* for September 2, 1943, carries the headline, "Bedbug Nuisance in Ottawa Grows Owing to Overcrowding."

LETTER 63

1. E.K. Brown, "A Review of A.J.M. Smith's (ed.) *The Book of Canadian Poetry,*" *American Literature,* vol. 15 (March 1943-January 1944), pp. 439-42.

2. "FG" is Frederick George Scott, clergyman and poet, born in Montreal in 1861, rector of St. Matthew's Church, Quebec, from 1896 to 1934, appointed archdeacon of Quebec in 1925. In the First World War he had served overseas with distinction as senior chaplain to the Canadian forces. Author of numerous volumes of poetry of high moral purpose and impeccable religious orthodoxy, he had published a last edition of *Collected Poems* in 1937. In the ranks of Canadian poets he was by this time very much one of the old guard, having lived to see his son, F.R. Scott, together with A.J.M. Smith, pioneer the coming of modernism to poetry in Canada in the late twenties. There is perhaps a touch of irony in the fact that it is Smith himself who in the present context of the new anthology has set the archdeacon on a higher pedestal than Brown will allow. In a biographical note, Smith had written that he "liked the consistency and discipline of the poet's world view." Brown, in his review (pp. 440-41), arguing that the archdeacon is only "a slight figure" in poetry, and suspecting Smith of praising this kind of "thoughtful" poetry at the expense of "nature poetry," attacks the latter for his "anti-romantic bias." F.G. Scott died in 1944.

LETTER 64

1. In the published review (*American Literature,* p. 441), the sentence reads: "It would be ungracious not to add that Mr. Smith's rigor will help to clear the air north of the border, deflate some very swollen reputations, and force critics to a greater awareness of the standards they employ."

2. This is probably the very popular *Lift Up Your Hearts,* first published in 1941. Promoted enthusiastically by the Canadian Legion, it sold a quarter of a million copies during the early years of the war.

3. Five of Scott's poems were included in the first edition of *The Book of Canadian Poetry:* 'The Piper of Arll,' 'At the Cedars,' 'Night Burial in the Forest,' 'At Gull Lake: August, 1810,' and 'At Delos.'

4. Sir John Collings Squire (1884-1958), journalist, poet and playwright and, in his capacity as editor and critic, an influential figure amongst the Georgians. For this group of poets, the *London Mercury,* which Squire edited from 1919 to 1934, was an important rallying point in the second decade of the century. Scott had kept in touch with Squire from time to time since their first meeting in London in 1934 (see Letter 93). In the *London Mercury* the title given for Elise Aylen's poem is 'Dusk of the Gods' (vol. 30, no. 177 [July 1934], pp. 199-200). It is in all other particulars the same poem as the 'Ode' referred to here.

5. *Brébeuf and His Brethren,* Pratt's epic poem on the Jesuit missions to the Hurons in the seventeenth century, had been published in 1940. On September 28, 1943, it was presented by the CBC as a dramatic reading for radio, with incidental music by Healey Willan.

LETTER 65

1. The last line from Lampman's 'September.' The correct reading, which Scott used when he first quoted the line to Brown, is: "October with *the* rain of ruined leaves."

2. The back page of the cover presented, without omissions, the opening paragraph of Scott's Foreword. It is a long paragraph.

LETTER 66

1. Lampman's sister.

LETTER 68

1. In his book, Brown uses the "MacMechan incident" as a lead-in to his section on D.C. Scott. Archibald MacMechan, professor of English at Dalhousie University since 1889, had published in 1924 a pioneering critical and historical study entitled *Headwaters of Canadian Literature.* Brown notes that in the list of forty or more poets who are at least referred to, and in some cases studied with care, there is no mention of Scott. Brown respects MacMechan and will not attribute the omission to "personal spite"; "it simply reflects," he says, "the long failure of the Canadian public and Canadian critics to do anything like justice to Scott's powers" (*On Canadian Poetry,* pp. 108-9).

2. MacMechan was for twenty years book critic for the *Montreal Standard.* The review, in the February 26 issue, is headed "A Poet of Real Significance," and the whole piece is full of praise. In the final paragraph "The Dean" writes: "And let me make a confession. I was not attracted to Mr. Scott's work at first; I approached it in a very critical mood. . .but in the end I was won over. Mine is a case of genuine conversion."

3. *The Oxford Book of English Verse,* first edition, chosen and edited by Sir Arthur Quiller-Couch (Oxford: at the Clarendon Press, 1900). This was the second of two expeditions Scott made in 1905 and 1906 in his capacity as an Indian Commissioner of the Department of Indian Affairs for the purpose of negotiating treaties with Cree and Ojibway tribes in northern Ontario. At Scott's request, Pelham Edgar had been appointed secretary of this second expedition. Scott had published his own account of the 1905 trip in *Scribner's Magazine* (December 1906) and would reprint it with the essays included in *The Circle of Affection.* Edgar's account of the 1906 trip, under the

title "Twelve Hundred Miles by Canoe," was first published in eight instalments in *Canada* (IV and V) between November 24, 1906, and March 16, 1907; and subsequently in the autobiographical and posthumous *Across My Path* (ed. Northrop Frye, 1952) under the title "Travelling with a Poet." Diaries covering both trips are housed with the papers of the Department of Indian Affairs in the Public Archives of Canada.

4. The passages Scott has in mind are the following:

> Hear beyond the silver reach in ringing wild persistence
> Reel remote the ululating laughter of the loons;

and

> She would be mine for ever and for ever,
> Mine for all time and beyond the judgment day.

5. These pages in *The Poems of Duncan Campbell Scott* (1926) contain the final six stanzas of 'Spring on Mattagami.' The offending passages are doubtless those in which the speaker pictures himself making passionate love to his lady on a "deep couch heaped of balsam fir. . . ."

LETTER 69

1. See "A Lampman Discovery," by J.E. Middleton, published in "The Bookshelf" column of *Saturday Night,* vol. 59, no. 10 (November 13, 1943), p. 28.

LETTER 70

1. Douglas Bush was at this time teaching at Harvard University, where he had been a member of the Department of English since 1936. Prior to that, he had been at the University of Minnesota. Brown had come to Minneapolis several times to visit his fiancée, Margaret Deaver, and it was on one of these occasions that he had met Douglas Bush. Bush has left a record of this meeting in a recent article, "E.K. Brown and the Evolution of Canadian Poetry," *The Sewanee Review,* LXXXVII, 1 (Winter 1979), p. 186.

2. The dedication to the first edition of *On Canadian Poetry* reads: "To Arthur/who set me the task/and to/Peggy/who held me to it."

3. William Arthur Deacon, who had been associated with *Saturday Night* (1922-28) and the old *Mail and Empire* (1928-36), had earned himself a solid reputation as an essayist and reviewer. He was at this time literary editor of the Toronto *Globe and Mail.* The review of *At the Long Sault* was headed "Archibald Lampman's Notebooks Yield Poems for New Volume," and it had appeared in the Saturday edition for October 30, 1943, p. 21. Although Brown found the review "not very interesting," Deacon was by no means indifferent to the subject. He was a great admirer of Scott, and especially of *The Green Cloister.* He was to visit Scott at 108 Lisgar Street in the spring of 1946.

LETTER 71

1. Scott now turns to the first two sections of *On Canadian Poetry.* The opening section is called "The Problem of Canadian Literature"; the second, "The Development of Poetry in Canada."

2. See Brown's postscript to Letter 56.

3. In this passage, Brown tries to disprove the "easy answers" often used to excuse the unpalatable fact "that in this country the plight of literature is a painful one." To those who argue that we have been too busy "making a new world," he points out that the United States had by 1843 produced a considerable number of authors who had "written works of the first order" — and that in the preceding century and a half Americans had been "just as busy building the material structure of a nation as we have ever been."

4. "A great literature is the flowering of a great society, a mature and adequate society" (p. 26).

5. Brown had quoted with approval A.J.M. Smith's charge to "the younger poets":
   Set higher standards for yourself than the organized mediocrity of the authors' associations dares to impose. Be traditional, catholic and alive. Study the great masters of clarity and intensity. . . . Study the poets of today whose language is living, and whose line is sure. . . . Read the French and German poets whose sensibility is most intensely that of the modern world. . . . Read, if you can, the Roman satirists. . . .
   And remember lastly that poetry does not permit rejection of every aspect of the personality except intuition and sensibility. It must be written by the whole man. It is an intelligent activity, and it ought to compel the respect of the generality of intelligent men. If it is good, it is good in itself (p. 74).

6. The passage Scott cites is from Collin's essay on Smith in *The White Savannahs:* "His problem is the eternal problem confronting a sensitive mind: to find significant expression for emotions set up by contact with the sophistries, the tacit beliefs, all the impurities that make an age what it is" (p. 239). Smith's *News of the Phoenix and Other Poems* was published by the Ryerson Press in 1943.

7. Archibald Lampman's grave is in Beechwood Cemetery, Ottawa.

8. William Douw Lighthall, like Scott, had his roots in the last decades of the nineteenth century. Though he was eighty-six at this time, he was still practising law in Montreal, and despite the illness referred to he was to outlive Scott by seven years. Poet, novelist and anthologist, and an eccentric propagandist in realms of political and moral philosophy, his *Songs of the Great Dominion,* compiled for the British "Windsor" series and published in 1889, remains a landmark in the record of the development of poetic practice in Canada. Scott and Lighthall were not close friends. But Lighthall had been an early champion of Lampman, as Scott notes, and this fact, together with their common membership in the Royal Society for nearly forty years, provided an enduring bond of sympathy between them.

9. *The New Treasury of War Poetry: Poems of the Second World War.* Edited, with an introduction and notes, by George Herbert Clarke (Boston: Houghton Mifflin, 1943). Elise Aylen's contribution is 'Ganelon' (pp. 40-42); Scott's is 'Hymn for Those in the Air' (pp. 129-30). A probable date for Lighthall's visit is indicated by an inscription in Scott's copy of *The New Treasury,* presently located in the Library at Carleton University: "Duncan C. Scott 10 November, 1943."

10. A reference to the dedication; see Letter 70, note 2.

LETTER 72

1. J.A. Froude, *Thomas Carlyle: a History of the First Forty Years of His Life* (2 vols.) and *Thomas Carlyle: a History of His Life in London, 1834-1881* (2 vols.) (London: Longman & Co., 1882 and 1884).

2. I have not been able to identify the "young communist" with any certainty. Professor A.G. Bailey, who knew Brown at the University of Toronto in the early thirties, suggests Henry Noyes and Stanley Ryerson as possibilities.

LETTER 73

1. This letter exists only as an undated carbon copy in the SAP, filed with other letters in random order. The clue for dating is the reference to the "short article" which has just been published in *The Educational Record.* The article had been solicited by W.P. Percival, Director of Protestant Education for the province of Quebec, early in 1943, and published in the October-December issue, pp. 221-25. Percival is to recall the 1943 contact with Scott when he writes towards the end of 1945 and early in 1946 to

ask for Scott's help in lining up persons who might agree to write short biographical studies of Sangster, Mair, Campbell, Cameron and Wetherell (SAP, "Lampman" file). The maturing of the project was the publication of Percival's *Leading Canadian Poets* in 1948. The reference in the present letter to "Yours of the 2nd" confirms the placing of it between Letter 72 and Letter 74. The conjectural date for the letter therefore lies somewhere between the 4th and the 15th of December.

2. The "idea" is a kind of doctrine of the crucial moment. It is a moment in the experience of a writer which provides "new influences" leading to the "strengthening and enrichment" of the writer's essential genius, "without diverting the stream from its main channel." Scott felt that in Lampman's case the crucial moment was his coming to Ottawa in 1883.

3. The *Canadian Forum,* begun in 1920, had called itself "A Monthly Journal of Literature and Public Affairs" and had built itself a solid reputation throughout the twenties and thirties as an organ of controversy and cautious avant-garde opinion. It had at the same time served as an important outlet for some of the new voices in poetry of these years: F.R. Scott, A.J.M. Smith, A.M. Klein, etc.

4. Scott's complete ignorance of Northrop Frye may sound strange to present day ears. The author of *Fearful Symmetry, Anatomy of Criticism* and more than a dozen other books, Frye is recognized now as one of the major critical voices of our time. But *Fearful Symmetry,* the study of Blake which was the cornerstone of his reputation, was not published until 1947. In 1943, he was thirty-one years old and had only recently been promoted from lecturer to assistant professor at Victoria College, University of Toronto. The reference for Frye's *Forum* article is: "Canada and Its Poetry," *Canadian Forum,* XXIII (December 1943), pp. 207-10.

LETTER 74

1. Walter J. Phillips, born in England in 1884, came to Canada in 1913 and settled in Winnipeg. His orientation was westward, towards the Rockies and the Pacific Coast. Recently, he had joined the staff of the Calgary Institute of Technology and become an instructor at the Banff School of Fine Arts. Over the years, he was to earn wide recognition for his water-colour paintings, and especially for his wood engravings and colour woodcuts. Scott's friendship with Phillips dated back to at least 1920, when the poet had belatedly sent the painter a copy of his 1915 volume, *Lundy's Lane and Other Poems.* In 1945 Scott was to undertake the writing of a brochure on Phillips for Ryerson's Canadian Art Series. It was published in 1947. There is an extensive file on Phillips, including many letters both ways, in the SAP.

LETTER 75

1. David Milne was born in Bruce County, Ontario, in 1882. In 1943 he was living in Uxbridge, near Toronto, where he was enjoying the fruits of a public recognition that had been denied him most of his life. Before this, he had lived for years in seclusion on Six Mile Lake, near Georgian Bay. His landscapes, delicate and evocative, are quite unlike those of the Group of Seven.

2. Douglas Duncan (1902-68), founder, with H.G. Kettle, and for many years director of the Picture Loan Society of Toronto; patron of art and promoter of young talent; collector extraordinary; bibliophile and master of the craft of bookbinding. In 1935, impressed by some of Milne's work he had seen in a Toronto gallery, Duncan had sought out the artist in his Muskoka retreat; and in 1938 he had become Milne's agent — Brown's "homme d'affaires." The connection with Brown probably began at the University of Toronto, where Duncan took a degree in art in Brown's time. Both were students in Paris between 1926 and 1928.

3. *The Civil Service Review* (December 1943), p. 471. T.R. Loftus MacInnes was at this time editor of the magazine and had written this review. I have let Brown's misspelling of MacInnes's name stand; he corrects himself in subsequent letters.

4. The Ottawa branch of the Canadian Authors' Association met in the old Dominion Archives on Thursday, December 16, 1943, to honour Duncan Campbell Scott. L.W. Brockington paid tribute to the poet, and Pelham Edgar gave an appreciation of Scott's poetry. The next day, the *Citizen* carried an account of the gathering. Julia Murphy had read selections from the poet's work, and Dorothy Lampman McCurry had sung several of Scott's "songs" that had been set to music. Gustave Lanctot, president of the Ottawa branch and long-time friend of Scott, was chairman. The *Citizen* regretted the absence of Dr. Scott himself, "owing to indisposition."

5. The first note had appeared in *Saturday Review of Literature*, 26 (September 1943), p. 28, where Benet had written: "In a recent anthology of Canadian poetry I have 'discovered' the poetry of Dr. E.J. Pratt of the University of Toronto, Canada's leading poet. I am ashamed that I did not know his poetry before this; but I am getting some of his books. His whale poem, 'The Cachelot,' is one of the best things I have read lately." A month later, in *Saturday Review*, 26 (October 16, 1943), pp. 23-24, Benet returned to the subject in the course of a general review of recent anthologies. He thought Smith's *The Book of Canadian Poetry* "an excellent compilation." "But I consider E.J. Pratt's work," he went on, "so exciting as to make most of the other collected poets in the volume pale to comparative insignificance." He then dealt with *Brébeuf and his Brethren* at some length. William Rose Benet had been associate editor of *Saturday Review* since 1923. Poet and novelist himself, he had produced several anthologies of verse and prose, including (with Norman Pearson) *The Oxford Anthology of American Literature* (1938). His novel-in-verse, *The Dust Which Is God*, had been awarded a Pulitzer Prize in 1941.

6. The American edition of Pratt's *Collected Poems,* with an introduction by W.R. Benet, was to be published by A.A. Knopf in 1945. Macmillan of Canada published the first Canadian edition in 1944, but without an introduction. When they reprinted the volume in 1946, Benet's introduction was included. Knopf's edition was a shortened version of Macmillan's.

LETTER 76

1. *Still Life and Other Verse* was published by Macmillan in 1943. James Hope & Sons Ltd. described themselves in 1943 as "Manufacturing Stationers, Printers, Bookbinders and Booksellers." Located at 61 Sparks Street, they were an Ottawa institution; but the store did not long survive the new conditions of the book trade in the postwar period.

2. The 'Twelfth Anniversary' sonnets were published in *The Circle of Affection*.

LETTER 77

1. Deaver Brown was born on December 30, 1943.

2. One of the Lampman "scribblers" temporarily in Brown's hands contained prose pieces, and amongst these was the address entitled "Two Canadian Poets," a study of Charles G.D. Roberts and George Frederick Cameron. The Ottawa Literary and Scientific Society came into existence on December 24, 1869. Its roots were in the Ottawa Mechanics' Institute (formerly the Bytown Mechanics' Institute, begun in 1843) and the Ottawa Natural History Society (begun in 1863). With E.A. Meredith, L.L.D., as president, the first meeting of the new society was held in January 1870. The "transactions" of meetings were not kept until 1897 — six years after Lampman had presented his paper. These documents are housed in the "Ottawa Room" of the Ottawa Public Library.

3. Carl Y. Connor, *Archibald Lampman: Canadian Poet of Nature* (Montreal: Carrier, 1929).

4. The review was to appear in the *University of Toronto Quarterly,* XIII, 4 (1943-44), pp. 221-29.

LETTER 79

1. Scott has forgotten. In his introduction to the 1925 edition of *Lyrics of Earth* (pp. 8-9), he had quoted a paragraph in which Lampman described the effect on him of his first reading of *Orion* and in a note had attributed it to an "unpublished essay." The reference is obviously to the manuscript of "Two Canadian Poets," which at that time, together with other Lampman papers, was in Scott's possession.

2. The *Queen's Quarterly,* in a review article dealt with five books: *The Autobiography of Oliver Goldsmith* (Myatt), *At the Long Sault, News of the Phoenix, The Book of Canadian Poetry,* and *On Canadian Poetry.* See G.H.C. (George Herbert Clarke), "Canadian Poets and Their Critics," *Queen's Quarterly*, vol. 50 (Autumn 1943), pp. 432-37.

3. Clarke writes: "The chief value of Professor Brown's book is to be found in the intellectual quality of its criticism, which is orderly, reasonable and persuasive. In his comparisons of poetic quality, however, he does not always draw steadily on his imaginative faculty" (p. 437).

4. The review of *On Canadian Poetry* is by Chester Duncan. The review of *At the Long Sault* is by Alan Creighton. A.M. Klein deals briefly with *The Book of Canadian Poetry* in a piece entitled "The Poetry of A.J.M. Smith." *Canadian Forum,* XXIII (January 1944), pp. 237-38.

5. Probably J. Burns Martin, later identified as the "B.M." of the *Dalhousie Review* who writes about Pratt's *Still Life* and *At the Long Sault.* Arthur Bourinot's dedication to *At the Mermaid Inn,* published in 1958, reads: To the Memory/of/my friend/Burns Martin,/Ph.D./late of the University of King's College, Halifax,/whose idea this was.

6. *The White Savannahs.*

7. The word Scott is reaching for is not "rascal" but "scoundrel." In a letter to Robert Bridges (October 18, 1882) Hopkins writes: "But first I may as well say what I should not have said, that I always knew in my heart Walt Whitman's mind to be more like my own than any other man's living. As he is a very great scoundrel that is not a pleasant confession. And this makes me the more desirous to read him and the more determined that I will not." (C.C. Abbott, ed., *The Letters of Gerard Manley Hopkins to Robert Bridges* [London, New York: Oxford University Press, 1955], p. 155.) Scott's reference to Goethe and Burns seems also to have been prompted by Hopkins and suggests, at the same time, the source for Scott's "rascal." Writing to R.W. Dixon on February 27, 1879, Hopkins comments on Tennyson: "To be sure this gives him vogue, popularity, but not that sort of ascendancy Goethe had or even Burns, scoundrel as the first was, not to say the second; but then they spoke out of the real human rakishness of their hearts and everybody recognized the really beating, though rascal, vein" (C.C. Abbott, ed., *The Correspondence of Gerard Manley Hopkins and Richard Watson Dixon*; London, New York: Oxford University Press, 1955, p. 25).

LETTER 80

1. *The Poems of Archibald Lampman* went through at least four printings between 1900 (the year of the Memorial Edition) and 1915. The "second impression" must have been issued very soon after the first printing of June 1900. A second edition, known as the Holiday Edition, came out early in 1901. The copy of the Lampman poem which Brown says he is enclosing does not seem to have been preserved.

2. Edward William Thomson (1849-1924), journalist and short-story writer, was an important figure in the life of Archibald Lampman and, to a lesser degree, D.C. Scott. The friendship with Lampman dated from the publication of the latter's *Among the Millet* in 1888 and is admirably documented in the correspondence which took place between the two men after Thomson's removal to Boston in 1891 to take up the job of revising editor and story writer for *Youth's Companion*. See Arthur S. Bourinot's *Archibald Lampman's Letters to Edward William Thomson (1890-1898)* and *The Letters of Edward William Thomson to Archibald Lampman (1891-1897)* (Ottawa: the Editor, 1956 and 1957). By 1904, Thomson had been back in Canada for three years and was living in Ottawa, where he worked as Canadian correspondent for the Boston *Transcript*. His son, Bernard St-Denis Thomson, had returned to Canada earlier and had married Ethel Wright of Ottawa (Bourinot, *The Letters of Edward William Thomson*, p. 20).

3. In his introduction to *Lyrics of Earth*, published in 1925, Scott had described "the principle of the 1900 collection": "In this first book almost everything that [Lampman] had written was included. The critical faculty was in suspension." *Lyrics of Earth*, on the other hand, was to be selective. Now, many years later, in his foreword to *At the Long Sault*, Scott had invoked the earlier principle of the 1900 collection: what was offered here was to be "a gathering together. . .of all that is left of the poet's work." This was not quite so, of course. The discovery of additional Lampman papers in the early seventies, and the re-examination of the copybooks and scribblers, would yield new poems.

4. George Frederick Cameron died in 1885 at the age of thirty-one, and two years later his brother, Charles J. Cameron, published a collection of the poet's verse under the title, *Lyrics on Freedom, Love and Death*. I do not know what "trail" Brown was following. The *Union List of Manuscripts in Canadian Repositories* (Ottawa: PAC, 1975) records that there is some unpublished material amongst the manuscript poems by G.F. Cameron held at the University of British Columbia.

5. Probably Clarkson College, which currently mounts a U.S. Army "ROTC Instructor Group" within a department of the Army. But a search of Army Historical Files and the Clarkson College Archives (kindly carried out by Lieutenant Clark J. Bailey and the Clarkson College Historian, Mr. Donald Stillman) has drawn a blank on any reference to Brown or his "inspection visit" to Potsdam in 1944.

6. "People continue to ask," Frank Chamberlain wrote in the January 29, 1944, issue of *Saturday Night*, " 'Who's going to be the new general manager of the CBC?' " He added: "Leonard Brockington, K.C., is silent these days." The question of Brockington's appointment had been raised intermittently for more than a year. The appointment never materialized.

LETTER 81

1. J. Burns Martin reviewed Brown's *On Canadian Poetry*, together with A.J.M. Smith's *News of the Phoenix*, in "New Books," *Dalhousie Review*, Vol. XXIII, no. 4 (January 1944), pp. 478-79.

LETTER 82

1. Bernal or Bernard? Thomson had only one child, a son, and in his letters to Lampman he refers to him as "Bernie." Bourinot, with his "Bernard St. Denis," seems sure of his ground, and so I give the additional information which he supplies: that Bernard was a graduate of Harvard, in Law; that he was "for many years on the editorial staff of the *New York Times*"; that he had died "about fifteen years ago" (i.e., about 1942); that his widow, Ethel Wright of Ottawa, "did not long survive him"; and that there is, Bourinot is given to understand, a grandson, Mr. Edward Wright Thomson. I have

tried to follow Bernard Thomson's trail to the *New York Times,* where he is said to
have been sports editor for a number of years, but a quick search of the records by the
present sports editor, Mr. James Tuite, has drawn a blank.

2. Charles J. Cameron, ed., *Lyrics on Freedom, Love and Death* (Boston: Moore;
Kingston: Shannon, 1887).

3. Scott is of course working from a typescript version of the lecture. In the printed
version (*University of Toronto Quarterly,* Vol. XIII [July 1944], pp. 406-23) the
section on Cameron begins on p. 418. It is in fact a patchwork of extravagant praise
and extended quotation. Having quoted some very weak lines, for example, Lampman
describes them as "touched with Cameron's rare gift of expression, that largeness of
utterance, that great way of saying things, which is characteristic only of the master
poets" (p. 422).

4. Brown had dealt sympathetically but rather severely with Cameron in the second
chapter of *On Canadian Poetry.*

5. In a paragraph in which he considers some of Roberts' shortcomings, Lampman cites
two love poems, 'Tout ou rien' and 'In Notre Dame,' as instances of the poet's "want
of tenderness and genuine delicacy" (pp. 417-18).

6. The sonnet begins: "Wisdom immortal from immortal Jove" (p. 420). See *Lyrics on
Freedom, Love and Death,* p. 148.

7. The Royal Society of Canada was formed in 1882 to promote the development of
science and literature in Canada. Lampman became a member in 1895, Scott in 1899.
In 1926, Lorne Pierce had made provision, under the aegis of the Society, for "a gold
medal in annual recognition of achievement in imaginative and critical literature."
Audrey Alexandra Brown, a native of Nanaimo, B.C., and by that time author of three
volumes of poetry and the autobiographical *The Log of a Lame Duck* (1938), was the
first woman poet to receive the Lorne Pierce award. Ira Dilworth had helped to get her
started, and it was through him that Scott became acquainted with her work. Though
not on the Committee, it was Scott who had proposed her name for the present
competition (SAP, Audrey Brown file).

8. "Our Peerless Leader" was Scott's sobriquet for William Lyon Mackenzie King. As
much a Conservative as his civil service job would allow him to be, Scott was no great
admirer of King. The "something else" King had to think about was doubtless the
conscription crisis developing in these final months of the war.

LETTER 83

1. Collin's review begins: "The Ryerson Press are to be complimented on their beautiful
presentation of Dr. E.K. Brown's book *On Canadian Poetry.* Dr. Brown is one of our
most promising scholars." *University of Toronto Quarterly,* Vol. XIII, no. 4
(1943-44), p. 221.

2. Collin saw Lampman as essentially a poet of nature whose achievement was limited by
his failure to reflect in his poetry the shifting currents of ideas and beliefs which
marked the last decades of the nineteenth century in Europe. See the chapter on
"Natural Landscape" in *The White Savannahs,* pp. 3-40.

3. The books were Pratt's *Still Life* and Ralph Gustafson's *Anthology of Canadian Poetry
(English).* Mr. Gustafson has drawn my attention to the fact that both books are
referred to in Brown's article "To the North: A Wall against Canadian Poetry," which
appeared April 29, 1944, in *Saturday Review of Literature* (Letter from R.G. to R.L.
McD., August 8, 1977). But the review which Brown is talking about here seems to
have been placed with *Voices,* the periodical to which Scott had contributed a poem
when Gustafson had served as guest editor for a special Canadian issue in the spring of
1943. *Voices* was published in Brattleboro, Vermont, but its editorial offices were in

New York City. For the review reference, see David Staines' bibliography in "E.K. Brown (1905-1951): The Critic and his Writings," *Canadian Literature,* 83 (Winter 1979), p. 185, where the title of the piece is given as "Recent Poetry from Canada" and the date as spring, 1944.

4. A complaint had been lodged about the noises made by mating frogs in the garden of P.A. Taverner at 43 Leonard Avenue, Ottawa. In an interview with a *Journal* reporter on February 3, 1944, Dr. Taverner explained that his singing frogs were in fact toads (pp. 1 and 12).

LETTER 84

1. This letter has not been kept. Brown's last to Scott, in the present sequence, is his letter of February 15, in which there is no reference to Scott's "comments on the A.L. lecture." We may try a reconstruction. When Brown writes on February 15, Scott's letter of the preceding day (Letter 82) is still in the mail. The next night Brown is to leave for Brooklyn. Scott's letter arrives in the afternoon, and Brown writes a hasty reply.

2. Bliss Carman is dealt with on pp. 52-56 of *On Canadian Poetry,* where his work is variously described as "jaunty," "cloying," and "monotonous."

3. A.F.B. Clark, though nearly twenty years older than Brown, had had a similar background: University College, Toronto, University of Paris, and a thorough training in romance languages. After a brief spell of teaching in Toronto (he was lecturer in English at University College, 1914-17) he had gone west, first to the University of Washington, then to the University of British Columbia, where he was to be a mainstay of the Department of French for the next thirty years. Clark was the author of books on Boileau and Racine and a frequent contributor to the *University of Toronto Quarterly.* Eric Trevor Owen, distinguished classicist, was from 1923 almost until his death in 1948 professor of Greek at University College, Toronto.

4. F.G. Scott.

5. Scott returns this letter to Brown. A later letter is preserved in the E.K. Brown Papers at the PAC. The date is February 26, 1944, and the writer is Stanton A. Coblentz, editor of a California-based little magazine called *Wings.* Coblentz has been going through the back files of his publication in search of two articles he had written many years before on Lampman. We must assume that he is doing this because he has noted the recent appearance of *At the Long Sault.* He has found the "opening article" in the autumn issue of *Wings,* 1934. This issue he sends to Brown, who in due course passes it along to Scott. The second article, Coblentz says, was published in the winter issue of *Wings,* 1935, but this issue he has been unable to find. He thinks the Library at Cornell University will have a complete file of the magazine. He mentions in passing that "some years ago" he had spoken to the Musson Book Company about bringing out a selection of Lampman's poems. Hence Brown's inquiry of Scott as to whether he knew anything about "the negotiations mentioned."

6. Wilfrid Eggleston, who was to found the School of Journalism at the newly established Carleton University later in the decade, was from 1940 to 1943 chief English press censor in Ottawa. An experienced reporter and a prolific writer himself, Eggleston took an early and keen interest in Canadian literature. He was to make an important critical contribution to the field in 1957 with the publication of *The Frontier in Canadian Letters.* He was on friendly terms with Scott through their association in the work of the Canadian Writers' Foundation.

LETTER 86

1. Margaret Whitridge, in her bibliographical note to a reprint of the Lampman poems for the Literature of Canada series of the University of Toronto Press, reproduces the

circular. See *The Poems of Archibald Lampman* (Toronto: University of Toronto Press, 1974), pp. xxx-xxxiv. Samuel Edward Dawson, nearing seventy at the time the Memorial edition appeared, had acquired the kind of reputation as a publisher and man of letters that might be expected to lend weight to the enterprise Scott had launched on Lampman's behalf. He had been Queen's Printer since 1891 and a Fellow of the Royal Society of Canada since 1893. Co-signer of the circular, with Scott and Dawson, was W.D. LeSueur.

2. The extracts are from *London Spectator, London Academy, Boston Transcript, Philadelphia Press, New York Independent, Collier's Weekly* and *Harper's Magazine.* Two short notes of commendation are signed, respectively, by W.D. Howells and Hamlin Garland.

3. Bourinot, who reprints this letter, omits the reference to the MacInneses, cutting the text from "and you might think" to "you will understand" (*Some Letters,* p. 34).

4. The Lampman File of the SAP contains an undated and unsigned typescript copy of a letter from Scott to Natalie MacInnes which is relevant here. Scott writes that he is sending Natalie "two precious books" which have been in his keeping since Lampman's death; "and you will see," he says, "that I have had them bound." "One," he continues, "is his last notebook in which he made pen copies of the poems. The last in the book is I think likely to be his last bit of writing, it is certainly his last completed poem. The other is a copy of *Alcyone* bound with the proof-sheets and you will find a note explaining the contents." Although there is no mention of the Memorial edition, the transfer recorded in Scott's letter to Natalie must surely be the same one Scott represents to Brown as having taken place "a month or so ago," which is to say around Christmas 1943. *Alcyone* is the Lampman volume which was in press at the time of the poet's death. Publication was stopped in favour of the forthcoming Memorial edition. The manuscripts which Scott is holding back, the "two which A.L. made for me," are the two which he will later present to Trinity College, Toronto.

5. The "Canadian Poets" series.

6. F.A. Hardy was born in England but had come to Canada as a child and had received his education at Halifax Academy and Dalhousie University. Appointed to the staff of the Library of Parliament in 1919, he became librarian on February 18, 1944; and he was to continue in this position until his retirement in 1959. He died in 1969.

LETTER 87

1. This copy of the Memorial edition, with Brown's notations scattered thickly through it, remains in the possession of the Brown family.

2. The correct title is *Lyrics on Freedom, Love and Death.*

3. 'Cloud and Sun.'

4. 'Even Beyond Music.'

5. Dorothy Livesay had been publishing poetry since the late twenties. Her political radicalism, nourished by the bitter years of the Great Depression, is strongly reflected in the volume to which Brown refers. The title is *Day and Night,* and it was to win the Governor General's Award for Poetry in 1944. That was her third volume, and there were many more to come. Livesay published her *Collected Poems: The Two Seasons* in 1972.

6. *Full Tide,* a publication which had been launched in 1936. Roberts had died November 26, 1943. On February 5, 1944, *Full Tide* brought out a memorial number (vol. 8, no. 2), "Dedicated to the Memory of Charles G.D. Roberts." Scott's tribute takes its place among others from Elsie Pomeroy, Lorne Pierce, W.A. Deacon, Lionel Stevenson and Watson Kirkconnell. Scott never had a great deal to say about Roberts, though certainly they were on friendly enough terms; and Roberts' death goes all but

unnoticed in the present correspondence. The tribute written for *Full Tide,* a masterpiece of guarded praise, is worth quoting in full.

I am glad to join your Symposium in honour of the late Sir Charles G.D. Roberts. I shall leave to others appreciation of his writings and take up my small allotted space in mentioning two personal characteristics. I could hazard the opinion that few writers have used oftener the term, fellowcraftsman; this word was an index of one of his qualities; he thought of all poets and versifiers as members of a guild, and if he praised indiscriminately it was for that reason. I think the praise came from a sense of comradeship and from a felling of kindness for writers of all calibers. He had, so far as known, no literary jealousy. My second point is — He was a leading Canadian for Canada and Canadians; as he wrote:

"But first in my heart this land I call my own!
Canadian am I in blood and bone."

This was generally recognized and I note its record in a late issue of The Literary Supplement of the London Times. "His aim — early and late — was to give Canada a sense of nationhood — and Canadian literature its own distinction." This was a worthy aim and one can only hope that he was satisfied, after a long and strenuous life, with its accomplishment, in degree at least, for its full attainment would be impossible for any man.

LETTER 88

1. Again there seems to be a letter missing, this time on Scott's side of the correspondence. On February 27 (Letter 86) Scott writes to say that he has two letters from Brown to answer, presumably those of February 15 and 20, but that he wants "to write now a Lampman letter and reserve my comments on these reviews until a later time." The "later time" appears to have come on March 6, for that is the date Scott scrawls across the top of Brown's letter of February 20: "Ansd Mar 6th." But I have not been able to find such a letter, original or carbon copy, and Scott's query here and Brown's response in Letter 89 therefore remain without anchorage in the text.

LETTER 89

1. *Wings* occupied a rear-guard position amongst American literary magazines of the thirties and forties. A quarterly, issued from Mill Valley, California, it described itself as "an independent poetry magazine, owned and published by the editor, and without patrons or outside financial support." Stanton A. Coblentz, owner and publisher, presented himself as the author of *The Mountain of the Sleeping Maiden and Other Poems.* In literary taste he was conservative, even reactionary. As late as 1950 we find him lamenting the rift "between present-day technique or its lack and the oldtime traditions of workmanship." He was in fact to fight a rear-guard action against modernism in poetry until the magazine ceased publication in 1957. Lampman's appeal must have been that of a craftsman and a gentle traditionalist offering peace where "much fruitful territory has been ravaged by the raging currents." See *Wings,* Vol. IX, no. 9 (Autumn 1950), p. 6.

2. See Letters in Canada, *University of Toronto Quarterly,* XIII (April 1944), p. 315.

3. Watson Kirkconnell was at this time head of the Department of English at McMaster University and a member of the newly created Governor General's Awards Board. He was born in Port Hope, Ontario, in 1895, and educated at Queen's University and Lincoln College, Oxford. Prior to coming to McMaster, he had been for nearly twenty years at Wesley College, Winnipeg, where he had served as both professor of English and professor of Classics. He was in fact an accomplished linguist and became a regular contributor of reviews of "other language" literature to the Letters in Canada Supplement of the *University of Toronto Quarterly.* He was a close friend of A.S.P. Woodhouse, with whom he collaborated in the preparation of *The Humanities in*

Canada (Ottawa: Humanities Research Council, 1947). Elected F.R.S.C. in 1936, he had been more recently honoured as recipient of the Lorne Pierce Medal for 1942. The Governor General's Awards had originally had three categories of awards: fiction, poetry and drama, and non-fiction. In 1942 the non-fiction category had been divided into "creative non-fiction" and "academic non-fiction." But the new terminology did not work well, and in 1959 the original categories were restored.

4. This is the article entitled "To the North: A Wall Against Canadian Poetry" which appeared in the *Saturday Review of Literature* on April 29, 1944.

LETTER 90

1. The note was written, in Scott's hand, on the back of the second page of Brown's letter of March 13, which is Letter 89 in this sequence. On the first page, upper left margin, Scott has written "Ansd 20-3-44." This answering letter, however, has not turned up. It was undoubtedly a letter of congratulation which followed hard upon Brown's disclosure "in confidence" that he was to receive a Governor General's award. Although its faintly plaintive tone disturbs the sequence a bit at this point, this note nevertheless helps to bridge the considerable gap between Brown's letter of March 13 and Scott's letter of April 1. Did it represent some first thoughts for what would become Scott's letter of the 16th? Perhaps; there are some echoes. My own inclination is to place the note somewhere between the missing letter of March 20 and the renewed-congratulations letter of April 16. Brown is silent; he will be on holiday for three weeks. Scott is a little gloomy. Certainly, the note underlines his growing dependence on hearing from his friend. Events were at any rate to develop quickly: soon after Scott had mailed his letter of the 16th, Brown was in Ottawa.

There is an anomaly about the provenance of Brown's letter of March 13 (Letter 89) which should be recorded here. This letter was not in the SAP, where the bulk of Brown's letters to Scott are filed. It turned up, surprisingly, amongst the residue of E.K. Brown papers still in Mrs. Brown's hands in 1975. Somebody, presumably after Scott's death in 1947, must have sent the letter back to Brown; either that, or Brown picked it up himself in Ottawa. Did the note on the back of the first page have something to do with this unusual disposal of the letter? Perhaps Mrs. Scott, sorting her husband's papers, thought that Brown should see these few lines. The original (TLS) is now with the E.K. Brown Papers, PAC.

LETTER 91

1. We must assume that Brown, who will be in Ottawa within a few days, has sent no word of his coming. This letter will reach him on his return to Ithaca. There is a typed draft of this letter, unsigned, in the SAP. Except for two minor differences in punctuation, it is the same as the holograph version. It is rare for Scott to proceed from a typed to a written text. One senses another ripple effect from that curious note affixed to Brown's letter of March 13.

2. In a letter dated November 8, 1905, John Masefield had written Scott asking permission to include 'The Piper of Arll' in a collection of poems of the sea to be published soon (*A Sailor's Garland*. Selected and edited by John Masefield [Methuen & Co. London, 1906]). He recalled having read 'The Piper of Arll' in 1895, when he was working in a carpet factory in Yonkers, New York. "I had never (till that time) cared much for poetry," he had written in his letter to Scott, "but your poem impressed me deeply, and set me on fire." The story, highly acceptable in the context of a diffident Canadian criticism, was to become widely known. It was used for the publicizing of the collected *Poems* of 1926 and gained further currency in Masefield's preface to the English edition of the same volume in the following year (*The Poems of Duncan Campbell Scott*. With a foreword by John Masefield [J.M. Dent & Sons: London, 1927]). When Masefield was appointed poet laureate in 1930, the *Journal* of

Ottawa gave the story another run: "Canadian Poem turned Masefield to Poetry, He Says." Scott's contact with Masefield was maintained, intermittently, throughout these later years. They met only once, briefly, in Florence, in the early thirties; at least so says Elise Aylen Scott to Bourinot (see note 5 of Letter 155). But in Letter 155 Scott tells Brown that Masefield "has probably never seen my visage." Masefield gives an account of the Yonkers happening in his autobiography, *In the Mill* (1941), pp. 59-60.

3. John Purves (Scott misspells the name) was reader in Italian Studies at Edinburgh University between 1921 and 1947. Editor, anthologist and lexicographer, he was interested in the relation between Italian and English literature, and his best scholarly work was done in this area. Scott had known Purves since 1932, when they had begun a correspondence on the question of Scott's representation in an anthology Purves was editing. There are some interesting letters in the Scott papers held at the Fisher Rare Book Library, University of Toronto.

4. For a possible Canadian edition of *In the Village of Viger*.

LETTER 92

1. There is no record at Rideau Hall of a formal presentation of the Governor General's awards having been made about this time. All we can know for certain is that Brown was in Ottawa between April 16 and April 20.

2. I cannot identify the "gift." Brown later calls it a "brochure" and links it with the summer of his brief stay in Ottawa, in 1942; it may be the sixteen-page booklet, *Addresses Delivered at the Dedication of the Archibald Lampman Memorial Cairn at Morpeth, Ontario,* published by The Western Ontario Branch of the Canadian Authors' Association (London, Ont., 1930).

3. At the head of the present letter, above the salutation, Scott has written in pencil:

$\frac{4 \text{ ordered}}{2}$ 6

1 Masefield
2 on hand
1 RH Coats
1 Stanstead—Prof Arnason
1 Sir J. Squire

4. Brown, discussing Pratt's 'The Roosevelt and the Antinoe' (*On Canadian Poetry,* pp. 143-44), dismisses the idea of Pratt as "a local Masefield." "I do not find the comparison illuminating," he writes, "and in some respects it seems to me to be dangerously misleading. Masefield's is essentially a tender nature, lacking in humour; and when he exalts strength, as he often does, there is something *maladif* in his tone as there is in Henley's or Swinburne's. Tenderness is almost absent from Pratt's poetry: his approach is much more masculine than Masefield's. . . ."

5. George Herbert Clarke of Queen's University.

6. The lectures did not result in a book. In 1945, however, Brown was to publish "James and Conrad" in *Yale Review,* XXXV (Winter 1945), pp. 265-85; and in 1946, "Two Formulas for Fiction" in *College English,* VIII (October 1946), pp. 7-17. The work on Forster bore fruit in "Rhythm in the Novel," the Alexander lectures which Brown was to give at the University of Toronto in 1949.

7. Guy Sylvestre, a pioneering figure in the appreciation of Québecois literature, was to be responsible for a "series of chronicles" scheduled to appear from time to time in the Saturday edition of *Le Devoir* under the title "A travers les livres et les revues." The review which Brown refers to was headed "La poésie *canadienne* anglaise." See *Le Devoir* (Samedi, 15 Avril 1944), p. 8. The second article, a review of *At the Long Sault,* was headed "Un poète anglais de Dollard." See *Le Devoir* (Samedi, 27 Mai 1944), p. 8. Guy Sylvestre is currently National Librarian. I have let Brown's misspelling of the name stand. He corrects himself later.

8. *Anthologie de la poésie canadienne d'expression française* (Montréal: Beauchemin, 1943).

9. The move to Chicago was to take place towards the end of June.

LETTER 93

1. "To the North: A Wall Against Canadian Poetry," *The Saturday Review of Literature,* 29 April 1944, pp. 9-11 (reprinted in David Staines, *E.K. Brown: Responses and Evaluations,* 1977).

2. The volume referred to is probably *Greater Poems of the Bible,* which was published by Macmillan in 1943. Wilson MacDonald (1880-1967) was paying the price at this time for an inflated reputation in the twenties, when he had been widely acclaimed for carrying on the traditions, both in subject matter and style, of the poets of the Confederation. His best work is reflected in *A Flagon of Beauty* (1931) and *The Song of the Undertow* (1935). To an engraved letter of promotion for *A Flagon of Beauty* which he had sent to Scott in the Fall of 1931, MacDonald had added a postscript: "I am speaking about you during Author's week. Let me know what you have written lately." I have no copy of a reply from Scott, nor can I imagine one. MacDonald stood at the distant edge of his interests.

3. Pratt shared space with six American poets, whose names, with the possible exception of Robert Nathan, are forgotten today. The review was entitled "Seven Good Poets."

4. J. Burns Martin had reviewed Pratt's *Still Life* in the April number of *Dalhousie Review* (vol. 24, no. 1, 1944). Amongst other books dealt with in the same article (pp. 117-9) is Wilson MacDonald's *Greater Poems of the Bible.*

5. Amongst the poems by Scott published in *The London Mercury* were: 'The Eagle Speaks,' 4 (June 1921), pp. 127-28; 'Permanence,' 5 (March 1922), pp. 458-59; and 'The Journey,' 17 (December 1927), pp. 130-31. 'The End of the Day' was quoted in a piece by Arthur Stanley called "Our Canadian Poets," 26 (October 1932), p. 542. Elise Aylen's contribution was 'Dusk of the Gods,' 30 (July 1934), pp. 199-200. When a selection of poems published in *The London Mercury* between 1919 and 1930 was brought out by Macmillan (London) in 1931, under the title *The Mercury Book of Verse,* Scott's poem 'Permanence' was included, pp. 228-29.

6. The funeral service for Sir Charles G.D. Roberts, who had died on 26 November, 1943, had been held in Toronto, followed by cremation. On May 15, 1944, the ashes lay in state in the cathedral, Fredericton, where Roberts' father had been an honorary Canon. A state Memorial Service for Bliss Carman had been held in the same cathedral in 1929.

7. Nathaniel Benson (1903-66), teacher, poet, playwright and freelance writer. Born in Toronto, he was by 1944 living in New York, where he was to remain until 1948. He had been president of the Canadian Authors' Association, 1941-1943, and managing editor of the *Canadian Poetry Magazine,* 1937-1943. A collection of Benson's poems, *The Glowing Years,* had been published in 1937. The elegy referred to, entitled 'The Last Parting (In Memory of C.G.D.R.),' had appeared in a recent issue of *Saturday Night,* 59 (April 15, 1944), p. 3. The poem was reprinted in *Canadian Poetry,* 7 (June 1944), pp. 10-12.

8. *Love's Labours Lost,* V, ii.

9. I do not know what these "old books" were, or whether they were ever passed on to Brown. Most of the valuable and interesting books in Scott's considerable library went to the Library at Carleton University when the Lisgar Street house was sold in 1957.

10. The picture is now with the National Gallery, Ottawa.

240

11. Norman Platt Lambert, born in 1885, had had a distinguished career as a journalist and businessman and had been appointed to the Senate on January 20, 1938. On May 4, 1944, in the afternoon session of the Senate, he had quoted extensively from Brown's *On Canadian Poetry* in support of a motion calling for a uniform textbook in history for Canadian schools. See *Debates of the Senate / Dominion of Canada,* Session 1944-1945, p. 150. The quoted passage is from pp. 22-23 of *On Canadian Poetry* and begins: "Canada is not an integrated whole."

LETTER 94

1. Abraham Moses Klein (1909-72), poet and novelist, was born in Montreal and educated at McGill University and the Université de Montréal. In the thirties he had become identified with a small group of writers to be known later as the "Montreal Poets." The others were A.J.M. Smith, Leo Kennedy and F.R. Scott, and in 1936 they contributed to and published (with E.J. Pratt and Robert Finch) *New Provinces,* a volume soon to be recognized as a landmark in the development of modern poetry in Canada. But Klein, deeply traditional and Jewish, was really of no school. He had published *Hath Not a Jew* in 1940 and would publish *The Hitleriad* and *Poems* in 1944.

2. Brown had written: "The poetry of the Montreal group and their disciples and associates is the core of Canadian verse during the past twenty years" (*On Canadian Poetry,* p. 67). That was the old group. By 1944, as Smith's remark and Brown's comment reveal, there were new alignments; and of course some new poets on the scene. It is difficult to be certain what Brown had in mind when he spoke of "the newest Montreal group." One group, which included Louis Dudek, Irving Layton and Raymond Souster, was flaunting a boisterous animism, anti-puritan and anti-philistine, which would find expression in a volume called *Cerberus,* in 1952. Another group, which included F.R. Scott, John Sutherland, Neufville Shaw and Dorothy Livesay, and which was led by the charismatic Patrick Anderson, recently arrived from England, had accepted Marx and Freud and a strong social commitment as the "new" direction for their poetry. A.J.M. Smith was uneasy about the new allegiances and so was Brown.

3. The *Journal* carried an account of Senator Lambert's citing of E.K. Brown in the Chamber.

4. Norman Alexander Robertson (1904-68), born in Vancouver, educated at Oxford and Harvard, was Under Secretary of State from January 1941 to August 1946.

5. Scott's question (Letter 86) was not about what poems from the Memorial edition Brown thought might have been left out (i.e., in *Lyrics of Earth*) but rather what poems from *At the Long Sault* Brown would like to see reprinted in the shorter Lampman Scott was now working on for Pierce, and what poems from *Lyrics of Earth* he would like to see cancelled.

6. Brown is referring to the index of titles supplied at the end of *Lyrics of Earth,* pp. 273-76.

7. 'April Night,' as Scott recognizes in a pencilled note in the margin, had in fact been brought forward to *Lyrics of Earth,* where it appears on p. 111.

LETTER 95

1. The text of this talk was published in the *Civil Service Review,* vol. 17, no. 3 (September 1944), pp. 306, 308-9, 339. It was repeated (with slight variations in title) in *Canadians All* (Autumn 1944), pp. 28, 62, and in *Echoes,* 176 (Autumn 1944), pp. 12, 48.

2. This is the lecture "Two Canadian Poets."

3. "A Legend of Welly Legrave," first published in *Scribner's* in 1898, was included in Scott's second collected volume of short stories, *The Witching of Elspie* (Toronto: McClelland & Stewart, 1923).

LETTER 96

1. This may have been the beginnings of the Arts Reconstruction Committee, which was to be constituted officially in 1945 "to present a brief to the Dominion Government with respect to the promotion and encouragement of the cultural and artistic life of local communities." Later, the Committee's work was assumed by the Canadian Arts Council. See the *Canadian Almanac, 1947*, p. 698. These are the preliminaries whose sequel is the *Report* (1951) of the Massey Royal Commission on National Development in the Arts, Letters and Sciences, and the establishment of the Canada Council in 1957.

2. Brown had written "9.30."

3. *The Witching of Elspie*.

4. "A Legend of Welly Legrave" was accepted by *Scribner's* in a letter dated September 17, 1897 (SAP) and was published the following April (1898), no. 23, pp. 470-79. "The Vain Shadow" was accepted October 24, 1899 (SAP) and was published the following July (1900), no. 28, pp. 72-83. "Expiation" (originally entitled "The Recompense") was not published in *Scribner's*. It appeared in *Munsey's Magazine*, 38 (1907), pp. 25-28.

5. Thoreau MacDonald, the "T.M." referred to below.

LETTER 97

1. Miss Ellen Elliott was an old-timer at Macmillan of Canada. Born in England, she had come to Toronto in 1920 and had joined the company in that year. She had served for many years as the secretary to the president, Hugh Eayrs, and in 1942 she had been appointed to the company's board of directors. She turns up amongst F.P. Grove's correspondents. See Desmond Pacey, *The Letters of Frederick Philip Grove* (Toronto: University of Toronto Press, 1976), p. 251.

2. Brown writes first "by a soldier," then corrects "soldier" to "sailor" (ink over type). The reference is to Frederick Balmer Watt's *Who Dare to Live* (Toronto: Macmillan, 1943). It is a narrative poem.

3. This probably became "English Studies in the Postwar World," *College English*, 6 (April 1945), pp. 380-91. See David Staines' bibliography of Brown's writings, *Canadian Literature*, 83, p. 185.

4. Russell Sutherland Smart, a graduate of the University of Toronto and Queen's University in the first decade of the century, later a prominent Ottawa lawyer in the firm of Smart & Biggar, had died May 18, 1944, in his fifty-ninth year.

5. It is difficult to know at this point what review of Smith's poems *(News of the Phoenix)* Brown is talking about. He was a great recycler of his own material. Perhaps it was the one Brown published about this time in the *Manitoba Arts Review*, III (1944), pp. 30-32 (reprinted in Staines, *E.K. Brown: Responses and Evaluations*) under the title "A.J.M. Smith and the Poetry of Pride."

LETTER 98

1. "The Revival of E.M. Forster," *Yale Review*, XXXIII (Summer 1944), pp. 668-81.

2. In the poetry section of "Letters in Canada: 1943," *University of Toronto Quarterly*, vol. XIII, no. 3 (April 1944), p. 315, Brown had tried to answer those who had complained "that the comments on Sir Charles' work in these surveys were grudging." But after a few general remarks flattering to the subject, Brown had

escaped further commitment by saying that he could not do better than quote extensively from Scott's tribute to Roberts published a few months earlier in *Full Tide*. This tribute, as Brown well knew, was just about as evasive as his own.

3. *Full Tide,* vol. 8, no. 2 (February 5, 1944), p. 11.

4. On June 21, 1944, the Ottawa *Journal* had carried an item under the headline, "Artists Ask $10,000,000 Grant To Cultivate Canadian Culture." The proposal was contained, the *Journal* said, in a brief prepared for presentation to the "reconstruction committee" of the House of Commons and was supported by "16 national associations of artists, authors, musicians, architects and players" (p. 7).

5. The Canadian Authors' Foundation (later to be called The Canadian Writers' Foundation) had been established in 1931 "to provide financial assistance to needy Canadian writers who have made a worthy contribution to the nation's literary heritage" (*Encyclopedia Canadiana,* vol. 4, p. 241). The CWF was to be incorporated by letters patent in 1945.

6. This is the manuscript that will appear eventually as *The Circle of Affection.*

7. The Keats lecture would not be published until the summer of 1946.

8. Professor Alexander had died on June 28.

9. Not much is known about the Dinner Club. The arrangements seem to have been informal, and the list of the fifteen or twenty men involved seems to have changed fairly frequently. Dr. J.J. Mackenzie recalls that when he came to Ottawa in 1939 to begin his long association with the National Research Council of Canada, Scott and Sir Lyman Duff were the oldest members. Dr. Mackenzie was an engineer and scientist, Duff a jurist, Scott a civil servant and poet, Smart a lawyer. The club seems to have had no other purpose than to provide congenial occasions for the meeting of good minds. The setting was usually the Country Club, across the river, on the Aylmer Road.

10. This letter from Masefield is in the Scott collection at the Thomas Fisher Rare Book Library, University of Toronto. It is dated June 3, 1944. Masefield is grateful for Brown's book and is sure that it will "turn a good many people to study some of the poets treated. . . ." With this nod to criticism taken care of, he devotes the rest of his short letter to the present state of poetry:

> But the ploughing and the sowing are the vital things; and what seems to me to be continually needed is just such a gathering of young poets, as you and Carman; or Shakespeare and Southampton; or Ronsard and Du Bellay, or Keats and Reynolds; with a few standards and many hopes and much enthusiasm. What all lands need now are multitudes made enthusiastic about poetry and about the standards and hopes of these groups of young men. It seems clear to me, that the main approach must be made by the voice; some exciting swift poetry must be made to be spoken; it may be centuries before any large proportion of any people will be readers, as you and I are readers.

11. See "Culture and Books," Times Literary Supplement (May 27, 1944), p. 259.

LETTER 99

1. Brown's interest in the Lampman notebooks never flagged. Here he discovers the "dramatic fragment" on King Seleucus and finds embedded in the text ("like pearls in putty," as MacInnes was to say) the two love lyrics which in January 1943 he had belatedly put forward for inclusion in *At the Long Sault*. The question of the "dramatic fragment" is referred to MacInnes. For MacInnes's reply, see Appendix F (p. 287). To the best of my knowledge, the King Seleucus poem is not extant in any form.

2. To be published in Arthur S. Bourinot's *Archibald Lampman's Letters to Edward William Thomson (1890-1898)* (Ottawa, 1956), pp. 48-52. Bourinot records that it was

first published in *Harper's* in 1896. The most recent reprinting is in *Archibald Lampman: Selected Prose,* ed. with an introduction and notes by Barrie Davies (Ottawa: Tecumseh Press, 1975).

3. 'With those cold eyes, my dear' and 'You cannot answer to my love.'

4. In his introduction to the *Lyrics of Earth* collection of 1925, Scott speaks of the high quality of Lampman's letters to Thomson and records that the latter "has generously given them to me." One has the impression that they are still in Scott's hands since he says categorically in Letter 103 that Lampman "does not refer to it [the King Seleucus 'fragment'] in the Thomson letters." Bourinot's acknowledgement to his 1956 edition of the Lampman-Thomson letters (Lampman's to Thomson, that is) makes it clear that they are by now in the hands of Mrs. T.R. Loftus MacInnes. For a scholarly edition of the complete Lampman-Thomson correspondence, see Helen Lynn's M.A. thesis, "An Annotated Edition of the Correspondence Between Archibald Lampman and Edward William Thomson (1890-1898)," Carleton University, 1980.

5. "In Memoriam: William John Alexander." I. Memoir, by M.W. Wallace. II. Critic and Teacher, by A.S.P. Woodhouse. *University of Toronto Quarterly,* vol. XIV, no. 1 (October 1944), pp. 1-33.

6. Beyond 'The Fable of the Goats' and 'The Great Feud,' there were no further omissions in the American edition.

7. George Moore (1852-1933), novelist, journalist and poet, perhaps best known as the author of *Esther Waters* (1894) and the autobiographical *Confessions of a Young Man* (1888) and *Hail and Farewell* (1911-1914).

LETTER 100

1. Sugar had been rationed in Canada since 1942. This is one of the few reminders in this correspondence that there was a war on.

2. Harry Adaskin, violinist, and Frances Adaskin, pianist, were both accomplished performers. Mr. Adaskin had been a member of the original Hart House Quartet and had toured extensively with the group between 1923 and 1938. He and Frances were old friends of the Scotts. Mr. Adaskin was to become Professor of Music at the University of British Columbia in 1946. Still active in the musical life of Vancouver, the Adaskins are among the last of the living links with D.C. Scott.

3. In the U.S. presidential election Republican Governor Thomas E. Dewey of New York was running against F.D. Roosevelt, who was trying for his fourth term of office.

4. The "dreadful condition" was the recurrence of the conscription question, which had surfaced in 1942, and which in 1944 was moving towards a new crisis threatening the unity of the country. There was to be an election in Quebec in August. The premier of the province, Joseph Adélard Godbout, was a Liberal, though he had spoken against Mackenzie King's proposal for another plebiscite on conscription for overseas service. If Godbout (as a Liberal stalwart) were defeated, King might feel justified in forcing conscription on the country, in particular Quebec, by the arbitrary means of an Order-in-Council. Godbout was defeated. King began implementing a modified conscription policy in November 1944, and there were riots in Montreal. The end of the war was in sight, however, and the crisis passed.

5. Scott has inserted the word "fairly" in ink above the line. But in the end Scott was to be very pleased with Thoreau MacDonald's work. Five letters from Scott to the artist, covering both the *Viger* connection and the later publication of *The Circle of Affection*, are in the MacDonald collection at the PAC.

6. Emily Carr, westcoast painter, was born in Victoria, B.C., in 1871 and died there on March 2, 1945. There are three letters from her to Scott in the SAP, dated respectively March 22, 1941; July 2, 1941; and July 23, 1944. The Scotts acquired an Emily Carr

painting in the course of their visit to the West in the winter of 1940-1941. Miss Carr shipped the canvas to them — and with it a second canvas, "as a good wish from me for your anniversary and also as a tribute to the beauty and pleasure Dr. Scott has given to Canada through his poems." Both paintings are now amongst the holdings of the National Gallery in Ottawa: "Forest Landscape I" (N.G. 5041) and "Forest Landscape II" (N.G. 5042). The photograph reproduced by *The Studio* was a black-and-white of "Forest Landscape II." See Donald Buchanan's "Contemporary Painting in Canada," published in the Special Canadian Issue (edited by Geoffrey Holme) of *The Studio,* vol. 129, no. 625 (April 1945), pp. 98-111.

7. For A.S.P. Woodhouse's presentation to the Royal Society, see "The Approach to Milton: A Note on Practical Criticism." *Royal Society of Canada Transactions,* 3rd series, vol. 38, section 2 (1944), pp. 201-13.

LETTER 101

1. Writing from Chicago, Brown frequently uses letterhead of the Department of English. At other times, he uses plain paper with no address given, only the date. He had followed similar practices in Ithaca. It would be interesting if we could tell from the kind of paper used whether Brown was writing from his office or his home, but of course we cannot. Having settled Brown at the University of Chicago, therefore, I use "Chicago" as an abbreviated form of address unless there is reason to show a different location. I use square brackets where, in the absence of evidence to the contrary, Chicago is the assumed location.

2. The reference is to Lampman's connection with Katherine Waddell.

3. It was to be Margaret Whitridge. See her *Lampman's Kate* and her introduction to *The Poems of Archibald Lampman.*

4. Henry John Cody (1868-1951). Educated at the University of Toronto, H.J. Cody was ordained in 1894 in the Church of England. He served as rector of St. Paul's Church, Toronto, later as canon of St. Alban's cathedral and archdeacon of the diocese of York. He became a member of the Ontario legislature in 1918. A member of the board of Governors of the University of Toronto from 1917, and chairman from 1925, he became president of the University in 1932. At the time this letter was written, he had just been appointed chancellor.

5. Joris-Karl Huysmans (1848-1907), autobiographical novelist and art critic, was born in Paris and lived nearly all his life there. Huysmans' best known novels, *A vau-l'eau* (1882) and *A rebours* (1884), and the prose piece *Là-bas* (1891), are said to epitomize the aesthetic and spiritual decadence which was a mark of French culture at the close of the nineteenth century.

6. *The Hitleriad.* New York: New Directions, 1944.

7. Victoria Sackville-West (1892-1962), English poet and novelist. Married Harold Nicholson in 1913 and became associated with the Bloomsbury group of writers. *The Land* was a volume of "British Georgics" published in 1926. The review appeared in *The Observer* 21 May, 1944, p. 3. Basing her judgment solely on the quotations used by Brown in his essays on Lampman, Scott and Pratt, Sackville-West concludes: "Lampman would be my choice." The occasion of the lecture in Canada was probably the visit which she and her husband paid to Montreal in the course of a North American lecture tour early in 1933.

8. Hatchards Ltd., of 187 Piccadilly, was a very old firm of printers and booksellers. It is still in business. Brown's use of the apostrophe is wrong.

LETTER 102

1. Beside this paragraph, in the left-hand margin, Scott has written: "Later he withdrew

the ltr to make a change and has not yet sent me a copy." The note is dated the 15th. In due time there was to be a "Copy for Dr. Scott," and this is the copy reproduced in Appendix F. The only evidence of alteration I can find in this copy occurs in the second and third lines of the main text, where there appears to have been a deletion, the words "fragment by Lampman" appearing in original (rather than carbon) typescript.

2. "War Needs Will Curtail Production of Liquor. Fact Alcohol Required for Synthetic Rubber Forces Step Government Hesitates to Take." Headlines, *Globe and Mail,* Sat., July 18, 1942. Rationing was in force by 1944.

3. Scott fails to identify the bookshop with the agency (which is to say, publisher). The roles were, in those days, often combined.

4. John and Edward Bumpus, Ltd., Booksellers to His Majesty the King, 477 Oxford St., London.

LETTER 103

1. This letter is represented by two carbon copies in the SAP. They have the same text, but one has a number of "typos" which have been corrected in black ink while the other is letter perfect. The corrected text is clearly from Scott's typewriter — the machine he used for the bulk of his personal correspondence. The original of this letter was mailed to Brown (it is in the E.K. Brown Papers at the Public Archives) and the carbon was put in Scott's files. The second carbon is from another typewriter and it is headed "Extra copy for Dr. Scott." My guess is that Scott had an extra fair copy of the letter made: the new "original" perhaps for Loftus MacInnes, the new carbon to be filed at Lisgar Street against contingencies. Scott was careful about such things, and these were delicate matters that were being discussed.

2. The "personal drama" is of course the Katherine Waddell affair.

3. The first and last are 'With those cold eyes, my dear' and 'You cannot answer to my love.' The third lyric, the "middle one," has as far as I know never been published.

4. See Letter 99, note 4. Scott probably acquired the Lampman letters from Thomson just before the latter's death in March, 1924. When he talked with Brown at Lisgar Street in August, 1942, he was as knowledgeable about the Waddell affair as these letters could make him. But how much did the letters have to tell? Dr. Whitridge suggests they had a great deal to tell, though the passages she quotes from the extant letters are not convincing evidence of the intimate liaison between Archie and Kate she would like to have us see. But she goes on to hint darkly at the destruction of some letters and the mutilation of others. It is true that Thomson, Scott and the MacInneses all had the opportunity to destroy or remove from the correspondence letters by Lampman which they saw as touching on "indelicate" matters. On the question of the mutilations, however, Dr. Whitridge needs correction. When the Lampman-Thomson letters eventually reached the Public Archives they indeed showed a number of excisions. Dr. Whitridge implies that either Scott or Natalie MacInnes had been at work with scissors at what she calls "critical points." But having examined this material, I do not find the points at all critical. The mutilations appear to be the result of a careless removal (but by whom?) of stamps from the corners of envelopes without in some cases removing the letters which they contained. I am grateful to Mr. David Boll, a former graduate student of mine, for suggesting this simple explanation. For Dr. Whitridge's discussion of the Lampman letters to Thomson within the context of the Waddell affair, see the introduction to *Lampman's Kate,* pp. 19-20.

5. First published in *The Poems of Archibald Lampman* (1900), p. 229.

6. Maud E. Playter, married to Lampman in 1887. She died November 22, 1910.

7. Scott is referring to the conversations of the summer of 1942, and especially the one

of August 11, about which Brown had written a note for his files. Scott's remarks on the present occasion are consistent in all important respects with Brown's record of the earlier conversation.

8. For the trip to Lake Achigan, east of Maniwaki, in September 1897, see Scott's Memoir to *The Poems of Archibald Lampman,* p. xx.

9. William Dawson LeSueur (1840-1917), civil servant and man of letters. Educated at the University of Toronto, LeSueur entered government service at a very early age. He was secretary of the Post Office, in Ottawa, from 1888 to 1902, when he retired. In these early days he had been in close contact with Scott through membership in the Literary and Scientific Society of Ottawa and the Royal Society, and through his collaboration with Scott and Pelham Edgar in the editing of the Makers of Canada series, to which LeSueur contributed the volume on Frontenac. His revisionist study of William Lyon Mackenzie, also written for the Makers of Canada series, was suppressed by a court injunction obtained by Mackenzie's descendants. See A.B. McKillop, *A Critical Spirit: The Thought of William Dawson LeSueur* (Carleton Library Original, 1977). McKillop has also published an edition of LeSueur's study of Mackenzie: *William Lyon Mackenzie* (Toronto: Macmillan, 1979).

10. In *Lyrics of Earth,* Scott makes many references to Lampman's "inward trouble." He concludes: "These quotations will prove the existence but not the plot of an intense personal drama" (pp. 22, 23, 37).

11. In the foreword to *At the Long Sault,* Scott writes: "The series, 'Portrait in Six Sonnets,' is evidently the record of a friendship strong in affection, and, to judge by the last Sonnet, high in emotional value" (p. ix).

12. Arnold Lampman died in August, 1894, at the age of four months.

13. Otto Archibald Lampman.

14. *Alcyone* was to have been published, at Lampman's expense, by Constable & Co. of Edinburgh. But the poet's death intervened. So did Scott, who arranged for a limited Ottawa edition of twelve copies and went on to the planning of the Memorial edition.

15. Brown's list is on the page appended to Letter 94.

LETTER 104

1. In the introduction to *At the Long Sault,* p. xvii.

2. This must have been a marginal notation by Scott on Brown's transcript of the "dramatic fragment." The Gilbert of "Gilbertian" is presumably W.S. Gilbert of Gilbert and Sullivan, masters of English light opera.

3. *The Civil Service Review.*

4. For the second edition of *On Canadian Poetry.* See the preface to this edition, which is dated August 1944, at Wieboldt Hall, The University of Chicago. The 1944 edition has been reprinted by the Tecumseh Press (Ottawa, 1973).

5. Francis Joseph Sherman (1871-1926), poet and banker, was born in Fredericton and educated at the University of New Brunswick. He rose to become assistant general manager of the Merchants' Bank of Canada and later of the Royal Bank. He served in the First World War and retired in 1919. Virtually all of his verse was written prior to 1899, the year in which Sherman was posted to Havana. *The Complete Poems of Francis Sherman,* edited by Lorne Pierce and with a foreword by Sir Charles G.D. Roberts, was published by the Ryerson Press in 1935.

6. The Pre-Raphaelite Brotherhood dated back to 1848, when the artists Dante Gabriel Rossetti, William Holman Hunt and John Millais had rebelled in the cause of "truth to nature" in art. Their work had pleased the public and scandalized the Royal Academy. Later, Rossetti had applied the ideals of the Brotherhood to poetry, and by the 1860s

and 1870s the movement was a potent force in English literature. The influence was noticeable in Canada by the last decade of the century. The imprint is strong in Scott's *The Magic House* of 1893 and Sherman's *Matins* of 1896.

7. "Satirical Verse," *Poetry,* LXV, pp. 54-56.

8. Earlier referred to as the address on "the future of the liberal arts in university education."

LETTER 105

1. "Two Canadian Poets: a lecture by Archibald Lampman (edited from ms. with preface and notes by E.K. Brown)" *University of Toronto Quarterly,* vol. XIII (July 1944), pp. 406-23.

LETTER 106

1. Creighton quoted the passage in which Lampman recalls the excitement he felt when he first came across Roberts' *Orion and Other Poems.* See D.G. Creighton, *Dominion of the North* (Toronto: Macmillan, 1944), p. 370.

2. Collin had refused to see evidence in 'At the Long Sault' of either great elegiac or great dramatic powers. See his review of *On Canadian Poetry* and *At the Long Sault* in *University of Toronto Quarterly,* vol. XIII, 4 (1943-44), p. 225 and p. 229. The new material Brown is now trying out on Scott was to form the basis of a new second paragraph to section VII of the chapter on Lampman in the second edition of *On Canadian Poetry.* In the Tecumseh Press reprint the paragraph is on p. 108.

3. The impressive phrase seems to have got lost in the redrafting of this paragraph for the new edition. See Letter 79, where Scott records his defence of the great merits of 'At the Long Sault' during talks with Clarke at Lisgar Street. And compare Scott's close comments on the "new material" in Letter 108.

LETTER 107

1. Brown's "last" is his letter of September 2, 1944 (Letter 104). His letter of 11 October is still in the mail.

2. Robert Graves' *The Story of Marie Powell: Wife to Mr. Milton* (London: Cassell, 1943) is one of five books reviewed by A.S.P. Woodhouse under the title "On Milton's Poetry; Milton Today" and published in *University of Toronto Quarterly,* vol. XIII (July 1944), pp. 462-67.

3. The letter is identified by Brown in his reply of October 22 (Letter 109) as a "request from Buffalo." In response to an advertisement I placed in the *Times Literary Supplement* during my search in 1978 for random locations of D.C. Scott letters, I received a note from Mr. K.C. Gay, Curator of the Poetry Collection at the Lockwood Memorial Library of the State University of New York at Buffalo. The Collection had one holograph letter by Scott, addressed to C.D. Abbott, late director of the Lockwood Library, and dated October 27, 1944. It was Scott's "polite reply," in which he turns down the request, citing reasons similar to those he gives Brown in this letter. The compete text is interesting, and I give it in its appropriate place as a footnote to Letter 109. There is a second letter from 108 Lisgar Street in the Buffalo Collection. It is from Elise A. Scott, and it is dated October 29, 1947. It is addressed to Mr. Abbott, who in a letter of October 22 had asked if he might see Scott on the occasion of a visit he hoped to make soon to Ottawa. Mrs. Scott says her husband is "ill and confined to bed." She is not sure if he will be well enough for a visit and suggests Mr. Abbott phone Lisgar Street on his arrival.

4. This may have been an economy edition, issued in difficult times of depression or war. I have not been able to locate a copy. The first edition, 1925, has a very decent cover.

5. The exclusion of 'The Land of Pallas' meant that this long visionary poem would

remain pretty well unknown until John Sutherland, Louis Dudek and Irving Layton sparked an interest in the "other" Lampman, the poet of social concern, in the late forties.

6. The reference is to the *Quarterly*'s payment for rights to the manuscript of "Two Canadian Poets."

7. Lampman's sister.

LETTER 108

1. In the absence of the interim draft, it is difficult to know how much of this advice was taken. The phrase "despite adverse criticism" remained. Probably the remarks relating to Clarke were softened and Scott's presence in the paragraph reduced.

2. At the head of the letter, above the date, Scott has written "Sunday." Pencilled at the bottom, very lightly, is Brown's note: "Arrived Tues. morning."

LETTER 109

1. Scott took Brown's advice and sent nothing to Buffalo. The text of the letter of refusal is as follows:

> Dear Mr. Abbott,
> Your letter of Aug. 15 reached me some weeks ago but I have not had the opportunity of answering it until now. I regret that I have no m.s.s. to add to your Collection much as I would like to send something. My drafts, such as exist, are in pencil & in notebooks; they would have to be separated and I fear explained for many of the lines are now indistinct. I am obliged to you for writing me in this matter and I hope you will have many encouraging replies.

LETTER 110

1. See postscript to Letter 104.

2. Emil Ludwig, *Mackenzie King, A Portrait Sketch* (Toronto: Macmillan, 1944).

3. "Pratt's Collected Work," *University of Toronto Quarterly*, XIV (January 1945), pp. 211-13.

4. A.J.M. Smith, "Colonialism and Nationalism in Canadian Poetry before Confederation," Canadian Historical Association *Report*, June 1-2 (1944), pp. 74-85.

5. James Cappon (1855-1939) came from Scotland in 1888 to Queen's University, where he was professor of English until his retirement in 1919. He was for many years editor of *Queen's Quarterly*. He published *Bliss Carman and the Literary Currents of his Time* in 1930. On the question of Roberts, Brown probably has in mind Cappon's *Roberts and the Influences of his Time* (1905) which is very short but which is usually preferred to the longer *Charles G.D. Roberts* contributed by Cappon to the Makers of Canadian Literature series in 1925.

6. The post of Professor of Poetry established in 1808 at Oxford University. Arnold held the position from 1857-67.

7. Brown's interest in Arnold dated from his post-graduate days in Paris, where a major part of his work had involved close textual analysis of Arnold's prose. From 1930 on into the early forties, scarcely a year passed in which Brown did not return, by way of new editions or articles or reviews, to this writer he so much admired. In 1948 he was to make a major contribution to the field with the publication, by the University of Chicago Press, of *Matthew Arnold: A Study in Conflict*.

8. Halldor Hermannsson, born in Iceland, 1878, was Professor of Scandinavian Languages and Literature at Cornell University when Brown took up his appointment there as chairman of the Department of English in 1942. He was an old-timer then, having held the post since 1921. He died in 1958.

LETTER 112

1. 'Estrangement' and 'Persistence'; and 'Cloud and Sun' and 'Loneliness'. 'Estrangement' was not included in the Ryerson edition of *Selected Poems of Archibald Lampman*. All other poems indicated by Brown were.

2. "A Portrait in Six Sonnets," written for Katherine Waddell.

LETTER 113

1. George Vertue (1684-1756), English engraver and collector of materials on the history of art in England. In 1714 he produced a line engraving, based on the Charles Jervas oil painting of Alexander Pope, which became the source of a whole family of subsequent reproductions — amongst them, presumably, the one of 1741 which Scott is now sending to Brown.

LETTER 114

1. This was the translation of Balzac's *Le Père Goriot* which Brown was preparing for the Modern Library series. He had been working on it for almost a year.

2. F.O. Matthiessen, *Henry James: The Major Phase* (London, New York: Oxford University Press, 1944).

3. Throughout the preceding months, Mackenzie King had faced mounting political turmoil over the conscription issue, and specifically over the question of whether men drafted for home service only should be sent overseas as reinforcements for active force units whose ranks had become seriously depleted. J.J. Ralston, then Minister of National Defence, thought that they should be sent, and when King seemed hesitant Ralston resigned. General A.G.L. McNaughton, now "retired" as G.O.C. First Canadian Army, was to take his place. This was in the early part of November. Three weeks later, in the face of mounting pressure, King's government tabled in the House of Commons an order-in-council which stated that men drafted for home service only were to be sent to the U.K. for service "in the European theatre of war." There was an uproar both in and out of Parliament. On November 27, King asked the House to approve what was essentially a motion of confidence in the government. After heated debate, the motion passed on December 7.

LETTER 115

1. 'These are in the beginning,' sent as a gift to Brown on January 18, 1941.

2. James Anthony Froude (1818-94), English historian and man of letters. He was the author of the four-volume study of Carlyle which Brown thought "irresistible."

3. *University of Toronto Quarterly,* XIV (January 1945), pp. 211-13.

4. Edmund Kemper Broadus (1876-1926) had been appointed professor and head of the Department of English at the University of Alberta in 1908. He was the editor, with Eleanor H. Broadus, of *A Book of Canadian Prose and Verse* (Toronto, 1923). Garnet Gladwin Sedgewick, born in Nova Scotia in 1882, was at this time head of the Department of English at the University of British Columbia, a position he had held since 1930. He was a champion of Marjorie Pickthall, a poet Brown considered "derivative" and therefore safe to deal with. Malcolm Wallace had just retired as head of the Department of English at University College, Toronto, where he had been an influential figure for more than two decades. Cyrus MacMillan, born in Prince Edward Island in 1882, had taught English literature at McGill University, where he had been first appointed in 1909. Later, he had entered politics, and in 1930 he became a member of King's cabinet. He was the editor of several volumes of Canadian folk music and tales.

LETTER 116

1. Both the carbon copy and the original of this letter are dated, in Scott's hand,

"30-1-*44*," an easy slip of the pen in the first days of the new year.

2. Arthur Vine Hall, born in Yorkshire in 1862, had gone to South Africa as a Congregational Minister in 1890. His collection of "so called poems," *The Poems of a South African,* had been published by Longmans in 1926. It was described by critics as sentimental, didactic and turgid.

3. The suggestion had come from Lorne Pierce as far back as September 1943, but Scott may have other details in mind, imparted to Brown in conversation, and notably the freeing of copyright which came about when McClelland & Stewart refused a proposal for a Canadian edition of *Viger* in 1926.

4. Charles Lamb (1775-1834), English essayist and critic. *Selected Letters of Charles Lamb,* chosen and edited by G.T. Clapton, was published in London by Methuen in a three-volume edition in 1925. Scott's first quotation is from Vol. III, p. 328. The second quotation is from the same volume, p. 203.

5. *Camille Pissarro: Letters to his son Lucien,* translated from the French manuscript by Lionel Abel (London, New York: Kegan Paul & Co. Printed by Routledge, 1944). Pissarro, perhaps one of the most influential of the French Impressionist painters, was born in 1830 and died in 1903. Paul Cézanne (1839-1906), *Letters.* Edited by John Rewald, translated from the French by Marguerite Kay (London: Bruno Cassirer, 1941).

6. John Butler Yeats (1839-1922), *Letters to his Son W.B. Yeats and Others, 1869-1922* (London: Faber & Faber, 1944). There had of course been earlier editions of J.B. Yeats' letters: in 1917 and 1920; but here, as in the case of the other books mentioned, it seems clear that Scott's reading has been prompted by the appearance of new or recent publications.

7. Sir Donald Francis Tovey (1875-1940), English musicologist, pianist, composer, and compiler of *The Oxford Companion to Music*. His *Beethoven,* with an editorial preface by Hubert J. Foss, was published by Oxford University Press in 1944.

8. This is Squadron Leader J.W. Thompson, R.C.A.F., to whom Scott had apparently sent a copy of a poem by Stephen Spender, perhaps on the basis of a chance encounter in Ottawa. Dr. Thompson sent his thanks August 15, 1944 (SAP). Scott's copy of Auden's *For the Time Being* is in the Carleton University Library. The inscription reads: "Duncan Campbell Scott/with best wishes/from/W.H. Auden/Sept 1944." On the end-paper of the book are some jottings in Scott's hand. These, if I interpret them correctly, suggest: that Scott wrote Auden on October 19, 1944, at Swarthmore College, Pennsylvania, presumably to thank him for the autographed book; that Scott wrote Dr. Thompson on October 20, 1944, presumably to thank him for his part in securing the book; that Scott wrote Thompson again on November 2, 1944, enclosing a photograph of Rupert Brooke, one of the several taken on the occasion of Brooke's visit to Ottawa in 1913.

LETTER 117

1. Brown's review in the *U.T.Q.* is of course of the first Canadian edition, brought out by Macmillan in 1944. There was to be a second edition in 1946. The "remarks about the arrangement" are concerned chiefly with Brown's objection that the rationale for the division of the book into its four sections is unclear, and with his disappointment at the separation, in different sections, of 'The Cachalot' and 'The Great Feud.'

2. After a lengthy attack on Canadian critics for their neglect of Pratt, Brown had written: "The Americans will see a collected edition of his work later in the year and they may be counted on to do now the job we should have done long ago."

3. Brown uses Scott as his lead-in: "In the career of a poet the first collected or selected edition appears late. The *Poems* of Duncan Campbell Scott came out in 1926 when he

was sixty-four; the *Collected Poems* of E.J. Pratt, the next of the masters, belong to his sixty-second year.''

4. The manuscript of *The Circle of Affection* was in the end taken by McClelland & Stewart, not by Oxford University Press.

5. Ira Dilworth, ed., *Twentieth Century Verse: An Anthology,* with an introduction and biographical notes (Toronto: Oxford; Clarke, Irwin, 1945). Representation is as follows: 15 Canadian; 18 American; 51 British, Irish and other Commonwealth. Six of Scott's poems appear: 'After Battle,' 'The Forsaken,' 'Spring in the Valley,' 'A Song,' 'Hymn for Those in the Air,' and 'Old Olives at Bordighera.'

6. Philip Albert Child, novelist, poet and teacher, born in Hamilton, Ontario, in 1898, had been Chancellors' Professor of English at Trinity College, Toronto, since 1942.

7. The plaque was the work of R. Tait McKenzie, and was installed initially in the old College Chapel on Queen's Street. When Trinity stopped using this chapel in 1925 it was placed in storage (perhaps in the "temporary" chapel) pending the construction of a new College chapel. The new chapel was long delayed, however, and when it finally opened on November 20, 1955, the Lampman plaque was not put in place on the north walls, as other memorial plaques were. In 1961, it was taken from its box and mounted on a rather obscure wall in the basement library of the College. And there it remains at the time of writing.

8. Early in December, 1944, the seat of Grey North had been cleared for a by-election by the resignation of W.P. Telford, the Liberal M.P. McNaughton was to run and was expected to win easily. The seat, however, was strongly contested. Election day was February 5, 1945. The winner, by a narrow margin, was W. Garfield Case, Conservative, Mayor of Owen Sound.

9. In ink, above the name "Russell," Scott has scribbled, in brackets, "A.E.," George William Russell's pseudonym.

LETTER 118

1. James Joyce's *Ulysses* was first published in Paris in 1922. It was judged "obscene" in the United States until the famous Woolsey trial of 1933. An uncensored edition appeared in both the United States and the U.K. in 1937.

2. The American edition retained the arrangement of the Macmillan edition but omitted 'The Fable of the Goats' and 'The Great Feud.' The Introduction by W.R. Benet was of course new. It was to be incorporated in the second Canadian edition.

3. William Henry Clarke, publisher, was born in Lindsay, Ontario, in 1902. He was manager of the Canadian branch of Oxford University Press between 1936 and 1949, a position which he held coincidentally with the presidency of Clarke, Irwin & Co. Ltd.

4. A non-denominational, revivalist movement founded by Frank Buchman in the 1920s. After winning strong support at Oxford University, the movement became known as the "Oxford Group." The name was changed to "Moral Re-armament" in 1938.

5. Robert Hamilton Coats (1874-1960), a prominent statistician, was educated at the University of Toronto, where he took his first degree in 1896. After a brief spell as a journalist, he had gone to Ottawa in 1902 to be assistant editor of the *Labour Gazette.* It was Coats who had organized the Dominion Bureau of Statistics in 1918, continuing as its head until his retirement in 1942. He was a Fellow of the Royal Society and the recipient of several honorary degrees. He was a close friend of Scott.

6. Harold Adams Innis (1894-1952) was at this time head of the Department of Political Economy at the University of Toronto. A brilliant economist and historian, he was the author of *The Fur Trade in Canada* (1930), *The Cod Fisheries* (1940) and numerous other books on staples production in Canada and on theories of communication which

252

greatly influenced the thinking of his time. A member of the Royal Society, he was to be elected president in 1946.

7. "Cephalus: A Prologue," presidential address, Royal Society of Canada, Section II, by R.H. Coats, 1944. *Proceedings and Transactions of the Royal Society of Canada.* Third series, vol. XXXVIII, Section II, pp. 1-36.

LETTER 119

1. Since the book came directly from the publisher, one must suppose that the "inscription" was sent in the form of a label of some kind. In Scott's files (SAP) there is a rough draft of most of the first page of this letter, and some of the differences between this text and the version sent to Brown are interesting. The judgements of Sherman and Smith which follow in the present paragraph were initially quite harsh. Of Sherman Scott had written: "As you know I am unmoved by his work, but I think he stopped writing because he had nothing more to say, his fount of feeling was dried up." Of Smith he had written: "I think A.J.M.S. should be pleased with the space you have given him, and I hope he will humble his pride and realize that you have done him justice. I think we shall be surprised if he does any more poems; I think his fount of feeling is also gone dry." "Of course," he had added, "these careless criticisms are for you only." But it is clear that Scott did not at all like what he had written, and so the criticisms were rendered harmless in the final version.

2. The passage Scott is referring to concerns 'Spring on Mattagami.' In the first edition of *OCP,* Brown had written about "stanzas which flame with his longing for some one in Ottawa, whom he pictures in the midst of wild nature. . . ." In the second edition, the passage reads: "stanzas which flame with his longing for some ideal woman whom he pictures in the midst of wild nature. . . ." The source of this correction is Scott's note on 'Spring on Mattagami,' included in the letter he wrote to Brown giving his reactions to the newly published *On Canadian Poetry:* "I think and hope the passion is sincere but you will have to count the lady as imaginary. . . ." (Letter 68).

3. The passage appears on page 101 of the Tecumseh Press edition and begins: "In a lecture he gave to the Ottawa Literary and Scientific Society in 1891 Lampman calmly took stock of the society round about him."

4. In the United States, the decision of Judge John M. Woolsey in 1933 had cleared the way for the lifting of the ban on *Ulysses* in the following year. In Canada, the prohibition on the book was to be "quietly lifted" in 1949. See Wilfred K. Kesterton, *The Law and the Press in Canada* (Carleton Library No. 100). Toronto: McClelland & Stewart, 1976, p. 103.

LETTER 120

1. Miss Marjorie White's mother was Florence Waddell, sister of Katherine. For a fuller account of the "green" volume, and its place in the story of Lampman and Kate Waddell, see Margaret Whitridge's introduction to *The Poems of Archibald Lampman,* pp. xxi-xxii, and her introduction to *Lampman's Kate,* pp. 18-19. Arthur Bourinot gives a detailed description of this ms book in *Some Letters of Duncan Campbell Scott,* p. 42, note 1. His tally of the poems is 93, as against Brown's 92 (though Brown is to say 93 in Letter 124). Dr. Whitridge says 92 (*Lampman's Kate,* p. 19).

2. William Stewart Wallace (1884-1970), distinguished historian, editor and biographer, was chief librarian at the University of Toronto from 1923 to 1954.

3. Norman Fee, born in Ottawa in 1889 and educated at Queen's University, had been appointed to the Dominion Archives in 1907. He became Assistant Dominion Archivist in 1945.

4. The passage begins: "I have been severely reproved by a critic in the *University of Toronto Quarterly*. . . ." See pp. 162-63 of the reprint of the revised edition of *On Canadian Poetry*.

LETTER 121

1. This should read "24th inst."
2. James White (1863-1928) was appointed geographer of the Geological Survey of Canada in 1894 and chief geographer of the Department of the Interior in 1899. A skilled cartographer and an expert on Canadian place-names, he supervised the publication of *The Atlas of Canada* (1906, 1915) and played an important part in the litigation over the locating of the Labrador boundary between Canada and what was then the Crown Colony of Newfoundland.
3. In the left margin, Scott has written: "She got her price: $15,000." The pictures had eventually been purchased by Col. R.S. McLaughlin of Oshawa, Ontario. See Robert Pilot, *Notes on Clarence Gagnon,* National Gallery of Canada Library, n.d., p. 2. A letter from Mrs. Gagnon to Scott (SAP) makes it clear that this transaction had been completed by March 10, 1945.
4. In the original, there are eight typographical errors in this sentence. All are corrected, either by the over-typing of a letter or by pen.
5. Bourinot, ever sensitive to the repercussions of the Waddell story, omits the phrase, "for the girl he loved." See *Some Letters,* p. 42.
6. Bourinot omits all of the postscript material, including the superscribed note.

LETTER 122

1. Natalie Lampman was born in 1892. See Scott's Memoir in *The Poems of Archibald Lampman* (Morang, 1900), p. xviii.
2. MacInnes and his wife had gone to California for an extended holiday. But as Brown later points out (Letter 124) Miss White's approach to Wallace was made before the MacInneses left Ottawa.

LETTER 124

1. Bourinot, alert as usual to possible sources of offence, omits the latter part of this sentence (*Some Letters,* p. 43).
2. The Banff School of Fine Arts, established on a grant from the Carnegie Corporation to the University of Alberta in 1933, offered summer courses in the theatre arts, music, art and crafts. By 1945, it was regarded as one of the leading fine arts centres in North America. The first Special Writers' Conference was held there in 1944. It was intended specifically for the encouragement of Alberta Writers. A second conference, similar in purpose, was to be convened in the summer of 1945. Brown and John Murray Gibbon, amongst others, were to address students and delegates in the writing divisions of the school. See *The Canadian Author and Bookman,* vol. XXI, no. 3 (September 1945), pp. 24-25.

LETTER 125

1. The letterhead is that of the College English Association. Brown's name appears on the list of directors, as does also the name of Odell Shepard, which Brown has circled and provided with a scribbled note: "Do you remember his book on Carman?" Shepard's book was *Bliss Carman,* published by McClelland & Stewart in 1923.
2. These letters seem to have vanished. Brown goes on to cite MacInnes's reference to "personal relations," and in the next letter Scott identifies them only as "the letters from A.L." which he cannot see until they "get unpacked." Other matters intervene, and the subject is not brought up again. Thomson had given Scott a batch of

Lampman letters in the early twenties. Were some letters held back, then passed to MacInnes in 1945, perhaps by Thomson's grandson? But MacInnes was in California, and Thomson's grandson was most likely to be in the east. The only Lampman connection with California seems to have been Stanley A. Coblentz, editor of *Wings,* and this is not a likely source for "personal" letters. It appears that we are again in the presence of the "Waddell affair," but this is mere speculation until the letters are found.

3. "Poetic Sensitivity to Time," *Saturday Review of Literature,* vol. 28, no. 17 (April 28, 1945), p. 11. Hillyer (1895-1961) was a distinguished poet, novelist and critic who had held the post of Boylston Professor at Harvard from 1938 to early 1945. He had been awarded the Pulitzer Prize for Poetry in 1934.

4. The "peerless leader" is of course Mackenzie King. King had left Ottawa April 19 to attend the opening of the San Francisco Conference, where the United Nations organization was to emerge from the ashes of World War II. He arrived in San Francisco April 23 and remained there until May 14, when he went to Vancouver to begin his election campaign. See *The Mackenzie King Record* (Pickersgill and Forster) vol. 2, p. 374 ff. The day in Chicago must have been fitted into the itinerary of his journey to the west coast, probably April 20, though I have not confirmed this.

5. Alexander Grant Dexter was doubtless a member of the press corps accompanying King on this occasion. Born at St. Andrews, Manitoba, in 1896, he was at this time associate editor of the Winnipeg *Free Press* and doing a tour of duty as Ottawa correspondent.

LETTER 126

1. Bourinot (*Some Letters,* p. 44) omits Hillyer's name.

2. The following advertisement appears on the end dust-jacket of the Ryerson edition of *In the Village of Viger:* "In his work. . .there is a mixture of restraint and intensity which grasps at one and will not let go. . . . A search for the adequate theme and the adequate form in which restrained intensity may express itself — here is the emotional centre of Scott's work. . . . Of all Canadian poets, indeed all Canadian imaginative writers, he has best succeeded in making great literature out of such distinctively Canadian material as our aborigines supply. . . . The perfection of his best Indian pieces is matched in his best nature-verse." The passage is a pastiche of statements chosen (somewhat inappropriately, as Scott notes) from widely separated passages in *On Canadian Poetry.* The dots of omission are as given in the original.

LETTER 127

1. "The impeccable one" is Scott's sobriquet for Thoreau MacDonald. Chicoutimi, high up on the Saguenay River, is considered the gateway to northern Quebec. To Brown, the *Viger* stories suggest a more southern and more congenial setting, perhaps that of the eastern townships.

2. The river, that is, which flows through the fictional village of Viger. There is also a Rivière Blanche which flows into the Ottawa River at Templeton, Quebec, just across from the capital.

LETTER 128

1. Scott had mentioned the Keats paper as early as January 1944. In July of that year, the essay on "Two Canadian Poets" taken care of, he had asked Brown: "Can you do anything with his Keats?" (Letter 98). Brown had responded favourably, but the project had not surfaced again until the present date, nearly a year later.

2. Connor writes: "At that time [the winter of 1892-93] he received an invitation from Kingston, to deliver a lecture on Keats and his Boston friends, hearing of it, proposed

that he repeat it there." See *Archibald Lampman* (Borealis Press edition, 1977), p. 166.

LETTER 129

1. Compare Connor: "That winter he completed the Keats paper, but it was never given in Boston, and though Mr. Scudder, of the *Atlantic Monthly,* gave it praise as a lecture he did not buy it" (*Archibald Lampman,* p. 166).

2. A reproduction of this marked copy of Brown's draft introduction is included as Appendix G (P. 290).

3. Two editions of *Letters of John Keats to Fanny Brawne,* one "printed for private distribution" and the other "public," had been brought out by Reeves and Turner in 1878. Harry Buxton Forman was the editor. The 1895 edition to which Scott refers is the complete and revised edition of the Keats letters.

4. Opposite this sentence, in the left margin, Scott has written: "I have a high regard for her."

5. Scott, in 1925, had drawn on one of Lampman's letters to E.W. Thomson: "The Keats at the beginning was very natural, for I could not write anything at that time without writing Keats. I am only just now getting quite clear of the spell of that marvellous person and it has taken me ten years to do it. Keats has always had such a fascination for me and so permeated my whole mental outfit that I have an idea that he has found a sort of faint reincarnation in me." See Bourinot, *Archibald Lampman's Letters to Edward William Thomson (1890-1898),* pp. 25-26. Lampman's letter is dated April 25, 1894.

LETTER 130

1. *Le rouge et le noir,* published in 1830, was perhaps Stendhal's (pseud. Henri Beyle) most famous novel. Beyle claimed that he wrote for the "happy few" who could see themselves as free spirits, not bound by convention. There were many disciples of *Beylisme,* hence Brown's reference to "the cult."

2. F.A. Hardy, of the Library of Parliament in Ottawa.

3. It was published before the year was out. See "James and Conrad," *Yale Review,* vol. XXXV, (Winter, 1945), pp. 265-85.

4. I can find no record of the publication of this lecture under the title given.

5. In the general election of June 11, 1945, the civilian vote returned Mackenzie King to his seat in Prince Albert, which he had held since 1926. When the armed forces ballots were counted, however, King lost the seat to E.L. Bowerman (CCF) by 129 votes.

LETTER 131

1. This is a corrected dating. Scott's dating, handwritten in his customary black ink, is "6. 6. 45." But "June 6" is impossible in the face of the reference, later in the same letter, to Brown's letter of June 20. The present letter, moreover, which takes up in earnest the subject of the new edition of *Viger,* is clearly forecast in Scott's previous letter of June 14, in which he promises, after a brief reference to *Viger,* that he will "write about that subject later." I assume a simple confusion in Scott's mind between the sixth and seventh month of the year. His reference, towards the end of the present letter, to "*perfect June* weather" with its underscoring of the first two words, must then be taken to mean that the weather is cool and fresh, as it is at its best in June, rather than hot and muggy, as it is at its worst in July.

2. The last line reads: "This is a book to own and read, to hoard and gloat over."

3. This is the first mention of the short story which is to provide the title for the miscellany of poetry and prose Scott has been working on for some time.

4. "The Circle of Affection," *Queen's Quarterly,* vol. 52, no. 2 (Summer 1945), pp. 141-57.
5. The Christmas gift of 1943.
6. *La Chartreuse de Parme* was published in 1839.
7. "Eight Quebec Independents Back In The Fold To Give Mr. King Lead Of Four In Commons." Headline, Ottawa *Journal,* June 12, 1945.
8. Jan Christian Smuts (1870-1950), South African statesman, was Prime Minister, Minister of Defence and Commander-in-Chief of South African forces from 1939 to 1948.

LETTER 132

1. The brief notice had appeared in "The Bookshelf" of *Saturday Night* under the heading "Tales of a Poet." The complete text is as follows: "This collection of short tales and character sketches is a reprint of a volume published first in 1896, which has been long cherished by friends of the poet and deserves wide circulation. The book is illustrated by Thoreau MacDonald" (*Saturday Night,* June 23, 1945, p. 24).

LETTER 133

1. Robert Seymour Bridges (1844-1930), English poet, and poet laureate from 1913 until his death. The work referred to is *John Keats: A Critical Essay* (London: privately printed, 1895). The length of the essay, in this edition, is 97 pages.
2. The Lampman volume was now confirmed as the second in the Ryerson series of selected editions of the major Canadian poets. The foreword was to be followed by the Memoir which Scott had contributed to the 1900 edition of Lampman's poems. The only significant change to the text of the Memoir would be a change in the date of the death of Lampman's father from 1895 to 1897.
3. Jesse Edgar Middleton, journalist, critic of music and the drama, poet, novelist and historian, was literary editor of *Saturday Night* from 1942 to 1946. Middleton was seventy-two at this time.
4. B.K. Sandwell was to continue as editor of *Saturday Night* for another six years.

LETTER 134

1. Scott had written: "In Professor E.K. Brown's Introduction to *At the Long Sault* there is a critical review and in a Foreword I give an account of his discovery in the poet's notebooks of many of the poems there included. In making the present selection I have welcomed and accepted the advice of Professor Brown and of Mr. T.R. Loftus MacInnes. . . ." Foreword, *Selected Poems of Archibald Lampman* (Toronto: Ryerson Press, 1947).

LETTER 135

1. Drawing a line from this point to the top of the page, Scott identifies the girl as Elizabeth Serson. The write-up of the interview, signed "E.S.", appeared in the Saturday edition of the Ottawa *Journal,* 4 August, 1945, p. 5.
2. The sonnets, four in number, would be published later in *The Circle of Affection.* They had been written, more or less at one sitting, on November 12, 1943. 'Old Olives at Bordighera,' another of the poems written in the decade following the publication of *The Green Cloister*, Scott's last collection, would likewise be included in *The Circle of Affection.* "The Bobolink" was a short sketch from *In the Village of Viger.*

LETTER 136

1. Gull Lake, Saskatchewan, is a small town on the C.P.R. main line between Swift

Current and Medicine Hat. Brown of course has in mind Scott's 'At Gull Lake: August 1810,' published in *The Green Cloister*.

LETTER 137

1. Gwendolyn Pharis Ringwood, born in 1910, was already known for her one-act play *Still Stands the House* (1938) and for her full-length drama *Dark Harvest* (1945). She was to gain considerable critical attention in the 1950s, when she wrote prolifically for CBC radio and television, as well as for the theatre.
2. Georges Bugnet, born in France in 1879 and educated at the Sorbonne and the University of Dijon, had come to Alberta in 1904. He had written two novels about the Canadian west and northwest, *Nipsya* (1924) and *La forêt* (1935), and for these and other literary achievements he was to receive the award of Chevalier dans l'Ordre des Palmes Academiques from the French government in 1970.
3. Brown has clearly typed "Maskeg" and has attempted no correction. I have not been able to get hold of a copy of the book to check the title-page. The only bibliographical entry I could find gives the following: *Le Pin du Muskeg* (Montreal: Garand, 1924).
4. David Staines, compiler of the bibliography of Brown's writings on which I have already drawn, places the pieces on Arnold, the Brontës and Meredith in *The American Peoples Encyclopedia* (Chicago: Spencer Press, 1948). There is no mention in this entry of the article on Canadian literature. See Staines, "E.K. Brown (1905-1951): The Critic and His Writings." *Canadian Literature*, 83 (Winter 1979), p. 187.
5. A.Y. Jackson (1882-1974) had been a moving spirit in the early work of the Group of Seven. At the time of the present correspondence he was already something of a legend, and in the nearly thirty years that remained to him he would become the grand old man of Canadian painting. Jackson and Lawren Harris and J.E.H. MacDonald (Thoreau's father) were close friends from the first decades of the century. Jackson's connection with Scott appears to have been slight.
6. Lake O'Hara lay in the mountains just above Chateau Lake Louise. With its modest community house and handful of log cabins, it was a favourite destination for painting excursions. W.J. Phillips went there often.

LETTER 138

1. Peter Aylen was Elise Aylen's older brother. He and his wife lived in Ottawa during the early years of the war. They were to move later to Victoria, B.C.
2. *Queen's Quarterly*, LII (Summer 1945), p. 254.
3. *Dalhousie Review*, XXV (July 1945), p. 262. "B.M." is J. Burns Martin.
4. The letter is from Henry Beston to Thoreau MacDonald. It is dated July 8, 1945, at Chimney Farm, Nobleboro, Maine. Scott has made his own copy, and it is in the "Viger" file, SAP. Beston writes:

   The life of Viger (which is not *pleine campagne* but near a great town) again put me in mind of the social picture of France as it is given by Balzac. Isn't it curious how that French Romantic Age has impressed itself on French Canada? I spoke of this in the "St. Lawrence." The French eighteenth century and the French Canadian eighteenth century were superficially related — the beau monde and the black flies simply dont go together — but these men and women of Viger could easily be a part of La Comedie Humaine. And oh what a blessing to come upon something written with real literary skill and Power!

   Beston was an American writer, for the most part of children's books. He had been associated with the *Atlantic Monthly* and *Living Age* in the 1920s. The *St. Lawrence* was published in 1942.

5. Barely discernible in the left margin, in Brown's hand, is the following: "that the prose was balanced by poetry, purity of style and tone."

6. Robert Charles Wallace was principal of Queen's University from 1936 to 1951. He had been professor of Geology at the University of Manitoba, 1912-1928, and president of the University of Alberta, 1928-1936.

7. The "agreeable para." is in *Saturday Night,* 15 September, 1945, p. 3. A draft of Scott's letter to Sandwell is in the "Miscellaneous Correspondence" file, SAP.

8. Edgar had been censoring German correspondence (presumably in connection with the Canadian prison camps) since 1942. See his letter to Scott of May 7, 1942, in which he looks forward gloomily to "reading countless German letters in their hateful script." (SAP)

9. Gustave Lanctôt, historian and distinguished public servant, was Dominion Archivist and deputy minister of the Canadian Archives from 1937 to 1948. Born in 1883, he was educated at the University of Montreal, later at Oxford and the University of Paris.

10. The projected book was probably *Across My Path,* a collection of essays and reminiscences. The manuscript was incomplete at the time of Edgar's death in 1948. Northrop Frye took it in hand, and it was published in 1952 by the Ryerson Press.

LETTER 139

1. Arthur R. Ford had followed Scott's work from the vantage point of the *London Free Press.* On June 18, 1945, he had sent Scott a copy of a column he had written that day on the new edition of *In the Village of Viger.* "I want to tell you," he wrote, "how much enjoyment I obtained in reading the republished volume of short stories. I have to confess I had not read them before." (SAP)

2. Walter Pater was widely reviewed in the early nineties as a result of the publication of his *Appreciation* (1889) and *Plato and Platonism* (1893). His death in 1894 had given rise to a spate of "Pater items" in magazines on both sides of the Atlantic. On the question of the *Viger* pieces in "their original dress," it is safe to say that Brown has been into *Scribner's.* In his introduction to the New Canadian Library edition of *In the Village of Viger* (1973), Professor S.L. Dragland notes that seven of the ten stories in that volume "had been previously published, a few at a time, in *Scribner's Magazine.*" The items Brown was most likely to have seen were "The Wooing of Monsieur Cuerrier" (published in the March issue of *Scribner's* 1891) and "Sedan," "The Pedler" and "The Bobolink" (published as a group in the October issue, 1893). If his search included issues of the late eighties, he would have encountered three more *Viger* stories: "The Little Milliner," "The Desjardins," and "Josephine Labrosse," all of which appeared in the October issue of *Scribner's,* 1887.

3. This is the Lampman "fair copy" book, source of the text which Brown has now made ready for the *University of Toronto Quarterly.*

4. Brown was to become interested in the variant readings for many of the Lampman poems which the Waddell manuscript supplied. In his copy of the Memorial volume (still in the possession of the Brown family) he gives "Waddell" as the source for quite a number of his pencilled notes.

5. I cannot account for Brown's description of this manuscript book as "black." In March, 1945, before he had seen the book and presumably on the authority of Stewart Wallace, he had described it as "bound in green calf and cloth." My research assistant examined the book in the summer of 1977. She describes it as "bound in green cloth, with tan leather spine and corners."

6. It is not often that Brown nods: the title is not absurd. The phrase "Gants du Ciel"

originated with Jean Cocteau. To explain the phenomenon of Raymond Radiguet, a brilliant young writer who died at the age of twenty, Cocteau used as a metaphor for the artist the image of a glove drawn over the hand of heaven in order that the divine force, protected from the contamination of direct contact, might yet communicate with mankind. In a short introduction to the first number of the periodical, Sylvestre states that the title *Gants du Ciel* in this context signifies the ideal of reaching towards those eternal spiritual values, "qui, plus que le pain, sont nécessaires à l'homme."

7. Northrop Frye was to contribute an important article: "La tradition narrative dans la poésie canadienne-anglaise." Brown's contribution was published under the title, "L'âge d'or de notre poésie." The special edition was No. 11 (Spring 1946). The original English version of Brown's article, "The Poetry of Our Golden Age," appears for the first time in Staines, *E.K. Brown: Responses and Evaluations*.

8. The review, headed "Poetry and Event," was by Winfield Townley Scott; *Poetry*, no. 66 (Summer 1945), pp. 329-34. The suggestion of "1850 vintage" occurs in the following passage:

   There is another comparison which may seem at first less plausible but which, I should like to suggest, actually is illuminating in several directions, and that is to Longfellow. It is illuminating, I believe, not only because it further defines the kind of verse E.J. Pratt writes but also denotes the point in time he actually occupies: mid-nineteenth century.

   Citing the "complexity" of Canadian society and the "primitiveness" of the country as sufficient reasons, Mr. Scott considers it inevitable "that [Canada's] major poet at mid-twentieth century should be by our standards a hundred years out of date." Pratt is an advance on Drummond and Carman. "Yet one must say," Scott concludes, "without condescension as without dishonesty, that his verse is dull."

9. *They Are Returning* (Toronto: Macmillan, 1945).

10. William Arthur Irwin, born in Ayr, Ontario, in 1898, was educated at the University of Manitoba and the University of Toronto. He was associate editor of *Maclean's* magazine from 1925 to 1942, managing editor from 1943 to 1945, and editor from 1945 to 1950. In the latter year he became chairman of the National Film Board, a post he occupied until 1953. For the next ten years he represented Canada abroad as high commissioner to Australia, ambassador to Brazil, Mexico and Guatemala. He is married to the poet P.K. Page.

11. The last line of Lampman's 'September.'

LETTER 140

1. On October 9, 1944, Philip Child, professor of English at Trinity College, Toronto, had written Scott to ask "whether it would be possible, now or in the future, to obtain some of the Lampman papers for Trinity." Scott replied October 16, saying that he thought something could indeed be done. He had spoken to Loftus MacInnes and had learned that there was "a certain quantity of MS in Mrs. MacInnes's hands." But since the MacInneses were on the point of moving to a new flat, it might be "some little time" before the matter could be pursued. The following February (Letter 117) Scott had brought Brown into the picture. The MacInneses remained favourably disposed to a gift of some manuscripts, but Natalie has just left for four months in California, where she will be joined shortly by Loftus, and there is to be a further delay. It is at about this point that Scott devises "a little scheme of my own," and of this he gives Brown brief notice in the February letter. Work on the presentation, however, is not completed until October. On the 15th, Scott writes Child to say that the material is ready. It is mailed on the 24th. I give this account of the evolution of the Trinity gift because I think it throws some light on the slightly injured tone of Scott's remark that "Loftus forestalled my plan." What was intended as a surprise for Brown has been disclosed by someone who had "no part" in this particular scheme. When was the

disclosure made? MacInnes had telephone conversations with Brown on his way to California on the 24th of March and on his way back to Ottawa on the 8th of May (Letter 120 and Letter 125). On one or the other of these occasions he must have told Brown what Scott was up to. The relevant correspondence with Child is in the SAP.

2. The two ms. poems presented to Trinity College were 'April' and 'Between the Rapids.'

3. Here, as elsewhere, Scott emphasizes the passage by underlining it in ink. Bourinot, responsive, omits "Major Lanctôt the Archivist" in his version of the letter. See *More Letters,* p. 72.

4. The text of Scott's handscript "note of presentation" is given in Appendix H (p. 291). The original copy, together with a typed version showing minor variations in wording, is in the Lampman File of the SAP.

5. 'Old Olives at Bordighera.' This is a late poem, one of Scott's favourites, read by Dilworth on the occasion of the recent birthday (Letter 135) and singled out for praise by Brown when it is published in *The Circle of Affection* (Letter 178).

6. *The Sweet Cheat Gone* and *The Past Recaptured* were both published in English translations in 1941, the last of the nine-part series.

7. George Santayana, philosopher and critic, published his three-volume autobiography, *Persons and Places,* between 1944 and 1955.

8. Charles M. Doughty, *Travels in Arabia Deserta,* 2 vols. (Cambridge: University Press, 1888). In the biographical sketch of W.J. Phillips he was about to begin, Scott would link Phillips' skill in colour woodcuts with Doughty's description of Arabs and Bedouins as men with "witty hands." See *W.J. Phillips,* Canadian Art Series (Toronto: Ryerson Press, 1947), p. 39.

LETTER 141

1. First published in 1943.

2. Walter de la Mare (1873-1956) was counted among the Georgian poets, his work appearing frequently in J.C. Squire's *Georgian Poetry* between 1912 and 1922. Traditionalist in form, he dealt characteristically with strange states of consciousness in poems of dream and fantasy. His new volume was *The Burning Glass* (London: Faber and Faber, 1945). Brown's review was entitled "The Epilogue to Mr. de la Mare's Poetry." See *Poetry,* LXVIII, (May 1946), pp. 90-96.

3. It was to hold until "quietly lifted" in 1949.

4. The First Series of Arnold's *Essays in Criticism* brought together a number of essays from scattered sources in nineteenth-century reviews and magazines. The four editions of this book published between 1865 and 1884 carried distinct texts. See E.K. Brown, *Studies in the Text of Matthew Arnold's Prose Works* (Paris: E. Droz, 1935). Brown's interest in Arnold never flagged. At the time of the present letter, he has just seen through the University of Manitoba Press a new edition of his *Representative Essays of Matthew Arnold,* first published by Macmillan in 1936 and re-issued in 1940. Within the next few years he will publish *Four Essays on Life and Letters by Matthew Arnold* in the Crofts Classics series (1947) and an important monograph, *Matthew Arnold—A Study in Conflict* (University of Chicago Press, 1948).

5. Buridan's ass was said to have starved to death between two haystacks which it found equally attractive.

LETTER 142

1. The enclosure is a Christmas card reproduction of A.Y. Jackson's "April, Petite Rivière." It is inscribed "To Peggy & Edward/affectionate greetings/from/Elise & Duncan."

LETTER 143

1. See *Trinity University Review*, Christmas issue, 1945. 'April' was chosen for reproduction because Scott considered it "the better specimen of Lampman's handwriting" (Scott to R.S.K. Seeley, November 6, 1945; Lampman File, SAP).

2. The extract is not preserved in the E.K. Brown Papers, but amongst some miscellaneous papers in the SAP I found a typescript carbon copy of the following:

   EXTRACT FROM A LETTER OF MOZART'S

   Music may be full of horror, effervescence, and young passion, nevertheless they must not be expressed to the extent of disgusting the audience, and music, even in the most trying situations, should not attract the ear aggressively, but flatter and charm it, and therefore remain music forever.

3. Bourinot (*More Letters*, p. 74) omits the final clause of this sentence.

4. Compare Bourinot, "but I must be a burden" (*More Letters*, p. 74).

LETTER 144

1. A novel, published in 1921 by W. Collins Sons.

2. Howard Robert Lawrence Henry, K.C., was at this time registrar of the Exchequer Court of Canada. He had joined the secretariat of the Prime Minister in 1927 and was King's private secretary from 1930 to 1945. In that year his son, David Howard Woodhouse Henry, married Elizabeth Pequegnat of Stratford, Ontario. The younger Henry is now the Honourable David Henry, Justice of the Supreme Court of Ontario since 1973.

3. The Keats essay appeared in the July issue.

LETTER 145

1. John McClelland (1877-1968) was a pioneer in the field of Canadian publishing and over his long career as president of McClelland & Stewart did much to encourage the development of Canadian literature.

2. Walter J. Turnbull, forty-nine years of age at this time, had served in the Prime Minister's Office since 1936, and since 1941 as principal secretary. In 1945 he had been appointed Deputy Postmaster General, a position he was to hold until 1957.

3. I cannot find any particulars about Ann. In the left margin, opposite her name, Scott has written, "10 yrs. with us."

4. Brockington was badly crippled.

5. In September 1945, Igor Gouzenko, a cipher clerk with the Soviet Embassy in Ottawa, revealed to the RCMP details of Soviet espionage activities in Canada. A Royal Commission was appointed in February, 1946, to study and evaluate the evidence. The findings of the Commission were published on the 27th of June following, by which time Scott appears to have lost interest in the affair.

6. Squadron Leader F.W. Poland, an American of English parentage, had come to Ottawa in 1942 and had been assigned to the post of Intelligence Officer with the RCAF. Later, his name appeared in connection with the Gouzenko disclosures, and on April 23, 1946, he was formally committed for trial under the provisions of the Official Secrets Act. Poland was acquitted the following January.

7. Gordon N. Ray, ed., *The Letters and Private Papers of William Makepeace Thackeray*. 4 vols. (London: Oxford University Press, 1945, 1946). I have let Scott's misspelling of Thackeray's name stand.

8. I. Norman Smith was at this time associate editor of the Ottawa *Journal*. He was the son of E. Norman Smith, who with Ross had built the fortunes of the *Journal* and helped establish its place on the Conservative side of the political fence. Norman

Smith Jr. was to become interested in Scott's work and would enjoy a short friendship with the poet in the time that remained before the latter's death in 1947.

9. John William Mackail (1859-1945) was a classical scholar and the author of *The Life of William Morris*. 2 vols. (London: Longmans, 1899).

10. This "travel note" joined others to make up the descriptive piece called "Wayfarers" in the essay section of *The Circle of Affection*. For the references to Buckfast Abbey and to Morris, see pp. 88-89.

11. In the chapter on Oxford in *The Life of William Morris*, vol. 1, Mackail writes: "Still the Oxford of 1853 breathed from its towers the last enchantments of the Middle Ages. . . ." Compare Arnold, in his preface to the 1865 edition of *Essays in Criticism* describing Oxford as "whispering from her towers the last enchantments of the Middle Age. . . ."

12. The passage Scott has in mind appears in Part IV of "The Rime of the Ancient Mariner," beginning "In his loneliness/and fixedness he/yearneth towards/the/journeying/Moon. . ." Without quotation marks or acknowledgement, Mackail uses nearly all the key words and phrases of this passage in constructing a final lofty sentence about Morris's death and his journey to join the immortals.

LETTER 146

1. As far as I can discover, Brown's fears were unnecessary. His copyright could be assumed with the publication of the book, unless he had otherwise assigned it. It is true, on the other hand, that he could have been called upon to defend his copyright if it had been challenged in the courts.

2. *Overture* (Toronto: Ryerson Press, 1945).

3. *Grey Ship Moving* (Toronto: Ryerson Press, 1945).

4. *Sandstone* (Toronto: Ryerson Press, 1945).

5. The edition Brown is referring to is probably *Selected Poems of Matthew Arnold* (London: Macmillan & Co., 1878). Arnold made the selection, and the edition ran to ten reprints between 1880 and 1889.

6. *The Adventures of Harry Richmond*, 1871.

7. Charles Frederick Harrold, *John Henry Newman* (London: Longmans, 1945).

8. Charles Hilton Brown, *Rudyard Kipling* (New York: Harper & Brothers, 1945). Brown's review, "Kipling and the Modern Reader," was published in *Yale Review*, XXXV (June 1946), pp. 740-42.

9. John W. Pickersgill was born in Wyecombe, Ontario, in 1905, and educated at the University of Manitoba and at Oxford. Returning to his alma mater, he held an appointment as lecturer in history, 1929-1937. He then joined the Department of External Affairs in Ottawa but was soon seconded to the Prime Minister's Office. Contrary to Brown's gloomy predictions, Pickersgill's career was to be highly successful. He was to be a member of the House of Commons for fourteen years and the holder of many important portfolios in the Liberal cabinet between 1954 and his retirement from politics in 1967. He is the author of *The Mackenzie King Record, 1939-44* (Toronto: University of Toronto Press, 1960).

10. Canadian historian John Bartlet Brebner (1895-1957) was at this time professor of History at Columbia University. His remarks on the failure, as he saw it, of the Royal Society to live up to the scholarly and cultural purposes for which it was founded appear in *Scholarship for Canada: The Function of Graduate Studies* (Ottawa: Canadian Social Science Research Council, 1945), pp. 65 ff.

LETTER 147

1. We do not have the note or letter from Mrs. Brown that must have accompanied the

263

photograph of Deaver. There is therefore no context for the reference to "the Truman family exploits" in the second paragraph of Scott's reply. Harry S. Truman had become President of the United States following the sudden death of Franklin D. Roosevelt on April 12, 1945.

2. The new Governor General was Viscount Alexander of Tunis (1891-1969).
3. Lady Bessborough was French-born, the wife of the Earl of Bessborough, Governor General of Canada, 1931-1935. The Bessboroughs were enthusiastic patrons of the amateur theatre movement in Ottawa and initiated the Dominion Drama Festival, a project in which Scott himself was deeply involved.

LETTER 148

1. Joyce Anne Marriott, poet, was born in Victoria, B.C., in 1913. She had joined the National Film Board in 1945. Scott would know her at this time as the author of four slim volumes of verse: *The Wind Our Enemy* (1939); *Calling Adventurers!* (1941); *Salt Marsh* (1942); and *Sandstone and Other Poems* (1945).
2. Following his return from overseas service in 1945, and a brief period on the staff of the International Service of the CBC, Birney had been appointed to the Department of English at the University of British Columbia.
3. There had been intermittent correspondence between Scott and Alfred Noyes since 1942, when the Noyes children had been at school in Canada. Noyes was born in 1880. His tastes in poetry, like Scott's, were conservative, and he watched the coming of modernism with misgivings. The anthology is *The Golden Book of Catholic Poetry* (Philadelphia: Lippincott, 1946). 'Compline,' doubtless chosen for its religious overtones, had appeared first in *The Green Cloister*.
4. Douglas Bush's *English Literature in the Earlier Seventeenth Century, 1600-1660* was Volume V of *The Oxford History of English Literature* (London: Oxford University Press, 1945).
5. 'Variations on a Seventeenth Century Theme,' one of Scott's most impressive poems, took as its tonic note a passage from Henry Vaughan: "It was high Spring, and all the way/Primrosed, and hung with shade." The poem appeared in *Beauty and Life*, 1921.
6. In some "notes" prepared the following summer for Arthur Stringer on Brooke's visit to Ottawa in 1913, Scott recalls the poet's "interest in John Donne." The full text of the "notes" is printed in Bourinot's *Some Letters*, pp. 58-60 and reprinted here in Appendix I (p. 292).
7. By 1946 there were five sections. Section II took in English Literature, History, Archaeology and Sociology. The "French Section" was Section I and had corresponding subdivisions.
8. The Dominion-Provincial Conference on Financial Relations had reconvened on April 25, 1946.
9. The clipping has not been preserved, but the *Journal* for April 29, 1946, carried a short piece on Dr. H.J. Cody that fits the context of the present letter. Cody, outgoing president of the University of Toronto, feared the loss of Canadian academics to greener fields. "Canada," he had written in his final report, "must increase the salaries of teachers and research workers or it will lose the best members of those groups."
10. *Deirdre of the Sorrows*. An Ancient and Noble Tale Retold by John Coulter for Music by Healey Willan (Toronto: Macmillan, 1944). Coulter, Irish-born playwright and poet, had written an earlier opera, "Transit Through Fire" (1942), and was to reach a wide audience in the sixties with his dramatizations for both stage and radio of the story of Louis Riel. He and Scott were good friends.

11. Augustin Frigon was general manager of the CBC, 1944-51. The work cited was the Piano Concerto in C Minor, first recorded in 1944.

LETTER 149

1. This is the piece Brown had referred to as a "short article" in Letter 144. There is a considerable gap between Scott's letter of May 1 and the present letter of June 10, with no word from Brown in the interim. Brown may have sent a note with the review; but if he did, it had not been preserved.

2. 'The Vision' appears on p. 98 of *The Burning Glass*. Scott may have been confused by the fact that Brown's review in *Poetry* begins on p. 90. On that page, one of de la Mare's poems is quoted in full, but the poem is 'Nostalgia,' not 'The Vision'.

3. *The Burning Glass,* p. 80.

4. *The Burning Glass,* p. 44.

5. The "enclosed lines" were published in *The Circle of Affection* under the title 'To Deaver Brown.' The other poems "written for children" and included in *The Circle* are: 'To Jane Edgar: For Her Album;' 'Slumber Song'/For Cynthia Joy Brockington/Christmas, 1945; and 'Rondeau'/For Primrose and Clare Coulter—written in a copy of *Deirdre of the Sorrows*. The text of the poem 'To Deaver Brown' is given in Appendix J (p.294).

6. See *The Circle of Affection,* p. 73: 'Spring Midnight: Deepwood'/To My Friend Arthur S. Bourinot.

7. 'On Hearing Bach's "Sheep May Safely Graze" ' was circulated first as a Christmas poem in 1940-41. The dedication is "To Ethel Bartlett and Rae Robertson," the remarkable team who in the thirties and early forties earned international acclaim in concerts for two pianos. I have let Scott's misspellings of the names stand.

LETTER 150

1. This was Scott's presidential address, delivered on May 17, 1922. See *The Circle of Affection,* pp. 123-47.

2. "Two Formulas for Fiction: Henry James and H.G. Wells," *College English,* VIII, no. 1 (October 1946), pp. 7-17. *College English* was listed in 1945 as "An official organ of the National Council of Teachers of English."

LETTER 151

1. The reference is to the special issue of *Gants du Ciel*.

2. "The marriage of Captain Lionel Vincent Massey, elder son of Mr. and Mrs. Vincent Massey, of Batterwood House, near Port Hope, (Ontario), Canada, and Lilias, widow of Flying Officer D.B. Van Buskirk, RCAF, and daughter of Mr. and Mrs. Franklin Ahearn of Ottawa, took place in Ottawa on June 15" (London *Times,* June 17, 1946).

3. Jean-François Pouliot (1890-1969) came from a family which had served for three generations in the legislative councils of the nation. By 1946, he had survived six general elections since taking his seat as the Liberal member for Témiscouata in 1924.

LETTER 152

1. Brown's letter is written on notepaper of the Alexandra Palace, University Avenue at Queens Park, an old hotel handy to the University of Toronto.

2. E.J. Pratt's appointment as Companion of the Order of St. Michael and St. George was announced in the Dominion Day Honours List for 1946. Scott's C.M.G. dated from June 2, 1934.

LETTER 153

1. The occasion of the dinner was the annual meeting of the Canadian Authors' Association.

2. Clarence Heber Dickinson, clergyman and publisher, was born in Anderson, Ontario, in 1899. He was general manager and Book Steward at the Ryerson Press form 1937 to 1964.

LETTER 155

1. The 1946 Annual Meeting of the Canadian Authors' Association, held at Hart House, University of Toronto, June 27-29, had closed with a dinner at the Royal York Hotel to celebrate in particular the 25th anniversary of the organization. The Ryerson Press, fulfilling its historic connection with the C.A.A., had played host for the occasion.

2. The Country Club has been mentioned several times by Scott, usually in connection with his birthday. It was on the Hull side of the river, on the Aylmer Road. Scott felt very much at home there, having been a member since 1915.

3. On the occasion of his eighty-fourth birthday, Scott was made a life member of the National Book League (Great Britain). John Masefield had written the invitation: ''The League asks me, as President, to say to you that it wishes to celebrate your birthday by making you a Life Member. Will you be so kind as to grant us that privilege, and will you also so far honour us, as to send us some photograph of yourself, which we may exhibit always, with other portraits of poets, in a room given over to the service of Poetry?'' The letter, which is part of the D.C. Scott holdings, Thomas Fisher Rare Books and Special Collections Department, University of Toronto Library, was dated July 20, 1946. The photograph (a portrait by Karsh of Ottawa) was sent August 24.

4. Augustus Edwin John (1878-1961), painter, muralist and print-maker, was perhaps best known for his portraits, which are very idiosyncratic and which show to perfection his fine draftsmanship. Though there is a visionary quality to much of his work, his mode remained to the end basically representational. During World War I, John had served for a time as official war artist attached to the Canadian Corps. Ralph Vaughan Williams (1872-1958), composer, was educated at Charterhouse and Trinity College, Cambridge. Traditionalist in form, his nine symphonies are rich in melodic invention and brilliantly scored. George Macaulay Trevelyan (1876-1962), historian, had been Regius Professor of Modern History at Cambridge from 1927 to 1940. His *History of England,* published in 1926, had become a classic. Geoffrey Faber (1889-1961), president of the publishing house of Faber & Faber, was chairman of the National Book League from 1945 to 1947.

5. Bourinot supplies the following note to this letter: ''Mrs. E.A. Scott tells me Scott and Masefield only met once, for a brief moment in Florence, where the latter was lecturing. The Scotts went to the lecture and spoke to him afterwards.'' See *More Letters,* p. 76. The date of this meeting, if it did indeed take place, must have been in the early thirties, just after Scott's marriage to Elise Aylen.

6. Added at the end of the carbon copy of this letter in the SAP is a note in Scott's hand, written at an angle across the page: ''wrote again on the 9th asking about Goriot and sending clipping from Gazette.'' In Bourinot's version (*More Letters,* p. 76) the note is reproduced as the concluding sentence of the main text, where of course it makes no sense. Yet it may have seemed to make some sense to Bourinot if we assumed that he had no access to the ''Goriot'' letter, which becomes Letter 156 of the present sequence but is not published in the Bourinot selection. That letter, a holograph, generated no carbon copy; and the original was amongst the residue of letters still in Mrs. Brown's hands in 1975. These were some of the first indications I had that Bourniot had worked solely from carbon copies of Scott's letters.

LETTER 156

1. The clipping was a favourable review of the English-Canadian Poetry issue of *Gants*

266

du Ciel. It was signed "Candide." Scott and Brown were not mentioned. See French Bookshelf, *The Gazette,* Montreal, August 9, 1946, p. 7.

LETTER 157

1. William Pate Mulock (1897-1954) had represented North York as a Liberal member in the House of Commons since 1930. From July 1940 until his retirement in 1945, he was Postmaster General in Mackenzie King's cabinet. Brown does not seem to have had word of his retirement.

2. Turnbull was Deputy Postmaster General at this time.

3. The article was to be published under the title "Homage to Willa Cather," in the *Yale Review,* XXXVI (September 1946), pp. 77-92. It brought a pleased response from the novelist that marked the beginning of an extensive correspondence which, as it developed, cast Brown in the role of more or less official biographer. It was from this still uncompleted work that Brown, when he recognized in 1949 that he had only a short time to live, turned aside in order to prepare a selected edition of Scott's poems and write the Memoir for it that was to remain the most important biographical and critical reference on its subject for the next twenty-five years. After Brown's death in 1951, Leon Edel was to complete the almost finished manuscript on Cather. It was published, under the title *Willa Cather: A Critical Biography,* in 1953. Cather's six-year silence as a novelist, to which Brown refers, dated back to *Sapphira and the Slave Girl,* 1940.

LETTER 158

1. This was the film version of Shaw's *Caesar and Cleopatra,* directed by Gabriel Pascal and starring Claude Rains and Vivien Leigh. The *Journal* for Friday, August 23, 1946, described it as a "gorgeous spectacle." The showing was at the Elgin theatre.

LETTER 159

1. This preface appeared in *Poems*, a volume which included 'Sohrab and Rustum,' 'The Forsaken Merman' and 'The Scholar Gypsy.'

2. Chauncey Brewster Tinker, seventy years old at this time, had published important books on Old English poetry, and on Johnson and Boswell and Fanny Burney, in the first two decades of the century. In 1940 he had joined with H.F. Lowry to publish *The Poetry of Matthew Arnold: A Commentary.* In 1950 he was to join with Lowry again, this time in the preparation of *The Complete Poetical Works of Matthew Arnold.* A complete edition (literary contents) of Arnold's notebooks was brought out by H.F. Lowry, K. Young and W.H. Dunn in 1952.

LETTER 160

1. This letter was amongst the papers which remained in Mrs. Brown's possession. It is an original signed typescript. Also amongst these papers was what I have called the "Goriot" letter, now Letter 156. It is a signed holograph. Both letters are dated August 9, 1946. Scott's note on his letter of August 8 about "asking about Goriot" and "sending clipping from Gazette" in a letter of August 9 established the claim of the "Goriot" letter to this date and gave it its place between Letter 155 and Letter 157. The other letter, on the basis of clear internal evidence, was easily placed a little later in the sequence as Letter 160. In dating this letter "August Ninth" (which is how the date is typed) Scott probably meant "September Ninth," and that is the date I have supplied. If, however, we assume a quick passage for Brown's letter of August 27 from New York (and a time of two days was not unlikely in 1946) a date of August 29 is also a possibility.

2. John Hunter-Duvar (1830-99), Scottish-born poet and dramatist, was best known for his verse plays: *The Enamorado* (1879) and *De Roberval* (1889). During the decade

between the writing of these two plays, he had been Dominion Inspector of Fisheries for Prince Edward Island, and he had remained an Islander throughout his retirement.

LETTER 161

1. John Watkins' friendship with Brown dated back to 1922, the year in which both began their academic careers at the University of Toronto; and they had kept in touch after they had gone their separate ways a few years later. Personal contact had been renewed during Brown's stay at Cornell. From a position as associate professor at the University of Manitoba, Watkins had moved to the Department of External Affairs in 1946. He was to have a distinguished career as a diplomat: Ambassador to the U.S.S.R., 1954-56; Undersecretary of State, Ottawa, 1956-58; Ambassador to Denmark, 1958-60. After Scott's death, Watkins was to be very helpful to Elise in the settling of her husband's affairs. Watkins himself died in 1964. For a review of his career and an account of the tragic circumstances of his death while under interrogation as a possible Russian agent, see the lead articles in "Focus," the Ottawa *Citizen*, June 13 and 15, 1981.

LETTER 162

1. Scott's grandfather was John Scott of Lincoln, England. The Rev. William Scott, Duncan's father, was born there on October 4, 1812.

2. This is Isabella Campbell MacCallum, whose daughter Janet married William Scott in 1859. Duncan was the second child by this marriage. His reference to being "about five" when he last saw his maternal grandmother places the latter's death c. 1867. She had been a Campbell, and Scott derived his second name from this source.

3. Print suppresses the troubled look of this page. The spacing is irregular, sometimes single and sometimes double. Towards the bottom, the lines begin to slant upwards to the right. I count eleven typographical errors, most of them corrected in ink.

LETTER 163

1. Brown's last letter is dated September 26. Scott's "28th ult." refers to the date he received it.

2. The Canadian première of Laurence Olivier's "Henry the Fifth" was held at the Avalon Theatre, on October 9, 1946, and attended by the Governor General, the Prime Minister and his cabinet, representatives of the diplomatic corps and, as the *Journal* noted, "several hundred people prominent in the social, educational and business life of the Capital." The editorial appeared in next day's *Journal*. It reads, in part: "One is glad to rejoice with the producers that here is the kind of movie to which one can invite the Governor General and the Prime Minister and—what is more—people like Duncan Campbell Scott and Pelham Edgar."

3. "Stories in Verse. E.J. Pratt: *Collected Poems*." *Times Literary Supplement* (Saturday, Sept. 14, 1946), 440.

4. *Shadows on the Rock* (1931); *Death Comes for the Archbishop* (1927); *My Ántonia* (1918).

5. Arthur John A. Stringer (1874-1950) was born in Chatham, Ontario, and educated at the University of Toronto and Oxford. He spent most of his life in the United States but kept up his Canadian connections. He was a prolific writer of poetry, plays, movie scenarios, short stories and novels. His biography of Rupert Brooke, entitled *Red Wine of Youth*, published in 1948, was to be his final work. Some letters relevant to the present context are preserved in the Rupert Brooke File of the SAP.

6. Richard Halliburton, born in Tennessee in 1900 and educated at Princeton University, was the author of several travel books. A flamboyant Byronic figure, Halliburton swam the Hellespont, ran the course of the original marathon, and rode an elephant

over the Alps in preparation for a book on Hannibal. Dead at the age of thirty-nine, he had left behind him much information and material relating to his idol, Rupert Brooke, whose mother he had persuaded to abandon a strict silence preserved for many years on the subject of her son.

7. The "few facts" became the "Notes. . .re Rupert Brooke's Visit to Ottawa," published by Bourinot in *Some Letters*, pp. 58-60 and reproduced here in Appendix I (p. 292). The originals of the Brooke letters are in the SAP.

8. Thoreau MacDonald was at this time designing for both Ryerson Press and McClelland & Stewart. Published, the text of *The Circle of Affection* ran to only 237 pages. It is difficult to see how MacDonald could have been so far out in his estimate. Perhaps Scott misread the figure.

9. Probably the notice of the death of Mrs. Isabelle Voorhis, widow of the Rev. Dr. Ernest Voorhis, formerly canon of the Cathedral of St. John the Divine in New York, and sister of Archibald Lampman. It appeared in the Ottawa *Journal* for October 1, 1946. Mrs. Voorhis had lived in Ottawa for many years, and for the last two years with her sister, Mrs. F.M.S. Jenkins (Annie), at 80 The Driveway. She was in her 83rd year. Other surviving relatives named are another sister, Mrs. W. LeBreton Ross, Vancouver, and two nieces in Ottawa, Mrs. H.O. McCurry (Dorothy) and Mrs. T.R.L. MacInnes (Natalie).

LETTER 164

1. Sir Mackenzie Bowell (1823-1917) was Conservative member of parliament for North Hastings from 1867 to 1892, when he was appointed to the Senate. He became Prime Minister on the death of Sir John Thompson in 1894. In January 1896, half of his cabinet, dissatisfied with his leadership, resigned. Bowell's own resignation followed in April 1896.

2. "Elsinore" is a mistake, but Brown types it clearly, and so I let it stand. Desmond Pacey, in *The Letters of Frederick Philip Grove*, cites a Mrs. Eleanor Haultain as advertising manager at the Ryerson Press during these years. See his note on Grove's letter to Lorne Pierce of February 11, 1939, p. 350.

3. *The Witching of Elspie*, a volume of short stories from Scott's middle period, had been published by McClelland & Stewart (with George H. Doran Company) in 1923. It was a relatively short book: large type, wide margins, 248 pages.

4. A.F.W. (Wynne) Plumptre (1907-77) was born in Montreal and educated at the University of Toronto and Cambridge. He had taught political economy at the University of Toronto from 1930 to 1941. After serving as financial attaché with the Canadian Embassy in Washington from 1942 to 1945, and as Secretary to the Wartime Prices and Trade Board in Ottawa from 1945 to 1947, Plumptre took over the assistant editorship of *Saturday Night*, a post which he was to relinquish in 1949 to become head of the Economics Division of the Department of External Affairs.

5. Lampman's essay on the Pre-Raphaelites is listed in the bibliographical appendix to Connor's *Archibald Lampman*. Together with the paper on Keats, it appears under the rubric of "Unpublished Essays." Connor quotes extensively from the essay to show that Lampman "was not in sympathy with the Pre-Raphaelites." See *Archibald Lampman*. Second edition (Ottawa: Borealis Press, 1977), pp. 135-37.

6. Alexander William Kinglake (1809-91), British traveller and historian, barrister and member of Parliament, was a contemporary of Thackeray and Tennyson at Cambridge. *Eothen; or, Traces of Travel, Brought Home from the East* was first published in 1844 and reprinted in numerous subsequent editions. It has been called "one of the great classics in the field of travel narratives."

7. The poem is called 'The Night Light.' *Yale Review*, XXXVI (September 1946), p. 37.

8. This article, and the short biographies which Brown goes on to mention, were to appear eventually in the 1950 edition of *Chambers' Encyclopaedia.*

9. Andrew Macphail was born in Orwell, Prince Edward Island, in 1864. He was educated at McGill University and the University of London. A physician by profession and professor of the History of Medicine at McGill from 1907 to 1937, he was at the same time one of the most influential literary figures of his generation in Canada. His literary interests were reflected in his long connection with the *McGill University Magazine* and in his friendships with Pelham Edgar, Stephen Leacock, John McRae and many other men of letters of his day. An early Fellow of the Royal Society, he was knighted in 1918 and received the Lorne Pierce Medal in 1930. Macphail had died in 1938. Hugh MacLennan was born in Glace Bay, Nova Scotia, in 1907 and educated at Dalhousie University, Oxford and Princeton. He was head of the Classics Department at Lower Canada College, Montreal, 1935-45. His first novel, *Barometer Rising,* had been published in 1941. In 1945, he had received the Governor General's Award for *Two Solitudes.*

LETTER 165

1. This was Mary Elizabeth Scott, first child of the Rev. William Scott's second marriage to Janet MacCallum. She was to linger on until the following spring.

2. The full entry for the Balzac volume in the Modern Library edition is as follows: *Père Goriot,* translated from the French by E.K. Brown and *Eugénie Grandet,* translated by Dorothea Walter and John Watkins. Watkins, an expert linguist, had probably been brought into the scheme by Brown. It is easy to see why he had an early copy of the book in his possession, though it is curious that neither Brown nor Scott, up to this point, has mentioned Watkins' share in the translation of *Eugénie Grandet.*

3. Bourinot, following the carbon copy, gives $300, a figure changed by Scott in the original to $500. See *More Letters,* p. 78.

4. In 1925, by an Act of Parliament, the majority of the members of Methodist, Presbyterian and Congregationalist churches were reconstituted as The United Church of Canada.

5. Probably *Matthew Arnold's Note-Books,* published by Smith Elder in 1902. The preface was by the Honourable Mrs. Woodhouse, who was Matthew Arnold's daughter. Alan Harris, in an article which appeared in *The Nineteenth Century and After,* CXIII, 1933, pp. 498-509, described these notebooks as "large size diaries in which, along with engagements, accounts and good resolutions he copied out passages from the books he was reading."

LETTER 166

1. The Albert Britnell Book Shop is located near the corner of Yonge and Bloor, not far from the University of Toronto campus. Brown would remember it from his college days as a favourite haunt of faculty and students.

LETTER 167

1. A handsome printing of an original poem by Scott entitled 'The Wren.' It is inscribed: "To Peggy, Edward & Deaver/affectionate greetings/from/Elise & Duncan."

LETTER 168

1. The books were: Earle Birney's *Now Is Time* (Toronto: Ryerson Press, 1945); Louis Dudek's *East of the City* (Toronto: Ryerson Press, 1946); Raymond Souster's *When We Are Young* (Montreal: First Statement Press, 1946); and John Coulter's *The Blossoming Thorn* (Toronto: Ryerson Press, 1946). The review was to be published in *Poetry,* LXIX (March 1947), pp. 349-53.

2. Arthur Irwin had become editor of *Maclean's* in 1945.

3. Lester Bowles Pearson (1897-1972) had joined the Department of External Affairs in 1928. From 1946 to 1948 he was serving in Ottawa as Under Secretary of the Department. John Watkins' "relation with Scandinavia" was his service with the American-Scandinavian Foundation in New York for a brief period following his graduation from the University of Toronto in 1927.

4. Frederick Philip Grove (later to be identified as Felix Paul Greve) was of German origin and came to America probably in 1909 or 1912. For the controversy which for a long time surrounded the circumstances of Grove's life before he left Europe, see Pacey, ed., *The Letters of Frederick Philip Grove,* preface and introduction; and D.O. Spettigue, *Frederick Philip Grove: The European Years* (Ottawa: Oberon Press, 1973). Settled in southern Manitoba as a teacher, Grove resumed the writing career he had begun in Europe and in the years that followed secured a place for himself as a major Canadian novelist through the publication of such books as *A Search for America* (1927), *Our Daily Bread* (1928), *Fruits of the Earth* (1933) and *The Master of the Mill* (1944). *In Search of Myself,* published in 1946, is an autobiography. Although obscure or deliberately misleading on the subject of "the European years," it remains perhaps the best work in the genre of spiritual autobiography ever produced in Canada.

LETTER 169

1. The Viger File of the SAP contains a clipping from the *TLS* of October 13, 1945, which describes *Viger* as: "Pictures of life and people in a French-Canadian hamlet." In the same list are Sir John Buchan-Hepburn's *The Time of Life,* a book of essays "on country life and pursuits in Scotland, Sussex and Surrey," and Kerry Wood's *Three Mile Bend,* "a description of the wild life and the changing scenes and seasons on a stretch of river near the town of Red Deer, Alberta."

2. The rainbow image is central in Scott's poem 'To Deaver Brown.'

3. The review appeared on February 1, 1947, and not on the "10th or 11th" as Scott suggests. It was highly favourable. Scott's "something queer about the Phillips book," which at first glance seems linked with the review, probably refers to pricing and royalty procedures. '

4. Amongst miscellaneous papers in the SAP I found the following typescript:
   BEN HUR LAMPMAN. WAS BORN IN BARRON WISCONSIN IN 1886.
   In 1912 he moved to Oregon where he has lived ever since. In 1916 he joined the staff of the Portland newspaper *The Oregonian* of which he is now the associate editor.
   There is no evidence of the origin of this extract.

5. "A.P.S.W.," obviously refers to A.S.P. Woodhouse. On the same sheet as the "Ben Hur" extract, Scott has typed the following:
   Extract from the notes to a paper read before the F.R.S.L. Apl. 1944 by Rt. Hon. Isaac Foot, P.C., on OLIVER CROMWELL AND ABRAHAM LINCOLN.
   Gardiner said that the discovery of the Clarke Papers threw every other accession of material into the shade. Unfortunately these four volumes published by the Royal Historical Society (1891-1901) have long since been out of print. This loss, however, has been in large measure made up by the fine volume *Puritanism and Liberty* by Professor A.S.P. Woodhouse, of the University College, Toronto (1938). This is a further debt we owe to trans-Atlantic scholarship.
   Again there is no indication of the source.

6. This must be a publication of the National Book League, but I have not been able to trace it.

7. The first Canadian edition of L.M. Montgomery's *Anne of Green Gables* had appeared in 1942. Ryerson's spring list for 1947 contained a section on Canadian

fiction. There is no classification by genre or type of novel. The lead item is Philip Child's *Day of Wrath,* joint winner of the Ryerson Fiction Award for that year. L.M. Montgomery dominates the list of thirteen other novels, seven of them being by her. But Scott's *Viger* keeps company with three books by F.P. Grove and one by his friend John Coulter.

8. The "note" by A.J.M. Smith is from *The Book of Canadian Poetry.* In the Ryerson list it reads: "Among the finest contributions to the art of the short story in Canadian literature." In the original, Smith couples *In the Village of Viger* with *The Witching of Elspie* in paying his tribute. There is no mention of Thoreau MacDonald's drawings in the Ryerson advertisement of *Viger*.

9. Bourinot (*More Letters,* p. 80) omits "from Flemington."

10. Bourinot omits this whole sentence.

LETTER 170

1. The question of the "kinship" comes up on page 6 of *W.J. Phillips.* Here Scott writes of the choice Phillips had to make as the son of a Methodist parson who was made to feel, like many of his kind, "that painting should be considered useless and effeminate." He was therefore compelled to choose either to accept parental blessing for a university career leading to the Church or "stick to his ambition to be a painter upheld only by his ability and determination." Scott at this point pauses to recognize his kinship with Phillips in their being sons of the Methodist parsonage. The failure of painting to demonstrate its utility he describes as "not alone the delusion of Methodist parsons;" and he adds, "it has too often obstructed and sometimes foiled talent or genius in all the Arts." But the observation remains general, and we are not encouraged to pursue its implications into Scott's own life. The way is in fact blocked in the second passage referred to by Brown, the "little tribute," which occurs on pages 33 and 34 of the Phillips essay. Here Scott goes out of his way to recall "the fortunate youngster," clearly himself, "whose early memory goes back to the days when *Good Words* and *Good Words for the Young* came every month into the home. . . ." For it was these illustrated books, and others such as *Works of Eminent Masters,* that had given and continued to give him great joy. "These books," he adds, "were the possessions of happy children brought up by indulgent parents whose influence was ever for the best in letters, music and art, who encouraged every evidence of talent."

2. In discussing the Japanese influence on Phillips' style, Scott relates two anecdotes about the European discovery of Hokusai's prints: one, that Bracquemond found a print wrapped around an imported oriental vase; the other, that Monet came upon several prints covering butter and cheese in a Dutch grocery. Scott adds: "My verdict goes to Bracquemond, probably because I dislike cheese and all its varieties, and I cannot separate the Monet legend from the malodeur of the Dutch cheese-shop." See *W.J. Phillips,* p. 40.

3. Phillips argued that pictures (small pictures at least) should be viewed individually and at arm's length. "A large number of estimable people," he is quoted as saying, "stick pictures all over their walls, all they like and may contrive to acquire. . . . They are like the lady who wears all her dresses at once." Scott remarks, "The words criticise the walls of the present writer and I should feel like stripping them bare and acquiring a solander box if I wholly agreed with them." See *W.J. Phillips,* p. 43.

4. "Letters in Canada: 1946," *University of Toronto Quarterly,* XVI, (January 1947), pp. 246-55.

5. Sister Maura (née Mary Power), *Initiate the Heart* (New York: Macmillan, 1946). Brown, however, does not mention the volume in his review.

6. Ontario Hospital, Woodstock, was opened in 1906. Originally designated for the

treatment of epileptic patients, it was enlarged to provide special care for tubercular patients and for the mentally ill and mentally retarded.

LETTER 171

1. Bourinot (*More Letters,* p. 81) omits "about The Ryerson Press and Dr. Pierce" and in the next sentence replaces Pierce's name with a dash.

2. Still intent on keeping Lorne Pierce out of the picture, Bourinot changes "Did he send you" to "Did you get. . . ." The catalogue referred to is *A Catalogue of Canadian Manuscripts Collected by Lorne Pierce and Presented to Queen's University* (Toronto: Ryerson, 1946).

LETTER 172

1. This continuation of the letter follows immediately (i.e., same page) the part just completed. Scott misdates it "Seventh *March*, '47."

2. William Saroyan, playwright and novelist, was born in California of Armenian parents in 1908. Among his best-known works are *The Daring Young Man on the Flying Trapeze* (1934) and *The Time of Your Life* (1939), and *My Heart's in the Highlands* (1940). Scott has in mind Johnny's Father in *My Heart's in the Highlands;* who at one point in the play says to Johnny: "You go on down there and tell that splendid scholar and gentleman your father is one of the greatest unknown poets living."

LETTER 173

1. The article was to appear under the title "Now, Take Ontario." *Maclean's* magazine (June 15, 1947), pp. 30-32. It is reprinted in Staines, *E.K. Brown: Responses and Evaluations.*

2. Henry W.Wells and Carl F. Klinck, *Edwin J. Pratt: The Man and His Poetry* (Toronto: Ryerson Press, 1947).

LETTER 175

1. This would be an inscription. The dedication was "To My Wife."

2. The setting of "The Return" is Viger, but it had not been included in the publication of the Viger group.

LETTER 177

1. Géza DeKresz, violinist, music teacher and conductor, was born in Hungary in 1882. At the time of his visit with the Scotts, he had behind him a long and distinguished career in Europe. He had given his first Canadian recitals in 1923, and in the following year he had become a founding member and leader of the Hart House String Quartet, a group which included Harry Adaskin, also a friend of the Scotts. DeKresz's most recent appointment (since 1941) had been as Director of the National Conservatory, Budapest, but early in 1947 he had left Hungary to undertake a series of concert tours in Canada. In 1948 he was to be appointed to the Faculty of Music, University of Toronto. Norah Drewett was an English concert pianist of great distinction who had married DeKresz in 1918.

2. The reference to "one of our foremost short story writers" suggests Raymond Knister, who in his introduction to *Canadian Short Stories* (1928) had singled out *In the Village of Viger* for praise because "it stands out after thirty years as the most satisfyingly individual contribution to the Canadian short story" (*Canadian Short Stories* [Toronto: Macmillan, 1928], p. xix). But Knister does not mention a specific story, and the story he chooses to represent Scott in his anthology is "Labrie's Wife," already published in *The Witching of Elspie* (1923) and therefore not included in *The Circle.*

3. John Almon Ritchie, lawyer, was born in Saint John, New Brunswick, in 1863. He

was the author of several plays, including *Dinner at Eight, After-Glow* and *The Worldlings.* Ritchie's lines "The wholesome sea is at her gates" are cut on the main entrance to the Parliament Buildings in Ottawa.

4. The play was entitled "Pierre," and it was published in Vol. 1 of *Canadian Plays from Hart House Theatre,* ed. Vincent Massey (Toronto: Macmillan, 1926). Scott is mistaken in his "only Vol." A second volume was published in 1927.

5. The review was published in the column "An Attic Salt Shaker," on July 5, 1947, p. 14.

6. Arthur R. Ford reviewed the book in the column "Over the Week-End," *The Free Press,* July 7, 1947. The *Gazette* notice was written by Neil M. Compton and appeared June 28.

7. The *Maclean's* piece.

8. "Forty years ago" places Scott's reading of "Self Reliance" in 1907, the year his young daughter Elizabeth died, under tragic circumstances, in Paris.

9. *The Belton Estate,* by Anthony Trollope, was published in 1865. His earlier novel, *Dr. Thorne,* was published in 1858. Scott's shift to the subject of Trollope is prompted by Brown's review of Michael Sadleir's *Trollope: A Commentary,* published in *Yale Review,* XXXVI, 4 (June 1947), pp. 753-55. Brown may have sent a copy, or perhaps Scott got access to the June number through the Library of Parliament, which he used frequently.

10. *Villette,* by Charlotte Brontë, was published in 1853.

11. Brown quotes an example of Sadleir's exaggerated praise: "in theme familiar, in treatment undistinguished, Trollope's work is nevertheless unrivalled in its power to hold the attention of readers of any kind and of any generation."

12. Scott writes "Mr." but then switches in the next line to "she." Although the lettering of the final "e" is blurred, "she" seems to be intended. Bourinot (*More Letters,* p. 82) changes "Mr." to "Mrs." and I accept his reading since he probably knew the Blackburns and was able to identify Mrs. Blackburn as the "devoted Trollopian." Russell Blackburn had been associated with the lumbering business in the Ottawa valley for many years. *Who's Who* of the time lists him as a "manufacturer." He was also sometime General Manager of the Ottawa & Hull Power Co., and Director of the Bank of Ottawa. The Blackburns lived at 102 Lisgar Street.

13. Sacheverell Sitwell, English poet, critic and essayist, was born in 1897. *The Hunters and the Hunted* was published in 1947. His brother Osbert, born in 1892, was the author of *Left Hand, Right Hand,* the beginning of the Sitwell family memoirs, which had appeared in 1944. Two volumes had followed, *The Scarlet Tree* and *Great Morning!* in 1946 and 1947.

14. *Selected Poems of Archibald Lampman,* in the Ryerson Library of Canadian Poets. The review had appeared in the *Journal,* July 19, 1947, p. 12. Ross deals extensively with Lampman, whom he calls "the greatest of Canadian poets." Scott, as editor, is briefly mentioned: "than whom there could be no better judge."

15. This is the 1925 selection of Lampman's poems, also edited by Scott.

16. Bourinot (*More Letters,* p. 83) omits the account of MacInnes's illness.

17. Fitzgerald's *The Rubaiyat of Omar Khayyam* (xxxviii):
> One Moment in Annihilation's Waste,
> One Moment, of the Well of Life to taste—
>   The Stars are setting and the Caravan
> Starts for the Dawn of Nothing — Oh, make haste!

18. See Ralph Gustafson, "Among the Millet," *Northern Review,* I, 5 (February-March)

1947, pp. 26-34. On July 17, Scott had written a long letter to Gustafson in which he sought to correct the latter on a number of misapprehensions which seemed to be gaining currency about Lampman's life. He dealt in particular with the social and physical environment which Ottawa offered Lampman, the nature of Lampman's frustrations, aspirations, and the like. The letter is an important one and was published under the title "Copy of a Letter from Duncan Campbell Scott to Ralph Gustafson" in *Fiddlehead*, XLI (1959), pp. 12-14. Notes for the letter and a carbon copy of the final version are in the Gustafson File of the SAP.

19. See *Saturday Night*, July 5, 1947. The short note identifies Scott as the "Dean of Canadian Letters" and adds: "many critics now regard him as second to no other Canadian poet."

LETTER 178

1. It is clear that Scott's letter of July 24 is still in the mails.

2. Scott will have a comment or two to make about most of the poems cited here by Brown. See Letter 182. Brown deals first with some "late poems," part of the group published in newspapers and periodicals between 1935 (the date of the last collected volume) and 1946.

3. The concluding stanza of 'Derwentwater' reads as follows:

> I thought on the ultimate secret,—
>   Long after the light had flown—
> That lies beyond all appearance
> And cannot be known.

4. The "early poems," nine in number, were poems which Scott had rejected in putting together the five discrete collections which had preceded the collected *Poems* of 1926. 'Early Summer Song' is dated "1890?" on the typescript version filed in the SAP. 'At Murray Bay' was rejected in the final drafting of *The Magic House* in 1892 or 1893.

LETTER 181

1. Alan B. Creighton, poet, editor and teacher, was born in 1903. In the thirties he had published two volumes of poetry: *Earth Call* (1936) and *Cross-Country* (1939). At this time, he was assistant editor (not editor, as Brown has it) of the *Canadian Forum*. Although Brown seems to have forgotten, Creighton had written a review of *At the Long Sault* for the *Forum* in 1944. The reference for Brown's review is *Canadian Forum*, XXVII (October 1947), p. 165.

2. The English Institute had met for the first time at Columbia University in 1939. It described itself as "an assemblage of persons interested in the serious study of the English and American language and literature." In subsequent annual meetings it showed itself less concerned with the results of research than with approaches and methodologies appropriate to its fields of interest. Postconference sessions were devoted to "a series of thoughtful and stimulating lectures by invited speakers on widely different aspects of literary scholarship." See *English Institute Essays 1939* (New York: Columbia University Press, 1940). Brown's paper was to be one of eight read at the 1947 meeting. Of these eight, four were to constitute the beginning of a two-year series on "The Theory of Fiction"; and Brown's paper was to take its place in this sub-group. Since the series was to be spread over two years, the publishing arrangements were to become complicated. The papers of the sub-group on "The Theory of Fiction" were to be reserved for publication with the complementary papers scheduled for the 1948 session. But Brown's paper did not appear in *English Institute Essays 1948* (1949), nor did it appear anywhere else, as far as I have been able to discover. Perhaps it was absorbed into the Alexander Lectures on "Rhythm in the Novel" which Brown was to give at the University of Toronto in 1949. The title given

in the Appendix to *English Institute Essays 1947* (1948) for Brown's lecture to the Institute is "Aspects of Victorian Fiction."

3. See *The Circle of Affection,* pp. 82-85. The context is a literary travelogue, entitled "Wayfarers," in which Scott describes places in England and Italy associated with some of his favourite authors. George Borrow, English novelist, whose *Lavengro* and *The Romany Rye* Scott greatly admired, is seen in the setting of Norfolk.

LETTER 182

1. For the text of this letter I follow the original sent to Brown. The carbon copy in the SAP, which is Bourinot's copy-text in *More Letters* (pp. 85-87), differs in several respects from the original: the inked corrections or additions, in this case quite numerous, do not always correspond. The dating of the carbon is "2nd to 8th Sept." The dating of the original is simply "2nd Sept." I have adopted "2nd to 8th" because I think the entry accurately reflects the period of the letter's composition.

2. The clause "wh. was sincere" is an inked superscription with an insertion mark after the word "loyalty" in both the original and the carbon copy.

3. In the original, the date "12 Mar '43" is a superscription with an insertion mark after the word "evening."

4. Ralph Gustafson was the guest editor. Scott changes "in *the* Canadian No." to "in *a* Canadian No." in the original but not in the carbon.

5. The carbon copy has brackets, in pencil, around the whole of this sentence; and Bourinot of course conforms. But they are not in the original, and so I omit them. In both the carbon and the original, "so long ago!" is a superscription above the word "here" — in pencil on the carbon, in ink on the original — but there is no mark of insertion. The date "Oct. '42" is, on the carbon, a superscription with an insertion mark after the phrase "until months afterwards"; on the original the insertion mark appears between "months" and "afterwards." The latter seems to be a slip, and so in this case I accept the carbon copy reading.

6. *The Magic House,* Scott's first volume of poems, was published in 1893. Scott did not begin his Notebooks, on which he was later to rely for dates, until after the publication of *Labor and the Angel,* his second volume of poems, in 1898. I do not know why he says that the "early poems" were written "of course after *The Magic House.*" I have already noted his tentative dating of 'Early Summer Song' as 1890 and his exclusion of 'At Murray Bay' (first published in *The Week* for 22 April, 1892) in the final drafting of his first collected volume.

7. I have not been able to find a place and date for the first publication of 'Early Summer Song.'

8. See *The Circle of Affection,* pp. 55-61.

9. Bourinot's version gives us "on 19," which is the reading of the carbon copy. But "19" refers to a stanza, not a page, and Scott has corrected the original, in pencil, to read "of 19."

10. Although the scansion marks appear on both the carbon and the original, Bourinot does not print them.

11. A printed version of this poem, under the heading '*A Song* by Duncan Campbell Scott,' is in the Clipping File (Poems) of the SAP. There is no date and no source, but Scott is right about *Saturday Night;* it was in the issue of March 17, 1928, p. 1.

12. In both the original and the carbon, the clause "i.e. if the CBC wld pay me for it!" is written in ink in the margin. In the original a mark of insertion is placed, in ink, after "Princess Elizabeth." There is no mark of insertion in the carbon, and Bourinot, making an educated guess and reading "or" for "i.e.," places the clause in the next

sentence, after "any commission from you." Princess Elizabeth was to marry Prince Philip on November 20, 1947.

13. 'Slumber Song' was written for Cynthia Joy Brockington, Christmas 1945. See *The Circle of Affection,* p. 76.

14. Scott has typed an upper case "H" over a lower case "h," and the blurred impression in the carbon looks very like an "N"; and so Bourinot prints "NEAT."

15. Masefield's letter is dated July 31, 1947, at Burcote Brook, Abingdon, Berkshire. The original, together with a carbon typescript "for E.K.B.," is in the Scott collection at the Thomas Fisher Rare Books and Special Collections Department, University of Toronto Library. Masefield, always attracted to the wilderness aspects of Canadian life, is particularly pleased to find in *The Circle* "so much about the Canadian Indians, and about the unrecorded and passionate life of the great primitive communities."

LETTER 183

1. Brown's copy of *The Poems of Archibald Lampman* ("Memorial" edition, 1900) remains in the possession of the Brown family, in Rochester, N.Y. It contains pencilled notes of dates, and a wide range of variant readings for a considerable number of the poems. A xerox copy of the book is in Special Collections, Carleton University Library, Ottawa. The total of 182 poems which Brown says he can date more or less precisely is out of 237 poems for the volume.

2. Brown's list has not been preserved. In Brown's copy of the *Poems,* however, tucked between front cover and flyleaf, I found a pencilled list in Scott's hand, and this must be the source for Brown's reference, at the end of the paragraph, to "the other poems you noted on the same sheet. . . ." On this sheet, Scott has supplied precise datings for fifteen poems, and these entries Brown has transferred to the text of the *Poems,* with the addition in each case of the note "D.C.S. memo."

3. The final entry of Scott's list is 'The Dead,' the poem which Brown cannot find "so entitled." The date entered here is "17 Aug. '94." On the back of the sheet, Brown has queried: 'Beechwood?' He probably has in mind the poem 'In Beechwood Cemetery,' which begins, "Here the dead sleep" (*Poems,* p. 288).

4. This was probably the last scribbler to come from Lampman's hand. It is really one-third of a scribbler and it contains both draft and fair copy of the poems included. It was at some point re-bound as an artist's notebook and is now deposited with the Public Archives of Canada. For this information I am indebted to Professor Bruce Nesbitt of the Department of English, Simon Fraser University, Vancouver, who is currently working on a scholarly edition of Lampman's poems.

LETTER 184

1. Bourinot prints this letter (*More Letters,* p. 84) but I cannot find the carbon copy which must have been his copy-text. He marks it "Undated." The signed version which was sent to Brown is dated in typescript at the bottom left-hand corner of the page (an unusual practice for Scott) and the date given is "16 Aug. '47." But internal evidence places the present letter unmistakably *after* Brown's letter of September 6, in which the question of the dating of the Lampman poems is first raised. Scott probably received Brown's letter on the 8th or 9th, since he tells Brown that he had "just posted" his own letter, which was finished on the 8th, when Brown's letter arrived. I have therefore changed Scott's "Aug." to "September."

2. Late in 1943, it will be recalled, Scott had transferred the bulk of the Lampman material still in his possession to Natalie MacInnes.

3. There is a half-erased upstroke after the "n" in "Duncan." Beneath, Scott has scribbled, "I was going to put my full signature!"

LETTER 185

1. Brown's *Matthew Arnold: A Study in Conflict* was to be released by the University of Chicago Press in 1948.

2. The finished piece, entitled simply ''David Copperfield,'' was to be published in *Yale Review,* XXXVII (Spring 1948), pp. 651-66.

LETTER 186

1. Scott has been silent for more than a month. Now, the Browns have sent word of the birth of another son. Whether the word was passed by telephone or telegram, or through John Watkins, I do not know. I have no further letters from Brown after Letter 185. Deaver's brother was to be named Philip.

DOCUMENTS

Appendix A

January 26, 1943

Dear Dr. Pierce.

When Professor E.K. Brown of Cornell University was in Ottawa last summer we were discussing Lampman's work and when I found that he was a great admirer of Lampman I told him of the M.S. we had given the Library of Parliament and of the Note-books in which Lampman worked. Mrs. Loftus MacInnes, generously and unreservedly, allowed Prof. Brown to use these Note-books. He discovered poems there which had never been written out fairly, some of great beauty and interest. We think these poems should be published, there are about fifty in all; and we have formed the plan of presenting them with a short preface by myself and with a critical Introduction by Professor Brown on these poems and on Lampman's work generally. I think such an Introduction would be of high value, as a new appraisal of Lampman's work by Professor Brown would be an important item in our literature. The book would not exceed a hundred pages but that would depend on the format. As you have the Lampman Poems now we would like you to issue this little book in the Spring. We should have the M.S. ready by the end of next month. Will you kindly let me know whether you are interested in our project.

> With kindest regards,
> Yours sincerely,
> D.C.S.

Dr. Lorne Pierce, F.R.S.C.
The Ryerson Press, Toronto.

(Source: carbon copy,
Lorne Pierce File, SAP)

Appendix B

DRAFT OF SCOTT'S LETTER TO BROWN OF NOVEMBER 1, 1942 (LETTER 14).
(The second page appeared on the verso of the single-paged draft. The date at the upper
right hand corner is probably a later addition by another hand than Scott's.)

[ı Nov 4ə]

Dear E.K.B.   Just as I was about to post my letter of the 3Ist the
Post man walked in with yours of the 28th so I opened the envelope (which
may show signs of the teakettld, in order to add a few words not in complete answer to yours. I read your article yesterday and like it much
and reflected upon it, its place in our scheme, and the Poems. I found not
for the first time the reading painful   I wish you would let me know soon
what you think of The Long Sault, you may keep this copy as I had several
struck off.   I will arrange the early Love Sonnets as I think they might
be used and you can consider them. You may have trouble with me
I am always pondering on the Canon, and the book takes form in my mind; I
mean the whole book, my share, yours and the poems. I would not care to
attempt a sonnet; I dont object to your setting me a task, but I have never
cared to use the form and you may have noticed I have made very few ,

[copy: inked over for
xeroxing]

In fact the opening & closing lyrics,
might be printed in *italics* so
~~after~~ detached are they but I don't
advocate that. I am very pleased
with what you say of this Poem & I want
to retain it all but more of this latter

(*Source:* SAP)

Appendix C

EXCERPT FROM LAMPMAN'S 'DAULAC'

From a text transcribed from the notebooks by E.K. Brown and sent to D.C. Scott for comment, October 1942.
(Reference: Letter 16, note 1.)
(The corresponding passage in the title-poem of At the Long Sault *begins at the bottom of p. 2.)*

And he turns at last in his track
Against a wall of rock and stands at bay,
And round him with terrible sinews and teeth of steel
They charge and recharge, but he with many a furious plunge and wheel

Hither and thither over the trampled snow
Tosses them bleeding and torn
Till, driven and ever to and fro
Harried wounded and weary grown
His mighty strength gives way
And they fasten upon him all together and drag him down
And he sinks outworn.

So Daulac turned him anew
With a ringing, piercing cry to his men
In the little raging forest glen
And his terrible sword in the twilight whistled and slew
And all his comrades stood
With their backs to the pales and fought
Till their strength was done
And the world that had seemed so good
Passed like a dream from their blinded eyes and was naught.
At last, at last!
The thews that were only mortal flagged and broke.
Each struck his last wild stroke and passed.
And they fell one by one
And then the great night came
With the triumph songs of the foe and the flame
Of camp fires — and out of the dark the soft wind woke
And the song of the rapid rose alway
And came to the spot where the silent comrades lay
Beyond help or care
With now but the red men round them to gnash their teeth and stare.

(Source: SAP)

284

Appendix D

SCOTT TO LORNE PIERCE
(Reference: Letter 35, note 1.)

February 20, 1943

Dear Dr. Pierce.

    Almost a month has gone by since I received yours of the 27th ult. I was pleased that your letter was so cordial to our Lampman project; since then Mr. MacInnes has seen you and preliminaries have been discussed. I had hoped to send you the M.S. before this but the delay was unavoidable. I am posting it today, registered. My opinion is that it will be an important item in Canadian letters. You will note that we added the word "new" to the phrase "And other poems," as we thought it important to make this fact part of the title. We would take it as a favor if you could come to a decision at an early date as to format etc. The sale price will we hope be reasonable. You will I know give all these questions the benefit of your long experience and correspond with me about them. Mr. MacInnes I can see at any time and I will write to Professor Brown.

    I appreciate your personal messages. The winter has been severe and we hope the worst is over; but I have been very well and as active as one can be in below-zero weather. I hope you can say the same as I note exceptional cold for Toronto.

                  With kindest regards,
                  Yours sincerely,
                      [Duncan Campbell Scott]

(Source: carbon copy,
Lorne Pierce File, SAP)

Appendix E

LORNE PIERCE TO SCOTT
Adknowledgement of "At the Long Sault" Ms.
(Reference: Letter 35, note 1.)

The Ryerson Press
299 Queen Street West
Toronto 2, Canada
February 24, 1943

Dr. Duncan Campbell Scott, D. Litt., F.R.S.C.,
108 Lisgar Street,
Ottawa,
Ont.

Dear Dr. Scott,-

I am very grateful to you for your letter, together with the manuscript of AT THE LONG SAULT AND OTHER NEW POEMS, by Lampman. Today I am sending it through for a lay-out and an estimate and shall write you at the earliest moment regarding format, list price and so on.

This is a note to you personally and in confidence. Does this manuscript unreservedly receive your okay? I like your FOREWORD. It is in splendid taste. I think, however, that Brown's INTRODUCTION could be shortened and I think it would be better with some adequate reference to yourself and your magnificent trusteeship, and also bracketing your name with those of Carman and Roberts in the opening paragraph. I find the selection very interesting. I wondered why some of the poems had been included. One of these days we shall have to prepare a selected edition of Lampman. I am hoping it can be done in 150 pages and I want to use your Memoir from the Morang edition adding whatever you thought was necessary from the Introduction to LYRICS OF EARTH. This will never be surpassed. It can only be supplemented. But in such a selected edition how many of the poems from AT THE LONG SAULT would be retained? Perhaps the title poem, 'The Silent Sequence,' 'The Growth of Love,' and half a dozen others.

We must have an attractive looking book and I should like to have it launched before the summer holidays, preparing the way just before publication by a publicity release through the Canadian Press and the radio, identifying you (if you do not object) very closely with this latest collection. After its publication I hope you will mark for me in his collected poems and in this those which you think must appear in a selected edition, in a small library of selected editions of Canadian poetry which we hope before long to launch. This will include the work of Roberts, Carman, Lampman, Campbell, Isabella Valancy Crawford and others on our list. The biographical and critical introductions would be written by such men as E.K. Brown, A.J.M. Smith, W.E. Collin and Philip Child.

I am very glad to hear your voice again.

With kindest personal regards,
Sincerely yours,
    Lorne Pierce,
    Editor

(*Source:* Lorne Pierce File, SAP)

Appendix F

T.R. LOFTUS MacINNES TO E.K. BROWN
Lampman's "Dramatic Fragment"
(Reference: Letter 29, note 2, and Letter 99, note 1)

August 8, 1944

Dear Dr. Brown:

As he has perhaps mentioned to you, Dr. Scott showed me the copy sheets you made of an unpublished dramatic fragment by Lampman.

I think I can throw some light on this, but first let me express my admiration of the keenness of your interest as exemplified by the perseverance, and, I might add, fortitude, required to decipher and transcribe the faded writing of that old note-book.

Now for the sources. The dramatic personae are all real historical characters: To begin with, King Seleucus — he was one of Alexander's generals, who after much jockeying for position with the others, grabbed off Syria and most of Asia Minor as his share of the spoils of conquest and founded the great city of Antioch, which under his successors, reached a population of more than half a million. He became one of the most famous and powerful kings in the ancient world and the development of his kingdom was comparable to that of his fellow general, Ptolemy, the first Greek King of Egypt and progenitor of Cleopatra.

Seleucus, *Nicator* or *Victorious,* apart from his warrings and intrigues, was a benevolent and progressive monarch, who created a great Empire, founded 34 cities, and was finally murdered 280 years before Christ, at the age of 78 after reigning 32 years, by a trusted servant upon whom he had bestowed wealth and favour, while enroute to conquer Macedonia; all of which shows what a vigorous old man he was in more ways than one.

And he did marry, as his second wife, in his grizzled years, the young, and, reputedly fair, daughter of his former military and political rival, Demetrius, *Poliocetes* (Destroyer of Towns), the lady whose end was on ice — these names need mnemonics — and it is authenticated that a while after the nuptials, his son by his first wife, Prince Antiochus, grew pale and spectre-thin (but did not die) from an unaccountable malaise which perplexed all the old folks; and that is where old irresistible Doc Erasistratus comes in. Dr. Erasistratus, properly handled, is far and away the best character in the piece. He was a grandson of Aristotle, no less, (well-connected, as Dr. Scott drily observed). He was the most popular society physican in Antioch — a modernist and strong opponent of purging and bleeding, which, however, remained the common treatment for most everything almost down to our own times. Also, as will be shown, he was the first psycho-analyst in a big way. He observed that the pulse of Antiochus accelerated irregularly whenever his new step-mother, Stratonice, came in to his sick room, which apparently was quite often. It was then no trick for the good doctor to diagnose the case as common love sickness, although he gave it more scientific terms befitting the fee of 100 talents, evidently an all-time high in the profession up to that date, which he charged Seleucus for his services. Seleucus not only paid the fee gladly, but promptly turned Stratonice over to Antiochus — "that his immoderate love might not cause his death" — this by Royal Proclamation, followed by a public holiday, and that was that. Perhaps there wasn't much connubial bliss between Seleucus and Stratonice anyway as he had slain her grandfather, Antigonus, and was holding her father, many years his junior, captive, and she may have held these incidents against him, so that it might not have been such a sacrifice for him to part with her. Presumably the marriage of Antiochus and Stratonice turned out all right, but, quite apart from his early neurosis, Antiochus was not hearty like his father as he predeceased him by 11 years.

I think you will readily agree that the original is much more lively, intriguing and spicier dramatic material than Lampman's adaptation of it. The theme is right down O'Neill's psychological alley and it is a wonder he did not hit on it. He might have given it a modern transposition as in "Mourning Becomes Electra" and "Desire Under the Elms."

As for Lampman's effort, it is easily his worst. He was both by nature and period unable to cope or play around with such sophisticated nineteen-twentyish stuff. His lines have no poetic or histrionic merit, except for the spirited martial Chorus with the choice rhymes; abysses and Issus; Pindus and Indus; torches and Persian porches; (incidentally, as Dr. Scott pointed out, these verses, both in matter and metre, would fit into "War"; note the soldierly discipline of the unrhymed penultimate line in each stanza, like a halt on the march breaking the clangorous rhyme scheme); and then, of course, there are the lovely gothic and utterly unhellenic love lyrics 'With those cold eyes, my dear,' and 'You cannot answer to my love,' unhappily set, like pearls in putty, perhaps in a naive attempt to obscure for the record their true associations and connotations. Dr. Scott, however, was closer to the events and could speak of them better than I.

I think I can tell you though the immediate explanation of what you found in the note-book. Lampman liked to read Lemprière's Classical Dictionary, in fact used to pore over it. I still have his copy. This admirable book contains all the relevant information on this as on other classical subjects, in a more concise, pithy and readable form than will be found elsewhere.

I certainly do not think that Lampman's MSS should be published but I hope somebody will do something with the story for the stage.

Natalie and I enjoyed listening to your excellent broadcast on Canadian literature. I should be much obliged if you would let me have a copy of it for our Lampman records, also, if you are agreeable, for publication in the Civil Service Review.

Please accept our hearty congratulations on your new appointment which represents advancement and recognition in your chosen field and which I hope you are finding entirely congenial.

It affords me another reason for revisiting Chicago some day.

With best wishes from us both,

Sincerely,

T.R.L. MacInnes

Dr. E.K. Brown,
Department of English,
Chicago University,
Chicago, Ill., U.S.A.

(*Source*: carbon copy
E.K. Brown File, SAP)

Appendix G

COPY OF BROWN'S DRAFT INTRODUCTION TO LAMPMAN'S ESSAY ON KEATS
Sent to D.C. Scott for comment, June 2, 1945.
(Reference: Letter 129. Scott to Brown, June 14, 1945)

N.B. In the original, circled numbers in pencil appear in the left margin: 1 at l. 10; 2 at l. 13; 3 at l. 15.

KEATS, by Archibald Lampman
with an introductory note
by E.K. Brown

"The Character and Poetry of Keats" was written on one hundred and thirty-two large sheets, subsequently bound into a notebook with flexible brown covers; the script is large and bold, and there are scarcely any corrections; on the obverse of a few sheets there are false starts. The only study of Keats to which Lampman refers is Lord Houghton's *Life and Letters of John Keats* (1848); and the principle of organization in his essay is Houghton's, the chronological. The text he used for his quotations from the poems was the Aldine, or some reprint of it; for the text of the letters he depended on Houghton.[1] He does not quote from the letters to Fanny Brawne.

Keats was the strongest literary influence upon Lampman, except perhaps in the last years of his life. In 1894, the year after this essay was written, [he confessed that it had taken him ten years to free himself from the spell Keats had cast upon him, and fancied, quaintly, that he might perhaps be some "faint reincarnation" of the poet.][2] For the man Keats, beset like himself by money difficulties and by illness, ~~and, again like himself, unappreciated at anything like his true merit by the literary opinion of his time,~~ he felt an intimate sympathy and a reverent respect. For the student of Lampman, the man and the poet, his judgment of Keats is of high importance. In Professor Carl Connor's biography, some aspects of the essay are summarized;[3] but it is now thought wise to make a large part of the text available.

1. The quotations have been corrected and are given in H.W. Garrod's text for the poems and M.B. Forman's text for the letters.
2. See *Lyrics of Earth,* edited by Duncan Campbell Scott, pp. 31-32.
3. Carl Connor, *Archibald Lampman, A Canadian Poet of Nature,* pp. 139-42.

(Source: E.K. Brown Papers, PAC)

Appendix H

TO THE PROVOST
TRINITY COLLEGE TORONTO
Text of handwritten "note of presentation" for two autograph poems by Archibald Lampman
(Reference: Letter 140, note 4.)

I take pleasure in presenting to Trinity College two autograph poems by Archibald Lampman. He gave them to me in 1884 and 1886. 'April' was the first of his poems that I admired and committed to memory. The other poem without title of which the first line is "The point is turned; the twilight shadow falls" was written after a vacation trip we took to the upper waters of the River Lièvre. When he made this copy for me in June 1886 he had not found a title for the poem but afterwards he called it 'Between the Rapids' and it was published in his first book, *Among the Millet,* 1887. It may be of interest to record here that this poem received special praise from a reviewer of the book in *The Spectator* of January 12th 1889. The writer compared it to Clough's poem 'Ite domum Saturae venit Hesperus.' Other records of that inland voyage are the poems 'Morning on the Lièvre' and 'A Dawn on the Lièvre.'

It gives me pleasure to know that these poems in the author's handwriting will remain in the custody of Lampman's Alma Mater.

Duncan Campell Scott

Ottawa
20th August 1945

(Source: copy, Lampman File, SAP)

Appendix I

NOTES BY DUNCAN CAMPBELL SCOTT RE RUPERT BROOKE'S VISIT TO OTTAWA
JULY, 1913
(Reference: Letter 27, note 3, and Letter 148, note 7.)

He was introduced by John Masefield with whom I had corresponded for some time. The only other introduction he had in Ottawa was to Sir Wilfrid Laurier. Sir Wilfrid asked him to lunch at the Chateau Laurier; there was no other guest. The House of Commons had prorogued on Friday 6th June. Lady Laurier had probably gone away for the summer and Sir Wilfrid may have been living at the Chateau; but I am not sure about this. Brooke was very favorably impressed by Laurier but as I remember he said the talk was very general and rather conventional.

R.B. registered at the Windsor Hotel, Metcalfe St., but after he called on me he was not often to be found there. He never made any remark about accomodation at this Hotel, and seemed to be satisfied with the comforts he found there. I cannot now tell what day he arrived in O. I failed to get the date of his registration when, after learning of his death, I got the Manager to let me cut out his signature from the register. He signed Rupert Brooke Cambridge England. From a reading of the letters to Edward Marsh I think the date was Wed. 9th July. He stayed here a full week and maybe a day over; I note he left Toronto on the 23rd for Niagara; meanwhile he had travelled to Toronto by water and made his visit at T. I gave him letters for Toronto to Edmund Morris, the painter, J.S. Willison, Editor of *The Globe*, Newton McTavish, Editor of the *Canadian Maga.*, and perhaps others. I also gave him an Open Letter to all Indian Agents in the West and later a special letter to Mr. Waddy, the Indian Agent for the Stoney Indians at Morley, Alta. I wanted him to visit one of our Indian Industrial Schools, and I gave him a letter to the Principal at Brandon; I was anxious that he should see Indians at the Blackfoot and the Blood Reserve but he could not find time for these visits.

It is over thirty three years since R.B. left Ottawa and I [had] seen the last of him and my memory does not recover any striking incidents of his visit. He called at the house the day he arrived, I did not see him then, he had tea, and the next day I found him by appointment at the Hotel. After that he was constantly with us and a few friends but he was content to look at the city and the country and did not want entertainment in the usual meaning of the word. He had many of his meals here and at the Royal Ottawa Golf Club. We visited the Gatineau Region as far as Meach's Lake and Kingsmere by motor; but there was little pleasure in motoring in those days: the roads were unpaved and the dust was unbearable. Brooke mentions the "execrable roads" around here in his W[estminster] G[azette] article on Ottawa.

In this house and for these few days he became a familiar, and I remember no one who so readily accepted the friendship offered him and gave everything in return without the slightest feeling of strangeness. Afterwards considering his background and his current friendships in England I thought and still think it remarkable. He was 25 years younger than I; our birthdays were consecutive in August, his on the 3rd and mind on the 2nd; although to quote Gilbert "that has nothing to do with the case," I can be "factual" in giving the opinion that he was homesick when he got here and he went away with a different feeling for the opening vista of his journey. He read us poems from the 1911 book and some new poems but he always had to be coaxed to read. He was delighted to find on my shelves several of W.W. Gibson's small books; he had a great affection for Gibson. Our talks on literature were many but their substance has evaporated. The only things I recall were his interest in John Donne and his desire to do some dramatic work, in fact I may say confidently that he was determined to make that a chief interest in his future.

As for his personal appearance so much has been said that any portrait of mine would be superfluous. When I spoke of "gush" I meant the Apollo, and the "young Greek god" sort of stuff. There was no doubt that he was handsome and everything about him went together harmoniously. Henry James in his introduction to the W.G. articles says some most excellent things wh. I will quote for you: P XII "young, happy, radiant, extraordinarily endowed and inevitably attaching" — P XXVIII "he was predestined and condemned to sociability" — P XXIII "social sincerity" — P XXIV "the pages from Canada, where as an impressionist, he increasingly finds his feet," and finds, XXX, *"a certain comfort of association."*[1]

For me the close of his article on Niagara is remarkable in many ways, you have only to reread it to know what I mean. I do not mean to even hint here at any derogation of descriptions of his good looks or of his fascinating personality. I do not find anywhere the tally of his height; a remark of no moment may be made that I remember him as not as tall as I am (5 foot 10 inches) but little less; of course the military authorities will have his height and other physical measurements.

The last memory of him in this house is of his last evening when he lay on his back on the library rug and played with the kitten called Skookum (this Chinook word meaning strong amused R.B.); they were great friends.

D.C.S.

1. Scott has written in the left margin: "The italics are mine. D.C.S."

(*Source:* typescript copy, Rupert Brooke File, SAP)

Appendix J

(Reference Letter 149, note 5.)

To Deaver Brown

TO DEAVER BROWN

Sweet child, unseen though loved as dear
As any that are known and near,
How can I send
To you so far in space and time
This burden of a rainbow-rhyme,
A love that bears
The seven diaphanous lines that bend
Above the treasuries and hold
The mystic hoard of gold.
In after years of fullest life
With all the joy amid the strife,
When you may see a rainbow hung
Between the mist-cloud and the sun —
Beauty of earth yet far above —
The pure, prismatic arc of love
That bears the promise in the glow,
May you recall these lines and know
He sent such love when he was old
To me when I was young.

(DCS 1946)

Source: The Circle of Affection

INDEX

INDEX

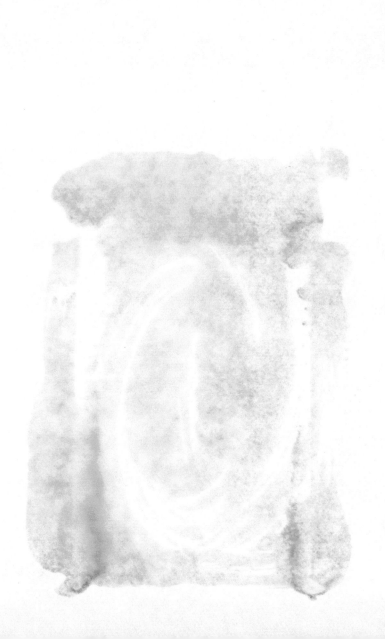